LIBRARY OF
RELIGIOUS AND PHILOSOPHICAL THOUGHT

PRIMITIVE CHRISTIANITY

VOL. III

PRIMITIVE CHRISTIANITY

ITS WRITINGS AND TEACHINGS IN
THEIR HISTORICAL CONNECTIONS

BY

OTTO PFLEIDERER, D.D.
PROFESSOR OF PRACTICAL THEOLOGY IN THE UNIVERSITY OF BERLIN

TRANSLATED BY
W. MONTGOMERY, B.D.

VOL. III

WILDSIDE PRESS

CONTENTS

JEWISH HELLENISM.

CHAP.		PAGES
I.	THE THERAPEUTÆ AND THE ESSENES	1–22
II.	THE BOOK OF WISDOM	23–35
III.	PHILO	36–74
IV.	JEWISH APOCALYPTIC WRITINGS	75–100

SYNCRETISM AND GNOSTICISM.

V.	THE RELIGION OF MITHRA	101–112
VI.	THE BEGINNINGS OF GNOSTICISM	113–141
VII.	THE PRINCIPAL GNOSTIC SCHOOLS	142–169

APOCRYPHAL ACTS AND GOSPELS.

VIII.	THE ACTS OF JOHN	170–190
IX.	THE ACTS OF THOMAS	191–206
X.	THE ACTS OF PETER	207–213
XI.	THE GOSPEL OF PETER	214–224
XII.	THE GOSPEL ACCORDING TO THE EGYPTIANS	225–228
XIII.	THE GOSPEL ACCORDING TO THE HEBREWS, AND OTHER GOSPEL FRAGMENTS	229–244
XIV.	THE ACTS OF PAUL	245–256

DOCTRINAL AND HORTATORY WRITINGS OF THE CHURCH.

CHAP.		PAGES
XV.	THE RELATIONS OF THE CHURCH WITH GNOSTICISM	257–271
XVI.	THE EPISTLE TO THE HEBREWS	272–299
XVII.	THE EPISTLES TO THE EPHESIANS AND COLOSSIANS	300–322
XVIII.	THE IGNATIAN LETTERS	323–364
XIX.	THE LETTER OF POLYCARP TO THE PHILIPPIANS	365–372
XX.	THE PASTORAL EPISTLES	373–399
XXI.	THE APOCALYPSE	400–475

PRIMITIVE CHRISTIANITY

JEWISH HELLENISM

CHAPTER I

THERAPEUTÆ AND ESSENES

THE Therapeutæ are described by Philo in his work *Concerning the Contemplative Life.* Their name, he says, was derived either from their being physicians of souls or from their rendering service to God. The latter is no doubt the true explanation; just as many religious associations in contemporary heathendom called themselves *cultores deorum*, this Jewish order gave themselves the name of Therapeutæ, which has a similar significance. Like the Bacchants and Corybants, Philo says, they were enthusiasts, transported by heavenly love. In their yearning for the immortal and blessed life they looked on their mortal life as already done with; they therefore made over their property to their relatives or friends, left their brethren, children, wives, parents, relatives and friends, and their ancestral cities, and withdrew, from fear of dangerous intercourse with men of the world, into gardens or lonely country places outside the walls. These people are found, he says, in numerous localities among both Greeks and barbarians, but they are most numerous in Egypt, and they have their chief colony there, on an eminence beside the Mareotic lake near Alexandria. Here they live in very simple dwellings, placed at a short distance from one another. In each there is a sacred apartment, called "semneion" or "monasterion," in which each celebrates for himself alone the mysteries of his consecrated life. Into that apartment they bring neither food nor drink, nor any of the other necessaries of the bodily life, but only the Law and the revelations of the Prophets, and the Psalms and other writings which serve to foster their religious insight. Their thoughts dwell continually upon God; even their dreams have no other subject than the beauties of the Divine virtues and powers (*i.e.* intermediate beings of an angelic nature); indeed, many of them talk when in a sleeping condition (hypnosis, ecstasy) of the lofty doctrines of sacred philosophy, which are revealed to them in dreams. It is their custom to pray twice daily, in the morning and evening. At sunrise they pray for a day of true happiness, that their minds may be filled with heavenly light; at sunset they pray that their soul, set free from the burden of sensuality, turning towards its inmost part and taking counsel with itself, may be able to search out Truth. The intervening time between morning and evening is entirely given up to religious contemplation; they study the holy Scriptures and investigate the meaning of the laws given to the Fathers by the aid of the allegorical method, for they hold the literal sense to be a mere symbol of the hidden reality which is allegorically revealed in it. They possess also writings of men of earlier times, the founders of their sect, who have left behind many monuments of allegorical wisdom which they use as patterns. They do not confine themselves to speculation, but also compose hymns to the praise of God in all kinds of metres. For six days they philosophise each alone in his own cell, but on the seventh day they come together for general discussion, and take their seats with dignity and order, according to age. Then the eldest and most deeply versed in their doctrines stands up and delivers a discourse full of understanding and insight, but void of rhetorical art; the others listen in silence, indicating their approval only by their looks and by nodding the head. The sanctuary where they come together on the seventh day has two divisions, one for the men and one for the women, for the latter also listen and are filled with the same zeal; these two portions are divided only by a wall ten or twelve feet high, so that the modesty of the women is preserved and at the same time they can hear the speakers. Moderation they make the basis of all the virtues. None of them take food or drink before sunset, for only philosophy is regarded by them as worthy of the light of day; the satisfaction of the bodily needs is more appropriate to the darkness. Many continue for three days without nourishment; some few, indeed, are so sustained by wisdom that they are able to extend their fast to twice that period. But the seventh day they hold to be worthy of peculiar honour, treating it as a festival, and on that day they care not only for the soul but also for the body, granting it, "like the cattle," rest. Their food is very simple, consisting of bread and salt and, for the weakly ones, a little hyssop, and with it they drink spring water. In eating and drinking they seek only to satisfy hunger and thirst; they avoid excess as an enemy of soul and body. Their dwellings and their clothing are equally simple, serving only as protection against cold and heat, for in all things they esteem modesty, which is the child of truth. Further on Philo describes, and contrasts with the wanton luxury of heathen banquets, the festal meal of the Therapeutæ, for which they assemble after (every) seven weeks, since they hold sacred not only the number seven but also its square. This is a preparation[1] for their great feast, which falls on the fiftieth day (Pentecost). They assemble in white garments, and first utter a prayer standing, raising their eyes and hands to heaven. Then they seat themselves in order of age, not, that is, of their actual years but of the length of time since their reception into the fellowship. At this feast women also are present, most of them being aged virgins who have preserved their virginity voluntarily from love of wisdom, which they prefer to sensuous pleasures, not desiring mortal children but immortal, such as the soul beloved of God brings forth out of itself, fructified by the spiritual beams of the Father, by which they are enabled to behold the doctrines of wisdom. The men sit on the right, the women on the left. They are not served by slaves, the possession of which they consider contrary to nature, since nature made all free, but by freemen, carefully chosen to this end from among the younger members of the community, who joyfully

---

[1] It has been much debated whether this passage refers to a feast which recurred every seven weeks, or exclusively to the celebration of the annual Feast of Pentecost. *Cf.* Conybeare, *De Vita Contemplativa*, p. 336 ff., and Herzfeld, *Gesch. Israels*, iii. 409.

serve the elders as their fathers and mothers. Wine is not set on the table on these occasions, but the purest water, cold for the majority, warm for the more delicate of the elders. Nor is any flesh set upon the table; there is only bread and salt, and a root of hyssop for the delicate ones; wine is considered a drink of madness. When they have taken their seats, all preserve the deepest silence and give their attention while some passage from the holy Scriptures is explained, or some question which has been suggested is answered. In explaining the sacred Scriptures they use the allegorical method, for the whole legislation seems to these people like an organism in which the literal command is the body, while the soul lies in the hidden sense of the words. Then, when the president thinks that enough has been said, he rises and sings a hymn, either a new composition, or by one of the ancient poets, who have left behind many compositions of this kind. After him follow the others in order, the listeners remaining silent and only joining in the closing words. When all have sung their hymns, the young men bring in the table as aforesaid, upon which is the holy food—leavened bread with salt and hyssop, the leavened bread being used in contradistinction to the unleavened "shewbread" in the Temple, the use of which is the prerogative of the priests. After the meal they keep the holy night in the following fashion: they all rise up and form two choruses, one of men and one of women; each chorus chooses as its leader the most respected member who is also skilled in music. Then they sing hymns to the praise of God in various metres and to various airs, sometimes together, sometimes in alternate strophes, first one chorus alone, then the other, then both united into one whole, in imitation of the choral songs of Moses and Miriam at the Red Sea after the destruction of the Egyptians. When the deep voices of the men blend with the high voices of the women there is a harmonious and truly musical symphony. Very beautiful are the thoughts, beautiful the words, beautiful the choric movements, all tending to piety. When they have thus drunk deep, until the morning, of this noble enthusiasm, at the first glimpse of the rising sun they raise their eyes and their hands towards heaven, and pray for a day of happiness, and for sincerity and keenness of spirit. After this each returns into his consecrated cell to apply himself to his customary study of philosophy. So much, says Philo, in closing his report, for the Therapeutæ, who live wholly for the contemplation of the reality of things, and of the soul, citizens of Heaven as well as of earth, friends, through their virtue, of the Father and Creator of the world.

The existence of these Therapeutæ has been questioned, but without justification. The hypotheses of Grätz and Lucius that the *De Vita Contemplativa* is a forgery, issued under Philo's name by a Christian of the end of the third or beginning of the fourth century, has found wide acceptance among German scholars, but has been so decisively refuted by the researches of Massebieau and Conybeare that it may be considered as no longer in the field. These writers have proved by numberless parallels that the language and thought of this work correspond so exactly with those of the other Philonian writings that, even if it had not come down to us under Philo's name, we could have ascribed it to no other than to him.[1] And why should a forger have fathered his work, which he intended for Christian readers, upon Philo, whom no Christian thought of as a weighty authority? And what need was there for a defence of Christian asceticism, which at that period was universally held in high esteem? Moreover, the Therapeutæ, as they are here described, were something quite different from the Egyptian anchorites of the end of the third century; they were rather monks and nuns, such as did not yet exist in the Christian world. Finally, how curious it would be that in a recommendation of Christian asceticism all that is specifically Christian should be lacking! All that distinguishes the Therapeutæ from other cultus-associations (θίασοι) such as were common in Philo's time is of an exclusively Jewish character. What reader could have understood that when the author of the *De Vita Contemplativa* spoke of the Law he meant the Gospel, when he spoke of the Jews he meant the Christians, that by the Sabbath he meant the Sunday, by the Pentecostal feast the Eucharist? How could he exclude the wine of the Eucharist as a "drink of madness" without falling into rank heresy? And how, as a Christian apologist, could he explain the leavened bread of the feast of the Therapeutæ by saying that they wished to avoid trenching upon the prerogatives of the Jewish priests,

---

[1] This disposes also of the opinion of Friedländer (*Zur Entstehungsgeschichte des Christentums*) that the author was an Alexandrian contemporary of Philo. Apart from this, his criticism of the hypothesis of Lucius, and his explanation of the reasons for its undeserved success, are quite to the point.

who alone were permitted to eat the unleavened shewbread? And does not this explanation point to the fact that in the time of the author the Jewish Temple-service was still being carried on? In short, it is quite impossible to think of the Therapeutæ as Christian ascetics, whereas all becomes intelligible when we take them to be what Philo represents—a cultus-association formed of Egyptian Jews and Jewish proselytes, the members of which had withdrawn from the worldly life and banded themselves together for the common pursuit of religious contemplation, adopting in the process some peculiarities of the Orphic-Pythagorean associations which were at that time widely diffused everywhere, and especially in Egypt. To their influence is due the abstinence from flesh and wine and the high estimation of virginity and voluntary poverty,[1] the religious meals and hymns, the white garments, the interest in mystical and allegorical writings, which had been handed down by tradition, and which were used as a model for the allegorical interpretation of the Old Testament Law. It was doubtless by means of these methods that the Therapeutæ found a way to dispense with the sacrifices of the ritual law, while their residence in Egypt relieved them from the necessity of taking up a definite attitude towards the sacrificial system at Jerusalem. But in regard to this we have no particulars.

In contrast with the contemplative, monastic life of

---

[1] This is not carried out to its logical conclusion, as each member has a dwelling of his own. Whether their needs were supplied by alms or in some other way is not clear from Philo's description.

the Egyptian Therapeutæ Philo sets the practical life to which the Jewish order of "Essæans"[1] devoted themselves. He treats of these latter in the writing *Quod omnis probus liber*, and in a fragment preserved by Eusebius (Mang., ii. 457-9, 632-4). In the former he says that they avoided the towns and lived in villages; in the latter, on the contrary, that they lived in many towns and villages of Judæa, in large communistic settlements. The two assertions may perhaps be reconciled by supposing that the Essenes preferred to place the houses of their Order in the country, but also had them in some of the towns (Josephus says, indeed, in every town). Apart from this, the two accounts given by Philo agree. They lay special stress upon the description of the complete community of goods in which the Essenes lived together as an Order. None of them, he says, has a house of his own, or any other property; all that they have they make over to be the common possession of their Order, and whatever they gain by their work they pay in to a common purse, out of which are provided their common dwellings, meals, clothes, and all necessaries of life. The next point which Philo emphasises as a peculiarity of the Essenes is that they rejected marriage, since they saw in it the chief hindrance to the communistic life, as the selfishness of the wife disturbed the resolution of the man: "He who is fettered by the charms of a woman or has to care for the needs of children is no longer the same towards others, but from a freeman has become a slave" (Mang., ii. 634). Nor were there any slaves

[1] This is the form used by Philo. For the explanation of the two forms (Ἐσσαῖοι, Ἐσσηνοί), see below, p. 18.

among the Essenes. They held slavery to be unrighteous, nay iniquitous, since it distorted the order of nature, which had made all men brethren. Herein they had affinities with the Therapeutæ, and they were distinguished from them principally by the fact that their life was not exclusively dedicated to spiritual contemplation, but throughout the week they engaged in practical work, especially agriculture and the care of cattle and bees, but they also engaged in handicrafts which provided for the simple needs of their peaceful daily life; they avoided occupations, however, which minister to war, luxury, or avarice, among which they reckoned trade and shipping. Of theoretic philosophy they did not think much; logic they left to pedants as not necessary to the acquirement of virtue; similarly physics (natural philosophy), as something which transcends human understanding, they left to those who love cloudy speculations; they philosophised only on the being of God and the origin of the universe. They occupied themselves chiefly, however, with ethics, using as teachers the laws of their fathers, which cannot have been discovered by the human soul without Divine inspiration. These they study at all times, but especially upon the seventh day, which they keep holy. On that day they rest from ordinary work and assemble in holy places, called synagogues, where they seat themselves in order of age and in solemn silence. Then one of them reads from the holy Scriptures, and another, who is well versed in such studies, rises and explains what is obscure. Most things they explain by symbols (allegories), according to the method which has come down from antiquity. They are instructed in piety, purity, righteousness, the true knowledge of the good, the bad, and the indifferent, in which love to God, to virtue, and to man form the threefold standard. To the love of God belongs the purity of the whole life, abstinence from oaths and from lying, and the belief that God is the cause of all that is good and of nothing that is wicked (or evil); the love of virtue shows itself in self-mastery, moderation; freedom from avarice and ambition; the love of man is seen in good-will, fairness, sympathy, helpfulness towards the sick and those who are unable to work, reverence for the old. While the Essenes sought to shape their thoughts and lives into a practical service of God, they despised the ceremonial service of the bloody offerings. This point Philo significantly places in the forefront of his description of the Essenes (Mang., ii. 457); obviously he found this divergence from the Mosaic law especially striking in the case of Jews who were in other respects a model of piety, as he represents the Essenes to have been. Why, then, does he not mention this point in the case of the Therapeutæ? Is it possible that they held a different opinion from the Essenes in regard to the bloody offerings? That is very unlikely, since, according to Philo, they rejected the use of flesh-meat; they seem therefore to have kept the Pythagorean command not to slay animals, whether for sacrifice or food, still more strictly than the Essenes (for there is no proof that the latter rejected the use of flesh for food); but their distance from the Temple at Jerusalem and their retired monastic form of life made the question as to the rightness of the Temple sacrifices of no practical significance for them, and therefore, if they were heretics on this point, their heresy would more easily escape attention than in the case of the Essenes.

The picture which Philo draws of the Essenes is confirmed and supplemented in respect to several important traits in the accounts which Josephus has given of them in two passages (*Ant.*, xviii. 1. 5, and *B.J.*, ii. 8). He, too, begins with the remark that the Essenes (this usual form of the name is his) sent offerings to the Temple (at Jerusalem), but did not offer sacrifices, since they held their customs of purification to be more important. For this reason they were excluded from the common sanctuary and offered their sacrifices by themselves. By their sacrifices Josephus probably means the common meals which, as being consecrated by prayers and lustrations and thus becoming religious ceremonies, the Essenes may have considered to be a substitute for the bloody sacrifices of the Temple. The latter they despised as a less worthy form of service to God, which was out of harmony with their purer religious ideas—an explanation which agrees so exactly with the statement of Philo that there is no reason to doubt its accuracy and seek the real motive of the Essenes in the Pythagorean prohibition of the slaughter of animals. The rejection of slavery, too, and abstinence from marriage are explained by Josephus in exactly the same way as by Philo: slavery they held to be an injustice; marriage and the rearing of children they did not condemn *per se*, but rejected them because of their pessimistic view of women as never being faithful to any man. Yet Josephus remarks that a part of the Essenes, who in other regards shared their way of life, formed an exception in this respect, and entered into marriage for the sake of leaving posterity, but only after they had tested the woman for three years, especially as regards her capability of bearing children (*B.J.*, ii. 8. 13 compared with 2). As Josephus only mentions this exception in one place, and elsewhere speaks as definitely as Philo of the Essene rejection of marriage, and as this would almost be necessary in view of their community of goods and their dwelling together in monastic institutions, it may be supposed that celibacy was the rule among the regular members of the Order, while the married were only related to these as lay brothers of a laxer rule, similar to the Tertiaries of the Franciscan Order.[1] After mention-

[1] *Cf.* on this point Friedländer, *Zur Entstehungsgeschichte des Christentums*, p. 126. It appears from other indications also that there were among them various classes, owning different degrees of allegiance to the strict rules of the Order. We hear of Essenes who lived in the towns, and again of those who fled the towns on account of the vices which were prevalent there, betook themselves to lonely places in the country, and made their dwelling in the wilderness. We hear of a class of Essenes who entirely rejected marriage, and of another who permitted it. We are told of an Essene community, the members of which were all men of mature age no longer assailed by the storms of life and of passion, "among whom no child, no boy, was to be found," and again of another which received the children of others in their tender years and trained them up in its principles. On the one side, we are assured that the Essenes numbered in all about four thousand members; on the other, that there were "myriads" of Essenes. All these apparent contradictions disappear if we admit the hypothesis that, alongside of the Order itself, there were innumerable adherents of Essenism who were less strictly bound by the stern rules of the Order. Without doubt there were a number of Essenes who lived in towns, and again others who led an ascetic, anchorite life in the wilderness, surrounded by a troop of eager disciples who, like Josephus, passed through a novitiate of three years' duration.

ing the celibacy and community of goods among the Essenes as their most striking characteristics, Josephus proceeds to give (*B.J.*, ii. 8. 5 ff.) a vivid picture of their way of life and the organisation of their community. At the first appearing of the sun they turn to it and recite some ancient prayers for its rising. The administrators chosen from among them allot to each his work, according to what each is capable of doing. After five hours' work, they assemble again, and, girded with linen aprons, take a cold bath, and after this purification pass into the room where they eat, as into a holy temple into which no unconsecrated person is permitted to enter. After the priest who presides over the meal has recited a prayer, they consume in silence the food which is laid before each by the person who is charged with this office. What the food consisted of, is not said; neither Josephus nor Philo reports that they abstained from flesh, while the latter expressly asserts this in regard to the Therapeutæ. That is certainly no reason for assuming that the same was the case in regard to the Essenes, whose way of life was so totally different, and who practised agriculture and stock-raising; nor is it implied by their rejection of bloody sacrifice, in view of the motive assigned for this above. After the mid-day meal, continues Josephus, they lay aside

These disciples were not, indeed, Essenes, but along with the Greek culture which they acquired among them, they carried with them into active life the Essene system of thought, and secured for it a very wide expansion. Both John the Baptist and Banus the teacher of Josephus were among these Essene anchorites.

again the holy garments which they have worn at table and go back to their work again until evening, when the common meal is taken in a similar way, and at this meal guests of the Order who may be present (probably only brethren of the Order from other "monasteries") take part. In consequence of the "moderation in food and drink" which prevails (this seems to imply the use of wine rather than otherwise), there is no noise in the whole house; the stillness which prevails impresses strangers as something solemn and mysterious. Here everyone is master of his passions and a friend of peace. In all their work the brethren obey the directions of their superiors; only acts of kindness and mercy are left to their own discretion. Truthfulness in every word is strictly enjoined; oaths they reject, and hold them worse than perjury. They occupy themselves much with the study of ancient writings, especially those which refer to the uses of soul and body; from them they draw a knowledge of medicinal roots and of the properties (medicinal effects) of minerals (this shows that the rejection of physics which Philo attributes to the Essenes refers only to speculative natural philosophy). Entrance into the Order is preceded by a three years' novitiate; in the second year the candidate receives the girdle and white robe, and takes part in the ceremonial lustrations but not in the sacred meals. Only after two more years of probation is he received into the Order. On his reception the candidate takes a fearful oath, by which he binds himself to honour God, to practise righteousness towards men, always to hate the unrighteous and to help the righteous, to be faithful in his relations with all, especially towards those who are set over him, since none receive authority apart from the will of God, and if he himself comes to a position of authority (in the Order) not to be arrogant or fond of display; ever to love truth and to convict liars, to keep his hands from stealing and to keep his soul pure from all unclean gains, to conceal nothing from the brethren of the Order, and to betray nothing to strangers. Further, they vow not to communicate any traditional teaching to others in a different form from that in which they have received it, and to safeguard ($συντηρήσειν$ = either to keep unchanged or to keep secret; either suits the context) both the writings of their sect and the names of the angels. Anyone who commits a serious offence is expelled from the Order after a trial in which at least a hundred members of the Order take part; which for many involves death through starvation, since they feel bound by their oath not to partake of food which has not been prepared by a member of the Order. As a crime worthy of death they distinguish especially disrespect towards Moses the Law-giver. The law of the Sabbath is kept by the Essenes even more strictly than by the rest of the Jews; they do not suffer themselves on this day to prepare any food, to kindle any fire, to move any vessel, or even to evacuate. This incidental necessity of our physical existence gave these curious devotees much trouble; they have rules to regulate its performance in such a way as not to "affront" the rays of the god (the sun), and the act itself they regard as a religious pollution from which they must free themselves by a lustration. They also carefully avoid spitting towards the right, as the holy region. We have already seen that they regarded the use of food which had not been prepared and consecrated by their priests as a religious defilement. This zeal for ceremonial purity, which puts a barrier between them and the outer world, draws lines of demarcation also, within the Order, between the ranks of their hierarchy, of which there are, according to Josephus, four. The elder members feel themselves so far above the younger that the touch of one of the latter, even as of a stranger, involves ceremonial defilement, which must be wiped out by a religious lustration. The strict Jewish legalism, which in these ceremonial matters seems to reach a pitch of fanatical meticulosity, was preserved by the Essenes during the Jewish war by many heroic acts of martyrdom. What gave them their power of yielding up their life with a smile, even amid tortures, was the conviction that only the body perishes, the soul lives on immortally. They believe, Josephus tells us (*B.J.*, ii. 8. 11), that the soul is derived from the finest ether, and being drawn down by a kind of natural magic, is fettered to the body. When, however, it is released from the fetters of the flesh, it rises joyfully, like one set free from long imprisonment, to higher regions. After death, the good look forward to a blessed existence in a land beyond the ocean, where they shall no longer need to suffer cold nor heat, but a soft zephyr from the ocean shall refresh them; where the wicked shall suffer ceaseless torments in a place of darkness and cold—conceptions which Josephus rightly compares with the Greek legends of the Islands of the Blest and of punishments in Hades, and in which he finds the strongest attractions of the Essene philosophy. Finally, he remarks that many Essenes are able to foresee the future, and that they cultivated the power of doing so by the study of the holy Scriptures and prophetic responses of oracles, and by special ceremonies of initiation.

The close affinity of the Essenes with the Therapeutæ is at once obvious. Even the names have a similar significance, for "Essenes" or "Essæans" is derived from the Syrian word *chase*, the plural of which has the two forms *chasēn* and *chasaia* (whence come the two forms of the name), and that means the same as the Hebrew *chasid* = pious, God-fearing; just as Therapeutēs = worshipper of God. But in spite of the resemblance of the two, the distinction must not be overlooked. Whereas the Therapeutæ dwelt alone throughout the week, each in his own cell, occupied with religious studies and meditations, and only assembled on the Sabbath to unite in worship and in common meals, the Essenes lived together in houses of their Order and engaged throughout the week in worldly occupations—agriculture, cattle-tending, and handicrafts; and whereas the Therapeutæ practised fasting, never ate before sunset, and even at their common meal on the Sabbath used only bread, salt, and water, without flesh or wine, nothing of this kind is found among the hard-working Essenes, who had their common meals twice daily, at which they ate, indeed, moderately, but sufficiently to satisfy their hunger, and probably did not altogether eschew the use of flesh and wine. Further, while the Therapeutæ, before entering their monkish Order, made over their property to their relatives, and therefore doubtless lived subsequently upon alms, in the regular fashion of mendicant monks, the practical Essenes, on the other hand, gave their property to their Order, which thus had at its disposal such considerable means that it not only provided its members with an assured subsistence and employment according to their skill, but was also able to exercise benevolence towards sick and poor persons outside of the Order. Whereas among the Therapeutæ only faint beginnings of an organisation of the Order are discernible in the distinction of elder and younger members, and the office of the president who spoke first at the holy meals, the Essenes, on the other hand, had a hierarchic organisation and a strict discipline: all members were bound to render absolute obedience to the authorities (priests, stewards, treasurers); four classes are distinguished by definite gradations of sanctity; reception into the Order was preceded by a three years' novitiate; a court of at least a hundred members judged all cases of transgressions meriting expulsion; frankness between the members of the Order and secrecy towards those without was a strict law. Whereas the Therapeutæ permitted unmarried women to have access to, and take part in, their sacred meals, the Essenes were exclusively a male Order. Whereas the Therapeutæ, besides the allegorical interpretation of the sacred Scriptures, also occupied themselves with the original composition of religious poetry and sang numerous hymns at their high festivals in choruses and with choric dances, nothing of this kind is reported of the Essenes; instead, they engaged in medical studies, and sought to cultivate, by the study of apocalyptic writings and the practice of ceremonies of initiation, the gift of prophecy, that is, they practised magic and divination after the fashion of the Orphic priests, who similarly performed cures and gave oracular responses.

The Essenes cannot be explained, any more than the Therapeutæ, as a development of pure Judaism; both were equally, though in ways which are to some extent different, influenced by the Orphic-Pythagorean mysticism and asceticism. Thence springs in both cases the impulse to flee from the world, the regarding of the earthly life as an imprisonment of souls which come from above, and of death as a release and entrance into a better existence; the effort to free the soul even now, so far as possible, from the fetters of sense and the cares of the world; to sanctify it by withdrawal from the world, by ascetic abstinence and mystical initiation. The Therapeutæ went furthest in this direction, with their strict fasting and their constant solitary meditation. The Essenes, on the other hand, made a compromise between this extreme asceticism and the needs of practical life; they desired to combine mundane occupations with renunciation of the world and of self; to this end men of like aims banded themselves together in a common cloistral life under the rules of an Order and with common property. And for this they found a suitable model in the ideal of a religious social brotherhood with complete community of goods, such as the Pythagoreans had conceived of and associated with the mythical beginnings of the Pythagorean school. Naturally, they took from this model only what suited themselves as Jews, and omitted the rest. In the

place of the authority of Pythagoras they put that of
Moses, and in the place of the sacred writings of the
Pythagoreans they put the Mosaic Scriptures; in
the place of their natural philosophy and arithmetical
speculations, the Biblical belief in God and creation; in
the place of the demons, the angels; and in place of the
transmigration of souls, the simple immortality which
was the more common belief among the Orphics also.
At the same time there remains a good deal which
is common to the Essenes and Pythagoreans; besides
the community of goods, there is the high estimation
of celibacy and the simple, temperate life (though
not perhaps a complete abstinence from flesh and
wine, which cannot be definitely proved in the case
of the Essenes), frequent washings for religious purification, prohibition of oaths and inculcation of truthfulness, division of the community into various classes,
strict subordination to the authorities, a novitiate of
several years before admission to the Order, strict
preservation, and (probably) keeping secret, of the
traditions of the Order, practice of a (partly magical)
art of healing and prophecy, allegorical interpretation
of the ancient sacred writings, worship of the sun as
a form of manifestation of the Divine light and consequently a symbol of the Deity, and finally, rejection
of bloody sacrifice. These last two points are so
surprising on Jewish soil that they would alone
suffice, alongside of the Essene doctrines of the soul
and immortality, to place foreign influence beyond
doubt. That this is to be sought nowhere else than
in contemporary Pythagoreanism Zeller long ago
clearly showed.[1] But in contradistinction to Zeller,

[1] Zeller, *Gesch. der griech. Phil.*, iii. 2. 279 ff.

JEWISH HELLENISM

and in agreement with Herzfeld,[1] Gfrörer,[2] and Friedländer,[3] I believe that the Hellenistic influence upon Judaism from which Essenism originated in the second century B.C., had its origin, not in Judæa in some kind of Hellenistic development of Jewish theology there, of which no other traces are found, but in Egypt, the native home of a syncretistic Hellenistic Judaism. The Egyptian Order of Therapeutæ was doubtless the first product of it. Palestinian Jews travelling in Egypt, who learned to know and highly esteem the earnest piety and ascetic way of life of the Therapeutæ, but did not approve of their contemplative idleness, and were more attracted by the active social and ethical ideal of the Pythagoreans, may have endeavoured to introduce this combination of practical activity and asceticism, along with some other customs from the same sources, among pious men of Judæa who were weary of the world, and to organise them in an orderly fashion. We shall therefore have to seek the roots of Essenism, if not precisely among the Therapeutæ, at least among the same circles of Hellenised Egyptian Judaism from which these sprang. Accordingly the origin of both is to be referred to very much the same period, namely, the first half of the second century B.C.

[1] Herzfeld, *Gesch. des Volkes Israel*, iii. 402 f.
[2] Gfrörer, *Das Urchristentum*, i. 2. 343 ff.
[3] Friedländer, *Zur Entstehungsgeschichte des Christentums*, p. 109 ff.

CHAPTER II

THE BOOK OF WISDOM

THIS writing, which has come down to us under the name of Solomon, is derived from an Egyptian Jew of the last pre-Christian century, and contains an apologetic and polemical diatribe or sermon against heathenism, whether of doctrine or practice, and on behalf of the true (monotheistic) religion and morality. In the first part, chaps. i.–v., the way of thought and life of the righteous and the ungodly is pictured, and their rewards, eternal life being in store for the one, and eternal death for the other. The second part, chaps. vi.–ix., begins with the exhortation to seek Wisdom, as the teacher of righteousness; thereupon Solomon recounts how he himself became a partaker of the Spirit of Wisdom, and describes in detail its character and its work in the world and in the soul of man. The third part, chaps. x.–xix., describes the administration of the Divine Wisdom in sacred history, from Paradise onwards to the experiences of the Israelites at their coming forth from Egypt and in the wilderness, in connection with which the happiness of the pious Israelites is contrasted with the unhappiness of the ungodly Egyptians, and in a lengthy excursus the foolishness of idolatry is pilloried.

The central point of the whole is formed by the description of the character of Wisdom in vii. 22 ff. "In her there is (or she is) a spirit, understanding, holy, like none other, manifold, subtle, mobile, transparent, stainless, bright, invulnerable, loving the good, keen, unfettered, beneficent, friendly to men, stedfast, unfailing, free from care, all-powerful, ruling all things and transfused through all intelligent, pure, and delicate spirits; more mobile than all motion, she penetrates all things by reason of her purity, for she is a breath of the power of God, a pure effluence of the glory of the Ruler of all things. Therefore nothing that is defiled enters into her, for she is a reflection of the eternal light; a spotless mirror of the power of God and an image of His goodness. While herself one, she is capable of all things, and remaining in herself she renews all things; from generation to generation she enters into holy souls and makes them friends of God and of the prophets, for God loves nothing else save one who dwells with Wisdom. Wisdom is more splendid than the sun and all the stars, better than the light, for the light gives way to the darkness, while against wisdom wickedness is powerless. Mightily does she extend her power from one end (of the world) to the other, and excellently orders all things. I have loved wisdom and sought her from my youth, and her would I have for my bride, for I was enamoured of her beauty. She exalteth her nobility, dwelling with God, and the Lord of all things loveth her. She is initiate into the knowledge of God and chooseth what works He shall do. Who is richer than she, who maketh all things, and is the fashioner of all? She also inspires the virtues, teaching moderation, prudence, righteousness, and valour. She knoweth the past and the future, cunning speech and the interpretation of dark sayings; she knoweth beforehand signs and wonders and the course of Time."

Wisdom is here pictured as an independent spiritual being alongside of God, the mediator of revelation in the creation, preservation, and ruling of the world. Wisdom had already been introduced in a similar way in Prov. viii. 22 f. and Ecclus. xxiv., as sharing in the work of creation and mediating the revelation of God; as, in a sense, a personification of the law which regulated the administration of the world and the ordering of Israel's life. It is possible that this thought, which was foreign to pre-exilic Judaism, passed into the Jewish Wisdom-literature from the Persian religion, for the hypostatising of abstract ideas into spirits which stand beside God as His angels is characteristic of the Zarathustrian religion, and the spirits of wisdom and of the good law are among the highest of the heavenly spirits of Parseeism.[1] In any case, the author of the Book of Wisdom has made the conception of the mediating Wisdom, which had already been taken up into Jewish speculation, the central point of his eclectic system, endowing it with the attributes of the Stoic Logos. This was on the one hand an extremely fine, ethereal and all-penetrating substance, on the other a thinking, world-ruling principle or intelligence; similarly, our author, in his description of the Spirit of Wisdom, combines material predicates which suggest a substance having

[1] *Cf.* Cheyne, *The Religious Life of the Jews after the Exile*, pp. 157 and 209; Stave, *Einfluss des Parsismus auf das Judentum*, p. 205 ff.

extension and movement in space, with others of a non-material character, which presuppose it to be a "personal" spirit. But we ought not, of course, in considering hypostases of this kind, to make our modern conception of personality the standard, for the ancients, with their animistic prepossessions, had not yet formed the conception of personality in our sense, and therefore spoke quite freely of spiritual beings as at the same time material, aerial in substance and possessing extension, divisible ("of many parts"), and moving in space. We shall find the same thing in the Philonian Logos, with which "Wisdom" is very closely connected. By these material predicates the Spirit of Wisdom is described as a cosmic metaphysical principle; by the moral and spiritual predicates, a principle of Divine revelation and communication of grace to the religious and moral life of men in general and the Jews in particular. For the Egyptian Hellenists, Wisdom is no longer so exclusively confined to the Jews and incorporated into the law of Moses as for the Son of Sirach [Ecclus.], but is "friendly to men" in general, and everywhere, in every nation, enters into holy souls and makes them prophets and friends of God. Only "into wicked souls she does not enter, and dwells not in a body which is held in pledge by sin" (i. 4), but "she lets herself be found by those who seek her, yea she comes to meet them, for she herself goes about seeking such as are worthy of her, and appears to them, full of grace, in their ways, and in every thought she aids them. For the beginning of Wisdom is the sincere desire for (ethical) instruction, desire for instruction is love, love is the keeping of her commandments, the strict keeping of the commandments is the assurance of incorruption, incorruption brings us near to God; thus the desire for Wisdom leads to royal dignity" (vi. 12–30).

The ultimate end of the way of salvation along which Wisdom leads those who love her is incorruption, that is, the immortal life of the soul in the presence of God. This belief is a very strong ground of consolation to the teacher of wisdom amid the perplexities of our earthly existence, a conviction which was scarcely found on Jewish soil except in the circles of the Therapeutæ and Essenes, and which originated from Greek — to be more precise, from Orphic-Platonic—speculation. The author has only adopted it, however, in so far as it was serviceable to his religious view of the world. Whereas the ungodly in their carelessness and arrogance suppose that they have the advantage over the suffering righteous and count their death a misfortune, an annihilation, the wise man, on the other hand, knows that God has tried the righteous and proved their worth, that in His mercy He has removed them after a short period of suffering and placed them in safety; for the souls of the righteous are in God's hand, and no pang can touch them; they are numbered among the children of God, and have their reward in the Lord; the Most High makes them His charge, they receive from His hand the most glorious royal dignity and crowns of beauty, He will shield them with His right hand and protect them with His arm. In the day of requital they shall shine as the light and judge the peoples (iii. 1–9, v. 5, 16 ff.). The godless, on the other hand, shall stand trembling on that day of reckoning, when their transgressions shall rise up against them as accusers, when they shall see the righteous whom they despised set in honour, but themselves have to repent their delusion in pain and shame (iv. 19–v. 15). It is only upon this contrasted fate of souls in the next world that our author lays stress; of a transmigration of souls or of a resurrection of the body he has nothing to say. But he is acquainted with the Platonic counterpart to immortality—the pre-existence of the soul. In viii. 19, 20, Solomon says of himself: "I was a child of good disposition and had received a good soul, or rather, because I was good I had come into an unstained body." Here, just as in Plato, the moral character of the pre-existing soul determines its earthly fate, and even the bodily dwelling-place which it shall receive. It is a natural consequence of this presupposition of the descent of the soul from higher regions that the author should say, quite in harmony with Plato (*Phædo*, lxxxi.): "This corruptible body weighs down the soul and the earthly tabernacle weighs heavy upon the care-encumbered mind" (ix. 15), and that he should attribute to this very imprisonment in the body the incapacity of man to gain a true knowledge of heavenly things without the aid of the Holy Spirit sent down from above (ix. 16 f.), and that, in contrast with the regular Jewish estimation of long life and the blessing of children, he should not hold these to be a desirable good (iii. and iv.). In all this there is apparent the point of view, the tone and temper, of the Orphic-Pythagorean-Platonic Hellenism of the time, its spiritualistic dualism, its contempt for the earthly life with its natural aims and goods, its desire for liberation from the fetters of sense, its want of confidence in the inherent spiritual powers of man, its longing for Divine help and illumination.

This Hellenistic spiritualism which holds the earthly body to be a fetter, and death a deliverance, a transference of the immortal soul to a better state of existence, seems, however, to be crossed by another view according to which death was foreign to the original creation of God, and came into the world through a hostile power. For in i. 13 the author of " Wisdom " says: " God is not the creator of death, and He takes no pleasure in the destruction of living creatures, for He has created all things that they might have being, and all the creations in the world are salutary (serviceable to life), there is no deadly poison in them, and Hades has no power over the world. For righteousness is immortal, but the ungodly have brought death upon themselves by word and deed; they counted death their friend, longed after him and made a pact with him, and they deserve to fall into his hands." Similarly in ii. 23 ff.: " God has created man for incorruption, to be the image of His own being, but through the envy of the devil death has come into the world, and is the fate of those who belong to the devil." According to this it appears that in the original plan of creation man was not intended to die, but even the body was to be immortal, and that in the constitution of the world only the means for the maintenance of life were provided, not the causes of death; the latter were first introduced into God's creation by the power of the devil, the enemy of God. But how are we to reconcile this with those other statements that the body is a burden to the soul, and that to die early is for the righteous not an evil but a sign of the Divine mercy, which desires to deliver their souls from the evil world, to bring them into safety and to eternal life in the presence of God? We can hardly fail to recognise that here two quite diverse views cross one another; one springs from Hellenistic spiritualism, the other partly from the ancient Jewish optimism and delight in life, partly from the Persian dualism. This, too, represented the purpose of the creation of Ahura Mazda, the Good God, as life only, the maintenance and advancement of the earthly, bodily life; death, however, was introduced into this good creation by the hostile spirit Angra Mainyu, and its power is increased by his adherents. It is well known that post-exilic Judaism took over from Persian Mazdeism, along with the doctrine of beneficent spiritual powers (angels and archangels, and intermediate beings such as hypostatised Wisdom), also that of evil spirits or demons and their ruler, Satan, and made more and more use of it the more difficult it became to reconcile the growing distress of the Jewish nation with the Divine administration of the world.[1] Whether the author of "Wisdom" was the first to explain death as a disturbance of the Divine creation caused by the devil, we do not know, but we certainly find, not only in the later Jewish theology, but even in the Jewish apocalyptic literature, the beginnings of which reach back into pre-Christian times, the doctrine of a seduction (variously conceived) of primeval man by demonic powers, whereby

[1] *Cf.* Stave, *Einfluss des Parsismus auf das Judentum*, p. 235 ff.

the poison of death was brought into the creation, and all was ruined and brought under the curse of corruption; that this was already an established doctrine of the Pharisaic schools in the time of Paul, may be inferred from his use of it in Rom. v. 12 and viii. 20 f. That these ideas, which belonged to the popular religion of the Jews of the time, should be retained by the author of "Wisdom" and combined with the Hellenistic ideas, which were of course of a quite different character, is not to be considered strange in the case of an unsystematic, eclectic, and practical controversialist, any more than the combination of similar ideas in the theology of Paul.

The same remark applies to his discussions of Divine grace and election. On the one hand the universality of the Divine mercy is very strongly emphasised, *e.g.* in xi. 24 ff.: "Thou dost have mercy upon all because Thou canst do all things; Thou dost have patience with the sins of men in order to lead them to repentance. For Thou lovest all things that are, and hatest nothing that Thou hast made, for Thou wouldst not have made it if Thou hadst hated it, and how could anything continue in being if Thou didst not will it? Or how could anything exist if Thou hadst not called it into being? Thou sparest all things because they are Thine, O Lord and Friend of souls! For Thine incorruptible spirit is in all things. Therefore Thou chastenest but mildly them that fall, and rebukest them, calling their faults to mind, that they, being delivered from their evil ways, may have faith in Thee, O Lord." In other passages the grace and mercy of God are confined to His "elect" (iii. 9, iv. 15), and these are, practically, only the Jews; whereas the heathen, Canaanites and Egyptians, are objects of rejection and hardening of heart. Of them it is said in chap. xii. that God commanded their extermination by the Israelites in order that the land of Canaan, which was His favourite land, might receive worthy inhabitants, children of God. It is true God might have annihilated the Canaanites at a stroke, but He had only executed judgment upon them little by little, leaving them time for repentance, although He knew that the race was corrupt, inherently evil, and would never repent, because it was from the first an accursed stock. The inexorable judgment of God upon the Canaanites is then justified by pointing to the absolute power and authority of God: "Who dare say, What hast Thou done? Or who dare oppose Thy sentence? Who shall reproach Thee because of the rejection of the heathen; are they not Thy creatures? For there is no god beside Thee who careth for all things, that Thou shouldst have need to prove (before him) that Thou hast not judged unjustly, no king or tyrant shall appear before Thee and be able to reproach Thee because of those whom Thou hast condemned to destruction. As righteous, Thou dost order all things righteously; for Thou holdest it unworthy of Thy power to condemn any who has not deserved punishment. For Thy strength is the very ground of Thy righteousness, and Thy lordship over all makes Thee gentle towards all," etc. (xii. 12–16). How little these various assertions agree with one another, is obvious to everyone; we can only see in them a laborious and unsuccessful attempt to reconcile the purer ethical notion of God and the demand for the universal destiny of men to salvation with the strict Jewish particularism and hatred of the heathen. "Thou didst prove them (the Jews in the wilderness) like a father who is training his children, but the others (the Egyptians) Thou didst condemn and punish like an implacable monarch" (xi. 10). The Pharisaic doctrine that God has predestined the heathen to destruction traverses, in the teaching of the author of "Wisdom," the higher view that God has mercy upon all, and that His incorruptible spirit is in all (xi. 24, xii. 1), while He is in a special sense the Father of every righteous man who is brought near to Him by the love of wisdom (ii. 18, iii. 9, vi. 18 ff.). The same inconsistency is shown in his judgment of heathenism, since he sometimes condemns it as a gross apostasy from God to idolatry, sometimes, on the other hand, admits that the heathen philosophers are less to blame, because they at least sought God and desired to find Him, though they went astray in their search, inasmuch as, in investigating His works, they allowed themselves to be so captivated by their beauty that their minds became wholly occupied with them, instead of rising to their Creator (xiii. 6 f.). But when he adds that they, too, were inexcusable, for if they were able to learn so much that they could investigate the world, they could the more easily have come to know the Lord of the world; he forgets that he himself has shortly before denied the capacity of the spirit of man, hampered as it is by the burden of the body, to attain to a knowledge of heavenly things without the aid of the Divine Spirit sent down from above (ix. 14-17).

Here, too, the milder Hellenistic view, which sees in the weakness of our sensuous nature a condition which calls for deliverance, but not deserving of punishment, is countered by the stern Pharisaic zeal which sees everywhere—at least among the heathen— guilt which deserves damnation.

Who the author of the Book of Wisdom was we do not know. In any case he was not a Christian, but an Egyptian Jew of Hellenistic culture, in whom acquaintance with heathen literature and philosophy had served not to diminish, but rather to intensify, the Jewish national self-consciousness. Many as are the points of contact between this Book of Wisdom and the letters of the Apostle Paul, who without doubt knew and used it, there is a vast difference between the points of view of the Christian Apostle of the Gentiles and the Jewish philosopher with his narrow sympathies. The hypothesis of Gfrörer[1] is worthy of mention, according to which he belonged to the Therapeutæ or Essenes. He has in common with them the doctrine of immortality, the world-weariness and yearning for heaven, the high estimation of virginity and the low estimation of the blessing of children, and the recommendation of a prayer of thanksgiving before the rising of the sun (xvi. 28). Finally, E. Pfleiderer[2] has called attention to the affinity of the Book of Wisdom with Ep. iv. and vii. of the pseudo-Heracleitic letters, in which a similar criticism is directed against heathenism from the standpoint of a Hellenistic Jew. Whether, indeed, this affinity is sufficient to justify the conjec-

---

[1] *Geschichte des Urchristentums*, i. 2. 266 f.
[2] *Philosophie des Heraklit*, Appendix, p. 346.

ture that they were written by the same author is to me doubtful; one passage in Ep. iv. gives ground for inferring a first-century authorship,[1] whereas the Book of Wisdom must be earlier than Philo and Paul, and belongs, therefore, to the last century before Christ. Moreover, there is found in these letters no trace of the conception, so important for the author of the book, of a hypostatised mediating Wisdom.

[1] Bernays, *Die heraclitischen Briefe*, p. 26.

CHAPTER III

Philo

In the religious philosophy of Philo the combination, which had long been aimed at by Egyptian Judaism, of Greek philosophy with the revealed religion of the Old Testament reached its consummation. The means of connecting these two so heterogeneous elements was found in allegory, which Philo was not indeed the first to employ, but which he applied more boldly than any of his predecessors to the interpretation of the sacred texts, in order to eliminate from them what was distasteful to his habit of thought, moulded as it was by a philosophic training, and to introduce into the text his own characteristic ideas. Philo does not in general deny (there are some exceptions) the literal and historic sense of the Old Testament, but he believes that he is able to discover in addition another, spiritual sense which the author himself desired to express by his language. Thus, for example, he interprets almost all the persons named in Genesis as standing for conditions of the soul ($\tau\rho\acute{o}\pi o\iota\ \psi\nu\chi\hat{\eta}s$), virtues or vices ; thus Adam is the sensuous man, Cain is selfishness, Abel submission to the will of God, Enoch penitence, Noah righteousness, Abraham is the soul which has grown wise through education, Isaac the soul which is wise by nature, and Jacob by experience. Egypt, again, is the symbol of the body; Canaan, of piety; Chaldæa, of worldly wisdom, and so forth. As a rule Philo admits, indeed, the literal sense alongside of the allegorical interpretation; but in cases where the former, by its too naïvely anthropomorphic sayings about God, contradicts the convictions of the Jewish philosopher, he entirely rejects it, and justifies his doing so by supposing that Moses accommodated his language to the comprehension of the many, who being themselves sunk in the things of sense can only conceive of God as having a sensible existence. "For there are two classes of men, the sensuous and the spiritual. The latter do not compare the truly existent (God) with any creature, but are content with the conviction that He exists, without desiring to form for themselves a picture of Him. Others are unable to form such a conception of a pure, simple, primary Being, without needs of any kind, but think of the Cause of all things as a being exactly like themselves. In the case of these dull-minded and unintelligent men the Legislator must play the part of physician and discover the appropriate cure for their malady. Let them hold false for true if they will, if only they are cured by so doing."[1] In many passages the allegorical interpretation is required, according to Philo, because the literal asserts something of God which is unworthy of Him; in others, because the literal sense is too commonplace to be attributed to the author of the Holy Scriptures.

[1] *Quod Deus sit immutabilis,* xi.–xiv. (Mang., i. 280-2; Richter, ii. 77-79).

Philo, however, with all his freedom of allegorical interpretation, remained a strict law-keeping Jew, and resolutely opposed those of his countrymen who held freer views and thought themselves dispensed, by their recognition of the hidden meaning of the law, from following its literal requirements; according to him, while the laws of the Sabbath, feasts, circumcision, have a higher spiritual truth, they also enjoin the outward usages. "We must regard the literal sense as the body, the mystical sense as the soul. As we must care for the body as the dwelling-place of the soul, so we must give heed to the literal sense of the laws, for only when this is observed can the inner truth be clearly recognised, and only in this way can we escape the censure of the multitude.[1] We see from this that Philo, like many philosophers before and since, purchased liberty for many theoretical heresies and innovations at the price of conservatism in practice.

That in spite of his earnest efforts Philo did not entirely succeed in reconciling Greek philosophy (Platonism) with the revealed religion of the Jews is manifest especially in his doctrine of God, in the unresolved antinomy between philosophic agnosticism and the belief in a religious revelation. On the one hand, God is for Philo so exalted above the world, so impossible to compare with any other object, that not only no finite limitation can be asserted of Him, but no definite quality of any kind whatever. He is better than the good and beautiful, more original than the monad, more pure than the One; therefore He can be known by no other, but only by Himself.[2]

[1] *De migratione Abraham*, xvi. (M. i. 451; R. ii. 312 f.).
[2] *De præmiis et pœnis*, vi. (M. ii. 414; R. v. 226).

"Human reasoning can only go so far as to recognise that God is, and that He is the cause of all things; to go beyond that and inquire regarding the attributes of God would be the height of folly." Nay, even Moses might not look upon His face, but only upon His back parts, that is, might not know Him according to His essence, but only according to the powers and influences which proceed from it.[1] On the other hand, as a Jew believing in revelation, Philo could not rest content with this empty agnosticism, but was obliged to describe his religious faith in God in terms denoting positive attributes. The Infinite Being ($τὸ\ ὄν,\ τὸ\ γενικώτατον$) receives determinations in consequence of its relation to the world; it is the efficient cause of all, and the reason ($νοῦς$) of the universe. Of all finite things, those which best admit of being compared with it are light and the human soul, but it differs from all finite things in that it is always active and constantly operative, never at rest, and never passive like the creature. God is above time and space; He precedes time, for He created time together with the world: He is bounded by no space but embraces all; is everywhere and nowhere; "although He is exalted above all things and has existence independently of that which is created, He has filled the world with Himself."[2] Inasmuch as God causes, comprehends, and penetrates all things, it can be said of Him that He is the One and the All ($εἷς\ καὶ\ τὸ\ πᾶν$),[3] which is not to be understood in the sense of a pantheistic identification of God and

---

[1] *De posteritate Caini*, xlviii. (M. i. 258; R. ii. 44).
[2] *Ibid.*, v. (M. i. 228 f.; R. ii. 6).
[3] *Leg. alleg.*, i. 14 (M. i. 52; R. i. 71).

the world, for Philo expressly rejects that as a heathen error.[1] In addition to the power that causes all things, the most important characteristic of the Philonian conception of God is beneficent goodness and mercy; this was the ground of the creation of the world, it maintains the world in harmony, it displays itself in the infinitely abundant beneficence which God exhibits towards the creatures, especially towards man. All good, whether natural or ethical, is a gift of God, and nothing that is not good comes direct from Him, penal evils being inflicted by subordinate spirits, who, however, of course act by Divine command. That mercy in God takes precedence of punitive righteousness, that He stretches out a saving hand even towards sinners and does not allow them to perish utterly, is one of Philo's strongest convictions,[2] to which the Platonic doctrine of the ungrudging goodness of the Deity[3] may have contributed as much as the theology of the best of the prophets and psalmists.

But of course this religious conviction of the beneficent goodness of God always stands opposed to the dualistic theory that the perfect God is separated from the imperfect world in such a way that it is not fitting for Him to come in contact with it or work upon it immediately. His activity, which religious faith is naturally bound to maintain, can therefore only be an indirect activity, mediated by those "incorporeal powers which are properly called ideas."[4]

---

[1] *De dekalogo*, xii. (M. ii. 189; R. iv. 257).
[2] *Quod Deus sit immutabilis*, xv. f. (M. i. 283 f.; R. ii. 81 f.).
[3] See especially *Timæus*, 29 E.—TRANSLATOR.
[4] *De victimas offerentibus*, xiii. (M. ii. 261; R. iv. 355).

But that Philo did not understand by these merely the Platonic "ideas" or Stoic "modes of activity" (*modi*) manifesting the one primal source of power, but thought of independent beings and servants of the Deity of an angelic order, is seen with especial clearness in the passage of the writing *De confusione linguarum*, xxxiv.,[1] where he explains the plural form in God's self-designation *Elohim* (Gen. i. 26, iii. 22, xi. 7) as indicating the plurality of the powers or angels who surround God. "There is only one God, but this one God has about Him innumerable powers as helpers and saviours of all created existences. Among them are punitive powers (punishment itself, however, is not intended to destroy, but to prevent sin and to convert sinners). By these 'powers' the incorporeal intelligible world was built, which is the pattern of this phenomenal world, the former being composed of invisible ideas as the latter is of visible substances. Many, carried away by the glorious nature of these two worlds, have deified the whole or its fairest part, sun, moon, and sky. Glancing at their folly, Moses says, 'Lord, Lord, King of the gods,' and thus points to the distinction between the Ruler and His subjects (namely, the 'powers'). There is, moreover, in the air a high and holy choir of incorporeal souls in attendance upon the heavenly powers—'angels,' as the prophetic Scriptures are accustomed to call them. This whole organised host forms the retinue, the attendant ministers, of the Lord and Ruler. The King communes with His 'powers' and uses them as His servants for the performance of such duties as are not appropriate to God Himself.

[1] M. i. 431; R. ii. 286.

It is true that the Father of all that is has need of no one, but with a view to what is seemly for Him and for the creature He has left some things to the subordinate 'powers,' though without according to them a complete independence, lest they should make any mistake in what they do." According to this passage the intermediate powers are of two orders, the heavenly ones who are also called "ideas" and who form the intelligible world, and the spirits of the air, who are called "angels." The two together form the serving retinue, the subjects of God, who permits them to perform specific functions with a relative independence. Among these numberless powers Philo distinguishes two as the highest in rank, the "henchmen" ($δορυφοροῦντες$) of God, sometimes describing them as creative and kingly power, sometimes as Might and Goodness ($ἀρχή$ and $ἀγαθότης$), sometimes as powers of blessing and punishment ($χαριστική$ and $κολαστική$), sometimes as God and Lord ($θεός$ and $κύριος$, with allusion to the double name Elohim-Jahwe). Elsewhere[1] he allegorises the six free cities of the Levites as the six highest powers, among which the highest of all is the Divine Logos, standing at the head of five others, distinguished as the Creative Power, the Sovereign Power, Mercy, Legislation, and a fifth which is not here named, but which may be concluded from other passages to have been the Punitive Power, or the Righteousness ($δίκη$) which has its throne beside the Ruler of all. How came Philo to set up these six hypostatised abstractions, which, though conceived as separate beings alongside of God, yet represent only His self-manifestation in providence, and which are

[1] *De profugis*, xviii. (M. i. 560; R. iii. 130).

immanent as metaphysical powers in the world and uphold it,¹ sometimes, however, take human form, and appear in that shape to Abraham?² Involuntarily we recall the six Amesha Spentas which surround the throne of Ahura Mazda, among whom the three chief are Vohu Mano, the Good Thought, or Divine Logos; Asha Vahista, the Highest Righteousness; and Kshathra Vairya, the Kingdom of Good-will—representatives, that is, of creative intelligence, power and goodness, just as the highest Powers of Philo are. Even the mediating position of these Powers between God and the world is the same as in the case of the Persian Amesha Spentas, which, like Persian Satraps, stand at the head of the whole system of administration, and direct the exercise of providence without infringing on the rights of Ahura Mazda, since they only carry out His will and act as agents of His creative and ruling activity.³ It is possible that this Persian conception of heavenly intermediate beings, like others of a similar kind, arose from the Spirits of the animistic popular religion being ethicised and represented as subordinate to the highest God and serving Him as His instruments. This is, in fact, the common root from which spring all the numberless hypostases and personifications among which the Persian Amesha Spentas and the Philonian "Powers" became the most important and most fruitful for later times. They cannot be explained on the basis of Greek philosophy, which had in itself (apart from its

---

¹ *De migratione Abr.*, xxxii. (M. i. 464; R. ii. 331).
² *De Abrahamo*, xxiv. (M. ii. 19; R. iv. 28 f.).
³ *Cf.* Chantepie de la Saussaye, *Religionsgeschichte*, 2nd ed., ii. 176 f.

connection with the popular religion) no tendency to personify its abstractions. The Platonic ideas are passive prototypes of the visible world, not active powers, and still less acting subjects. The Stoic Powers or "logoi," again, do not reach the level of independent subjects and intermediate beings, but are merely modes of manifestation (*modi*) of the primal power. Thus, what is specially characteristic of the Philonian Powers is lacking in the Platonic as in the Stoic philosophy, whereas it is found in almost exactly the same form in the Amesha Spentas, Yazatas, and Fravashis of the Persian religious system, which was the first to endeavour to effect an organic combination of the ancient popular animism with ethical monotheism, and thus made the first step in the direction which was afterwards followed by the various syncretistic attempts at reform made by Paganism in its decline. But Jewish theology, too, with its doctrine of angels and of Wisdom, had long ago taken the same direction. That Philo should follow in the steps of these predecessors was the more intelligible, because he stood in pressing need, in order to bridge the gap between God and world, of intermediate beings who had the incorporeal spirituality of the Divine and the creaturely finiteness of the world. It was equally natural that he should seek analogues for these creations of the syncretistic heathen-Jewish Gnosis in the Greek philosophy, and should find them, to some extent at least, both in the Platonic "ideas" and also in the Stoic powers of nature and reason. It is therefore not to be denied that these two influences worked upon the Philonian doctrine of intermediate beings and strengthened it on the metaphysical side, just as in the case of the older Wisdom-doctrine. It has to be said, however, that the peculiar religious significance of the Philonian doctrine of intermediate beings has its roots not only in the Greek philosophy, but also, and more immediately, in Oriental-Hellenistic-Jewish syncretism.

What applies to the " Powers " as mediators and instruments of the Divine activity applies especially to the " Logos," which Philo counts as the first among the six highest Powers, and names the ruler of the Powers. Especially instructive, as evidence of the central position which this conception occupies in the Philonian system, is the passage[1] where the pillar of cloud, which stood between the Israelites and Egyptians, is interpreted as meaning the Logos. " To the archangel and eldest Logos the Father of all has given the prerogative of standing in the midst to divide the Creator from the created. He is the advocate of distressed mortality in the presence of the Immortal, and the envoy of the Ruler to His subjects. Neither unbegotten, like God, nor begotten, like the creature, acting as surety to both parties, to the Creator as security that the whole race shall not perish and the world return to chaos, to the creature as a pledge of hope that the God of mercy will not forget His own work. ' For ' (so speaks the Logos) ' I will declare peace to the creature from the side of God, who is able to make an end of strife and keep peace for ever.' " The Logos is therefore as decisively separated from God as from the world; he is the eldest or first-born son of God ($\pi\rho\epsilon\sigma\beta\dot{\upsilon}\tau\alpha\tau\sigma\varsigma$, $\pi\rho\omega\tau\dot{\sigma}\gamma\sigma\nu\sigma\varsigma$ $\upsilon\dot{\iota}\dot{\sigma}\varsigma$), the eldest of the angels, the Beginning,

[1] *Quis rer. divin. hæres,* xlii. (M. i. 501; R. iii. 45 f.).

the Word and the Name of God, the image of God and the prototype of man; therefore "if we are not yet worthy of being called children of God we may at least become the children of His eternal image, for God's image is the eldest Logos"[1] As the revealer of God, the Logos is concerned in the creation, and indeed in several aspects, both as the epitome of the prototypes of all things—the "idea of the ideas"—which is identical with the intelligible world, and as the creative power, the demiurge who moulds matter into a world according to the Divine idea. "Strictly speaking, the intelligible world is nothing else than the Logos of the God who is engaged in making the world, just as the design for a city is nothing else than the image in the mind of the architect who is drawing out the plan of the visible city." This doctrine rests, in the opinion of Philo, not merely on his own authority, but on that of Moses, for if, according to the words of Moses, man is the image of the image of God (i.e. of the Logos), much more must the world be so, of which man is but a part.[2] In reality, of course, Philo did not take this doctrine from Moses, but from Plato, with whose world of ideas, or supreme idea, he frequently identifies his Logos. From this we might no doubt draw the inference that the Logos is not a separate being alongside of God, but only God's own reason, or the sum of the Divine thoughts which form its content. But this interpretation would contradict all that Philo says elsewhere of the independent mediating activity of the Logos in the creation, as in the ruling, of the

[1] *De confus. ling.*, xxviii. (M. i. 427; R. ii. 279).
[2] *De mund. opif.*, vi. (M. i. 5; R. i. 9).

world. He expressly says elsewhere that the Logos was the organ of God in the formation of the world; he names Him the image, shadow, dwelling-place, of God, the eldest angel, nay, the eldest creature.[1] An attempt has been made to harmonise this vacillation in his conception of the Logos between that of an independent intermediate being and that of the immanent Divine reason or idea, by ascribing to Philo the distinction between two forms of the Logos, that within the Godhead and the external (ἐνδιάθετος and προφορικός). But this distinction is found in Philo merely with allusion to the thought and speech of man, it is never expressly transferred to the Divine Logos. Moreover, the question whether Philo gave casual thought to the distinction is of little importance, since it is in any case certain that it is just this indeterminate ambiguity of the Logos, as at once philosophical idea and mythological intermediate being, which is the characteristic feature of his Logos-doctrine. It is not therefore to be set aside, but to be explained on the ground that Philo sought to rationalise the conception of an intermediate being ("Wisdom") which he had taken over from Persian-Jewish speculation, by combining it with Platonic and Stoic theories, and thus to make it more acceptable to the Greek culture of his contemporaries. It is quite possible that the leap from the one line of thought to the other might not be consciously recognised by his imaginative, rather than scientific, mind. This ambiguity runs through all the utterances of Philo regarding the relations of the Divine Logos to

[1] *De ling. confus.*, xxviii. (M. i. 427; R. ii. 279); *De migr. Abr.*, i. (M. i. 436; R. ii. 293); *Leg. alleg.*, iii. 61 (M. i. 121; R. i. 174).

the world and humanity. We have already spoken of the creation; in the maintenance and administration of the world the Logos works as the Divider (τομεύς) who separates the simple original form into more and more widely contrasted classes, and also as the Bond and Law (δεσμός, νόμος) which holds together the antitheses and unites the manifold into a harmony. If the Logos is in this the Law of Nature (ὀρθὸς τῆς φύσεως λόγος), the intelligence which informs the world-order, he manifests himself at the same time to the pious mind as the angel who is charged with the administration of the Divine providence, and bestows gifts and blessings upon men. He was, especially, the real subject of all the theophanies and miraculous interpositions in the history of Israel: he appeared, in company with two other angels, to Abraham at Hebron, to Jacob at Bethel, to Moses in the burning bush, to the Israelites in the fiery cloud; he was the manna, the bread from heaven, which was given to the Israelites in the wilderness in order that they might learn that "man does not live by (natural) bread alone, but by every word that cometh out of the mouth of God," *i.e.* that man is sustained by the whole Logos as well as by each part of him; the whiteness and sweetness of the manna indicate that the Divine Logos both enlightens the soul and satisfies its hunger and thirst with the sweetness of virtue; the name *manna* (τί) indicates that the Logos is the universal substance (τί), the γενικώτατον, the supreme idea. This allegory, to which Philo frequently reverts (in the *Leg. alleg.* and *De profugis*), is very instructive; it combines the most naïve animism (embodiment of a spiritual being in an edible substance) with the most fine-drawn speculation (this spiritual being is universal existence, Plato's "highest idea") and the most edifying mysticism (the word of God which illuminates the soul and satisfies it with virtue). Had Philo borrowed the Logos as a purely speculative conception from Plato and the Stoics, it would be difficult to understand how he came to make it appear in the rain of manna, in flames of fire and visible angels. On the other hand, it becomes quite intelligible, if he found this mythological hypostasis (under whatever name) already present in Jewish theology, that he should seek to combine it with philosophical ideas, thus elevating it into a spiritual principle and a fitting subject for edifying reflections. That this was the actual history of the genesis of the Philonian Logos, becomes the more probable when we observe that in *Sapientia Salamonis* " Wisdom " figures in precisely the same way as a mythological hypostasis, appearing under all kinds of various shapes and forms in the sacred history, while, on the other hand, as a cosmic principle it is endowed with all the predicates of the Platonic "idea," and of the cosmic reason of the Stoics. We observed the same thing above in the case of the Philonian " Powers." In all these instances the basis is to be found in the mythological hypostases or spiritual beings of the animistic popular metaphysics, these being subsequently elevated by cultured thinkers into bearers of spiritual attributes and subjects of spiritual activities (as we should say, into ideal principles), without, however, entirely repudiating their animistic origin. Here, too, is to be found the very simple solution of the much-discussed question concerning the " personality " of the Logos. He is just as much and as little "personal" as any of the other spiritual beings of animism, which no doubt resemble what we call a "personality" in so far as they are thought of as active, thinking and willing subjects; but, on the other hand, as having an aerial substance and being extended and divisible and capable of taking various forms, they have the closest affinity with wind, breath, fire, light, and other similar physical phenomena. That this ambiguity is shared also by the hypostatised conceptions of the religions and philosophy of antiquity,[1] and that our distinction between spiritual and material existence was not yet current, and consequently our conception of "personality" was still foreign to them, is known to everyone who has made an unprejudiced study of the sources. As to why Philo put his Logos in the place which in older Jewish speculation was occupied by the hypostasis of Wisdom, various reasons may be suggested. In the first place, the masculine form of the name may have appeared to him more appropriate than the feminine Σοφία for the godlike intermediate being; since the angels were thought of as masculine, the highest archangel ought not to have a feminine name. Another reason was that in many passages of the Old Testament there was ascribed to the authoritative Word of God a creative, life-giving, healing effect, which made its personification at least not unnatural; indeed, this personification seems to be actually accomplished in Wisd. xviii. 15, where

---

[1] As regards "wisdom," see above, p. 26. The same applies to the Logos of Philo, as also to that of Heracleitus and the Stoa. Cf. De cherub., ix. (M. i. 144; R. i. 205), ὀξυκινητότατον καὶ θερμὸν λόγος . . ., ἔνθερμον καὶ πυρώδη λόγον.

the destroying angel is described as the almighty Word of God (παντοδύναμος θεοῦ λόγος). Then there were many non-Jewish analogues which may have served as contributory motives. It is true that the Logos of Heracleitus and the Stoics, which was a pantheistic world-intelligence and at the same time a kind of self-vivifying matter, was something different from the Philonian Logos, which stood between the supramundane Deity and the material world as an intermediate being; so that this philosophic conception cannot have been its immediate source. But even in the Stoic theology, as systematised by Philo's contemporary Cornutus, the Logos is identified with Hermes, the messenger of the gods, and in this form is made the personal Word, or mediator of revelation, of the Godhead.[1] In this theological adaptation as the personified word of revelation, the Stoic Logos-Hermes had affinities with various figures of mythology: with the Egyptian Thoth, the god of the creative and wonder-working Word, and of science, who, united with Hermes, later became Hermes Trismegistos and was made the mythical author of various theosophical writings; and with the Persian Vohu Mano, the "Good Thought," the first of the six Amshaspands or archangels of Ahura, of whom we

[1] On this point compare the essay of Reitzenstein on the myths of the creation and the idea of the Logos in *Zwei religionsgeschichtliche Fragen* (Strassburg, 1901), where the derivation of the Logos doctrine of Philo from the Hellenistic-Egyptian religion, especially from the combination Logos = Hermes = Thoth, is clearly shown; but the philosophic side of the conception is too much relegated to the background. Wendland has lately maintained the same conclusion in his lecture on *Hellenismus und Christentum* (p. 7, note 4), which also contains other valuable suggestions.

were reminded above (p. 43) by the six Highest Powers of Philo; finally, with the Babylonian Nabu, son and revealer of Marduk, who, as the god of prophecy and astrology, became the special god of the Chaldæan priests. We may conclude from this that the idea of a personal Word of revelation and mediator between the Deity and his worshippers was part of the common material of the religions of Asia Minor and of the Greek-speaking peoples generally at that period. It was from this that Philo took his Logos-conception in the first place, but he then proceeded to combine this religious conception, the personification of the Word of revelation, with the Platonic doctrine of ideas and the Stoic world-reason, and thus extended it into a philosophic conception, a principle of cosmic interpretation. This accounts quite naturally for the ambiguity and vacillation of the Philonian use of the term; for Philo the philosopher it signifies the Divine world-principle, the intelligence which created and rules the world; for Philo the theologian it signifies both the personal mediator of all Divine revelation in nature and history and the principle of all human wisdom, piety, and virtue.

Philo's doctrine of man is somewhat confused, from his having combined the Platonic with the Stoic and both with the Old Testament teaching in various ways which do not harmonise with one another. But the Platonic idealism predominates. Man is related to the world as regards his body, which consists of the four elements of the world; by his intelligence, however, he is related to the Divine Logos, inasmuch as he is an image, emanation, and reflection of the blessed nature (the Deity).¹ "How could it be possible that the human spirit, which is so small and is confined within the brain or heart, could take in the greatness of the heaven and the earth, if it were not an effluence, unseparated from its source (ἀπόσπασμα οὐ διαιρετόν), from that Divine and blessed soul, for nothing is separated from the Divine by division, it only extends itself. The human spirit also extends itself, when contemplating the world, to the furthest limits of the universe, without being broken, for its power is extensible."² That reminds us of the Stoic theory of the emanation of souls from the Divine cosmic ether. Philo expressly says the same thing in several places:³ "The soul is not composed of the same elements as the rest of the world, but of a purer and better substance from which the heavenly natures (the stars) are created." "According to the sayings of wise men of old, the stars and the whole heaven are created from a fifth element purer than the other four, and consequently the human soul must also be an effluence from this." Yet he seems unable to rest content with this theory, and improves it by borrowing from the Old Testament: "The intelligence, the most perfect work, is an effluence from the soul of the All, or rather, as it better befits the pupil of Moses to say, an imprint of the Divine image."⁴ The Mosaic dictum that the blood is the soul of all flesh (Lev. xvii. 11) is variously explained by Philo, who separates the intelli-

[1] *De mund. opif.*, li. (M. i. 35; R. i. 47).
[2] *Quod deterius pot. insid.*, xxiv. (M. i. 209; R. i. 292).
[3] *Quod Deus sit immutabilis*, x. (M. i. 279; R. ii. 75); *Quis rer. div. hæres*, lvii. (M. i. 514; R. ii. 62).
[4] *De mutat. nom.*, xxxix. (M. i. 612; R. iii. 202). Still more definitely in *De plantat.*, v. (M. i. 332; R. ii. 148), which is cited below.

gence from the soul as the principle of life, either as a second additional soul or as the highest part of the whole, "the soul of the soul," so to speak. This division into a sensuous and an intelligent soul is crossed by several others: the Platonic threefold division into intelligence, courage, and desire; another division into spirit, utterance, and meaning; finally, a Stoic eightfold division which recognises, along with the intellectual ruling part, the five senses and the powers of speech and procreation as the seven parts of the nonintellectual or sensuous soul. But these are in Philo rather exercises in learned trifling than a theory seriously conceived and logically carried out. The main point is always for him the distinction between the intelligent soul or spirit which is peculiar to man (λογισμός, νοῦς, πνεῦμα) and the sensuous nature which has its seat in the body. Of this mind or spirit (νοῦς) it is said that it is "breathed into us from above, from heaven," or "has descended" from above, that it has "left the heavenly place and entered into the body as into a strange country, and is therefore but a sojourner and pilgrim upon earth." As to the motive which has led the blessed spirits to descend from the ethereal region into the prison-house of the earthly body, Philo speaks uncertainly; sometimes he says (like Plato) that they sink down from an inclination towards the sensuous; again, that they descend from desire for knowledge in order to make acquaintance with the world, and then, after they have beheld the world of sense, return to their heavenly fatherland, whence they had come forth, so to speak, on an exploring expedition.[1] This ingenious theory would, it

[1] *De confus. ling.*, xvii. (M. i. 416; R. ii. 265).

is true, ascribe to the world of sense rather more value for the education of the heavenly spirits than can easily be reconciled with the anti-sensuous spiritualism of our author, for elsewhere he constantly and with great variety of expression speaks of the world of sense as a prison of the spirit and as the ground and seat of all evil. From the passage in Gen. xv. 13, "Thy seed shall be sojourners in a strange land," he draws the twofold doctrine,[1] first, that God does not permit the pious to dwell in the body as in his home; secondly, that the earthly dwelling-place of the soul is a source of servitude, injury, and bitter humiliation to it, for the passions are foreign to the spirit and have their root in the flesh. It is, indeed, a fourfold servitude, since there are four powers of passion: pleasure and desire, pain and fear. These passions exercise an oppressive domination over their slaves until the time when the judgment of God shall separate the oppressor from the oppressed, setting free the latter, and sentencing the former to punishment. From this derivation of all evil from the body follows logically the doctrine of a universal and inborn sinfulness. "No man's life continues without failure from beginning to end; some fall voluntarily, others involuntarily; for that reason the race of mortals could not stand the test if God were to judge them by strict law and without mercy, but in God mercy takes precedence of justice."[2] The child, it is true, is (up to its seventh year) in a condition of relative freedom from guilt, good and evil are not yet developed;[3] from that age

---

[1] *Quis rer. div. hæres,* liv. (M. i. 511; R. iii. 59).
[2] *Quod Deus sit immutab.,* xvi. (M. i. 284; R. ii. 81 f.).
[3] *Quis rer. div. hæres,* lix. (M. i. 515; R. iii. 64).

onward, however, evil begins, the soul both producing it out of itself and freely adopting it from its environment. Even without teachers it falls of itself (αὐτομαθής) into transgression, so that it is always loaded with a burden of iniquity, for "the imagination of man's heart is evil from his youth" (Gen. viii. 21).

How, then, did Philo combine this view of man, derived from the Platonic-Neo-Pythagorean system, with the Old Testament doctrine of Creation and Paradise? The wide discrepancy between them could not escape his observation, but he takes refuge, here as elsewhere, in bold allegories, which probably were current even before his day in Jewish speculation. He interprets the account of the Creation in Gen. i. as referring to the origin of the heavenly or prototypal man, that of Gen. ii. as referring to that of the earthly man, who is the image of the heavenly. When it is said here (ii. 17) that God made man by taking the dust of the earth, it is clear that there is a great difference between the man so formed and the one who was made before (i. 28) in the image of God. The former is sensuous, consisting of soul and body, made in the two sexes, and by nature mortal; the one made in the image of God is an "idea" or a type or a seal (imprint, mould), intelligible, incorporeal, asexual, by nature immortal.[1] This intelligible man, many hold to be identical with the Logos, who has the same predicates (γένος, ἰδέα, σφραγίς), and is even called the "man of God."[2] But Philo certainly made a distinction (even if he did not perhaps always strictly maintain it) between the

---

[1] *De mund. opif.*, xlvi. (M. i. 32; R. i. 43 f.).
[2] *De confus. ling.*, xi. (M. i. 411; ii. 257).

ideal man and the Logos who is his prototype. He expresses himself most clearly on the point in *Quis rer. div. hær.*, xlviii. (M. i. 505; R. iii. 50), where he allegorises the birds in Abraham's sacrifice in Gen. xv. 10 as representing a twofold Logos; "the one is above us, our prototype, the other the image in us. Moses names the one who is above, the image of God, the one which is in us the likeness of the image. For he says that God made man, not as His image, but after His image. Thus our spirit ($νοῦς$), which is the real actual man, is only at second hand a likeness of the Creator, between stands he who is man's pattern and God's image (the Logos)." In another passage he contrasts the philosophic theory of the relationship between the human soul and the ether with the truer teaching of Moses, who did not compare the rational soul with any created being, but spoke of it as the image of God and of the invisible world, "made and formed by the seal of God, whose imprint is the eternal Logos."[1] But the vagueness of the ideal man who stands between the Logos and the actual earthly man is shown, *e.g.*, by the fact that Philo sometimes goes so far as to identify him with the tree of life in Paradise, since both are immortal and "stand in the midst"[2]—one of his favourite allegorical ingenuities. Regarding the creation of the actual man we find various statements. Sometimes Philo closely follows the narrative of Gen. ii. and speaks of man as formed directly by God, his body being made of earthly matter, his soul of Divine spirit inbreathed into

[1] *De plant.*, v. (M. i 332; R. ii. 148).
[2] *Ibid.*, xi. (M. i. 336; R. ii. 153).

the body; thus man stands in an intermediate position between mortal and immortal natures, and partakes of both, being mortal as regards his body and immortal as regards his spirit.[1] On the other hand, in several passages he explains the mixture of good and evil in man by supposing that the angels had a share in his creation, appealing to the plural form in Gen. i. 26, "Let *us* make man in *our* image."[2] But in this he has failed to notice that these words are found in Gen. i., where, according to his explanation elsewhere, there is no reference to the creation of the natural man, but only to the heavenly ideal man, in whom no such mixture of good and evil takes place. Again, it is not evident how this Old Testament account of the Creation is to be reconciled with the above theory of the pre-existence of human souls and their descent from their heavenly home. Here as elsewhere Philo is unable to bridge the gulf between the Jewish religion with its basis of revelation and the idealistic speculations of Greek philosophy.

The two streams of influence—idealistic philosophy and Jewish religion—come nearest to a reconciliation in the ethic of Philo; to the former is due its ascetic, world-renouncing character, to the latter its faith in Divine revelation and the help given by Divine grace, and both concur in their goal and summit, ecstatic mysticism. The end set before man is to follow God and become like Him; in this, too, consists his true happiness. That happiness is only to be attained by the practice of virtue, Philo

---

[1] *De mund. opif.*, xlvi. (M. i. 32; R. i. 44).

[2] *Ibid.*, xxiv. (M. i. 16; R. i. 24 f.). Similarly in *De profugis, De confus. ling.*, etc.

holds to be the fundamental truth which is common to Moses and the philosophers.¹ Quite in the spirit of the latter he says² that the true good does not lie in any outward or bodily things, indeed not in every part of the soul, but only in the ruling part (ἡγεμονικόν), in the dominion of reason over sense, so that the latter becomes, in a measure, rational, in so far, that is, as it follows the direction of the reason. When it is said of Abraham that he walked according to God's commandment, the commandment means the same precept which is praised by the philosophers —to live according to nature (ἀκολούθως τῇ φύσει ζῆν). That is fulfilled when the spirit, advancing along the path of virtue, walks in the steps of right reason (ὀρθὸς λόγος) and follows God, constantly giving heed to His commandments and fulfilling them always and everywhere in word and deed.³ Therefore, as Philo, in agreement with the Stoics, says, the fundamental virtue and mother of all the virtues is wisdom; but, further, this wisdom is, according to him, identical with the true faith in God which Abraham had. This primary virtue divides itself, as the river in Paradise divided into four streams, into four chief virtues, righteousness, temperance, prudence, and courage. But to these four cardinal virtues of philosophy Philo adds (as became customary later in Christian ethics) three theological cardinal virtues, which he sometimes⁴ calls hope, penitence, and righteousness, sometimes

---

¹ *Quod det. pot. ins.*, xvii. (M. i. 203 ; R. i. 284); *De migrat. Abr.*, xxiii. (M. i. 456 ; R. ii. 321).
² *De nobil.*, i. (M. ii. 437 ; R. v. 258).
³ *De migr. Abr.*, xxiii. (M. i. 456 ; R. ii. 320).
⁴ *De præm. et pœn.*, ii.–vi. (M. ii. 410–12 ; R. v. 220–4).

faith, joy, and the vision of God, sometimes simply piety, which exhibits itself in love to God and to man. Faith, in particular, Philo holds to be the royal virtue, because, as firm trust in God and grateful acknowledgment of the good that we owe to Him, it binds us to God. It was the link by which Abraham held fast to God, it was the most immaculate and fairest sacrifice which he offered to God, the only good that does not disappoint and never changes, the consolation of life, the fulfilling of fairest hopes, the sum of all goods, the knowledge of piety, the inheritance of blessing, the guide of the soul in the pathway of improvement.[1] To withdraw oneself from the finite, not to put one's trust in created things, which are wholly unworthy of it, and only to put one's trust in God, who alone is worthy of it, that is the act of a great and heavenly spirit, which is no longer fettered by any of the charms of the earthly.[2] Philo, however, often places love on the same level with faith as a fundamental religious virtue, which, as love to God, is joyful piety, as love to man, the primary ethical principle. "Among the innumerable precepts and maxims the chief are—in relation to God, piety and holiness; in relation to man, love and righteousness; each of them divides itself into many other virtues."[3] Following the example of the Therapeutæ, Philo describes piety as a being possessed by heavenly love, as a Bacchic enthusiasm, which does the good from an inner impulse, not because of a

---

[1] *De Abrah.*, xlvi. (M. ii. 39; R. iv. 56); *De migr. Abr.*, ix. (M. i. 442; R. ii. 301); *ibid.*, xxiv. (M. i. 456; R. ii. 320).

[2] *Quis rer. div. hær.*, xviii. (M. i. 486; R. iii. 22).

[3] *De Septenario*, vi. (M. ii. 282; R. v. 26).

commandment from without. Of Moses he says that he was a friend of God, inspired by heavenly love, honouring the Ruler of all things above all else, and being honoured by Him in return. The pious are free, as being the friends of God. They are not servants of God, but partakers in His power; in a certain sense, themselves gods.[1] "Most closely related to piety, nay indeed her twin-sister, is love to men"; in it is manifested our gratitude for God's goodness to us. "When the Creator of all things, looking in mercy on thy weakness, grants thee, out of His glorious power, that which serves to satisfy thy wants, what does it beseem thee, who hast brought nothing into the world, to do for men who are thy kinsmen and made of the same clay?"[2]

If we ask how man attains to virtue, Philo points, on the one hand, to moral freedom, the chief point in which man surpasses other creatures, which he has received from God and in which his likeness to God consists;[3] on the other hand, to the Divine mercy, apart from whose compassion the sinful race would be irrevocably lost, and whose help we have pressing need of, for all good.[4] It is a constantly recurring thought of Philo's that all good in man is the work of God, and not derived from our own strength. It is God's work to implant and cultivate virtue in the soul; it is a self-satisfied and ungodly spirit which thinks itself like God and imagines that it is acting,

[1] *Quod omnis probus liber*, vii. (M. ii. 452; R. v. 278); *De vita Mosis*, iii. 1 (M. ii. 145; R. iv. 200).

[2] *De vict. offer.*, vi. (M. ii. 256; R. iv. 347); *De caritate*, i. (M. ii. 383; R. v. 185).

[3] *Quod Deus sit immut.*, x. (M. i. 279; R. ii. 75).

[4] *Ibid.*, xvi. (*v. sup.*, p. 40).

like God, whereas in reality it turns out to be passive. Since it is God who sows and plants good in the soul, it is a godless spirit which says, "I plant."[1] The Divine work in the soul is carried on by the Divine "Powers," who descend at the command of their heavenly Father into the soul as the temple of God, to purify and sanctify it and sow the seed of holiness in it; especially by the Divine Wisdom or the Logos, which are both described as the miraculous bread (manna) and miraculous water from the rock in the desert, because they satisfy the hunger and the thirst of godly souls with the knowledge and love of God. In this the Logos appears no longer as the historical mediator of revelation (*sup.*, p. 48), but as the principle of the true and good, of knowledge of God and virtue, working within man. He is called the stream which fills the whole world with blessedness, and, in especial, man with wisdom, the Divine cup-bearer who brings to mortals a draught of nectar, and himself is this nectar; he is the bread, the heavenly food which God gives to the soul, sweeter than honey and purer than the snow; he is the spouse who begets noble and good thoughts in the soul, the guide who shows the right way, the warrior who overcomes the passions, the admonisher who charges us with guilt and brings us back to the right way. In all these relationships the work of the Logos practically coincides with what we are accustomed to call the natural revelation in conscience, but nevertheless it would not fairly represent Philo's opinion simply to identify them.[2] We must not forget that the Logos

---

[1] *Leg. alleg.*, i. 15 (M. i. 53; R. i. 72).
[2] As Gfrörer seems inclined to do, *Philo*, 208 ff.

of Philo, however nearly allied to the immanent Logos of the Stoics, is yet essentially a transcendental hypostasis, which, like the Pauline πνεῦμα, "descends from above," is "sent down" into the spirit in order to aid its natural weakness with its own supernatural strength. On this presupposition the antinomy between human freedom and Divine grace cannot of course be solved; but we may perhaps see an effort in that direction in Philo's distinction of the three ways or stages of virtue. The first and lowest way is asceticism—virtue engaged in dubious fight with sensuality. Its representative is Jacob, whose vision of the ladder to heaven with the angels ascending and descending is a symbol of the varying strength of virtue. But Moses is also celebrated as a hero of asceticism, since he "sanctified not only the soul but also the body, keeping himself pure from all passion and from everything which belongs to the mortal nature, such as food and drink and intercourse with women; the latter, from the time when he came forward as a prophet, in order that he might always be ready to receive the Divine oracles."[1]

But the soul must free itself not only from sensuous passions but also from itself, as is shown in the example of Abraham, according to Gen. xv. 4. "If thou desirest to inherit Divine blessings, O soul, thou must not only leave thy land, that is the body, thy kinsmen, that is the senses, thy father's house, that is speech, but flee from thyself, go out of thyself, intoxicated like the corybants with a Divine enthusiasm. For only then does the soul inherit Divine blessings when, filled with enthusiasm, it is no more confined to itself,

[1] *De vita Mos.*, iii. 2 (M. ii. 145; R. iv. 200).

but drinks deep draughts of heavenly love and, guided by truth, is drawn upwards to God."[1] The second way of virtue is knowledge, and its representative is Abraham. Before he begot Isaac of Sarah, that is virtue, he must first associate with Hagar, that is devote himself to the study of all the sciences—grammar, music, geometry, rhetoric, and dialectic. "In these and similar branches of knowledge thou must exercise thyself, for perhaps we may succeed, as many have done, in making friends, through the subordinate virtues, of the royal virtues. Just as our body cannot at once bear solid food, but needs first in childhood milk; even so the soul needs the circle of the sciences as its nutriment in childhood.[2] The third way of virtue is that of the pure God-given nature, which does not need to occupy itself with lower acts and exercises, but, taught by itself (αὐτοδίδακτος), immediately becomes a partaker of the royal virtue, like Isaac, the type of joyful wisdom, who already possesses the perfect gifts of God bestowed on him by the prior influence of the Divine grace, and only desires to continue in them."[3] In addition to these three ways of virtue, Philo, like the Stoics, speaks of three grades: the beginners, the advanced, and the perfect. He explains, *inter alia*, Jacob's change of name to Israel as referring to these grades; as Jacob he stands for instruction and progress, as Israel, for perfection, the vision of God. The perfect are the "men of God" who receive the highest good, undisturbed peace, rest in God, the vision of God. Philo

---

[1] *Quis rer. div. hær.*, xiv. (M. i. 482; R. iii. 18).
[2] *De congressu erudit. gratia*, iv. (M. i. 521 f.; R. iii. 74).
[3] *Ibid.*, vii. (M. i. 521 f.; R. iii. 74).

frequently says that this is the perfection of virtue and happiness. He seems, however, to distinguish herein two varieties or stages, the mediate recognition of God from His revelation in the world, in which we see Him as in a mirror, and the immediate vision in mystical ecstasy. No doubt the soul which has not yet been initiated into the great mysteries, but still loves the lower levels, which cannot yet directly grasp that which is (God), by its own strength without external help, but only by means of His works, recognising Him as creator or cause—no doubt such a soul has a share in the Divine glory; but the highest glory and the truth are first attained when the soul, purified to the uttermost, transcends not only the multitude of numbers (the manifoldness of the finite), but even the Dyad which stands next to the Monad (the highest powers or ideas), and attains to the pure, simple, and self-contained Idea which needs nothing from without (Absolute Existence, God). Until it arrives at this perfection, it needs the Divine Logos as its guide; once it has reached this highest knowledge, it will keep step with its former guide, and both will stand in immediate communion with God, the Ruler of all.[1] That this highest can only be reached when the soul withdraws itself from all finite things and even transcends itself, in ecstatic enthusiasm, is often reiterated by Philo. Besides the passage quoted above from *Quis rer. div. hær.*, xiv., another very instructive passage is that in which Philo allegorises the saying in Lev. xvi. 17: "When the high priest goes into the Holy of Holies, he is no more a man

---

[1] *De Abrah.* xxiv. (M. ii. 19, R. iv. 29); *De Migr. Abr.*, xxxi. (M. i. 463; R. ii. 331).

until he comes out again."[1] That signifies, Philo says,[2] that " when the mind, laid hold of by the Divine love, penetrates in its ardour into the Holy of Holies, it forgets, in its enthusiasm for God, everything else, and even itself, and only remembers the Lord, to whom it offers holy virtues as an offering of incense; but when the enthusiasm comes to an end and the yearning grows weaker, it falls back from the Divine to the human." The same meaning is conveyed by his allegorical interpretation of Gen. xv. 12:[3] "When the Divine light shines forth the human grows dim, when the Divine light sets the human rises. So it is with the race of prophets: our human mind withdraws at the coming of the Divine Spirit, and only returns when the latter withdraws, for it is not meet that mortal and immortal should dwell together. When the prophet seems to be speaking, he is really passive, and another is using his vocal organs to communicate whatsoever he will."[4] No doubt Philo is here speaking primarily of prophetic inspiration, but the comparison of this passage with those quoted above warrants the conclusion that for him mantic enthusiasm and ecstasy were only a special form of the most exalted religious condition of the soul—the mystical ecstasy of the vision of God.

This theory is in Philo not a mere philosophic construction—indeed, it harmonises ill enough with

[1] E.V. "And there shall be no man in the tabernacle of the congregation when he goeth in to make an atonement in the holy place."

[2] *De somniis*, ii. 34 (M. i. 689; R. iii. 311).

[3] "And when the sun was going down, a deep sleep fell upon Abram; and, lo, an horror of great darkness fell upon him."

[4] *Quis rer. div. hær.*, liii. (M. i. 511; R. iii. 58).

his transcendental doctrine of God—but rests upon actual religious experiences which he had undergone himself and observed in the Therapeutæ, of whom he had so high an opinion,[1] just as the similar description of enthusiasm in Plato's *Symposium* is based on the orgiastic phenomena of the Dionysiac-Orphic mysteries. To this extent, therefore, it might be said that the Philonian, as also in a certain sense the Platonic, philosophy was an attempt to insert the phenomena of religious enthusiasm and mysticism into the general framework of a philosophic system, and thereby to fill them with an ethical content and to make them serviceable in the interests of an ethical treatment of life. And with a view to this end—to ethicise enthusiasm and in general to promote the alliance of the religion of revelation with reason—the central Philonian doctrine of the Divine Logos was of special service, for in it the two elements, religious supernaturalism and philosophical rationalism, are united in the most intimate manner possible, and with the greatest possible art. As a hypostatised, heavenly, spiritual being the Logos is the mediator of a supernatural revelation, which from time to time, in the past and in the present, comes to man from above in miraculous, catastrophic occurrences, superseding his natural spiritual life, communicating oracles and giving rise to those phenomena of enthusiasm which everywhere constitute the animistic basis of the belief in revelation in the positive religions. But as the rational law of the natural and ethical order of the world ($\dot{o}\rho\theta\dot{o}s\ \tau\hat{\eta}s\ \phi\dot{v}\sigma\epsilon\omega s\ \lambda\acute{o}\gamma os$ or $\nu\acute{o}\mu os$) the Logos is at the same time

[1] *De vita contemplativa*, ii. (M. ii. 473; R. ii. 306). *Cf. sup.*, p. 1 ff.

the principle of the continuous, immanent revelation in reason and conscience, in that highest power of the soul (νοῦς) which is essentially the Divine in man, the "effluence and the imprint of the Divine Logos," the principle of a revelation which is therefore practically identical with the development of the natural ethico-religious mental endowment of man. By the very fact that these twofold revelations, the supernatural-enthusiastic and the natural-rational, are carried back to one and the same principle in the Logos, the possibility is provided, and the duty imposed, of bringing them into a unity which shall be as harmonious as possible, of bringing what is irrational in the positive and enthusiastic revelation under the control of the practical reason, and of subordinating it to the ends of the ethical life; and this is always and everywhere the task of apologetic theology, of the Hellenistic-Jewish not less than, at a later time, of the Christian apologetic. On this ground we can explain *a priori* the important place which the conception of the Logos received in Christian apologetic and theology; it played the very part with a view to which Philo had constructed it. The apologetic task which confronted Christian theologians was, however, on the one hand more difficult and complicated, on the other easier and more fruitful in result, than that of Philo. It was more difficult in so far as the Logos, by its identification with the historical person of Jesus, now first received the concrete personal definiteness of a Second Divine Being; and as a natural consequence of this, the apocalyptic-enthusiastic aspect of his work of revelation became more strongly marked, and was embodied in miracle-stories which were to form a permanent, insoluble, irrational element in Christian theology. On the other hand, the task of the Christian apologists was easier in so far as the ethical idealism which the Logos represented acquired a more definite norm and a more effectual motive force than had ever been possible in the abstract speculation of Philo. For this reason, if for no other, though it contained the kernel of the new religion, that religion could never have grown out of it alone; what was needed was an ethically impressive personality, which could be looked on as the bearer of the ideal, the embodiment or "incarnation" of the Divine Logos, and could thus become a nucleus round which might crystallise the dominant ideas precipitated from the ferment of the time. These it united into a new conception of the world, which had an immense advantage over the Philonian in that it was based upon the powerful impression made by a lofty ethical Personality and His tragic story.

In Philo we do not find any such association of the Logos with a historical person. His ideal picture of Moses, who by the inspiration of the Logos became prophet, priest, and king, goes some way in the direction of this thought, but there is no reference here to an incarnation of the Logos, any more than elsewhere in Philo; nor does he ever even hint at a union of the Logos with the Messiah. He believed, of course, like the rest of the Jews, in a future deliverance of their nation from the tyranny of the heathen, which should be effected by a victorious leader and king who should rule his people in righteousness and accomplish vengeance upon his enemies. In this connection he describes how the Jews of the dispersion should return from all quarters to Palestine, "led by a Divine figure exalted above all humanity, beheld only by the blessed while invisible to all others."[1] No doubt what suggested this to his mind was the leading of Israel in the wilderness by the fiery pillar, and since he saw in that pillar a form in which the Logos appeared (v. sup., p. 48), it is probable that in this leading of the return by a superhuman Divine appearance (θειοτέρα ἢ κατὰ φύσιν ἀνθρωπίνην ὄψις) we are to think of the Logos as the subject of the manifestation. Yet this has nothing in common with the idea of a human Messiah-king. The Messianic expectation remains for Philo wholly on the earthly plane, and follows the national and political lines of Jewish tradition. The Logos, on the other hand, "stands for him too high to allow him to contemplate his incarnation; he might hover in the air, in the pure heaven, but could not permanently descend upon the unclean earth."[2] This is the point at which the Christian doctrine of the Logos diverges from the Philonian; the latter remains in the transcendental region of religious-philosophical speculation, while the former comes down to the historical level, and so becomes the principle of a historical religion which overleaps the boundaries of Judaism and rises to the idea of universal God-Manhood.

Finally, another point which we have to notice is Philo's inconsistent attitude to the Jewish national law. On the one hand, he describes the aim of the Mosaic legislation as the bringing about of such a unanimity of thought and similarity of custom in all lands as would raise the whole human race to the highest

[1] *De execrat,* ix. (M. ii. 436; R. v. 255). [2] Gfrörer, *Philo,* p. 530.

happiness. That is no doubt, in the meantime, merely a pious aspiration, but it is certain some time to receive fulfilment if God grants increase of virtue. Now it is obvious, one might think, that the Jewish law could only lead men to this ethical unity on condition of parting with its national form, the ceremonial law, and retaining only the universal spiritual and ethical kernel, a critical distinction for which Philo's allegorical interpretation of the letter was calculated to prepare the way. But near as this inference lay, Philo himself was far from actually drawing it. On the contrary, we find many passages in which he sharply takes to task those Jews who think by a spiritual interpretation of the law to remove the obligation of the letter. "There are some who hold the written laws to be nothing but symbols of spiritual doctrines, and carefully seek out the latter while carelessly despising the former. Such people I can only blame. They ought to give heed both to the discovery of the hidden significance and the observance of the obvious sense. They live, however, entirely for themselves, as though they dwelt in a desert or were disembodied spirits; they set themselves above all that is valid for the many, and inquire only concerning absolute truth as such, whereas holy Scripture commands us to be careful to maintain a good repute and not to alter the laws given by inspired men." No doubt a spiritual sense underlies the commandments regarding the keeping of feasts and Sabbaths and regarding circumcision, but that is no reason for disregarding the outward observances which have been ordained for us. "We must look to the literal sense for the body, and to the hidden meaning for the soul. Just as we care for the body as the habitation of the soul, so we must give heed to the literal sense of the laws. For if these are observed we can the more clearly recognise the truths whose symbols they are, and, moreover, it is only in this way that we can avoid incurring blame and censure from the multitude."[1] Philo therefore recommends a middle position between the belief of the multitude, who only hold by the letter of the tradition without observing the deeper meaning, and a thorough-going gnosis which attaches weight solely to the ideal meaning and not at all to the letter, and thus makes a breach with the Jewish popular religion.

That there was a gnostic party of this kind among the Jews of the Diaspora at that period is unmistakably evident from Philo's language in the above passages. Probably the Therapeutæ belonged to it, since their spiritual piety was widely different from ordinary Judaism. If Philo, in his work on *The Contemplative Life*, nevertheless belauded them as an example of virtue, that may be explained from the fact that they as an esoteric and ascetic association did not assume a provocative attitude, and gave no offence to the people by freedom of morals. But there seem also to have existed at that period Jewish Gnostics who paraded their rejection of their ancestral law in an extreme libertinism; these, doubtless, were among the adversaries whom Philo opposed as "The seed of Cain who held himself to be wise"[2] in the work

---

[1] *De migr. Abr.*, xvi. (M. i. 450; R. ii. 312)

[2] περὶ τῶν τοῦ δοκησισόφου Κάϊν ἐγγόνων (M. i. 226 ff.; R. ii. 3 ff.). The passages cited below are from M. i. 232, 233, 235; R. ii. 12, 13, 15 f.

which bears that title. He certainly names the Sophist Protagoras, as being the originator of the godless opinion that the human mind is the measure of all things, "a successor in the delusion of Cain"; but it does not follow that his whole polemic is directed solely against Greek philosophers—how could it be said of them that they know how to make and to listen to lofty discourses about holiness and the worship of God, while they have in themselves a mind at enmity with God? Or that they dare to defend themselves against the accusation of ungodliness by asserting that they have been excellently trained by their teacher Cain, who taught them to honour that which is at hand more than the distant author of it, and who is the more deserving of loyalty because he clearly proved the might of his doctrine by manifest deeds, in that he was victorious over Abel the teacher of the opposite opinion?[1] Is not that an unmistakable allusion to a Jewish sect who must have expressly acknowledged Cain as their leader? That this was actually the well-known antinomian gnostic sect of the Cainites is clearly evident from Philo's further description, in which the story of Cain's founding a city is allegorically interpreted of the "foundation of his doctrine," which means, no doubt, the sect named after him, the "citizens" of which Philo describes as associates in ungodliness, self-love, boasting, falsehood, and delusion, men who hold themselves wise but do not know the true wisdom, and instead suffer from ignorance, want of instruction, and all allied disorders.

[1] The same proof of the higher origin and superiority of Cain over Abel is found also in Epiphanius' description of the gnostic Cainites (*Hær.*, xxxviii. ii.).

The laws which obtain in that city are: lawlessness, unrighteousness, iniquity, unchastity, impudence, delusion, incontinency in all sensuous lusts. "Such is the system of life which the ungodly build for themselves by their own strength and because of the wretchedness of their souls, until the wrath of God prepares for their sophistical arts a fearful fall; yea, that shall come to pass, even though they should build a city and a tower the top of which should reach to heaven. Moreover, they have gone so far in their accursed ungodliness that they have not only set up this way of life for themselves, but are endeavouring to compel the virtuous majority in Israel to accept it, and to force upon it, when leaders and teachers are being chosen, men of evil works." It does not seem to me possible to doubt that this polemic of Philo is directed against the Jewish gnostic sect of the Cainites, who sought by their "sophistical arts" to win adherents for their antinomian doctrine and practice among the Jews of the Diaspora, and endeavoured to influence the choice of the rulers of the synagogue in orthodox communities. As the Cainites belonged to the widely distributed Ophite Gnostics, Philo's polemic furnishes clear proof of the existence of the beginnings of that form of Gnosticism even in pre-Christian times in the Judaism of the Diaspora.[1] It did not arise solely out of the Alexandrian Judaism, but out of that Babylonian *cum* Jewish *cum* Hellenistic mixture of religions in which the various Christian Gnostic sects had their common source, as we shall see later.

[1] *Cf.* Friedländer, *Der vorchristliche jüdische Gnosticismus*, 1898.

JEWISH HELLENISM

CHAPTER IV

APOCALYPTIC WRITINGS

To defend Judaism as the one true religion against superstition and unbelief, whether Jewish or heathen, was the common aim of the Jewish literature of the Hellenistic period. But whereas the Jewish thinkers of Alexandria sought to attain this end by means of a speculative spiritualisation of Jewish tradition aided by Greek philosophy, other Jewish apologists had recourse to the more popular method of establishing and confirming the belief in the final victory of Judaism over all enemies, within and without, by means of a religious view of history, looking both to the past and to the future. In this religious view of the history of the past and its issue in the future the apologists followed in general the footsteps of the ancient prophets; but since the direct impulse of the prophetic spirit had lost its force, their revelations became more or less artistically composed visions, the borrowed and often unnatural symbolism of which was very different from the fresh and genuine religious poetry of the ancient prophets. "Apocalyptic is the aftermath of the ancient prophetism, and an artificial solution of a contradiction: on the one hand the later Judaism had lost the consciousness of a living fulness of the Spirit of God, while on the other hand, in a time of much unrest, a keen desire had arisen to lift the veil of the unknown, and learn what was in store for the oppressed people of God."[1] Closely connected with the secondary and dependent character of the apocalyptic writers is the pseudonymous form of their revelations; they seek to cover themselves with the authority of an ancient and honoured name. Under the names of the heathen Sibyl or the mythical Daniel or Enoch, or of Moses, Baruch, Ezra, and the Twelve Patriarchs, the anonymous authors profess to prophesy the whole course of history from beginning to end, the fulfilment of the professed prophecy up to the time of the writer serving as guarantee for the fulfilment of the prophecy of the future. They naturally attach themselves closely to the ancient prophetic and other sacred scriptures, but in the free interpretation of these, Apocalyptic rivals Alexandrian speculation. Moreover, in its cosmogony, angelology, and eschatology it has adopted so many new and foreign elements, derived from the Oriental-Hellenistic mixture of religions, and so worked them up into a mighty world-drama embracing heaven and earth, that it may be regarded as, in so far, a special form of the Jewish-Hellenistic syncretism which we shall have to discuss more fully at a later point.

The apocalypse or collection of Jewish oracles, sent forth under the name of the heathen Sibyl, which is preserved to us in the third, fourth, and fifth books of the (generally heathen) Sibylline oracles,[2] is the

[1] Hilgenfeld, *Die jüdische Apokalyptik*, p. 10. *Cf.* Schürer, *Neutest. Zeitgesch.*, ii. 610 f.

[2] Further details in regard to this and the following work may be found in the *Alttest. Apokryphen und Pseudepigraphen* of

work of several Alexandrian Jews, the earliest oracles having been written before the middle of the second century B.C., the latest about the middle of the second century A.D. Common to all of them is the aim of propagating Judaism among the heathen. This end is served by a sharp polemic against the ungodliness of heathen polytheism, the origin of which is explained by a euhemeristic interpretation of heathen mythology and theogony (the war with the Titans). As a punishment for their idolatry and their unnatural vices, the destruction of all heathen kingdoms and many individual heathen towns is announced; on the other hand, the Jews are belauded as the righteous nation which has held aloof from the follies of the heathen, and although at times it has met with misfortunes, is assured of ultimate happiness and victory. "Then when the fateful day of the End comes, God shall send a King from the rising of the sun who shall make an end of war over all the earth, slaying some and making treaty with others. The temple of the great God shall be filled full of glorious wealth, the earth and the sea shall be full of riches. A final assault of the hostile kings will be repulsed by a fearful judgment, with fire and sword, brimstone and hurricane; but the children of the great God (the Jews) shall dwell quietly round about the temple, protected by God, who is the sole ruler of all things, as by a wall of fire. But Hellas too, if it lays down its pride and turns to the service of the great God, may have a share in the great happiness of the people of God.

Kautzsch, ii. 177 ff. *Cf.* Schürer, *Neutest. Zeitgesch.*, ii. 792 ff.; Hilgenfeld, *Jüd. Apok.*, 53 ff.; Gfrörer, *Philo*, ii. 121 ff.; Delaunay, *Moines et Sibylles*, 169 ff.

There shall be no more war nor drought upon earth, but great peace and abundance of all good things; one law shall obtain over the whole earth, and the true God shall be Lord alone. From the whole world men shall bring incense and gifts to the house of the great God (in Jerusalem), which shall then be the sole temple for all humanity. The whole of the earth and of the sea shall be open to travel and shipping, for the peace which belongs to the good shall come upon earth. But those who shall put away the sword are the prophets of the great God, for they themselves are the judges of mankind and righteous kings. That is the judgment and rule of the great God" (iii. 652-784). The victory of the Jewish theocracy, in which the prophets shall rule over mankind as judges and kings, closes the world-drama, according to the oracle of the Jewish-Alexandrian Sibyl, who, it should be said, guards herself against being confused with the shameless Erythræan prophetess of lies, and professes to be a daughter-in-law of Noah (iii. 812 ff.).

The Palestinian apocalyptic literature begins with the Book of Daniel, which was written by an unknown author during the excitement of the Maccabean war, and was attributed to a mythical saint of the time of Nebuchadnezzar. After a series of edifying stories which centre in the fate of this hero regarded as a prototype of the Maccabean confessors and martyrs, there is a description of the visions in which Daniel sees in advance the course of the history of the world, that is, the history of the four world-empires—the Babylonian, Median, Persian, and Greek—down to the time of the enemy of the Jews, Antiochus Epiphanes, with whose persecution of the

Jewish religion the retrospective prophecy breaks off, since immediately after this time of oppression, the victorious coming of the kingdom of God is expected. When the beasts have been destroyed in which those four world-empires are symbolised, Daniel sees (vii. 13 f.) "one like unto a son of man" coming on the clouds of heaven, and brought before the Ancient of Days (God). "Unto him was given dominion, honour, and kingship, so that all peoples, nations, and tongues served him; his dominion is an everlasting dominion, which shall not pass away, and his kingdom shall never be destroyed." As immediately afterwards the same dominion is given to the "saints of the Most High" (18, 22) and to the "people of the saints" (27), it is probable that what is meant in verse 13 by the figure of a son of man is not a personal Messiah, but the Jewish people, which is symbolised by this figure just as the foregoing world-empires were symbolised by animal forms. That did not prevent the symbolic personification from being understood at a later epoch as referring to a personal Messiah coming upon the clouds of heaven, for we find, in the Similitudes of Enoch, the Messiah spoken of as the heavenly Son of man, undoubtedly with allusion to the passage in Daniel.

The Apocalypse of Enoch is a composite formation, in which we can distinguish three main strata: (1) the primary document, i.–xxxvi. and lxxii.–cv., the origin of which is ascribed by most critics to the last third of the second century B.C., under the reign of John Hyrcanus; (2) the Similitudes, xxxvii.–lxxi., which, according to the prevailing view, are to be ascribed to the first century B.C., either to the seventh decade (prior to 64) or the fourth (under Herod); others, however, incline to see in them a Christian apocalypse of the first century A.D., but this view can hardly be correct; (3) the Noachian elements which have been—perhaps by the redactor of the whole—interpolated into the Similitudes or added at their close (cvi. f.); after which follows a final word of exhortation (cviii.).

The book of Enoch in its present form consists partly of descriptions of things above and beneath the earth, which the patriarch Enoch, who is exalted by reason of his translation to God, saw in vision or in the course of an actual journey through heaven and hell, undertaken under the conduct of an angel; partly of prophetic narratives concerning future events, especially a universal flood (lxxxiii. ff.), and also concerning the history of Israel (vision of shepherds, lxxxv.-xc.), finally the whole history of the world down to the judgment (vision of the ten weeks, xciii., xci., xii.-xvii.); partly of discourses of exhortation, invective, and consolation (introductory and closing chapters). The cosmological visions are of special value for our knowledge of Jewish popular metaphysic, in which there is welded together an abundance of material drawn from Oriental and Hellenistic belief and superstition, animistic natural philosophy and theosophy, along with the monotheistic basis. Among the historical visions, the vision of the shepherds is of special importance for the determination of the date of the primary document. It describes the history of Israel and its conflict with the world-powers in a very artificial and tasteless allegory, in which the Jewish heroes are represented by tame animals, their heathen enemies by beasts of prey, and the angelic powers which watch over the fate of nations by " shepherds," who faithlessly neglect their duty as guardians, and therefore are sent to hell with the fallen angels. The number (seventy) of the shepherds probably has reference to the seventy years of bondage foretold in the prophecy of Jeremiah (xxv. 11), which are extended by Daniel (ix. 24) to seventy weeks of years, down to the commencement of the Kingdom of God. This time of bondage is divided, according to Enoch, into four periods: the first, down to Cyrus; the second, to Alexander; the third, to the domination of the Syrians; the fourth, to the establishment of the Kingdom of the Messiah. This is a rather different division from that of the four world-empires of Daniel, and it is therefore probable that the number four for the world-epochs, which is common to both, is to be referred to some traditional conception which may have had its roots in Parseeism, to which the doctrine of the punishment of the hostile angelic powers also seems to point.[1] At the end of the vision of the shepherds, after the judgment upon the earthly and heavenly enemies (angel-shepherds and star-spirits), the Messiah appears in the form of a white bull, to which all its race (the people of God) become like (xc. 37 ff.). The Messiah is therefore here the human head of the people of God, the representative, but not the cause, of its final victory and blessedness. It is otherwise, however, in the Similitudes (xlv.–lxii.), in which Messiah is described as the "Chosen" and

[1] *Cf.* Beer in the commentary on Enoch in Kautzsch's *Pseudepigraphen*, ii. 294; Stave, *Einfluss der Parsismus auf das Judentum*, p. 190.

the "Son of man," who was hidden in the presence of God before the world was created, whose glory is from eternity to eternity, whose power endures from generation to generation, who sits upon the throne of judgment and shall take vengeance upon kings and mighty men, but shall save the holy and righteous. Here, therefore, the Messiah is a superhuman being descending out of his Divine pre-existence, the instrument of the Divine judgment, and of the salvation of the people of God. In the vision of the ten weeks (xci. 12 ff.) there is no mention at all of the Messiah. Here the first, the earthly, judgment is carried out by the sword of the righteous themselves. Finally, however, in the tenth week there shall take place the great eternal judgment, in which the hostile angelic powers shall be punished by God. Thereafter there shall be a new heaven and an unending existence in goodness and righteousness. Here we have for the first time the thought of a preliminary earthly period of salvation of temporary duration, in contrast with the final eternal completion of all things. The coexistence of such different kinds of representations in one and the same apocalyptic writing shows how little need was felt for systematic order and logical unity in these eschatological conceptions. The same was the case in Christianity from the first, and it is therefore idle for the theologian to attempt to bring dogmatic order into this chaos.

The apocalypse which has come down to us under the title of the "Assumption of Moses" contains a prophecy of Moses, when about to depart, concerning the history of Israel from its entry into Canaan until the time of the author, which probably falls about the beginning of the Christian era (4 or 6 A.D.). It is only the close of this apocalypse which has an interest for us, inasmuch as here, in place of the representations, customary since Daniel, of a descent of the Kingdom of God from heaven to earth, what is predicted is rather a raising of Israel from earth to heaven. "The most high God shall arise, who alone is eternal, and will come forth to punish the heathen, and will bring to nought all their idols. Then shalt thou be happy, O Israel, and shalt mount upon the neck and the wings of the eagle (the Roman Empire), and the days of the eagle shall be fulfilled. And God shall exalt thee and cause thee to hover aloft in the starry heaven; then shalt thou look down from above and see thine enemies upon earth and recognise them, and rejoice and thank thy Creator." This transference of the future salvation of Israel to the heavens implies a deeply pessimistic conviction concerning the impossibility of deliverance from its earthly misery; and a similar view will be found in the next two apocalypses with which we shall have to deal. What, precisely, the author understood by the "hovering of Israel in the starry heaven," it is impossible to say, and it is equally impossible to discover the meaning of the enigmatic word "Taxo" (ix. 1). So much only seems clear, that it cannot be the Messiah,[1] for in connection with the hope of a transcendental salvation which is here in view there is no room for a Messiah.

Of the writings to which tradition ascribes the name Baruch, we have here only to do with the

[1] *Cf.* Clemen in the commentary on the "Assumption of Moses" in Kautzsch's *Pseudepigraphen,* ii. 326.

"Apocalypse of Baruch," which has come down to us in a Syriac text. It begins with the description of the first destruction of Jerusalem, and of the carrying away of the prisoners to Babylon. Baruch, who has remained behind among the ruins, is consoled in his trouble by various revelations concerning the future fate of Israel, which, under curious allegorical forms (the vine, the spring, and the cedar, xxxv.-xl., and the alternately dark and clear waters, liii.-lxxiv.), signify in sum that after manifold trials the Messianic judgment on the nations and the deliverance of Israel from all her troubles shall at length come to pass. A letter of Baruch to the nine-and-a-half tribes of Israel in the (Assyrian) captivity concludes the writing, which has perhaps not been completely preserved. It was written about 70 A.D., and gives a vivid picture of the struggles of the Jewish faith with the stern fact of the destruction of Jerusalem.

The same questions of theodicy, of the compatibility of the evils of the world in general, and of the misfortunes of the Jews in particular, with the righteous rule of God over the world, form the central interest of the Apocalypse of Ezra (the so-called Fourth Book of Ezra or Second Esdras), which is so closely related to Baruch in its main tenor as well as in many particulars, that one of them must be dependent on the other. As to which has the priority, the opinions of exegetes are divided;[1] I agree with those who hold Ezra's to be later, and therefore dependent on Baruch.

---

[1] *Cf.* Rothstein in the commentary on Baruch in Kautzsch's *Pseudepigraphen*, ii. 405 ff., with Schürer, Wellhausen, Kabisch, and Clemen. On the other side, Gunkel in his Commentary on 2 Esdr.

The historical allegory conveyed in the hackneyed vision of the eagle (xi. f.), which in confusion and tastelessness goes beyond even the earlier apocalyptic allegories (vision of the beasts and the shepherds, of the vine and the spring, of the clear and dark waters, and the like), points, according to the most probable interpretation (it is not possible to arrive at certainty) to the period of Domitian as the time when the Apocalypse of Ezra was composed.

The importance of this apocalypse and of that of Baruch lies in the deepening of theological reflection which they show. The special distress of the Jewish people forces upon pious thinkers the general question of the reasons for the evils of the world in general and the possibility of their being finally overcome, the question why so many are lost and so few saved. This most difficult question of theodicy lies heavy upon their hearts, and in order to answer it they survey the whole course of history from the beginning, and find that evil entered the world even with the first man, and caused so profound a corruption that it is impossible in the present world to overcome it, and salvation must therefore be looked for only in a wholly new world. "The promises for the future which are given to the pious are not such as can be fulfilled in this present age. For this age is full of trouble and confusion. Evil has been sown and its harvest has not yet appeared. Until the harvest has been reaped and the place where the bad seed is has disappeared, the field where the good seed has been sown cannot be seen. For a small grain of evil seed was sown in Adam's heart at the first, but how great a crop of sin that has already borne and shall yet continue to bear before the threshing floor appears! When Adam sinned the world was judged; the present age is (only) the evil way leading to the future. When Adam sinned, his fall not only came upon him but upon us, his posterity, for what doth it profit us that eternity has been promised to us if we have done the works of death?"[1] Yet this universal corruption inherited from Adam does not do away with the personal responsibility and guilt of individuals. For "in the judgment each one bears his own unrighteousness or righteousness without substitution. On victory in the fight which every man must fight depends his life or death."[2] These two points of view are explicitly combined in the Apocalypse of Baruch, liv. 15 f.: "Though Adam first sinned and brought untimely death upon all, yet of those who are descended from him each one singly has brought future torment upon himself, as, on the other hand, each one singly elects for himself future glory. For in truth the believer receives reward. Adam was therefore solely and only the cause of his own downfall, and we each of us become our own Adam." lvi. 6: "When, as a consequence of Adam's transgression, untimely death began, mourning began to be known, and tribulation manifested itself, and pain was created and affliction was perfected and boasting began. And since the underworld craved ever for fresh blood, child-bearing began, and sexual lust, and the loftiness of mankind was abased, and good withered. What can be darker than all this? And from this black darkness came ever more darkness, and so at last the blackness of

[1] 2 Esdr. iv. 27 ff., vii. 10, 118.   [2] 2 Esdr. vii. 105, 128.

darkness came to be. For Adam was a danger not to himself alone but to the angels; for they too, at the time when he was created, possessed freedom. And some of them descended and had intercourse with women, and then those who had so acted were handed over in chains to torment. But the rest of the angels hold themselves far aloof from such deeds." Here there is ascribed to the fall of Adam a fatal influence not only upon mankind, but also upon the world of angels, the fall of some of whom appears as a consequence of the fall of Adam. That certainly does not agree with the conception to which Wisd. ii. 24 bears witness (and which is alluded to also in 2 Cor. xi. 3), according to which Satan was the cause of man's fall, and sin therefore had its origin in the spiritual world prior to the commencement of human history. Still another version of the origin of evil is given in Enoch (vi.–viii., xv., lxix.) and in the Book of Jubilees (iv., v., x.), where it is ascribed to the seduction of the daughters of men by angels, and to the giants who sprang from these unions and became destroying demons and founders of idolatry. When in the same passage we are told of the judgment upon these fallen angels, and how they are fettered in dungeons beneath the earth until the final judgment, the affinity, and doubtless also the historical connection of this mythical conception with the Persian and Orphico-Pythagorean[1] demonologies (which are doubtless mutually connected) becomes unmistakable.

The richly developed angelology of the apocalypses points in general to Parseeism. In Enoch xx. six

[1] *Cf.* Dieterich, *Nekyia*, p. 211 f.; Stave, *Einfluss des Parsismus auf das Judentum*, p. 197 f.

archangels are enumerated, with special names and functions or spheres of authority, corresponding to the six Amesha Spentas; in Enoch xl. four "angels of the presence" are mentioned who sing praises before the Lord of Glory, and each one of whom has his special office; according to Enoch lxi. 10, God calls together to judgment "the whole host of heaven, all the holy ones in the height, the Cherubim, Seraphim, and Ophanim, all angels of power and might, the 'chosen' and the other powers who are upon the earth and over the water." These spirits of the elements are divided, according to lx. 12 ff., into spirits of the moon and stars, thunder and lightning, sea, frost, hail, snow, mist, dew, and rain. It was the primeval animistic belief in spirits, which in Israel was driven into the background by the religion of Jahwe, which now, reinforced by the influence of heathen demonology, came to the front again and, as angelology, allied itself with monotheism.

Although in theory this whole host of spirits is subordinate to the sole dominion of God, yet the prominence of this spiritualism does not indicate a glad confidence in the universal administration of the Divine providence, but, on the contrary, a gloomy feeling of the god-forsaken hopelessness and helplessness of this present world, which becomes more and more pronounced, especially in the later apocalypses. "Who is there among living men who has not sinned, who is there among men born of women who has not broken Thy covenant? Now I know that the future world shall bring little relief but much torment. For an evil heart has grown up in us which has brought us nigh unto destruction and has shown us the ways of death and led us far away from life; and that, not a few of us only, but almost all who have been created. ... Men are in worse case than the beasts, which have no judgment to look forward to, and know nothing of future torment or blessedness. But as for us, what profit is it to us that we have the chance of attaining blessedness, seeing that in reality we fall a prey to torment? For all who are born are defiled by ungodliness, full of sin, laden with guilt, and we should be in much better case if after death we had not to go into judgment."[1] To this complaint Ezra receives the answer that men fall under the condemnation of the righteous God just because they live godlessly in spite of the possession of reason and of the commandments; yet he himself need not fear on this account, for he has a treasure of good works which is laid up for him with God, and shall be revealed at the last day. But even before that, immediately after the death of each man a preliminary retribution begins; the souls of the ungodly go not to a place of rest, but must wander miserably about in the sevenfold torment of contrition, shame, anxiety, and fear, intensified by the contrast with the happier lot of the pious. The latter go immediately to rest in sevenfold joy, happy that they have finished the sore struggle against the innate evil disposition, that they enjoy deep peace under the protection of the angels, that they have escaped from mortality and are delivered from the trammels and troubles of earth, and look forward to future glory, being already blessed in beholding the face of Him whom they had served during their earthly life, and

[1] 2 Esdr. vii. 45–69.

from whom they are now to receive praise and reward, while their faces shine as the sun and the stars of light.[1] Similarly, in Baruch it is said the righteous go fearlessly forth from this life, and eagerly expect to receive the promised world because they have a treasure of good works laid up in the store-houses of God. This present world is indeed for them only toil and trouble, but the future world is a crown of victory with great glory. If there were nought but the life which each man has here, there could be nothing more bitter than that. For of what use is strength which turns again to weakness, satiety which turns again to hunger, beauty which turns again to ugliness. In the present existence evil is neither fully evil, nor good fully good; all things are constantly changing, pass into their contraries and turn to nought. Therefore nothing in the present life ought to engage us; we should wait quietly until that comes which has been promised. For what is future, we desire to be present, and place our hopes on that which is to come. For there is a time which shall not pass away, a new world which endures for ever. It is the inheritance of those who have provided themselves with stores of wisdom, who have not fallen away from grace and have observed the law with sincerity.[2] Therefore the exhortation goes forth, "Renounce this passing life, cast away mortal cares, throw off the burden of human existence, put off thy weak nature, lay aside torturing problems, and hasten to depart from this temporal life."[3]

[1] 2 Esdr. vii. 80-99.
[2] Apoc. Bar. xiv. 12, xv. 8, xxi. 13 ff., lxxxiii. 9, xliv. 10.
[3] 2 Esdr. xiv. 14.

In this world-renouncing mood and the hope of a super-earthly happiness for the individual souls of the pious, the Palestinian Apocalyptic is entirely at one with the Alexandrian-Jewish Hellenism, and was no doubt influenced by it; but along with this individualistic and transcendental eschatology, which for the Alexandrians is the chief thing, there is associated and interwoven in the Palestinian writers the traditional expectation of a forthcoming Messianic period of blessedness for the Jewish people. In this the ancient prophetic ideal conception of the future continues to exercise an influence, but in such a way that from the time of Daniel onward it is transferred from the natural, historical level to the supernatural, and has become in a measure transcendental, thus standing in no clear relation to the Hellenistic eschatology. The end is to be preceded by a time of fearful affliction, divided, according to Apoc. Bar. xxvii.,[1] into twelve periods. There shall be fearful signs in nature, tumult, murder, and violence among men, "then reason hides herself, and wisdom flees to her chamber, unrighteousness and unchastity are multiplied upon earth"; "confusion of mind comes upon all men, the humble are exalted above the men of reputation, the poor above the rich, the dissolute above the heroic, the wise shall be silent, and fools speak. Peoples shall war with their rulers. Whosoever escapes war, earthquake, fire and famine, shall be given over into the hands of the Messiah. He shall summon together all peoples and shall suffer only those to live who submit themselves to the Jews; the rest he shall put to the sword. Then

[1] *Cf.* lxx.; 2 Esdr. v. 1-13, xiii. 30.

when he has humbled the whole world and seated himself in peace upon the throne of his kingdom, bliss shall be revealed and peace shall appear. Sickness, care, and affliction of all kinds shall depart, and no man shall die before his time. Universal peace shall reign, not only among men but also in nature, wild beasts shall offer their service to man, women shall bear without birth-pains, work shall be easy and successful, the fruitfulness of field and vineyard shall be of fabulous extent; moreover, the two monsters behemoth and leviathan which were made on the fifth day of creation shall now serve as food for the righteous, and the rain of manna shall be repeated. But this time of earthly happiness is only the end (the closing period) of the era of transitoriness and the beginning (the prelude, introduction) of the eternal. Afterwards, when the time of the coming (earthly presence) is completed, he shall return to heaven in glory. Then those who have fallen asleep in the hope of his coming shall arise, those souls which are ordained unto life shall go forth once for all out of the storehouses where they have been kept, and shall rejoice that the end of time has come, but the souls of the godless shall perish because the time of their destruction has come." The distinction, which is only hinted at in Baruch,[1] between the period of earthly happiness under a victorious Messianic king and the completion of all things in the new world is more definitely taught by Ezra. He speaks of the Messiah in three passages. At the close of the vision of the eagle (xii. 31) he says that the lion who rebukes the eagle for his sins is the Christ (the

[1] lxxii.–lxxiv., and xxix., xxx., xl.

anointed one), whom the Most High has kept unto the end of days, who shall spring from the seed of David and shall come forth to bring the ungodly to judgment and convict them of their sins, and afterwards destroy them. But he shall graciously deliver the remnant of the people of God, and grant them peace, until the end, the day of judgment, comes.

In the next vision (xiii. 1) the seer beholds something in the semblance of a man (*tanquam similitudinem hominis*; *cf.* Dan. vii. 13) rise out of the heart of the sea and fly with the clouds of heaven. That is, as the interpretation proceeds to set forth (25 ff.), he whom the Most High hath long-time kept, purposing through him to deliver the creation and create a new order. "Whereas thou hast seen that out of his mouth came wind and fire and storm, and that he bore no sword nor any weapon, yet destroyed the assault of that host which came to fight against him, this is the interpretation: Behold the days come when the Most High shall deliver the dwellers upon earth. Then shall come great excitement upon them, so that they shall levy war upon one another, city against city, and kingdom against kingdom. Then when those signs which have been announced beforehand come to pass, my Son shall appear, whom thou hast seen rising up as a man. Then when all nations hear his voice they shall lay aside their sins and the wars which they are making upon one another, and an innumerable host shall be gathered together at one point to attack him. But he shall stand upon the top of Mount Zion, and shall rebuke the nations which have come against him for their sins, and declare to them their future torments, and shall destroy them without labour by a rebuke which shall be like fire; but the people of Israel, as many of them as are left, he shall protect and shall show them yet many more wonders" (alluding to Baruch's description of the Messianic blessedness). Finally, the Messiah's arising "out of the sea" is interpreted (*v.* 51 ff.) as meaning that he will come forth out of a hidden place, so that "none of the inhabitants of earth shall see my Son or his comrades (the angels) until the hour of his day" (of his visible appearing). In all this the question regarding his origin, whether he is from earth or from heaven, remains uncertain; "of the seed of David" (xii. 1), compared with vii. 29, "shall die," make for the former, but the retinue of angels which accompanies his appearance suggests the latter. Perhaps the author of the Apocalypse of Ezra designedly left this question open because both views existed side by side in Jewish tradition, as we have already seen in the different sections of the Apocalypse of Enoch, where, according to the vision of the shepherds, the Messiah is a "white bull" which comes forth from Israel, while according to the Similitudes he comes from heaven, where from the beginning he had been hidden and kept by God, as the "Son of man and the Chosen One." That the earthly dominion of the Messiah is to be only a limited transitional period, after which shall follow the judgment of the world, bringing in eternal retribution, is still more clearly taught in 2 Esdras vii. 26 ff. than in Baruch and Enoch (xci. 12–17): "Behold the days come when these signs of which I have told thee beforehand come to pass, the city which is now invisible and the hidden land shall appear (the heavenly Jerusalem and Paradise), and whosoever is delivered from the plagues shall behold my wonders. For my son Christ shall be revealed and those that are with him (the angels) and shall give joy to them that remain, for four hundred years. After these years shall my son, the Christ, die, and all who have the breath of life. Then shall the world be turned into the silence of the primeval time for seven days, as at the first beginning; so that no man shall remain. But after seven days the world, which is now sleeping, shall awake, and corruptibility itself shall be destroyed. And the earth shall deliver up those that rest in her, and the dust shall release those who sleep therein, and the chambers shall restore the souls that were committed to them. And the Most High shall appear upon the throne of judgment. Then cometh the end, and compassion is no more, and mercy removes afar off, and long-suffering is past. Judgment alone shall remain, truth shall abide, faith shall triumph. Reward follows, retribution appears, good deeds awake and evil deeds sleep no more. Then the pit of torment appears (the abyss of hell; *cf.* Enoch xviii., xix., xxii., xxvii.) and over against it the place of rest, the furnace of Gehenna is revealed and over against it the paradise of bliss." The description of the latter as an existence exalted above all change of day or night, of heat and frost, in the splendour of the glory of God, is an expanded and more florid elaboration of Enoch's description of the glorious lot of the righteous "in the light of eternal life," in equality with the angels of heaven (Enoch lviii. 51), in which the resemblance to the light-realm of Ahura and the Orphic "Islands of the Blessed" is immediately evident.

If, however, we recall that, according to the passage of 2 Esdras (vii. 80–99) quoted above (p. 89 f.), the souls of the righteous immediately after death enter into a "sevenfold joy," behold God's face, and shine like the sun and stars, it is hard to say what is the exact distinction between this blessedness of the righteous immediately after death, and that which only follows the last judgment and the resurrection, or what changes in their condition are made by the occurrence of this world-catastrophe and by the preceding earthly reign of the Messiah. It is exactly the same difficulty which we encountered before in the Pauline eschatology, and, in both cases, the solution is not to be sought in any harmonising dogmatic construction, but simply and solely by recognising the historical fact that two entirely different lines of religious thought and hope of the future have collided with one another and become entangled—the Hellenistic spiritual faith in immortality beyond the grave, and the blessedness of the souls of the good, such as obtains exclusively in the Book of Wisdom and in Philo, and the Jewish national belief in the earthly blessedness of the people of God under the reign of the Messiah. That the apocalyptists could not abandon this national ideal of the prophets is quite intelligible; but it is a remarkable evidence of the strength of the influence which Hellenism exercised on the whole of the Jewish theology that even Palestinian apocalyptic could not help placing the Hellenistic belief in the heavenly blessedness of the souls of the good alongside of the belief in the earthly Messianic kingdom, or even, indeed, before it. For that even they did tend to lay more and more stress on the Hellenistic view is evident from the interesting fact that the later apocalyptists limit the earthly Messianic kingdom more and more definitely to a fixed period (whether of 400 years or, as in the Apocalypse of John xx. 2-7, of 1000 years, is immaterial) and distinguish it from the final state in the new super-earthly world. This doctrine of "Chiliasm" is, according to Gunkel's penetrating remark, "a compromise between the ancient hope of the prophets, which they expected to be realised in the present world, and the transcendental hope of later Judaism; and the main emphasis falls upon the latter."[1] A compromise of this kind cannot of course escape inconsistencies, and of these one of the most striking is the doctrine that at the end of the 400 years the Messiah shall die, along with all other men (vii. 29). According to this, he seems to be thought of as an earthly man, and yet immediately beforehand his manifestation in company with "those that are his," *i.e.* the angels, and at the same time with the appearance of the heavenly Jerusalem and of Paradise, is described in such a way that it is more natural to think of a heavenly being, descending from his pre-existent state, than of an ordinary mortal man. Is it possible that the author thought of an incarnation of the Christ, the heavenly Son of God, in order to reign as an earthly Messiah? But, if so, why did he say nothing about it? And how strange it would be in this case that at the renewal of the world and the resurrection (vii. 31 ff.) this Son of God does not

[1] Commentary on 2 Esdr. in Kautzsch's *Pseudepigr.*, ii. 370.

come forth again as the first of the risen and take an active part in the judgment of the world,[1] but after his death at the end of the 400 years disappears completely and for ever from the scene! We are here confronted with an enigma of which the solution is probably to be found in the fact that the author of the Apocalypse of Ezra wavered undecidedly between the transcendental and the historical conception of the person of the Messiah. The author of the Similitudes of Enoch had taken the former side by hypostatising the symbolical figure of the Son of man in Dan. vii. 13 as a pre-existent heavenly being, and bringing it into such close connection with the Divine "Wisdom" that it almost seems to be identical with the latter. And, accordingly, he had asserted concerning this earthly, semi-divine being, not merely pre-existence before the beginning of the world, but also the eternal duration of his reign, and especially that he should exercise judgment upon the world.[2] But this transcendental view of the person of the

---

[1] In vi. 6 the holding of the judgment by God alone is so particularly emphasised that it reads like a protest against the New Testament Christology. *Cf.* Gunkel, *ut sup.*, p. 364.

[2] Enoch xlix. 2 ff., li. 2 f.: "The Chosen One standeth before the Lord of Spirits, and his glory is from everlasting to everlasting, and his power from generation to generation. *In him dwells the spirit of Wisdom* and the spirit of Him who giveth understanding, and the spirit of doctrine and of might, and the spirit of those who have fallen asleep in righteousness. He shall *judge* the things that are hid. He shall choose the righteous and holy among those who are risen; for the day of their redemption is at hand. In those days shall the Chosen One sit upon My Throne, and all the secret things of wisdom shall proceed out of the thoughts of his mouth, for the Lord of Spirits has granted it unto him and has glorified him."

Messiah, which was closely connected with Hellenistic speculation, seems never to have become popular in Jewish circles, for in the Psalms of Solomon, which contain the popular Messianic belief of the Pharisees, the Messiah appears, quite in accordance with the ancient prophetic ideal, as the victorious and righteous King of David's line. And it is of course immediately obvious that this view of the Messiah is much more suitable to the expectation of an earthly, national Messiah than the heavenly hypostasis of Hellenistic speculation, which has nothing to do with earthly kingdoms and battles, but belongs to the spiritual realm of the super-sensuous ideal world. Thus it is easy to understand how the Jewish apocalyptic, which derived from prophetism but was influenced also by Hellenism, retained on the one hand along with the popular expectation of an earthly Messianic kingdom an earthly and human Messiah, but on the other hand felt the attraction, along with the Hellenistic idealism, of the view of the Messiah as a mystical spiritual being descending out of his mysterious heavenly pre-existence. While the latter is the more prominent in the pre-Christian Similitudes, it seems to have lost ground later in consequence of the Jewish opposition to the Christological speculations of the New Testament, as may be gathered from 2 Esdras vi. 6. It is, moreover, clear that the combination which was effected in Christian theology from its beginnings (Paul), of the historical Messiah Jesus with the pre-existent heavenly Son of God, was so far prepared in Jewish theology that it appears as a natural and inevitable synthesis of the two Messianic views which there stood side by side. The Hellenistic theory of a Divine intermediate being and instrument of revelation, and the prophetic ideal of a human Messianic king, showed some tendency even in the Jewish theology to become united with one another, but this was not wholly possible because the link of connection was wanting. When this was provided in the person of the historical Messiah Jesus, who by His death and resurrection became the heavenly Lord of the new people of God, there began immediately a fusion of the two elements, the result of which is expressed in the words of the Fourth Gospel: "The Logos became flesh and dwelt among us." In this the Wisdom-doctrine of Judaism[1] attained its fulfilment and was transcended: the Christian faith in Christ offered the solution of the problems of Hellenism as well as of Hebraism.

[1] *Cf.* Enoch xlii.: "When Wisdom came to take up her abode among the children of men, and found no dwelling-place, she returned to her place (in heaven) and took her seat among the angels."

SYNCRETISM AND GNOSTICISM

CHAPTER V

THE RELIGION OF MITHRA

FROM the time of the conquest of Babylon by Cyrus, there began, along with the intermixture of nations, an intermixture of religions ("Syncretism") which, increasing with the lapse of centuries and extending itself westward, swept like a tidal wave over the ancient popular religions, sapping their foundations and preparing the way for new religious constructions. If the founding of the Perso-Babylonian Empire by Cyrus was the starting-point of this great movement in the history of the world, the overthrow of the Persian Empire by Alexander the Great gave a new and powerful impulse to its further extension towards the West. To the Perso-Babylonian mixture of religions there were added not only the Syrian and Phrygian cults of Western Asia, but also the Jewish and Hellenistic beliefs and systems of thought, as further elements in the conglomerate. Babylon, Seleucia, Antioch, Tarsus, Alexandria, and Rome mark the stages in the progress of this movement. Various Oriental cults had made their way to Rome during the last centuries of the Republic. About the middle of the first century A.D. Christianity made good its footing there, at first under the protection of Judaism. It was towards the middle of the second century, however, that Rome became the chief battleground of the three religions which, as the final products of the age-long movement of religious syncretism, struggled with one another for the mastery of the world—Mithraism, Gnostic Christianity, and the Christianity of the Church. The struggle between the two latter was decided after some decades in favour of the Church, but the rivalry between Christianity and Mithraism lasted for two centuries longer, and only came to a close during the reign of Julian, the last pagan who occupied the throne of the Cæsars. It seems to me advisable, as a help towards understanding the Gnostic religion and its relation to the Christianity of the Church, to cast a glance in the first place at the religion of Mithra, which resembled Gnosticism both in its historical point of departure and in its fundamental religious ideas.

The religion of Mithra was a syncretistic religion in which successive strata can be distinguished. The lowest stratum consists of the Iranian belief in Ahura Mazda which is associated with the name of the prophet Zarathustra; next comes a stratum of Semitic doctrines which became superimposed upon the former in Babylon; upon this again the local legends of Asia Minor deposited some alluvial layers, and finally there grew up out of this fruitful soil a rich vegetation of Hellenistic ideas.[1] The first stage was the fusion of the Iranian religion with the

[1] Cumont, *Textes et monuments relatifs aux mystères de Mithra* (1889), i. 240. The account which follows is based throughout upon this authoritative work.

Chaldæan mythology and theology. Ahura Mazda was united with Bel, the Lord of heaven, Anahita with Ishtar, and Mithra with the sun-god Shamash; the Chaldæan worship of the stars was taken over into the Persian religion, more especially the worship of the seven great gods, the sun and moon and the five planets, Mars, Mercury, Jupiter, Venus, and Saturn. Alongside of these seven principal gods, to whom the days of the week are dedicated, stand the twelve signs of the zodiac, each of which was worshipped in the appropriate month. Along with the worship of the stars, the belief in the world-directing power of the star-gods, and the astrological divination and magic associated therewith, passed over into the Persian religion, but not without undergoing an important modification in which the reflex influence of the Iranian religion of conflict is unmistakable. The astrological fatalism of the Chaldæans did not remain, as in Babylon, the central point of a quietistic faith, but became the dark background which served as a foil to the glad, hopeful, and courageous belief in deliverance which characterised the religion of Mithra. The central significance and the main attraction of this religion lay in the mythical figure of the light-god, Mithra, who even among the Persians was held to be a "mediator" between Ahura and mankind, and for that reason united himself the more easily with the Chaldæan sun-god Shamash, who occupied the same mediatorial position between gods and men in Babylon—or it should perhaps rather be said that he was confused with him (the relationship wavers between alliance and identity). Some legends of doubtful origin became associated with the Mithra myths and provided the material for certain observances and for the pictorial representations which have been preserved to us on numerous monuments. To these belong the legend of the miraculous birth of Mithra out of a rock, of the worship offered by shepherds to the newborn babe, of his victory over the aurochs and the sacrificial slaughter of it in a cave, which he performed at the command of the god of heaven. With this divinely commanded sacrifice there is associated a cosmogonic myth. From the body of the sacrificial bull there grew up useful plants, wheat from his marrow and the juice of the vine from his blood, while from his seed sprang animals of all kinds (whether man is included is uncertain). To this there are to be added two legends connected with water. In one Mithra appears as the deliverer of mankind from a parching drought by causing a mighty stream of water to gush forth from a rock; in the other as delivering men from a destructive flood, in which he plays the part of Noah. Finally, the mediator of creation shall also serve as mediator of the end of the world; he it is who shall raise the dead, hold a universal judgment, destroy the ungodly in a great conflagration, and bestow upon the righteous eternal life in a new world. How far this doctrine of resurrection, which is expounded in the Persian Bundehesh, played a part also in the Mithra-cult is doubtful; in any case it was of less importance than the belief in immortality, which, in association with the worship of the stars, formed the central point of the mystical cultus.

The souls of men, according to the religion of

Mithra, descended to the earth from the height of heaven, whether under the compulsion of an astrological fate, as the Babylonian doctrine asserted, or of their own free-will, in order to maintain the good fight against the demons of darkness, as the Iranians believed. After men's death, the dark " Devas " and the bright emissaries of God struggle for their souls. Hell with its tortures awaits the unclean, or, at the least, transmigration into the bodies of the lower animals, but pure souls mount up under the protection of the angels of Ahura through the seven star-worlds to the highest light-world of God. On the way they have to pass through seven gates, each of which opens only to the initiate, who can give the right password to the keeper of the gate. As it passes through these seven gates the soul gradually strips itself of all its earthly elements. It leaves its sensuous nature to the moon, its lower needs to Mercury, its desire for life to Venus, its intellectual capacity to the sun, its combativeness to Mars, its ambition to Jupiter, and its indolence to Saturn. Thus stripped of all earthliness, it passes in its original nakedness into the eighth heaven, the light-kingdom of the blessed gods, and is welcomed by " Father Mithra," its helpful ally in its earthly conflicts, "like a child who has returned from a long journey." The origin of this impressive doctrine is doubtless to be sought in the Babylonian myth of the descent of Ishtar to hell, who also had to pass through seven gates, and at each to strip off a portion of her garments ; but while there it is a descent of the goddess to the under-world, in the religion of Mithra it is an ascent of the god-related soul to the heavenly world. The reason for giving it this different turn lies most probably in the fact that the Iranian religion places the future dwelling-place of the good in the heavenly world of light; but it is also possible that the suggestion of this new version may have been found in the Babylonian myth which tells how the highest father of the gods, Ea, created, for the deliverance of his daughter Ishtar from the thraldom of the queen of the dead, his messenger Assusunamir, who freed the prisoner and brought her back rejoicing to the dwellings of the gods. This feature of the Babylonian myth is found in a more fully developed form in the Jewish-Gnostic sect of the Mandæans. With them, the divine hero Hibil-Ziva is called into being in order to descend into the under-world and overcome the dragon of darkness, shut up the lords of hell in prison, set free the good spirits, and lead them up to the world of light,[1] a conception which recurs in various modifications in the doctrine of redemption of the Christian Gnostics.

The seven gates through which the soul passes on its way to heaven correspond to the seven grades of mystic initiation which the believer in Mithra had to pass through in order to be assured of his future deliverance; at each of these stages he received a new title and appeared at the cultus-ceremony in a corresponding mask—as raven, griffin (? or "occult one"), soldier, lion, Persian, sun-courier, father. The putting on of the masks is a remnant of primitive animistic cultus-usage by means of which the par-

---

[1] Brandt, *Die mandäische Religion*, pp. 213 ff., 191; Kessler, *Vortrag über Gnosis und altbabylonische Religion*, in "Verhandlungen des v. Berliner orientalischen Kongresses," pp. 296, 299.

ticipant desires to identify himself with the God or magical power of which he assumes the mask and garb. It was only when they attained the grade of "lion" that the initiate became partakers of the sacred cultus-meals, at which the "fathers" took the highest places. The whole act of initiation was known as "sacramentum," *i.e.* military oath, because the believer was thereby received into the army of Mithra. Among the ceremonies associated with reception into the various grades of initiation were sacred lustrations, which served as means of cleansing from all guilt, and the marking of the forehead with a sacred sign as the symbol of their abiding loyalty to Mithra.[1] In the higher grades there was also the touching of hands and tongue with honey as a symbol of the purity and victorious might of the deeds and words of the mystics. One peculiar ceremony is the presenting of a wreath, which the candidate, however, must not place upon his head, but decline, explaining that the wreath belongs only to the god Mithra, and that his servant must, therefore, always refuse it. What is related, however, of difficult, painful, or alarming tests imposed upon the candidates in these mysteries seems, if not pure invention, to be at least much exaggerated.[2] They probably consisted only of dramatic representations of the descent into the dark depths of Hades, and of the ascent to the glory of the heavenly heights won by a victory

[1] Whether the marking of the forehead was done with anointing oil or by branding is doubtful. Cumont inclines to suppose the latter; but the analogy of the Mandæan practice of marking the forehead of the newly baptized person with oil of sesame (Brandt, *Rel. der Mandäer*, 103) is in favour of the former.

[2] Cumont, *ut sup.*, i. 322 f.

over the powers of death. The initiate of the higher grades had the right to take part in the sacred meals which formed the central point in the worship of Mithra; these were covenant meals ("communions") in memory and in imitation of the meal by which, according to the legend, Mithra himself had once sealed a covenant with the sun-god. Thus we find on a bas-relief which is still preserved, representing the sacred meal,[1] the two gods in the midst seated on cushions, side by side, each holding a cup in his right hand, in front of them a small table on which stand four small loaves, each marked with crossed strokes, while round about on both sides stand the believing communicants in their mystical masks. Whether the cup in this Mithra-communion contains water alone or mixed with wine is uncertain; Cumont conjectures ("sans doute") the latter, but he cites no proof. In favour of the former there is Justin's statement (*Apol.*, i. 86) that in the mysteries of Mithra bread and a cup of water are set forth with certain formulæ of blessing; Tertullian, too, *De Præscript. Hær.*, xl., speaks only of an oblation of bread in the Mithra-cult, without any mention of wine. Among the Mandæans, whose worship shows many points of contact with the Mithra-religion, the sacred meal consisted of ordinary bread and water for the laity, but of ceremonially prepared bread and a mixture of water and wine for the priests; only on special occasions, such as confession and marriage, was this also given to the laity (Brandt, *ut sup.*, 108 ff.). Something similar may perhaps be supposed in regard to the Mithra meals, but the question must be left open.

[1] See figure and explanation in Cumont, i. 157 f.

THE RELIGION OF MITHRA 109

There is another important point upon which the students of the history of religions are at variance. Up to a short time ago the prevailing opinion was that the most important feature in the Mithra-cult was the offering of a bull (Taurobolium, vulgar for Tauropolium), the blood of which was allowed to flow over the initiate, in order that by this "baptism of blood" they might become partakers in the pure and immortal life of the god Mithra, whom the bull represented; this cultural sacrifice was supposed to be the reproduction of the cosmogonic sacrifice and the prototype of the eschatological offering which the god himself would offer for the life and salvation of the world, or, at least, of his own followers, as is known from numerous representations.[1] But now the latest and most thorough investigator in this department, Cumont, has given it as his opinion that the taurobolium and blood-baptism never belonged to the worship of Mithra, but were peculiar to the savage cult of Artemis Tauropolos, which had its seat in Asia Minor, and to that of the Phrygian Cybele. Yet it is possible that the two views might be reconciled. Cumont himself mentions (i. 334) that in Ostia the shrine of the Phrygian goddess in which Taurobolia took place was closely connected with a Mithra-crypt;[2] and indeed the religion of Mithra, even in Asia Minor, and subsequently throughout the West, stood in such intimate alliance with the

[1] So especially Reville, *La religion à Rome sous les Sevères*, 93 ff.; similarly Gasquet in his work on the Mysteries of Mithra.

[2] The *spelæum* or underground portion of the sanctuary in which the mysteries were celebrated. See Cumont, *Monuments, etc.*, i. 57 ff.—TRANSLATOR.

religion of Cybele that the "sisters" of the latter take their place alongside of the "brethren" of the former. Under such circumstances, would it not have been easy for the originally Phrygian ceremony of the Taurobolium to find its way into Mithraism as a further means, additional to baptism and the communion, of securing salvation and a pledge of eternal life? The Phrygian blood-baptism may just as well have passed into Mithraism as did the asceticism which belonged to the cult of Isis, but was originally foreign to the Iranian religion (Cumont, i. 324). It was held among the believers in the mysteries to be a sacrament of such saving power that it might even be performed on one for the benefit of others.[1] All these sacred ceremonies were only different means to the end of securing an immortal and happy life in the other world; the initiate spoke of themselves as "born again for ever."

The adherents of Mithra had a well-organised hierarchy. The priests or presidents were not identical with the "fathers," but were taken from among them (as the bishops from among the presbyters in the Church). They had to make daily prayers to the sun (at morning, mid-day, and evening), to offer sacrifices of many kinds, to arrange the sacred initiations and meals, at which there were hymns accompanied by the music of flutes and cymbals. As holy days, they kept the day of sun, perhaps also a day in the middle of the month, and, especially, the

---

[1] The Mandæan religion, too, recognises a representative anointing and communion of the living for the benefit of the dead, in order to secure and hasten their ascent to the world of light—masses for the dead! (Brandt, *ut sup.*, 81 f.).

25th December as the birthday of the unconquered sun (*sol invictus*). At the head of the priesthood stood the high-priest or "father of the fathers," who was only permitted to marry once. According to Tertullian, there were also in the Mithra-community "virgins" (nuns), as well as men vowed to continence, but this is hard to reconcile with the fact that women took no direct part in the cult of Mithra, and could not be received among the initiate. Mithraism was a religion for men, which never belied its origin from the Iranian religion of conflict; contemplation was never so much in favour with it as the practice of the virtues which have to do with the battle of life, such as valour and self-mastery, fighting courage and contempt of death. Its morality, which aimed at hardening the feelings and disciplining the will, closely resembled the Stoic ethics, which were especially congenial to the Romans; and what Stoicism and Platonic philosophy were to the upper classes, Mithraism was to the lower classes of the Empire, among whom it won the majority of its converts: it strengthened the humbler people to meet the hard struggle for existence by enrolling them in the organised fellowship of the army of the warriors of the divine hero Mithra, of whom it was believed that as the helpful "mediator" he would stand by the side of his adherents in the battles of this life, and secure to each loyal and valiant warrior a blessed life in the world to come—a hope which was constantly anew assured and sealed to the believing soul amid the awe-inspiring experiences of the secret initiations.

We can well understand how this religion attained great influence during the period of the decline of paganism, and for centuries was a rival to Christianity; but it is equally easy to understand why it could not ultimately dispute the victory of the latter. No doubt the pagan worship of nature was here ethicised, but it was not overcome in principle, whether in doctrine or in cultus; it was in all respects a compromise with the heathen polytheism, and for that reason not on a level with Christian monotheism. It had indeed a personal mediator, but he was a hero of natural might, not of moral loftiness; his sacrifice was a cosmogonic myth, not the ethical self-sacrifice of the historical Saviour. No doubt it had its ceremonies of initiation, its signs and pledges of eternal salvation, such as the heart in search of consolation longs for; but they were crude rites, rooted in animistic superstition, to which a magical influence was ascribed, but in which it was scarcely possible to find an ideal meaning. No doubt, too, it had its organised community, which offered strength and support to the individual, but it was a union of men which excluded women—this circumstance alone must have seriously weakened its propaganda.

SYNCRETISM AND GNOSTICISM

CHAPTER VI

THE BEGINNINGS OF GNOSTICISM

THE close resemblance between the pagan syncretistic religion of the Mithra-cult and the pagan-Jewish-Christian syncretistic religion of Gnosticism was recognised even by the contemporary of both, the Greek philosopher and opponent of Christianity Celsus, who therefore classed them together in his polemical work. Origen, replying to him in his apologetic work, *Contra Celsum*, vi. 24 ff., has justly reproached him with using the singular and blasphemous tenets of the obscure sect of the "Ophians" as the basis of accusations against the Christianity of the Church, which was in no way responsible for them, since they were so far from being Christians that they were as hostile to Jesus as Celsus himself, and could not bear even to hear His name. This assertion of Origen can, however, only be held true under certain limitations. We know from other writers against heresy that there certainly was a Gnostic-Christian sect of Ophians or Ophites or Naasenes (from the Hebrew $Nahas = ὄφις =$ serpent), who held Jesus to have been born of the Virgin, and, in consequence of the wisdom, purity, and righteousness in which He surpassed all other men, to have been the appointed vehicle of the heavenly

Christ, who came down and dwelt in Him (*cf.* Irenæus, *Adv. Hær.*, I. xxx.). Unless, then, we suppose that the Church apologist has from intolerance caricatured the Ophians in making them non-Christian, the only alternative is to suppose that alongside of the Gnostic-Christian there was also a non-Christian sect of Ophites, who must doubtless in that case have been the older branch of this sect, from which the Christian branch was a later offshoot. With that agrees the statement of Philaster, who at the outset of his history of heretics describes the Ophites, Cainites, and Sethites as sects which had arisen before the coming of Christ. The pre-Christian origin of the Cainites, which we have seen reason to infer from Philo's writing, *De posteritate Caini* (*sup.*, p. 72 f.), tends to confirm this. Moreover, the statement of Hippolytus in the *Philosophumena* (v. 2, 6) also agrees with this, where he says that the Naasenes (= Ophites) gave themselves the name of Gnostics because they alone, according to their opinion, "know" "the deep things" (ultimate principles), and that from these, who were obviously the first Gnostics, many sects had branched off who had formed different dogmas upon the same subjects. We may recall in this connection the Apocalypse of John, which in the messages to the Churches at Ephesus, Smyrna, Pergamum, and Thyatira opposes certain teachers of error, who, under the names of Nicolaitanes, Baalamites, followers of the prophetess Jezebel, spread antinomian doctrines and gloried in knowing "the depths of Satan," and who, for that reason, are described by the writer of the Apocalypse as a "synagogue of Satan," while they themselves gave

THE BEGINNINGS OF GNOSTICISM 115

themselves out to be (Gnostic) Jews (Apoc. ii. 9, 14 ff., 20-24). As concerns the place of origin of these most ancient Gnostic sects, which were in existence prior to Christianity, not only does the content of their myths, as we shall see immediately, point to Babylon as their original home, but the statement of Origen (*Contra Celsum*, vi. 28) and Hippolytus (*Philos.*, iv. 2, v. 13), that the Perates and Ophites traced their origin to a certain Euphrates Peratikos, must be interpreted to the same effect. Indeed, Clement of Alexandria rightly recognised (*Strom.* VII. xvii. *ad fin.*) that this name did not originally refer to a personal founder, but to their place of origin, and this is confirmed by recent investigation. The orientalists Kessler and Brandt agree in explaining "Euphrates Peraticus" as referring to the district Forat-Maisan in Mesopotamia, the same neighbourhood in which the remnants of the very ancient Jewish-Gnostic sect of the Mandæans are still found.[1] If we provisionally accept as authoritative the account of Origen (*Contra Celsum*, vi. 30 ff.), who repeatedly boasts of his superior knowledge of the Ophite Gnosis, the most prominent point in their creed is the belief in the "seven world-ruling demons," to whom they gave the names Michael, Suriel, Raphael, Gabriel, Thautabaoth,

[1] Brandt, *Die mandäische Religion*, p. 192. "The most ancient Gnostic systems point to the land of the Mandæans as their place of origin." The statement of Origen and Hippolytus regarding Euphrates Peraticus "points directly to the region of Forat-Maisân in the land of Mesan, the present district of Basra. Here, therefore, we must seek the cradle, or at any rate one of the chief strongholds, of Chaldæan speculation." *Cf.* also Kessler in the report of the Fifth Oriental Congress at Berlin, 1882, p. 304. Anz has also attempted to prove the Babylonian origin of Gnosticism in Harnack's *Texte und Untersuchungen*, xv., Heft 4.

Erataoth, Onoel or Tartarooth, and whom they represented under the animal forms of lion, bull, dragon, eagle, bear, dog, and ass. These powers have command of the seven gates of eternity through which the soul has to pass; at each gate the soul must address to the guardian of it a prescribed prayer, of which the first, *e.g.*, runs: " I salute the king who has not his like, the fetter of blindness, the oblivion of all care, the first power, which maintains itself by the spirit of prudence and wisdom; may I be let go from here pure, a part of the light of the Son and of the Father; grace be with me, yea, Father, may it be with me."[1] The last two words form the standing refrain in each of the succeeding prayers, which request that the soul may be allowed to pass through each gate in turn, and that by means of their gnosis, *i.e.* through knowing the right password. On the other hand, souls who do not possess this gnosis will be swallowed by the archon who has the form of a

[1] With this may be compared the Mandæan prayer of the soul in its upward passage to the Kingdom of Light (Brandt, *ut sup.*, p. 76): " How joyful is my heart, how joyful am I on the day when the sentence is spoken unto me, and my going is to the place of life. I fly and go, I am come to the station of the sun (the place where he keeps guard). I cry a cry, 'Who will lead me past the ward of the sun?—Thy merit and thy works and thy righteousness and thy virtue lead thee past the ward of the sun!'" "Whosoever is signed with the sign of life, and over whom the name of the King of Light is named, and who stands firm and constant, and does good and beautiful works, him shall none hinder upon his way." Compare also the prayer of John at his departure (Acts of John; see below) for the safe-keeping of his soul on its upward path from the hostile powers which menace it in the other world. The similarity of this conception in the heathen, Jewish, and Christian Gnosticism clearly betrays the common origin of all Gnosticism from the Perso-Babylonian mythology.

THE BEGINNINGS OF GNOSTICISM 117

dragon; they serve as the food of the demons, from which these draw their life and strength[1]—a conception in which the most primitive animistic superstition may be recognised as the underground foundation of this gnosis. We are reminded, too, of the animal masks and names of those initiated into the mysteries of Mithra by the statement that some attained the forms of the archons, and consequently received the names lion, bull, dragon, eagle. bear, dog. Moreover, Origen is able to go beyond the information given by Celsus concerning the Gnostic diagram by his learned knowledge of the subject; he had seen upon such a diagram a fiery circle with a flaming sword for its diameter, on the two sides of which stood the tree of life and the tree of knowledge, and, in addition, a number of circles larger and smaller, beside one another or superimposed on one another, with the inscriptions " Father and Son, love and life, the prudence of wisdom and the nature of wisdom, knowledge and insight " (capp. xxxiii.-xxxviii.). The instructive remark of Celsus that the Gnostics use the names of all kinds of barbarous demons in magical formulæ— the magic papyri found in Egypt give astonishing examples of these formulæ [2]—gives the learned father occasion for an excursus on Greek and barbarian mythology which no longer has any interest for us.

A connected picture of the Ophite Gnosis is given by Irenæus (*Adv. Hær.*, I. xxx.), of which I may give at least the principal points. At the head stands

[1] As Epiphanius tells us in *Hær.*, xxvi. 10 and xl. 2, both of which passages are to be compared throughout with the account given by Origen.

[2] *Cf.* Dieterich, *Abraxas*, 1891.

the following trinity : (1) Father of all, or first man, or eternal light ; (2) Son, or reason proceeding forth from the Father, or second man ; (3) Holy Spirit, or mother of all living. Below the latter, as the antithesis to the divine world, lie the "four elements," water, darkness, abyss, chaos. From the union of the first two beings with the spirit, thought of as a female principle, springs the heavenly " Christ," and the " Sophia," who is thought of as both male and female. The latter sinks down into the waters of chaos, and there receives a body, the weight of which hinders her return to the heavenly mother ; struggling upwards, she remains suspended half-way between the abyss and the divine world, and her body, which is of an aqueous nature, forms the visible heaven. Then there come forth from her, by a series of self-begettings or emanations, the seven world-rulers, Jaldabaoth, Jao, Sabaoth, Adoneus, Eloeus, Oreus, Astapheus, each of whom inhabits one of the seven heavens. When the sons and fellow-rulers of Jaldabaoth, the chief of these, endeavour to dispute his sway, he begets out of matter a son and ally, the serpent-formed Nous, the author of all the evil and wickedness in the world. Thereupon he boasts himself the highest God, but is rebuked by his mother, the Sophia, and reminded of his subordination to the higher Father and Son. In order, nevertheless, to maintain his supremacy, he calls on his six fellow-rulers to make man in their image. This attempt at first succeeds but poorly : man crawls like a worm upon the ground. Then the Sophia (or, according to other versions, Jaldabaoth himself) takes pity on this miserable creature and implants in him a spark of light, whereupon he becomes a thinking and willing being, and at once begins, passing over his immediate semi-divine creator, to thank the true God and primal father or first man. Jaldabaoth, rendered jealous by this, seeks to weaken man by creating the woman, Eve, with whom then the other archons, in adulterous intercourse, begot demons (transferring to Paradise the myth of the union of the sons of God with the daughters of men in Gen. vi. 4). When, therefore, the Sophia saw that Jaldabaoth from jealousy was withholding from men the knowledge of their true divine maker (by forbidding them to eat of the tree of knowledge), she caused the serpent to tempt Adam and Eve to transgress the command of Jaldabaoth, whereupon they recognised the highest power and deserted their lower creator. (According to another version, the Sophia was herself the serpent who communicated to men the knowledge of all the higher mysteries which Jaldabaoth had withheld from them.) Thereupon men, along with the serpent, were thrust out of Paradise (thought of as in some way super-earthly) into the world, where now the serpent with his six sons formed a lower " seven," and set themselves in opposition to the higher seven archons. In this less exalted scene man grew coarser in body and soul; yet through the mercy of the Sophia there was given back to him a faint light which made him capable of self-knowledge, and of some knowledge of the world. Meanwhile there continued, generation after generation, the constant strife of the lower seven, at whose head stood the serpent, known also as Michael and Samuel, against the higher seven (the spirits of the stars, as they are now expressly called). Jaldabaoth, wroth at the diminution in man's service, sent the Flood; but the Sophia delivered by means of the ark the light-natures which were related to her. It was Jaldabaoth who made a covenant with Abraham and gave Moses the law, and both he and each of the other archons sent their prophets, each of whom looked to his sender as God and Father. At the same time the Sophia revealed, through the same prophets, many things concerning the divine Primal Man and the higher Christ and his future coming. Urged by her, Jaldabaoth at length sent, not knowing what he did, the son of the unfruitful Elizabeth and the son of the Virgin Mary. But the Sophia, who could never find rest either in earth or heaven, moved her heavenly mother to send down the heavenly Christ to her aid. He therefore descended through the seven heavens, making himself like unto the sons (rulers?) of each of them in turn, and gradually robbed them of all their power, because every vestige of light had a natural tendency to come to him. Then he allied himself with his heaven-born sister, the Sophia, and they rejoiced together like bride and bridegroom; having thus become one with the Sophia, the heavenly Christ descended into the man Jesus, who was born of the Virgin by the power of God, and was therefore wiser, purer, and more righteous than all other men. Through this descent of the heavenly Christ, which, however, remained unknown to many of the disciples of Jesus, the latter became Jesus Christ, and began to perform miracles and cures in order to reveal the "unknown father," and to acknowledge himself publicly to be the "son of the first man." Wroth at this, the archons, and the father of Jesus (Jaldabaoth), brought about his death; but this death was undergone only

THE BEGINNINGS OF GNOSTICISM 121

by Jesus, since the Christ and the Sophia had left him before its occurrence, and departed into the eternal age, whence they sent a heavenly power to raise Jesus from the dead in a spiritual body. His disciples, indeed, supposed that he had risen in his earthly body, for they did not know that flesh and blood could not attain the Kingdom of God. The risen Jesus remained with the disciples for eighteen months, and he taught the more able ones concerning the heavenly mysteries, then he departed to heaven, where Christ sits at the right hand of his father Jaldabaoth, in order to take unto himself the souls of those who acknowledged them (the further statements regarding Jesus, his father, and the souls of men are hardly intelligible). Then the consummation of all things will draw nigh, when all the dew of the spirit of light will be gathered together and removed into the eternal age.

It is clear that this "Gnosis" is not philosophy, nor sprung from Greek philosophy; and it is equally far from being a simple religious popular belief. It is an artificial mixture of legends and speculations derived from various quarters. In this mixture we can distinguish three kinds of elements: (1) theogonic and cosmogonic myths, (2) Old Testament stories regarding the early history of mankind, and (3) evangelical traditions. From the artificial connection of these various and contradictory elements result the numerous bizarreries and obscurities of this Gnosis, which are to be explained neither by dogmatic and speculative interpretation, nor by purely literary and historical criticism of the sources, but only by means of the study of comparative religion, which has before it here a rich and fruitful department of work. The myths of this Gnosis are not freely composed in order to embody deep speculative ideas, but are derived from the same Babylonian mythology from which the mixed religions of Mithraism, Mandæism, and Manichæism took their rise.

The seven archons are the planet-gods of the Babylonian astrology and theology; the seven heavens with their gates, through which the souls are allowed to go on giving a password, are already known to us from the mysteries of Mithra: we saw there that the seven gates of the lower world through which Ishtar passed on her descent into hell have been changed into the seven gates of heaven, which stand under the guardianship of the star-gods, whose favour souls must seek to win; if they did not, the gates remained shut to them, and they ran the risk of being devoured by a demonic dragon (p. 117), a trait in which the older form of the myth (gates of the under-world, not of heaven) may be recognised. The highest of the seven archons or gods of the planets is Jaldabaoth, an Aramaic name which signifies "born out of Chaos"; on the other hand, he is described in the Ophite myth as the son or emanation of the Sophia, a daughter of the heavenly deity who has partly fallen from her high estate. He is therefore not, properly speaking, a god, but a derivative and semi-divine being, who in consequence of his origin represents a mixture of divine and semi-divine beings. This demi-god is identified by the Ophite Gnosis with the God of the Old Testament, the Creator of men, the Law-giver and Ruler of the Jewish people. As to the difficulty that the God of the

THE BEGINNINGS OF GNOSTICISM

Old Testament is always represented as, if not the absolutely sole God, at any rate as the absolutely highest God, the only one who deserves to be called the true God, while Jaldabaoth certainly is not so represented, this Gnostic system seeks to solve it by relating that Jaldabaoth had falsely given himself out to be the true God, and caused himself to be praised and worshipped as such. There is thus a state of tension or hostility in the relationship between Jaldabaoth, the active God of Jewish history and religion, and the true but inactive deity of the original heavenly Trinity of Father, Son, and Spirit. Jaldabaoth is not indeed a power wholly opposed to God, like Ahriman or the Devil; he has as creator and law-giver a real though limited power and conditional authority. He is like an unruly vassal-prince who uses his *de facto* power in order to usurp the sovereignty to which he has no right. Occurrences of that kind were so frequent in the political world of Western Asia at all times, that it cannot be wondered at if they were transferred to the super-earthly divine world, especially as, in the popular religion, the gods were supposed to share the fate of the peoples who belong to them. At the same time the conception of the rebellious demi-god and intermediate being Jaldabaoth, differs so strikingly from the Old Testament belief in God, that the question inevitably presents itself: How could men of Jewish race, starting from the Old Testament religion (for it was only on such a soil that the Ophite Gnosis could spring up), come to degrade the sole ruling Jahwe of the Old Testament into the limited demi-god Jaldabaoth? One explanation which has been offered of this curious phenomenon attributes it to Christian influence—in order to emphasise the inferiority of the Jewish religion as compared with the Christian, Christian Gnostics depotentiated, it is suggested, the conception of the God of the Old Testament into that of Jaldabaoth. But this explanation is not satisfactory, for two reasons: first, because the inferiority of the Jewish religion as compared with the Christian was taught in the most definite fashion by the Pauline, the Johannine, and the Catholic theology, without any need of having recourse to a mythical apparatus of this kind; in the second place, because in the Jewish Gnostic teaching of the Mandæans, which was not influenced by Christianity, the creation was the work of a subordinate god, who had revolted from the supreme God, or it was the work (in part at least) of the seven evil spirits who were sprung from the Ruha Kodshah (holy spirit), who had become a demon.[1] Taking this into account, it may be conjectured that in the Ophite Gnosis also the doctrine of the seven archons and their head, Jaldabaoth, of their rule over the world and their half-hostile attitude towards the supreme God, may have had their origin, not in Christian dogmatic motives, but in the influence of the Babylonian mythology upon the Jews of the eastern Diaspora. That does not, of course, exclude the influence of religious motives; it merely means that we shall have to seek them in the first place in the circle of thought of the Jewish Diaspora itself. The more the educated Jews of the Diaspora found themselves forced to

[1] Brandt, *Rel. d. Mandäer*, §§ 17–27.

THE BEGINNINGS OF GNOSTICISM 125

realise the inconsistency between the national particularism of the Old Testament religion and the lofty conception of a single Deity common to all the world, the nearer at hand did the thought lie for them that this particularistic national religion, like all the rest, might be derived from one of the subordinate spiritual beings, whose limitations and imperfections might be the explanation of what was imperfect and obsolete in their traditional national religion. If in many circles in the Diaspora the Mosaic law in particular was felt to be an irrational barrier and fetter, not all who so felt were content, like Philo, to combine a spiritual interpretation of the letter with conservative practice; many drew the practical inference that the law should be rejected, and this tendency, to which Philo himself bears witness while condemning it (p. 71 f.), found its simplest justification in supposing that the God of the Mosaic law was a subordinate semi-divine being. Tendencies of this kind, which manifested themselves often enough in the Jewish Diaspora, both in the East and in the West, everywhere prepared the ground for the reception of new ideas; especially in the East they favoured the acceptance of Chaldæan speculations, which were imposing from their *aura* of deep and subtle wisdom. It was only necessary to identify their astrological and mythical figures with the Biblical Jahwe or with the angel, spirit, word, or name of Jahwe, in order to set up a mixed religion, lightened of its narrow national and historical limitations, but on the other hand weighted with heathen superstition.

When, later, this Jewish-Babylonian mixed religion,

which had originally arisen in the Jewish Diaspora of the East quite apart from Christian influence, and, indeed, prior to Christianity, came into contact with Christianity, there appeared to be so much in common between the two that there soon resulted a further mixture. The Pauline doctrine of redemption was sympathetic to the Jewish Gnostics on account of its antinomian tendency and the doctrine of a Redeemer and Son of God who had come down from heaven, and again, as victor over all powers above and below the earth, had returned thither, which found parallels and points of contact in more than one of the Babylonian myths. In the myth of the creation, Marduk, the god of the city of Babylon, "the first-born son" of the god Ea, appears as the victorious hero who overcomes Tiamat, the serpent of Chaos, the enemy of the gods, cleaves her in two, and makes heaven and earth out of the two halves. In the myth of the descent to hell, the heavenly goddess Ishtar goes down into the underworld, and is there held a prisoner, until Ea, the father of the gods, creates Assusunamir to be his messenger, who frees the prisoner and brings her up again from hell to heaven. These two myths find their application both in the Mandæan and in the Ophite Gnosis, and not only in the cosmogonic region but also in connection with redemption. Only in view of such an intermixture can the strange, many-sided, constantly changing figure of the Ophite Sophia or "Achamoth" (the Aramaic name for wisdom) be understood. Like Ishtar, she is the daughter of the heavenly deity and descends into the dark abyss, where she is held prisoner by the weight of the corporeal world, and is prevented from returning to the light-world until there is sent to her from the Supreme Father the Saviour and Son of God, " Christ," of whom she then becomes the bride, as Ishtar does of Thammuz, her beloved. In another aspect, however, the Sophia is to be compared with the sea-serpent Tiamat, for her body is formed of the water of the abyss which she has set in motion, and out of this her "aqueous body" she has formed the visible heaven by raising herself aloft and spreading it out. It is true that in Irenæus' account nothing is said of this division being made with the sword, as in the Marduk myth; but in Origen, *Contra Celsum*, vi. 34, there occurs the statement, which is doubtless to be interpreted in this sense, that Celsus had heard these people among others speak of the "fluid power" of a certain virgin named Prunikos (another name for Sophia or Achamoth), and of the cleaving of heaven and earth with the sword in order that there might be life. Nothing else can be meant by this than the well-known myth of the creation of heaven and earth by the splitting asunder of the body of the sea-serpent Tiamat (= Prunikos = Sophia); and therefore doubtless the same cosmogonic myth underlies the account of Irenæus (I. xxx.) of the formation of heaven from the aqueous body of the Sophia. Yet again, however, the Sophia is the serpent of Paradise, who is called "wiser than all creatures," because she alone has knowledge of all mysteries and can communicate them to men. In so far as this communication from the first took place against the will of the creator, Jaldabaoth, and in Paradise contrary to his express command, and had as its consequence the banishment of men from Paradise to the lower world, the Sophia appears as an evil principle which tempts men to transgress the law, and can thus become a demonic world-goddess, which is the form she takes in the Mandæan Ruha Kodshah (properly holy spirit). That the latter had originally the same significance as the Ophite Sophia-Achamoth, is obvious from the fact that the latter, like the former, is the mother of the seven archons. On the other hand, however, the Ophite Sophia is the saving power, originating from the heavenly light-world, who at the first creation of man implanted in the miserable being who had been brought into existence by the planetary spirits the spark of divine light, and who only led men into disobedience in Paradise in order to free them, by the gift of a higher wisdom, from the service of the false god; who in motherly pity bestowed upon fallen men the "sweet breath of the dew of light," by means of which they were enabled to know themselves and the world, and in spite of all their misery to shape their destinies and enjoy the world; and who in the history of Israel, while the prophets were proclaiming their own God, foretold without their knowledge much concerning the heavenly Father-God and his eternal son Christ, and the future descent of the latter; who afterwards by her earnest supplication obtained from the father the sending forth of the saving spirit, and uniting as a bride with the Christ at his appearance, made her dwelling in the man Jesus, whom she had prepared as a pure vessel for this use, and through him revealed the "Unknown Father"; who finally went up again with the Christ-Spirit into the eternal world from which she originally came, and by her power, operating thence, first raised

THE BEGINNINGS OF GNOSTICISM 129

from the dead the crucified Jesus, and took him to herself, and continues to gather together the "light" souls which belong to her until they shall all have been saved and transferred to the everlasting age. Thus the myth of the Sophia obviously embodies the profound thought that knowledge is a twofold principle, divine and demonic, the cause of guilt and evil as well as of redemption and salvation. These two aspects, however, are sometimes, again, divided between different figures; with especial clearness in the system of the related Mandæan Gnostics, where the bad side of the Sophia is incorporated in the arch-devil Ruha Kodshah, the antithesis to which is presented by Manda Chaje, the spirit of life and light. In the Ophite Gnosis, however, the Sophia is preponderantly a principle of deliverance and salvation, while the dangerous side of knowledge receives a special embodiment in the son, Nous (Reason), whom Jaldabaoth produces from matter, and who is the cause of all ill and evil among men.[1] The serpent form which is attributed to him, as to the Sophia, is a clear proof that he is essentially only the darker side, the side related to the material world, of the Sophia herself, that daughter of the light-deity who has sunk down into the elements. These ingeniously alternating

[1] The paradox which this involves finds its best explanation in the utterance of Goethe's Mephistopheles (Prologue in Heaven):

"Ein bischen besser würd' er leben
Hätt'st du ihm nicht das Fünklein Himmelslicht gegeben;
Er nennts Vernunft und braucht's allein,
Um tierischer als jedes Tier zu sein!"

"(Man) would live a little better hadst thou not given him the spark of heavenly light; he calls it reason, and uses it only to be more brutish than the beast."

aspects of the Gnostic Sophia are not, however, a product of free philosophical speculation, but resulted naturally from the combination of elements of different kinds drawn from the three sources of the Gnostic syncretism, the Babylonian Ishtar and Tiamat myths, the Old Testament legend of the serpent in Paradise, and the Hellenistic-Jewish doctrine of the Wisdom of God, the principle of the creative and educative revelation of God, and finally from the Christian doctrine of the Spirit (who exercised a preparatory activity in the history of Israel, but personally appeared in Jesus) of the heavenly Son of God, or Christ, who, having returned to heaven, draws thither after him those who are his. This conception of the descent of Christ from heaven and return to heaven has its unmistakable counterpart in the descent and ascent of the gods in the myths relating to the descent to hell and to the ascent of souls in the mystery-cults. This is especially clear in the hymn of the Naasene Gnostics which has been preserved to us in Hippolytus, *Philosophumena*, v. 11. In this there is first described the varied need of the human soul, which, having fallen into a labyrinth, wanders about without finding any outlet. "It seeks to flee from the awful chaos, and knows not how to escape; therefore, O Father, send me! Possessing the seal, I will descend, I will wander through all the æons, I will reveal all secrets, I will make known the forms of the gods and communicate the mystery of the holy way, which is called 'Gnosis.'" Here we have the sum of the Gnostic teaching about redemption; it consists in the communication of the secrets of the holy way which leads out of the labyrinth of the dreadful chaos, out of the thraldom of the world-powers which are hostile to God, up to freedom. This way has been opened by Christ, who reveals all the secrets of the upper world, which he himself has passed through upon his descent, makes known the forms of the gods (archons) who preside over it, so that the soul is enabled, by knowing the character of each of these powers, to authenticate itself at each of the seven gates and obtain admission. Hippolytus, however, gives a much more complicated account of the Gnosis of the Naasenes and Peratæ (the sect of the Ophites which is most nearly related to them) than that of Irenæus which we have given above. Probably he has in view a later and more developed phase, in which the Oriental Gnosis had combined with Greek mythology and philosophy, with the result of producing curious hybrid myths. He begins by stating (*Philos.*, v. 13) that this Gnosis is based on Chaldæan astrology, making from the relations of the stars myths about the revolt and fall of spiritual powers, and putting these forth as the teaching of Christ. All things that are in process of becoming are subject to the decree of fate determined by these powers; only the Gnostics, who have recognised the constraint of this condition and are instructed in regard to the way by which man came into the world, are able to get free and escape destruction. This destroying power of fate is sometimes identified with the primal water, which the Greeks call Chronos, and Heracleitus's saying is quoted, that water became the death of souls, and, as a further proof, the drowning of the Egyptians in the Red Sea is cited; sometimes the destroying power is interpreted as being the star-gods, whom Moses named the "serpents of the wilderness," and from whose deadly bite only the "true and perfect and universal serpent," viz. the "wise Logos of Eve," delivers those who believe in him and come forth out of Egypt, namely, from this body and from this world (v. 16). Of this wise Logos of Eve, *i.e.* of universal nature and the "mother of all life," it is further said (v. 17) that he sits in the midst between the Father and Hyle (Matter), for of these three, each of which has infinite power in itself, consists the universe. The Son, or Logos, or Serpent, who occupies the intermediate position, sometimes moves towards the unmoved Father and receives from him the formative powers, sometimes turns towards the formless matter, which is in perpetual movement, and impresses upon it the ideas which he has received from the Father. Just as painters transfer to their pictures the forms of animals without taking away anything from the animals themselves, so the Son transfers to matter the forms which he draws from the Father. Here, therefore, the Son or Logos plays the part of the Platonic demiurge; immediately afterwards, however, the demiurge and ruler of matter is identified with the "murderer from the beginning," the devil; thus we have in the figure of the Logos the same duality which we noticed in the Sophia, and again in the curious antithesis between the "true, perfect, and universal serpent" and the destroying serpents. Moreover, with the Hellenistic conception of the Logos or Son who turns now towards the Father and now towards matter, we may compare the theogonic and cosmogonic myth of Ocean, the primal source of gods and men, which turns ever upwards and downwards, and in its upward streaming produces the gods, in its downward, man (v. 7). Wide as are the differences between these two conceptions, it is impossible not to recognise a close relationship between them; and as the symbol of the moving serpent is as appropriate to the conception of the water moving up and down as it is inappropriate to that of the demiurge Logos, there can be no doubt which is the original, and which the later adaptation. The latter betrays itself finally in the interesting saying which Hippolytus twice repeats as a maxim of his Naasenes: "The beginning of perfection is the knowledge of man, the end of perfection is the knowledge of God" (v. 7, 8)—a thoroughly Greek thought, which is widely diverse from the astrological and cosmogonic myths from which this Gnosis took its rise.

The same is the case in regard to the sect of the Simonians, whose origin is referred by the Fathers of the Church to Simon the Magian, known to us from Acts viii., who gave himself out to be a manifestation of the Supreme God. The most detailed description of this sect is found in Hippolytus, *Philosophumena*, vi. 6–19, especially in chaps. 18 and 19, with which may be compared Irenæus' account (*Adv. Hær.*, I. xxiii. 2–4). Here the teaching of Simon is described, according to his work, "The Great Revelation" (ἀπόφασις), as follows:—At the head of the system stands "the infinite power," the eternity of which is expressed in three participles, as that which stands, and has stood, and shall stand. This primary being, which is also described as fire (cap. 9 ff.), divides into the first "syzygy," "Reason and Thought" (ἐπίνοια or ἔννοια, Iren.), and yet remains one in spite of this self-differentiation. Cruder, and therefore doubtless older, is the description of the first syzygy as Heaven and Earth (cap. 13), between which there stretches endlessly the intangible air, in which dwells the "Father who sustains and maintains all that is finite" (cap. 19), in whom, therefore, the original primal power (or, according to the most ancient myth, the primal fire) appears personified. Besides this first syzygy there are two others, each with a dual description, "voice and name," or "sun and moon," "deliberation and reflection," or "air and water." Above these three syzygies lies, as the common source of all, "the seventh power," or "the Spirit of God which hovers over the waters" (cap. 13 f.). It is not worth while to disentangle this confusion; it is enough that in it various strata, earlier and later, of the Simonian doctrine may be recognised: a cosmogonic-naturalistic stratum, a theistic-demiurgic, and an abstract-philosophic. Regarding the Ennoia which springs from the primal power, and which plays a part corresponding to that of the Ophite Sophia, we are further told that she gave birth to the angels and spiritual powers by whom the visible world was created. Afterwards the Ennoia was held fast in the thraldom of these lower powers, so that she could not again mount up to her father, but was compelled to undergo a transmigration through the bodies of many women; among others, she was incarnated in Helen of Troy, and finally in a harlot named Helen, whom Simon emancipated from a brothel in Tyre, the "lost sheep" of the parable. Then when the angelic powers, owing to mutual jealousies, administered the world too ill, the highest god resolved to appear in the world in his own person. On his way down he likened himself successively to the angelic powers, and finally appeared on earth as a man, without really being so. In Judæa he appeared as the Son, in the Christ who was only seemingly crucified; in Samaria, however, as the Father, in Simon; and among other nations as the Holy Spirit, though he allowed himself to be called among men by whatsoever name they pleased. The prophets were inspired only by the angels who created the world; those, therefore, who believe in Simon and Helen as the incarnation of the highest deity do not need to trouble about the laws of the prophets, but can do what they like, since they are saved and freed by the grace (Gnostic revelation) of Simon. Nothing is evil in itself, but is only counted so in consequence of the ordinances of the world-ruling angels, who thereby hold men in bondage to themselves. With this doctrine of the Simonians corresponded, according to the report of the heresiologues, their practice, in which, following the example of their founder Simon, they practised all kinds of magic and unbridled lust, calling it "the perfect love." They are also said to have worshipped Simon and Helen under the figures of Zeus and Athene.

We recognise here an antinomian, libertine gnosis of exactly the same character as that attributed to the Cainites, who made Cain, Esau, Korah, the Sodomites and Judas their patrons, and praised Judas's treachery as a wise and virtuous deed. They taught that evil was not a free act, but was due to the influence of an inborn nature, and that there was no other way of salvation than that of "experiencing all things," that is, committing all kinds of shameful deeds without scruple. This "solution of all things in heaven and earth" (we might call it "the Superman's transvaluation of all values") they described as "the Gospel of Judas" and the "perfect Gnosis" (Iren., I. xxxi. 1; Epiphan., *Hær.*, xxxviii. 3). If we compare with this the exactly similar description of the obscure "seeming wisdom" and shameless unchastity of the "Children of Cain" in Philo's work of that title (*sup.*, p. 72 f.), we shall find it very probable that the sect of the Cainites, which was nearly related to that of the Simonians, was known to Philo, and that the Gnosis which was common to both dated from pre-Christian times, and consisted in antinomianism with a Jewish-pagan syncretistic basis. That the non-Christian and pre-Christian origin of the Ophites and Cainites is explicitly evidenced by Philaster and Origen has been remarked above (p. 114), and Origen declares the Simonians with equal definiteness to be non-Christian, since they did not recognise Jesus as the Son of God, but professed that Simon was the power of God (*Contra Celsum*, v. 62). Whether this Simon was the Samaritan Magian who is known to us from Acts (whose birthplace, according to Justin, was the village of Gitta near Samaria), or another Magian of similar name, and whether he was really the founder of this Gnostic sect, or only their deified hero, like Pythagoras or Apollonius of Tyana, who were worshipped among the Neo-Pythagoreans, is a difficult question, and can hardly be answered with certainty. It is, however, beyond

THE BEGINNINGS OF GNOSTICISM 137

question, according to what we have seen above, that Simon Magus of Acts viii. was *not* the original founder of the Gnostic sects in general, whatever may have been the case in regard to the Simonian sect. This patristic legend makes shipwreck on the two well-authenticated facts that Gnosticism did not draw its origin from Palestine but from Mesopotamia, and that it did not arise in the Apostolic age but in pre-Christian times. On the other hand, we have no reason whatever to doubt the historical existence of a Samaritan Simon of Gitta. Moreover, the possibility is not to be denied that this wonder-worker may have come in contact in some way with the popular Gnostic system of the Cainites or Ophites, which was widely diffused throughout Western Asia, and by means of his magical arts and libertine principles have found such favour among them as to become the founder of a special sect who called themselves Simonians. It is equally possible, however, that without any historical connection of that kind an extreme antinomian sect of the Jewish syncretistic Gnostics of Western Asia took possession of the popularly venerated figure of Simon Magus in order to exalt him as their special prophet, and—in opposition to the Christian Son of God—to give him out to be a manifestation, nay "the great revelation," of the highest power or deity, exactly as at a rather later period the Neo-Pythagoreans did with Apollonius of Tyana and the Mandæans with John the Baptist. According to this, which is, as it seems to me, the most probable supposition, we have to regard the Simonians as by no means absolutely the first

Gnostic sect, but as the first which came into hostile contact with early Christianity. If this were the case, it would afford a very natural explanation of the origin of the patristic tradition which makes Simon the founder of all heretical Gnosis; and it would also, on this hypothesis, be very easy to understand how the Jewish Christians, who were hostile to Paul on account of his antinomianism, brought him into such close connection with the hero of the antinomian Gnostics, the deified Simon Magus, that finally they became identified in tradition, as is the case in the anti-Pauline Clementine romance, of which we shall have more to say below.

As a contrast to the radically antinomian Gnosis of the Simonians, we have the conservative legalism of the Elkesaites, of whom Hippolytus and Epiphanius[1] give accounts which are in the main agreed. According to the *Philosophumena* (ix. 13), the Syrian Alcibiades came in the time of the bishop Callistus from Apamea to Rome, and preached there a new baptism for the forgiveness of the grossest sins and at the same time for the healing of various diseases, such as madness and possession, on the ground of a revelation which had been given in the third year of Trajan to a pious Serian (Parthian) named Elkesai, and had been recorded by him in a book.[2] This revelation had been made by an angel, lofty of

---

[1] Epiphanius (*Hær.*, 19 and 30) brings the Elkesaites into such close connection with the Ebionites, Sampsæans, and Ossenes, that all these sects appear as but slightly different varieties of the same Gnostic-syncretistic Jewish Christianity.

[2] According to Origen, however, this book was supposed to have fallen down from heaven (Euseb., *H.E.*, vi. 38).

THE BEGINNINGS OF GNOSTICISM 139

stature as a tower, and by his female counterpart the Holy Spirit. This angel is identical with the "higher Christ" (x. 29; Epiph., *Hær.*, 19), the "Son of God, and Great King" (ix. 15), who as the first-created spirit rules over all angels, and has appeared at various times in a human body, first in Adam, then in the patriarchs, finally in Jesus, in whom he was crucified, rose again, and ascended to heaven (Epiph., 30, 53). According to *Philos.*, x. 29 and ix. 14, the higher Christ is partly God-born spirit, partly born of the Virgin as Jesus, partly transmigrates from body to body, is born in various forms, and appears at different periods in different incarnations—a theory of "transmigration of souls" similar to the Pythagorean doctrine, as Hippolytus remarks. Still closer is the parallel with the Buddhist teaching regarding the repeated appearances at different epochs of the heavenly Buddha or Saviour, one of which was the historical person of the Indian Saviour, Gautama Buddha, who was born of a virgin mother. That this Buddhist doctrine may have exercised an influence upon the Elkesaite Gnosis, whose founder was a Parthian, is, in view of the connection between India and Parthia, by no means improbable—much more probable certainly than that it should have been influenced by the Pythagorean philosophy. We are told, further, that the Elkesaites observed the legal (Jewish) manner of life, retaining, in particular, circumcision and Sabbath-keeping. They attached, however, supreme importance to baptism, which was performed in the name of the highest God and of his son, the Great King; and the candidate pledged himself to a pure life, calling on the seven witnesses—

heaven, water, the holy spirits, the angels of prayer, oil, salt, and earth. That this exalted estimate of baptism rests on a Gnostic-mythic foundation is to be inferred from the statement of Epiphanius that the Elkesaites "worship water as a god,"[1] saying that from it came forth life (Epiph., *Hær.*, 53). On the other hand, they held fire to be hostile to God. They rejected all sacrifices, and maintained that these had never been offered to God by the Fathers (*Hær.*, 19); and they applied a very searching criticism to the Mosaic law. They attached no weight to the prophets, nor to the apostles; and they used only the Gospel of the Hebrews (*Hær.*, 53, 30). Finally, we are told that they professed to cure the most serious illnesses, such as madness, consumption, or possession, by cold baths, which were to be repeated forty times within seven days, and were accompanied by appeals to secret powers; that in praying they were accustomed to turn towards Jerusalem; that they prosecuted astrological science, and held certain days to be unlucky; that they treated their doctrine as esoteric knowledge, carefully keeping it secret from strangers (*Philos.*, ix. 16, 17). All these traits point to the probability that this Gnosis, also, draws its origin from Jewish-Babylonian syncretism, and that Christian elements were only subsequently embodied in it. Whether Elkesai was the name of a historical founder, or the title of the book of revelations, or whether the word signifies a mythical hypostasis,

---

[1] This betrays Babylonio-Persian influence; the highest Babylonian god was Ea, who was also called Apsu = Ocean, and was therefore originally a water-god (the Oannes of Berosus). The Persians also worshipped water as a divine being, Apamnapat.

THE BEGINNINGS OF GNOSTICISM 141

"secret power," which was perhaps also identified with the "higher Christ," we cannot tell. That the sect first came into prominence in the beginning of the reign of Trajan, as both our informants testify, is quite credible.

SYNCRETISM AND GNOSTICISM

CHAPTER VII

The Principal Gnostic Schools

THE first well-authenticated names of Gnostic teachers and heads of schools are Menander, Saturninus, and Basilides. Menander was, according to Irenæus (I. xxiii. 5) and Justin (*Apol.*, i. 26), a pupil of Simon, was, like him, a Samaritan by birth, and had ensnared many persons in Antioch by his magical arts. He taught that the highest power or deity was unknowable, and that it was from the Ennoia, which was either united with this supreme deity or sprung from it, that the angels were derived who created the world. The conquest of these angels by means of magic knowledge was the end for which he himself, Menander, had been sent by the deity as the saviour of men. By baptism in his name his followers attained to the resurrection, in the sense that they were no longer subject to death, but lived on immortally without growing old ("ultra non posse mori, sed perseverare non senescentes et immortales"). Whether this was meant only in a spiritual or also in a bodily sense is doubtful; the phraseology, and the magical character of this Gnosis, are rather in favour of the latter. In any case it is clear that this magical Gnosis as yet contained no Christian elements whatever; its

THE PRINCIPAL GNOSTIC SCHOOLS 143

only possible relation to Christianity was that of a rival doctrine of salvation. It was only in the hands of the pupils of Menander, Saturninus and Basilides, that this syncretistic Gnosis took a Christian turn.

Saturninus or Satornilos taught, according to Irenæus (I. xxiv. 1 f. ; cf. *Philos.*, vii. 28) that the one father, who was unknown to all, created the angels, archangels, powers, and authorities. By seven of these, one of which was the god of the Jews, the world and man were created according to a pattern, all of light, which came down from heaven. But these world-creating spirits, owing to their weakness, were only able to make man in so miserable a fashion that he crawled like a worm upon the ground. Then the heavenly power took pity upon him and sent to this weak creature, who nevertheless was made after his image, a spark of higher life, which set him upon his feet and made him truly alive. This spark of life returns after death, when the earthly part of man undergoes dissolution, to its heavenly source. But it is not bestowed in equal measure upon all men, for just as the angelic powers have as their antithesis the demons, so, according to Saturninus' doctrine in its original form, there were created from the beginning two orders of men: the good, who were capable of being saved, and the wicked, who were allied with the demons and given over to corruption. From these demons, and especially from Satan, the enemy of the creative angels and of the god of the Jews, are derived marriage and procreation, and the use of flesh-meat. Some of the utterances of the prophets are their work, while others were given by the creative angels. But even the latter were so little able to resist the corruption caused by the demons and wicked men that they all united, including even the god of the Jews, in endeavouring to throw off the authority of the Supreme Father. The latter, therefore, in order to depose the god of the Jews and destroy the wicked men and demons, but to save good men, sent Christ, the deliverer, who, without being born or assuming a bodily form, only seemingly (putatively, δοκήσει) appeared as man (in Jesus) and brought redemption to those who believe in him, who have the spark of life in themselves. This redemption is not effected here, as in the earlier systems, by magic and libertine antinomianism, but by belief in the revelation of the Father and in the redeemer Christ Jesus, by whom the god of the Jews and the other creative angels are deposed, while at the same time Satan and his demons and all wicked men are annihilated and their works destroyed. As these included procreation and the eating of flesh, abstinence from both these is a logical consequence for the redeemed who have in them Christ's spark of life. Thus the libertinism of the Cainite-Simonian Gnosis is here transmuted into asceticism, a transformation which materially aided the propagation of this Gnosis in Christian circles ("per hujusmodi continentiam seducentes multos," Iren.).

The system of Saturninus was more fully developed by Basilides, who was his fellow-pupil at Antioch, but afterwards migrated to Alexandria, and there founded a school of his own, in which this Gnosis underwent an important transformation. Of its original doctrines we have clear information from Irenæus (I. xxiv. 3-7), with whose account that of Epiphanius (*Hær.*, 24) is in

THE PRINCIPAL GNOSTIC SCHOOLS 145

agreement, while Hippolytus seems to have in view a later form of the Basilidean Gnosis. Basilides taught that from the alone unbegotten Father there went forth first Nous (mind); from him, the Logos; from the Logos, understanding, wisdom, strength, righteousness, and her daughter peace;[1] and from these a further series of 365 angelic powers, who created, and inhabit, an equal number of heavens. The angels in the visible heavens nearest to us have, in turn, created all the parts of the (earthly) world, and divided its various countries and peoples among themselves as their special territories. The chief among them was the god of the Jews, who desired to make all other nations subordinate to his people, the Jews, and by that means caused universal uproar and confusion. For this reason the unbeginning and unnamed Father sent his first-born Nous, who was also called Christ, to free those who believe in him from the power of the creator of the world; this Christ appeared upon earth as a man, under the name of Jesus, and performed miraculous acts, but he did not suffer the death of the cross; in his stead Simon the Cyrenian, with whom he had exchanged outward appearance, was crucified, while he himself, mocking at his enemies, returned to his Father. Those, then, who know this are freed from the spiritual powers who made the world, and do not need to acknowledge the crucified; whoever acknowledges him is still in bondage to those powers, whosoever denies him is free, because he knows the ordinance

---

[1] The last two are, indeed, only witnessed to by Clement of Alexandria (*Strom.*, IV. xxv. 164), but certainly belong to the list, in order to make up the number seven; they are the seven star-spirits in an idealised form.

of the Father. Only the soul, however, is saved; the body is by nature corruptible (therefore there is no resurrection). The Old Testament prophecies are derived from the spirits who made the world; the law, in particular, from the god of the Jews, from whose rule the enlightened have been set free. From this Basilides drew, according to the writers on heresies, in contradistinction to the ascetic Saturninus, the libertine inferences of the Simonians: one might partake, without scruple, of idol sacrifice, and engage indiscriminately in all kinds of indulgences, including unchastity. Here, too, as among the Simonians, magic plays an important part. Anyone who knows the secret names of the angels (among them Kaulakau for the saviour and Abraxas for the whole of the 365 heavenly powers), and knows how to use them aright, can become invisible and intangible to all hostile powers, "Thou shalt know all, but none shall know thee," they said; and since they thought themselves exalted in their esoteric wisdom above the distinctions of all the positive religions, they desired to be neither Jews nor Christians. On this ground they rejected martyrdom incurred by confession, and held denial of their faith to be permissible. Only a few persons, indeed, were in possession of this higher wisdom—scarcely one among thousands; those who possessed it, moreover, were to keep their wisdom strictly hidden from the multitude. This Gnostic school was, therefore, at the same time, as regards those without, an exclusive mystery-association.

Quite different is the description of the Gnostic system of Basilides and his son Isidore given by Hippolytus, *Philos.*, vii. 10 ff. According to him, these Gnostics pretended to trace back their teaching to the secret tradition of the Apostle Matthew, whereas it really, in the opinion of their critic, was based upon the doctrines of Aristotle. But while the latter had taught that the world was without beginning, Basilides on the contrary, according to Hippolytus, taught that there was a time when nothing at all existed, and then the non-existent god willed to create the world. But this is only to be understood in a metaphorical sense, for the germ of the world arose out of non-existence without the exercise of will, thought, or feeling, and in this germ, as in a seed or an egg, all parts of the world were already present. This world-seed contained at the beginning a threefold sonship consubstantial with the primal god: the highest sonship took flight immediately after the creation to the primal god, drawn by his overpowering beauty; the second, lower, sonship was unable to rise by itself, but needed the wing of the holy spirit, who could not, however, quite attain to the highest, but remained as a boundary between the super-earthly and the world. The third and lowest sonship remained in the meantime in the material of the world-seed, because it had need of cleansing. Out of this there now arose the great world-ruler, who immediately, in order not to be alone, produced for himself out of the elements a son mightier and wiser than himself, with whose aid he created the ethereal world, the "Ogdoad." The same procedure repeated itself with a second archon and his son and creation, the "Hebdomad." Meanwhile, the third sonship remained still in the world-seed, yearning after the revelation of the sons of God (Rom. viii. 22). In the first Epoch, from Adam to

Moses, there ruled the great archon of the Ogdoad, who held himself to be the sole god, because all that was above the world was hidden from him. In the second Epoch, from Moses to Christ, there ruled the archon of the Hebdomad, the god in whose name Moses and the prophets spoke. Then came into the world the Gospel, but without a spatial descent of the blessed sonship of the non-existent God, which only communicated its powers to the son of the great archon. By this means the latter acquired the knowledge that he was not himself the highest god, but that above him there was the non-existent God and the sonship and the holy spirit. After this secret had been made known throughout the whole of the 365 heavens, the enlightening ray came finally to Jesus the son of Mary, who was the first to begin the process of division of the world-mixture, for through his suffering and resurrection the corporeal, psychic, and spiritual elements began to separate, and each to return to the part of the world-order to which it belonged. Thus, through him (through the continuation of the process of division which began with him), the third sonship, which had remained behind in the lower world, was purified and enabled to raise itself to the blessed sonship of the higher world. All that here below, in this mixed world, yearns after freedom and after the manifestation of the sons of God, must follow Jesus in being exalted to the blessed sonship in the region of the spirit. When that happens the course of the world will be completed and God will bring upon the whole world "the great ignorance," the result of which will be that every creature will thenceforth remain within the limitations of its own nature; none shall thenceforth, though yearning and striving beyond the limits of its nature, encounter suffering and corruption; that will be the Nirvana of the blessed eternity, in which all pains and desires of the restless, temporal spirit will be at an end. The early Christian hope of a general restoration of all things (Apokatastasis) in a new heaven and a new earth takes, in this curious Gnosis, a Buddhistic direction: by the cessation of all will and knowledge, the course of being and suffering shall come to rest. That these thoughts are not, as Hippolytus supposed, derived from Aristotle, is clear; nor is it possible to refer them to Stoicism, as some modern historians of heresy have endeavoured to do. On the other hand, their affinity with the Indian doctrine of Deliverance is so striking that it is hardly possible to avoid supposing a direct influence from that quarter. And this conjecture gains in probability when we learn from Clement of Alexandria and Origen that the Basilideans also taught the transmigration of souls; they interpreted the saying about retribution "unto the third and fourth generation" as a reference to the fate of souls in these reincarnations,[1] and the saying of Paul (Rom. vii. 9), "I was alive without the law once," as referring to a former life of his soul in an animal body.[2] If we recall how important a part is played in Buddhist legend (and here only) by references to former modes of existence and the fate of souls therein, we shall find a borrowing of this conception by the Basilideans from that quarter very probable—the more so as there are no grounds for it in the rest of

[1] Clem. Al., *Fragm.*, § 28 (*Op.*, ed. Klotz, iv. 14)
[2] Orig., *In Ep. ad Rom.*, v. (*Op.*, iv. 549).

their system. What is told us of their psychological theory, too, that there "grow into the soul," which is in itself simple and rational, many impulses and characteristics of animals, plants, and stones, finds its parallel in the Buddhist psychology. Finally, the ethical maxim of Basilides which Clement of Alexandria reports (*Strom.*, IV. xii. 28), that it is part of the so-called (*sic*) will of God that a man should love all things, because all things have a relation to the whole; a second, that he should desire nothing; and a third, that he should hate nothing—what is that but the quintessence of Buddhist ethics? This series of striking analogies seems to me to justify the conjecture that the later developments of the Basilidean Gnosis, of which the *Philosophumena* and the Alexandrians Clement and Origen give us information, are to be referred rather to Indian than to Hellenic influence. But it must be left an open question whether this influence was encountered in Syria or only later in Egypt, where Basilides settled between 120 and 130 A.D.; the one is as possible as the other.

Contemporarily with Basilides, Valentinus began to teach in Alexandria and to gather a following, without, however, at this time severing himself from the fellowship of the Church. It was only after his migration from Alexandria to Rome (*c*. 135 A.D.) that his breach with the Church took place; thereafter he worked in Rome for more than two decades as the influential head of a widely distributed sect. His doctrine was not, as Hippolytus asserts, drawn from Pythagoras and Plato, but is a development and fantastic elaboration of the older Ophite Gnosis, the roots of which, as we saw, reach back to the Babylonio-

THE PRINCIPAL GNOSTIC SCHOOLS 151

Jewish syncretism. Even within the school of Valentinus, his system underwent many alterations and developments, and the historians of heresy seem to tell us more of these than of its original form. Irenæus entirely confines himself to the teaching of the Valentinian Ptolemæus, whom he calls the "flower" of the school (*Adv. Hær.*, I., Præf.). The description of Hippolytus (*Philos.*, vi. 29-36) is somewhat simpler and less extravagant; therefore, probably, refers to an earlier stage of development. He frequently, also, remarks on divergences in certain points of doctrine. I consider it, therefore, advisable to follow his report for the most part.

The divergences begin from the outset. Part of the school placed at the head of their system the syzygy of the primal father or primal deep (Buthos) and the primal mother, Sigē (Silence) or Ennoia (Thought), or Charis (Grace); from this first pair proceeded three others, Nous or Monogenes and Aletheia, Logos and Zoe, Anthropos and Ecclesia; from the third of these pairs (Logos-Zoe) there proceed five others, and from the fourth (Anthropos-Ecclesia) six others, so that the whole sum of divine existence, the "Pleroma," consists of three groups, an ogdoad, decade, and dodecade; therefore in all of thirty æons. To these, in the progress of the theogonic drama, there were added the divine Æon Christ and his spouse, the holy Ruah (Spirit), and Horos the keeper of the boundary—all three offspring of the primal Father—and the common offspring of all the Æons, the Sotēr (Saviour) Jesus, not to mention the minor parts played by the Demiurge, the Devil, Beelzebub, angels and demons who, sometimes as supernumeraries and sometimes as actors, fill the stage of this Divine Comedy. So Irenæus; but Hippolytus remarks that in regard to the beginning the members of the school are at variance, some of them placing at the head, not a syzygy, but only the unbegotten Monad, the primal Father, and giving ethical explanations of the derivation of the further Æons from him. Since the primal Father did not love loneliness, he resolved to bring forth from himself the fairest and best that was in him, " for he was all love, but love is not love when there is not a beloved," and so he produced out of his sole being the first pair of Æons, Nous and Aletheia, from whom proceeded the other two pairs. Instead of the ogdoad, there is thus a hebdomad at the head of the system, to which are added the decade and dodecade as in the former scheme. As the primal Father, or primal Deep, is not reckoned with the Æons, their number amounts only to twenty-eight; afterwards, however, this is explicitly increased to thirty by the addition of the newly produced Æons, Christ and the Holy Spirit, from which it is obvious that this number is fixed *a priori* as a frame which must be filled in one way or another. The explanation of this lies, not, of course, in the thirty years which the Saviour had completed at the time of his public appearance (Irenæus), but in the thirty days of the month of the solar year, of which we were reminded also by the 365 heavens of the Basilidean Gnosis—yet another confirmation of the theory that all the Gnostic systems were ultimately derived from the lore of the Babylonian priests. The principal rôle in this theogonic or cosmogonic drama is played in the Valentinian, as earlier in the Ophite

Gnosis, by the Sophia Achamoth; her adventures are, however, elaborated in a considerably more fantastic fashion here than there. Here, too, her fall from the divine Pleroma gives the impulse to the whole process of world-formation, with all its consequences; but whereas that decisive act there appears as accidental, here it is due to a tragedy in the divine life before the world began. As to the details the reports waver. According to one account, the Sophia, forgetting in her vanity the distinction between the absoluteness of the unbeginning primal Father and her own limitation, desired to be in nothing behind him who had brought forth the Æons out of himself alone, and brought forth, out of herself alone, a shapeless abortion, to her own dismay and to the horror of all the Æons. To console her, the primal Father then caused the first pair, Nous and Aletheia, to produce the last pair, Christ and the Holy Spirit (a female principle), and these shaped the abortive offspring of the higher Sophia into a perfect Æon, which, however, remained outside of the Pleroma. Being abandoned by its creators, this lower Sophia fell into distress and yearning; to console her the Æons sent the " great High-priest Jesus," who was produced by them all in concert. He then set right her miserable condition, changing her by his heavenly power into psychic, material, and demonic beings. According to the description of Irenæus, the guilt of the higher Sophia consisted in a passionate desire to know the unknowable primal Father and to unite herself with him, not knowing that in such a union she must perish, like Semele in the arms of Zeus. She was delivered from this fate by the guardian of the boundary of the divine Pleroma, Horos, who made her retire within her limitations and caused her to come to herself and abandon her audacious passion. This forsaken passion of the higher Sophia now became a new being, the lower Sophia or Achamoth, which was given a form and brought to self-recollection by the Æon Christ, but remained banished from the heavenly world of the Pleroma, and in her loneliness fell into distress and yearning. From this point both accounts concur in representing that the material world arose from the sufferings of the lower Sophia, the watery element from her tears, the light from her laughter, corporeity from her trouble and terror. Irenæus adds that every one of these Gnostics imagines and recounts this tragedy in a different way. Students of heresy have indulged in further imaginations and speculations regarding this Valentinian myth, sometimes trying to find in it the Platonic doctrine of the fall of souls, sometimes the Hegelian doctrine of the origin of nature from the self-alienation of spirit. But while no one can be prevented from finding in the Gnostic fantasies as much philosophy as he likes, the primary fact in the case should not be forgotten: that, namely, the Valentinian Sophia Achamoth is derived from the Ophite, and the latter, as we saw above (p. 126 f.), from a combination of the Babylonian Ishtar and Tiamat myths with the Jewish doctrine of the creative Wisdom. The fall of the Sophia and her severance into a higher and lower, come from the myth of the descent of Ishtar to hell, and the formation of the world from her tears is a sentimental refinement of the nature-myth of the formation of

THE PRINCIPAL GNOSTIC SCHOOLS 155

the elements from the aqueous body of the Chaos-serpent, of which there are clear traces in the Sophia myth of the Ophites. The Valentinian cosmogony closes with the origination of the Demiurge out of psychic existence, his creation of seven heavens and angels (the hebdomad of the planetary spirits recurs under all sorts of variations), finally with the origination of the Devil or world-ruler and his demons out of a certain spiritual evil-substance, which, like the psychic and the sensuous, took its rise from the passion of the Sophia. We may spare ourselves further detail and now take a glance at the redemption myth, which, here as in other cases, is built up on the basis of theogonic and cosmogonic myths as a higher and final story.

Man was formed, according to the Valentinians, from psychic and material existence; the material part of man is in a sense the lodgment, sometimes of the soul alone, sometimes of the soul and the demons, sometimes of the soul and the powers of the mind (λόγοι in the Stoic or Philonian sense), which were planted in this world as the common fruit of the Pleroma and the Sophia. The latter indeed aids the Demiurge in all things in the making of the world, and without his knowledge contributes what is best in it. The prophets and the law spoke as instruments of the Demiurge; since the latter, as a merely psychic being, was by reason of his limitations in ignorance of things of the Spirit of God and the acts of the Sophia, the prophets were not able to reveal anything concerning the divine mysteries. When, therefore, the time for revealing these arrived, Jesus was born of Mary, not as a mere creation of the Demiurge like the posterity of Adam; he received from the Demiurge only his body, his inner being came from the Holy Spirit or Sophia, while as the heavenly Logos he sprang from the Ogdoad (the most divine of the Æons). Hippolytus remarks, however, that there was a difference of opinion on this point between the Eastern and the Italian branches of the Valentinian school. The Italians, among whom were Heracleon and Ptolemy, taught that the body of Jesus was psychic, and therefore at his baptism the Spirit, that is, the Logos of his higher mother the Sophia, descended upon him and raised from the dead that which was psychic. The Eastern school, on the other hand, among whom were Axionicus and Bardesanes, held that even the body of Jesus was pneumatic, because begotten by the Holy Spirit; they were therefore more decidedly Docetic than the Western Valentinians. The object of the birth of Jesus from Mary was that he should reveal the supreme Father, and thus bring all things in this lower world into order, as was done in the middle world by the Jesus who was produced by the Pleroma, and in the highest world by the Christ who was brought forth by the highest pair of Æons; each of these three worlds had therefore its own redeemer, Christ or Jesus, and the redemptive work of the historical Jesus, the son of Mary, is only an analogous repetition of the prototypal transcendental processes. According to Irenæus' account, some of the Valentinians taught that the psychic redeemer was the son of the Demiurge, and only passed through Mary as water passes through a tube; on him the redeemer who sprang from the Pleroma

THE PRINCIPAL GNOSTIC SCHOOLS 157

descended at his baptism in the form of a dove; there was also in him the spiritual seed which springs from the Achamoth. Our Lord was therefore composed of four elements; his spiritual part came from the Achamoth, his psychical part from the Demiurge; the visible body which was capable of suffering was prepared with the utmost skill, not from fleshly matter but from psychic substance; and finally the higher redeemer, who descended in the form of a dove. Neither this Christ-spirit nor the spiritual seed of the mother Achamoth took part in the sufferings of Jesus; only the psychic Jesus and his body, which was mysteriously formed out of psychic substance, underwent the sufferings. Even in the teaching of Jesus the redeemer, there was shown, according to the opinion of these Valentinians, the plurality of the elements which formed his being, for he sometimes spoke as the instrument of the highest redeemer, sometimes as the instrument of his mother Achamoth, sometimes as the instrument of the Demiurge. Moreover, they interpreted the Gospel discourses and narratives for the most part allegorically, with reference to the figures of their system of Æons, or to the three orders of men: the spiritual, psychic, and earthly, who correspond to the three sons of Adam, Cain, Abel, and Seth; of whom the earthly are subject to corruption, the psychic, when they choose what is good, are destined to find rest in the intermediate region, while the spiritual, when they have risen to perfection, shall become the brides of the redeemer's angels. The end of the world—such at least was their teaching, according to Irenæus—will come about when all spiritual men — that is, themselves — perfected by Gnosis, shall be initiated into the secrets of the Achamoth and attain to the knowledge of God. Psychic men, however, among whom are the Christians of the Church, since they have not attained to perfect knowledge, will be saved solely by faith and good works. They, the Gnostics, however, shall be saved, not by good works, but by their spiritual nature, which is incapable of corruption whatever they may do; just as dung cannot injure gold, so their spiritual nature cannot be lost by any kind of conduct. Consequently they allow themselves, according to Irenæus, to transgress all ethical rule and discipline. They eat things offered to idols, come together to keep heathen feasts, and practise unchastity under the pretext that it is necessary to give the flesh what belongs to the flesh, and the spirit what belongs to the spirit. This reproach does not, indeed, apply to all the Valentinians, but certainly to some, such as the notorious Marcus, who imposed on women by impudent charlatanry and robbed them of both money and honour (Iren., I. xiii. ff.; Hippol., *Phil.*, vi. 39 ff.).

Indulgence in libertine conduct and magic practices was common not only to the Valentinian Marcus and the Simonians, but also to Carpocrates and his son Epiphanes (both of whom taught in Alexandria). According to Irenæus (I. xxv.), he believed that the world was created not by the unbeginning Father, but by subordinate angels, and that Jesus was a son of Joseph, and was just like other men, except that he was distinguished by moral purity and the remembrance of that which he had seen when with the Father (in a Platonic pre-existence); therefore he

THE PRINCIPAL GNOSTIC SCHOOLS 159

was granted power to free himself from the dominion of the world-creating spirits, to ascend to God, and to remove the penal sufferings which had been imposed upon men. Those who follow his example in despising the creator of the world receive the same powers, and the apostles were not in any respect inferior to Jesus. The adherents of this Gnosis ascribed to themselves the capacity to coerce the powers that rule the world, by means of magical arts. They shared with the Basilideans the doctrine of transmigration, but with the peculiar modification that every soul was again and again imprisoned in a body until it had performed every possible action in this world; therefore the only way to escape reincarnation is to go through as much action, good and evil, in the present as is possible. The distinction between good and evil consists, not in the nature of the action, but in the intention of the doer; everything is in itself indifferent, it is only through faith and love that a man can attain blessedness; that is the secret tradition which Jesus gave commandment to communicate to those who are worthy.

The ultimate inferences from this libertine theory were drawn by Carpocrates' son, Epiphanes. As a "Super-man" he came to early maturity (he is supposed to have died at the age of seventeen), and wrote a work "On Righteousness," in which, according to the information given to us by Clement of Alexandria (*Strom.*, III. ii. 5 ff.), he proclaimed the most radical anarchism, communism, and libertinism.[1] The

[1] The statement of Clement that a shrine was erected to him in Cephallene and a cult held in his honour is not so improbable as to justify the supposition that he was a mythical moon-god.

Divine righteousness, so he taught, gave all things to be possessed and enjoyed by all creatures equally; it was human laws which first introduced into the world the distinction of "mine and thine," and therewith theft, adultery, and all other sins. As the Apostle said, "it was by the law that I knew sin" (Rom. iii. 20, vii. 7). As God Himself implanted in men the powerful sexual impulse with a view to the maintenance of the race, the prohibition of sexual lust is absurd, and the prohibition of lusting after one's neighbour's wife is doubly absurd, since thereby what is common is made a private possession. Monogamy is therefore, according to this Gnostic, as much a transgression of the community of women prescribed by the Divine righteousness as private possession of property is a transgression of community of goods. The conduct of the Carpocratians was, according to Clement, in accordance with these principles. At their "Agapes" they indulged in orgies of unchastity, and described these as "mystical communion" and as the way to the Kingdom of God. Clement closes (III. v. 40) his description of these libertine Gnostics (Carpocratians and Nicolaitanes, the latter a branch of the Simonians) with the remark that all these heresies may be reduced to two kinds; they teach either moral indifferentism ($ἀδιαφόρως\ ζῆν$) or an overstrained and hypocritical asceticism. As an example of the latter he mentions Marcion.

In immediate connection with Carpocrates, Irenæus (I. xxvi. 1) and the other anti-heretical writers mention the Gnosticism of Cerinthus, who, according to Hippolytus, *Phil.*, VII. vii. 33, brought his wisdom to Egypt, where Basilides, Carpocrates, and Valentinus

THE PRINCIPAL GNOSTIC SCHOOLS 161

taught; according to Irenæus, however, he taught in Asia, where he had a hostile encounter with John the Evangelist (III. iii. 4). According to the short account in Irenæus,[1] Cerinthus taught that the world was not made by the highest god, but by a quite subordinate power, which did not know the highest god. A distinction is to be made between the creator and the father of Christ; there is also a distinction between the son of the creator (Jesus) and the Christ who comes from above; also between the Monogenes as the beginning (of the Æons) and the Logos as the true son of the Only-begotten; thus the Logos holds the same position in the second rank of the divine Æons, inferior to the (Nous or) Monogenes who precedes him, as in the systems of Basilides and Valentinus (pp. 145, 151). Jesus was not born of the Virgin, but was Joseph's son, and was distinguished from other men only by wisdom and righteousness; after his baptism there descended upon him in the form of a dove the Christ, who came from the highest power, and made known his unknown Father and wrought miracles. Before the Passion, Christ, who as spirit could not suffer, departed from Jesus and flew back to the Pleroma, so that it was only the man Jesus who suffered and rose again. While this Christology has points of contact with that of Basilides, and, so far as concerns the manhood of Jesus, also with that of Carpocrates, Cerinthus diverged from both in the practical inferences which he drew from it. Although he, like

[1] I. xxvi. 1 and III. xi. 1. The latter passage forms a noteworthy supplement to the former, and clearly shows the relation of Cerinthus' teaching with the Basilidean Gnosis.

them and like all other Gnostics, represented the law as not given by the highest god, but by subordinate world-creating angelic powers, he rejected the antinomian inferences which were drawn by them, and held, like the Elkesaites and Ebionites, that the law was, in part at least, binding, and indeed—if we may trust the accounts of Epiphanius (*Hær.*, 28) and Philaster (*Hær.*, 36)—not merely the universal moral commandments, but also Jewish ritual ordinances, such as circumcision and the keeping of the Sabbath. As a consequence he had, of course, to reject the Apostle Paul. The same authorities tell us that Cerinthus taught that Christ had not yet risen, but would only rise at the general resurrection; which is, however, in contradiction with the statement of Irenæus that, according to Cerinthus, while the spiritual Christ did not suffer, Jesus both suffered and rose again. According to a statement of the Roman presbyter Caius preserved by Eusebius (*H.E.*, iii. 28. 2), Cerinthus taught a materialistic Chiliasm, for which reason he was regarded by some as the author of the Apocalypse of John, and even of the Johannine Gospel (Epiph., *Hær.*, li. 3). Against the latter assertion, made by the so-called Alogi, whose orthodoxy in other respects Epiphanius acknowledges, he raises the natural objection that the Gospel of John did not represent Christ, as Cerinthus did, as a mere man, but as the eternal Word which came down from heaven and became flesh. Cerinthus did not, however, deny that the divine Christ had come down from heaven; he only refused to identify him absolutely with Jesus. Doubtless the distinction which Cerinthus made between the two was intended to serve the purpose of softening the docetism of most of the other Gnostics and of doing justice to the picture of Jesus which is given in the Gospels. If Cerinthus, in this as in his conservative attitude towards the law, took up a mediating position between heretical Gnosticism and the belief of the Jewish-Christian communities, it is easy to understand how the contradictory legends arose regarding his relationship to the Fourth Gospel, one of which related that it was written to oppose Cerinthus (Iren., III. xi. 1, 3, 4), the other that it was written *by* Cerinthus (Epiph., *Hær.*, li. 3), for it is in fact a position such as this, mediating between Gnosticism and the faith of the Church, which was taken up, as we shall see later, by the author of the Fourth Gospel, though with much more skill and success than by Cerinthus. In its historical significance, therefore, the Gnosis of Cerinthus seems to me comparable with that of Marcion: each of them is a counter-current, or eddy, of the heretical Gnosticism,[1] a sobering-down of its fantastic features, a moderating of its extravagances, an effort to turn it into the same channel as the faith of the Church. In the case of Cerinthus, this was combined with the anti-Pauline Jewish Christianity of the Elkesaites and

---

[1] Lightfoot, *Apostol. Fathers*, i. 382, well remarks that a sharply marked type of docetism such as is combated in the Ignatian Letters is not a sign of late, but rather of early date "since the tendency in docetism was to became less pronounced as time went on." It may well have been the same with the Gnostic antinomianism. The contrary, traditional view, according to which pronounced docetism and antinomianism is a later phase of the development of Gnosticism, is closely bound up, in my opinion, with the mistaken traditional opinion regarding the Christian origin of Gnosticism, and must be abandoned along with the latter.

Ebionites, such as we encounter in the Pseudo-Clementine literature; in Marcion it follows the tendency of the Pauline and anti-Judaic Gentile Christianity, such as is represented especially by the Ignatian letters.

Marcion, a native of Sinope in Pontus, came about 140 A.D. to Rome, where at first he continued in fellowship with the Church, but afterwards, through his acquaintance with the Syrian Gnostic Cerdon, who held the same opinions as the Simonians, or perhaps as Saturninus (Iren., I. xxvii. 1, 4), allowed himself to be led into heretical views. After breaking with the Church, he founded a sect which became so widely extended and entered into so serious a rivalry with the Church that Marcion acquired the reputation of being the worst of heretics, " the first-born of Satan," as Polycarp is said to have called him when they met in Rome. The most dangerous point about this heresy, and that which incurred for it the special enmity of the Church,[1] was not especially extravagant speculation, but, on the contrary, the fact that Marcion abandoned the whole mythical apparatus of Pleroma and Æons, and the fall of the Sophia and the twofold or threefold Christ, and the grades of spiritual powers, etc., and laid all emphasis upon the practical side, on the recognition of what was peculiar to Christianity as a religion in contrast with Judaism, and on the practice of its

---

[1] To this are due the stories about Marcion's dissolute youth, and the suggestion of baffled ambition as the motive for his breach with the Church—stories which, in relation to heretics, are so much a matter of convention in ecclesiastical tradition that we may fairly ignore them.

ethic, interpreted as a strict asceticism. For this reason the question has been raised whether Marcion is to be considered a Gnostic at all. But that he is to be reckoned so cannot well be doubted. His well-authenticated dependence on the Syrian Gnostic Cerdon places his connection with the Gnostic heresies beyond doubt; but even in point of content Marcion's doctrine does not belie its relationship with the most ancient Gnostic ideas of the Ophites; but everything is simplified and popularised, and thus becomes, instead of the esoteric doctrine of a school, the faith of a church capable of attracting the masses.

Marcion has in common with earlier Gnostics that which Irenæus describes, with good reason, as the chief mark of heretical Gnosis: the distinction between the supreme God, the Father of Jesus Christ, and the subordinate divine power, which was at work in the creation and administration of the world. But the theogonic myths which are intended to explain the origin of the lower divine beings were abandoned by Marcion. At the head of his system he places only the distinction between the Father-god, who is only good and gracious, and the god of the Old Testament who is not good but only righteous, who is a strict judge, and whose righteousness has even a bad aspect, for Marcion, going beyond Cerdon in this, describes him explicitly as the author of evil, and as being fond of war, fickle, inconsistent with himself (Iren., I. xxvii. 2). We found something similar in the Ophite description of the Jewish god Jaldabaoth, whose jealousy, narrowness, and tyranny are there emphasised. It was indeed, from that mythological point of view, very natural, once the Jewish national religion was recognised as an inferior stage in comparison with the universal religion of Christianity, to embody this contrast in a corresponding distinction of their gods, especially as in this way the pressing problem of the origin of evil received a simple solution which discharged the good Father-god from all responsibility. It is, no doubt, too much to say that the whole of the Gnostic systems arose out of the question *Unde malum?*—they had a more general basis in the syncretistic tendency of the age—but this was certainly one of the contributory motives of the manifold Gnostic speculations, and especially of the dualism of Marcion,[1] which has so much resemblance to the Persian dualism that we might conjecture an influence from that quarter, mediated perhaps by the religion of Mithra, which was extending its influence in Rome in the time of Marcion. Hellenistic influence, however, is suggested by the assignment of a material substance as the third principle alongside of these two gods, which, as it affords the inferior god only a faulty material

[1] *Cf.* Tertullian, *adv. Marc.* I. 2 : " Languens, quod et nunc multi et maxime hæretici, circa mali quæstionem, unde malum, et obtusis sensibus ipsa enormitate curiositatis inveniens creatorem pronuntiantem : Ego sum qui condo mala (Isa. xlv. 7), . . . et in Christo aliam inveniens dispositionem solius et puræ benignitatis ut diversæ a creatore, facile novam et hospitam argumentatus est divinitatem in Christo suo revelatam." (He wearied himself, as many still do, and especially the heretics, about the question of evil, whence it is, and his perceptions being dulled by the morbid character of his inquiry, when he found the Creator declaring, " I am he that createth evil" (Isa. xlv. 7) . . . while in Christ he found a disposition of pure benignity quite different, as he thought, from that of the Creator, he hastily concluded that a new and previously unknown deity was revealed in Christ.)

for the formation of the world, serves as a further explanation of the evil of the world. Further, there is (introduced as a fourth principle in Hippolytus, *Phil.*, x. 19) Satan with his demons, creatures and emissaries of the creator of the world, who, acting as his instruments, moulded, in particular, man's body, which therefore is of demonic origin and nature. From this it may be seen that even the Marcionite Gnosis is not a homogeneous system, derived from pure religious idealism, but rests on the same basis of heathen-Jewish-Christian religious syncretism as all other Gnostic systems. It has also, in common with these, the second of the distinctive marks, a docetic Christology. In order to deliver men from the dominion of the creator of the world, the good god sent from heaven the redemptive spirit, who, without undergoing human birth or corporeal existence, suddenly appeared in Judæa in seeming human form as Jesus, was authenticated as a son of God by miracles, but not by the fulfilment of the predictions of the prophets, who had only promised a warlike Messiah of the Jews. It was not to fulfil, but to destroy, the law and the prophets and all the works of the creator of the world that Christ appeared; therefore the world-powers brought him to the cross, but, naturally, since he had no real body he could only suffer in appearance, and could not rise again in the flesh. For the same reason the salvation which he brought can only profit the souls, not the bodies, of those who believe in his teaching; the body, which is of the earth, can have no part therein. As all that has to do with the body is from the Demiurge, who is not good, it is the duty of the good to grieve him by abstaining from all his works and ways, especially from marriage and from the eating of flesh-meat (*cf.* Saturninus, p. 144 *sup.*). Christ also brought redemption to past generations by his descent into hell, and it was precisely the "ungodly," such as Cain, the men of Sodom, the Egyptians, and all the heathen, who entered into his kingdom, whereas the souls of the righteous, of Abel, Enoch, Noah, the patriarchs, and all the prophets, received no share in his salvation, because they did not believe the message of Jesus, but supposed it to be only another of the many temptations to which they were subjected by their God. This reversal of the religious estimate of historical characters was a feature which we met with also in the Cainite Gnosis (p. 135 f.). In both cases it is the expression of a radical antinomianism, in the latter, of course, of a libertine tendency; but in Marcion it is based on a deeply religious, but at the same time extremely one-sided and unhistorical exaggeration of the antithesis between law and Gospel, Judaism and Christianity. To prove the antithetic and mutually exclusive character of the two, Marcion wrote a work under the title of *Antitheses*, which has not, unfortunately, been preserved. He also, in order to provide his church with a substitute for the authority of the Old Testament, made, for the first time, a canonical collection of New Testament writings, though, of course, only of such as suited him, namely, ten letters of the Apostle Paul (excluding the Pastorals), with the Gospel of Luke, the only one which he accepted as Christian, and that not without mutilation. This proceeding of his had important consequences for the Church, for it occasioned the making of a collection—a more complete collection, however—of New Testament writings, and of setting them, not indeed in the place of the Old Testament writings, but side by side with them as a canon of equal value. The retention of the Old Testament for the Church was a matter of life and death; and the reconciliation of the differences which Marcion so strongly emphasised could only be effected, in the absence of our modern conception of historical evolution, by the allegorical method of interpretation. This ought therefore to be placed to the credit of the Church as for practical purposes an indispensable expedient, while, on the other hand, Marcion's rejection of it was not based upon better historical insight, but upon his theological antinomianism.

APOCRYPHAL ACTS AND GOSPELS

CHAPTER VIII

THE ACTS OF JOHN

IF we look only at the school-dogmas of the Gnostics as they are represented by the reports of their ecclesiastical opponents, it is difficult to understand how this mixture of wild imaginings and scholastic subtleties could make any deep impression on the Christian churches. It is otherwise when we turn our attention to the Gnostic popular literature, the remains of which have come down to us in the apocryphal Acts[1] and Gospels. The most important among them, the "Acts," ascribed to Leucius Charinus, of John, of Peter, of Thomas, of Andrew, of Paul, certainly date from the second century, and in part indeed from the first half of the century.[2]

[1] Tischendorf, *Acta apostolorum apocrypha*, Leipzig, 1851; Wright, *Apocryphal Acts of the Apostles* (Syriac version, with English translation), London, 1871; Lipsius, *Die apokryphen Apostelgeschichten und Apostellegenden*, 3 vols., 1883-90; Harnack, *Chronologie der altchristlichen Literatur*, i. 541 ff.; Zahn, *Geschichte des Neutest. Kanons*, ii. 2. 856 ff.; *Acta Johannis*, 1880.

[2] According to Zahn, *Acta Joh.*, cxliv. f., the Acts of John were certainly composed before 160, perhaps even by 130. In his *Geschichte des Neutest. Kanons*, ii. 864, he argues that there is not sufficient evidence for the earlier date, and holds to 160. Harnack, *Chronologie*, i. 542, says that both conjectures are in the meantime without sufficient foundation.

THE ACTS OF JOHN

They belong, therefore, to Early-Christian literature, and are of great importance for the understanding of that period of the growth of the Catholic Church. The composition of these writings served, as Lipsius remarks in his introduction to the above-named work, the special end of propagating the teachings and practices of the Gnostic schools within the Church, and a subsidiary purpose was to set alongside of the tradition of the growing Catholic Church another which equally laid claim to apostolic origin. As edifying and entertaining popular writings these apocryphal "Acts" were thoroughly adapted to the taste of the time, and to the religious needs, appetite for miracle, and curiosity of the multitude. Miracles of exorcism, raising the dead, healing and judgment, are multiplied endlessly; visions, appearances of angels, voices from heaven, animals that speak, wild beasts tamed and obeying the saints, demons in bodily shape, earthquakes, fire and water serving the saints, martyrs dying surrounded by heavenly splendour, and their enemies swallowed up by hell, appearances of Christ and of the martyrs in many guises—these constitute the miraculous apparatus of these edifying romances, the monotony of which is only occasionally broken by hymns, dialogues, and prayers of religious value or poetical merit. The romantic narrative is, however, nowhere an end in itself, but serves merely to dress out the Gnostic theological and moral teaching, which it was thus intended to popularise. Its characteristic marks are a docetic Christology, and an ascetic morality, which inculcates chastity (even to the rejection of marriage), fasting, and poverty as universally incumbent on all

Christians. Passing over the fantastic narratives, I shall confine myself to laying stress on the didactic elements which are characteristic of the Gnostic religion.

In the fragment Διήγησις θαυμαστή, newly edited by Dr James,[1] the Apostle John narrates in the first person his wonderful experiences in his intercourse with the Lord from the commencement of his discipleship. Even at his call (the account of which is based on the Synoptic, not the Johannine, narrative), Jesus appears to John and his brother James in different forms, as a boy and as an old man, sometimes small, sometimes reaching to heaven, sometimes soft, sometimes hard as a stone, sometimes wholly immaterial and incorporeal, as though nothing (perceptible) was present. On the mount of transfiguration John, who as the favourite disciple ventured nearer to Jesus than did Peter and James, saw Him in superhuman form, His feet whiter than snow, so that the ground was illuminated by them, and His head reaching into the heavens. At other times also it appeared to the disciple, when he was walking with Jesus, as though His walk was a movement through the air, His feet leaving no imprint upon the ground. For the present, however, he will say no more of these marvels, which must be treated as mysteries. Very curious is the account of the " Lord's departure " which here takes the place of the narrative of the Passion. Before

[1] In Robinson's *Texts and Studies*, v. i., " Apocrypha Anecdota," second series, edited by M. R. James, 1897. *Cf.* also P. Corssen, " Monarchianische Prologe zu den vier Evangelien," in Gebhardt and Harnack's *Texte und Untersuchungen*, xv., Heft 1 ; Hilgenfeld, " Der gnostische und der kanonische Johannes," in *Zeitschrift für wissensch. Theol.*, 1900, Heft i.

Jesus was taken prisoner " by the lawless Jews who received their law from the lawless serpent,"[1] He commanded His disciples to clasp hands and move round Him in a choric dance, responding to His words of prayer with an " Amen " (after each strophe). Thereupon He gave utterance to the following hymn :—

" Honour to Thee, O Father ! Honour to Thee, O Logos ! Honour to Thee, O Grace ! Honour to Thee, O Holy Spirit ! (or, to Thee, Spirit ! to Thee, Holy One !). Honour be to Thy Glory ! We praise Thee, O Father ; we thank Thee, O Light in whom dwelleth no darkness. That for which we thank Thee is this : I desire to be saved and to save. [I desire to be redeemed, and to redeem. I desire to be wounded, and to wound. I desire to be born, and to bear. I desire to eat, and I desire to be eaten.[2]] I desire to hear, and I desire to be heard. I desire to be understood, and I am wholly understanding. I desire to be washed, and I desire to wash. Grace leads the dance : I will flute, dance ye all. I will lament, do ye all smite upon the breast. An Ogdoad (of Æons) sings praise with us. The Dodecade leads the dance on high. It is the whole to which the dance leads. He who does not take part in it, knows not what comes to pass. I desire to fly and I desire to remain. I desire to adorn and to be adorned. I desire to be united and I will unite. I

---

[1] This means the Ophite " Ophiomorphos," son of Jaldabaoth, the God-opposing principle of the sensuous world and of legal religion (v. sup., p. 118).

[2] These four strophes are wanting in James's fragment, but are otherwise well supported.

have no house and I have houses. I have no dwelling and I have dwellings. I have no temple and I have temples. I am a lamp unto thee who seest me. I am a mirror unto thee who perceivest me. I am a door unto thee who knockest at me. I am the way to thee, the pilgrim. Join my chorus! Behold thyself in me, the speaking one; and when thou hast seen what I do, keep my secrets. Mark, O member of my chorus, what I do, for thine is this suffering of man which I have to suffer. For thou wouldest not at all have been able to understand what thou sufferest, had I not been sent unto thee as the Logos from the Father. Thou who hast seen what I suffer hast beheld me as a sufferer, and in this seeing thou dost not remain standing still but art all set in motion. Thou hast me as a place of rest: rest in me. Who am I? Thou wilt know it when I am gone away. What I now appear is not what I am; what I am thou shalt see when thou hast come to me. If thou didst understand suffering, thou wouldst possess impassibility. Learn to know suffering, and impassibility is thine. What thou knowest not, I myself will teach thee. I am thy God, not the god of the betrayer. I shall be in harmony with holy souls. In me shalt thou recognise the word of wisdom. Repeat with me again: Honour to Thee, O Father! Honour to Thee, O Logos! Honour to Thee, O Holy Spirit! Wouldst thou know what my meaning is? Once I played with all things and yet could never be harmed. I rejoiced, but do thou give heed to the whole, and then speak, saying: Honour to Thee, O Father! Amen."

After this hymn, as the John of the Leucian Acts narrates, the Lord went forth with them, and they fled hither and thither like men amazed. Even he, John, did not remain present at the suffering of the Lord, but fled, weeping over what had happened, to the Mount of Olives. And when the Lord was hanged upon "the thorn-bush (βάτος) of the cross," about the sixth hour of the day, a darkness came upon the whole land. And (suddenly) the Lord stood in the midst of the cave and illuminated it, and said: "John, it is only for the multitude down there in Jerusalem that I am being crucified and smitten with lances and reeds,[1] and given vinegar and gall to drink. But to thee I am speaking, and do thou give heed to what I say. I put it in thy mind to come to this mountain, that thou mightest hear what the disciple of the Lord has to learn, and the man of God." "Thereupon He showed me a cross of light set up, and a great multitude round about it; but Himself, the Lord, I saw above the cross, without a form, only with a voice of a strange kind, sweet and kindly and truly divine, which said unto me: 'John, one there is who must hear this of me. This cross of light I will call for your sakes sometimes Logos, sometimes understanding, sometimes Jesus, sometimes Christ,

---

[1] Whether this is an allusion to the lance-thrust spoken of in Jn. xix. 34 is doubtful. Against it we have to note (1) the plural λόγχαις, (2) the correlation with καλάμοις, (3) the placing of this ill-treatment before the giving to drink, and, further on, even before the crucifixion (at the close of the mystery of the cross of light). Is it not rather a variation of the scenes of Mk. xv. 17 ff. = Mt. xxvii. 28 that is suggested? This conjecture acquires the greatest probability when we read in the corresponding passage of the Gospel of Peter (see p. 213 below) ἕτεροι καλάμῳ ἔνυσσον αὐτὸν καί τινες αὐτὸν ἐμάστιζον. The νύσσομαι (I am being smitten) in the passage quoted above is to be compared with this ἔνυσσον (= smote), not with the Johannine ἔνυξε (= pierced).

sometimes door, sometimes way, sometimes bread, sometimes seed, sometimes resurrection, sometimes Son, sometimes Father, sometimes Spirit, sometimes life, sometimes truth, sometimes faith, sometimes grace. And it is so called with reference to (ordinary) men, but its true being, thought of in its essence and spoken to you (Gnostics?), is that which fixes the limits of all things, the strong necessity of that which, from mutable, has been made stedfast, and the harmony of wisdom. There are, however, powers and forces and authorities of the right hand and of the left, demons, energies, threatenings, passions, the devils and Satan, and the roots below from which proceeded the nature of that which is in process of becoming. This (Light-) Cross is he who has made all things secure through the Word, and separated out individual things from the process of becoming, and then reduced all things to unity. This is not the wooden cross which thou shalt see when thou goest down from here, nor am I he who is on the cross—I whom thou now seest not, but whose voice alone thou hearest. I was held to be that which I am not, I was not that which I was for many others. They say other things of me, base things which are not worthy of me. Even as the place of rest has as yet neither been seen nor pointed out, so shall I, much more than the lord of it, be neither visible nor to be expressed in words. The uniform heap round about the cross is the lower nature (sensuous humanity), and those whom thou seest on the cross have not yet a single form, for not every member of Him (the Christ) who descended has yet been taken up. But when the higher (spiritual) nature shall be taken up, and a race which is in harmony with me, then shall he who now hears me become this (higher race), and shall no longer be what he now is, but shall be exalted above it, as I now am. For so long as thou dost not call thyself mine own, I am not (actually) that which I (essentially) am. But if thou wilt listen to me, then thou shalt be as I am; but I shall be what I was, when I have united thee as completely with myself as I am united with myself, for (only) with my aid art thou this. Therefore trouble thyself not about the many, and despise those who stand outside of the mystery, for thou shalt know me that I am wholly with the Father, and the Father with me. I have not really suffered anything of that which they will say of me, but I would have that suffering, which I showed to thee and to others in the choric dance, to be called a mystery. For what thou seest I have showed unto thee; but what I am (in reality), that I alone know, and none other. Let me, therefore, keep what is mine, and what is thine do thou see through me; but thou shalt see me in truth, not as I said that I am, but as thou art able to apprehend me, in so far as thou art related (with me). Thou hearest from me that I have suffered, and yet I have not suffered; that I have not suffered, and yet I have suffered; that I have been smitten, and yet I have not been wounded; that I have been hanged, and yet I have not been hanged; that blood has flowed from me, and yet I have not bled; in short, that I have not had what they say of me, and, on the other hand, have suffered what they do not say. What that is I interpret to thee, for I know that thou wilt understand it. Behold then in me the becoming weak of the Logos, the being smitten of the Logos, the bleeding, wounding, hanging, suffering, the crucifixion and death of the Logos. And in truth I say this not having regard to men. First, therefore, fix thine eyes upon the Logos, then shalt thou think of the Lord, and in the third place of the man and of that which he has suffered.'" After the Lord—so the story proceeds—had spoken of this and of other things, which He was not able to speak of as He wished to do, He was taken up into heaven without any of the multitude seeing him. He, John, then went down (from the Mount of Olives) and laughed at all the others, for the Lord had told him already what they now said about Him; but one thing he kept firmly, that the Lord had done all things only symbolically and docetically, as a symbolic arrangement for the conversion and saving of men.

It would not be reasonable to demand that in a Gnostic mystery and hymn every word should be clear and intelligible to us. The fundamental idea is, however, quite intelligible. It is the docetic view of Christ and His sufferings. He was not that which He was supposed to be; what was said of Him is beneath Him and unworthy of Him. In particular, He was not really crucified; the crucifixion of Jesus in the presence of the multitude at Jerusalem was only a symbolical spectacle,[1] during which Christ Himself

[1] It is not clear whether the crucifixion of the man Jesus, without participation of the God Christ, was a real event, or a mere phantasmagoria, an illusion. The words of Christ in the hymn, "Once I played with all," can be interpreted in the one way as well as in the other. Nor is this point of great importance, since it is in any case certain that according to the Gnostics the Divine Saviour Christ did not really suffer.

was invisibly but audibly in intercourse with John upon the Mount of Olives, showed and interpreted to him the true cross, the "Light-Cross," which was wholly different from the wooden cross—a Gnostic conception which occurs also in the Acts of Philip and of Peter, and finds its explanation in the Valentinian system, where the Stauros (cross) is identified with the Horos (boundary), and is represented as a divine Æon who maintains the stability of the upper world or Pleroma, and divides it from the lower. To these two functions of establishing and dividing in the universe (Iren., I. iii. 5) there is a clear allusion in the esoteric interpretation of the "Light-Cross" as "division and the strong necessity of that which was insecure, but has been made firm, and the harmony of wisdom." Moreover, we may recall that Philo had attributed to the Logos the two functions of dividing and uniting. One coincidence—not exact but pretty close—with the Valentinian doctrine of the Æons may be found in the strophes of the above hymn in which it is said that the Ogdoad and the Dodecade take part above in the chant of praise and choric dance of the disciples of Christ. There is also a parallel to this choric dance and responsive choric song, which was certainly taken from the actual usages of Gnostic worship, in Philo's description of the Therapeutæ (*sup.*, p. 5). The subject of the chanted thanksgiving is clothed in the enigmatic words, "I desire to be saved, and I desire to save, to be redeemed and to redeem, etc." The key to their meaning must be sought in the conception of the (Ophite) popular Gnosis[1] according to which the

[1] See Lipsius' illuminating interpretation (*Apokr. Ap. Gesch.*, i. 529).

Sophia is, on the one hand, enclosed in pneumatic souls as a divine kernel and needs to be delivered, and, on the other hand, as the higher divine power, effects the deliverance. One must, however, guard against the temptation to find in this popular literature the special systems and doctrines of the different Gnostic schools; they are, rather, a practical working up of the fundamental ideas, for the most part common to the various schools, of the mystic philosophy of Gnosticism. One of the most interesting of these is, without doubt, the thought, which recurs again and again in the hymn we have quoted, that the true significance of the suffering of Christ consists in its being a symbol of the sufferings of mankind in general, and that the Logos was sent to us by the Father in order that we might learn to understand our human suffering and thus be set free from it. ("Learn to know suffering, and thou shalt be free from suffering. What thou dost not know I myself will teach thee. For thou wouldst not have been able to understand the suffering, had I not been sent unto thee as the Logos from the Father. Behold thyself in me!") As in Christ the meaning and significance of human suffering in general is revealed, so those who are His, who must suffer as martyrs for confessing Him, may be certain that Christ shares in the sufferings of all who are His, that He is not appealed to in vain by any who are His in their trouble, but graciously takes under his protection every suppliant; and He can do so because He is "omnipresent, unchanging, unconquerable God, higher than all power and might, more ancient and stronger than all angels and so-called creatures and the whole of the Æons; resting on Him and building yourselves up upon Him, ye shall keep your souls untroubled." From this it is quite clear that it is that same practical religious need of the soul for a guarantee of life, which underlies all the mystery-systems, which made the deity of Christ a postulate of the Gnostic communities and ultimately of the Church. That alongside of this mysterious deity of Christ His manhood is at first sublimated into a docetic appearance is entirely natural. Actual sufferings, especially, were found impossible to reconcile with the Divine subject, and the attempt was therefore made to allegorise, in one way or other, the evangelical tradition in regard to this—sometimes in the form that in the story of Christ's sufferings we should see only the symbol of human suffering in general; sometimes in the form that the Christ who is present in His Church shares in the martyr-sufferings of Christians; sometimes, again, in the form that the sin, weakness, and unfaithfulness of His people inflict upon Him ever-renewed sufferings. It is to this effect that the enigmatic words must be interpreted: " I have not suffered (namely, in the literal historical sense), and yet I have suffered (namely, in the sufferings and sins of Christians)." Ingenious and edifying as these thoughts were, it is quite intelligible that the teachers of the Church could not rest content with them, and were unwilling to surrender the reality of the historical sufferings of Christ. The relation of the God-Christ to God the Father is left obscure; frequently the expressions used have a Monarchian ring, as though Christ were simply and absolutely God, and Father and Son were only different names for the same Divine Person; again, however, as the

Logos sent from the Father, He is distinguished from Him as a different Person. It is not our business to solve this problem, but merely to note that the naive oscillation between different conceptions points to a relatively early period, where the question has not been clearly thought out how the divinity of Christ is to be reconciled with that of the Father, and when no definite antithesis was felt between a still naïve Monarchianism and incipient Trinitarianism. This naïveté and indefiniteness of view is common to the Gnostics and their earliest ecclesiastical opponents, such as Ignatius and the author of the First Epistle of John.

In the last fragment of the Acta Johannis, which deals with the departure (μετάστασις) of the Apostle, there are some further remarkable prayers and homilies.[1] On the last day of his life, a Sunday, the Apostle assembled his brethren about him to celebrate divine service, and delivered a discourse to them, in which he first reminded them of all the gifts of grace which had been given to them by the Lord through his ministry, adding an exhortation not to grieve, dishonour, and injure the Lord by disobedience to His commands. "Let not our good God be grieved, the gracious, the merciful, the holy, the pure, the stainless, the alone, the sole, the unchangeable, the sincere, the guileless, the unwrathful, who is high and lifted up above every name which can be said or thought by us, our God Jesus Christ! May He have joy and honour through our living in purity, chastity, temperance, and brotherly love!" Then follows the

[1] Tischendorf, *Acta apost.*, 272 ff.; Zahn, *Johannesakten*, 239 ff.; Wright, *Apocryphal Acts*, ii. 61 ff; Lipsius, *Apokr. Ap. Gesch.*, i. 533 ff.

THE ACTS OF JOHN 183

celebration of the Lord's Supper, at which the bread (there is no mention of wine) is consecrated with the following prayer: " What praise or offering or thanksgiving shall we name at the breaking of this bread save Thee alone? We worship Thy name which the Father has named (or "the name of the Father which Thou hast revealed," the latter being perhaps a Catholic variant); we adore Thy name which is expressed by " Son "; [1] we adore the resurrection which has been shown to us by Thee; we adore Thy seed, the word, grace, the ineffable pearl, the treasure, the plough, the net, the greatness, the diadem, the Son of Man who was so called for our sakes, truth, rest, knowledge, freedom, refuge in Thee. For Thou art the sole Lord, the root of immortality, the source of incorruption, and the seat of the Æons. For all this art Thou now called for our sakes, in order that we, naming Thee by this name, may make known Thy greatness, which is at present incomprehensible to us, which is only visible for the pure, and can only be seen in the man who belongs to Thee."

After the celebration of the Lord's Supper, the Apostle, so Leucius continues, took his disciples with him to a place outside the town, and bade them dig his grave. After that he offered the following parting prayer: "Thou who hast chosen us to be apostles to the heathen, who hast sent us out into the world, O God (Christ), who hast showed Thyself through Thine apostles; Thou who hast never rested, but always from the foundation of the world hast

[1] This appears to be the correct translation of the words σου τὸ λεχθὲν διὰ υἱοῦ ὄνομα; cf. Corssen, "Monarchianische Prologe" in Gebhardt and Harnack's Texte und Untersuchungen, xv. 1. 121.

been working salvation; Thou who revealest Thyself throughout all nature and makest Thyself known even among the animals; Thou who hast made our waste and desolated soul calm and still; Thou who hast given Thyself as the Logos to the thirsty soul; Thou who to the dead soul didst soon appear; Thou also didst show Thyself to the soul sunk in lawlessness in the place of the law, to the soul conquered by Satan hast revealed Thyself as a deliverer; Thou who hast slain the adversary of the soul that takes refuge in Thee; Thou who didst stretch forth Thine hand to her, and lifted her up from her hellish condition, and suffered her not to walk in the flesh (or "in transgressions"), who didst show her her proper enemy and didst give her pure knowledge concerning Thyself, God, Jesus, Father of those who are above the heavens, Father and God of those who dwell in heaven, law of the ethereal beings and path of the beings of the air, guardian of the dwellers upon earth and terror of those that are below the earth, grace of Thine own; receive the soul of Thy John, O Jesus, which perchance is found worthy by Thee! Thou who up to this hour hast also kept me pure for Thee, and unstained by woman; Thou who, when in my youth I purposed to marry, didst appear unto me and say unto me, 'John, I have need of thee'; Thou who, when the third time I was minded to marry, didst visit me with sickness, and on the sea didst say unto me, 'John, wert thou not mine I would suffer thee to marry'; Thou who didst open the eyes of my spirit and who wast the giver of my natural eyes; Thou who, when I looked about me in the world, madest me to know that to look upon a woman was something hateful; Thou who didst deliver me from the perishable and unreal, and preserve me for the life which endures for ever; Thou who didst free me from the foul frenzy of the flesh; who didst deliver me from bitter death, and didst bring to life again him that hath need of Thee; who didst put an end to the hidden sickness of my soul and didst prevent me from open doing (of evil); who didst force out and drive away him who did disquiet me; who hast preserved my love to Thee immaculate, and my walk before Thee without failure; who didst give me undoubting faith in Thee, and show me pure knowledge concerning Thee; who dost give to every work its appropriate reward, and hast put into my soul the desire for no other possession than of Thee alone, for what could be more precious than Thou? Now when I have finished the service which Thou, O Lord, hast entrusted unto me, honour me with Thy rest, grant me Thy perfect portion, unspeakable blessedness. And when I depart to Thee, let the fire (of hell) retreat, darkness be conquered, the abyss overcome, the furnace lose its strength, hell be quenched! May Thy angels accompany me, the demons be afraid, the rulers be cast down, the powers of darkness sink away, the regions on the right stand firm, those on the left not be maintained! May the Devil be stultified, Satan made a mock of, his rage be stayed, his wrath cease, his children be smitten, his whole root cut off! Yea, grant that I may complete the whole journey to Thee without suffering and injury, and receive that which Thou hast promised to those who have lived purely and loved Thee alone!"

"Do Thou be with me, Jesus Christ, our Lord! Peace be unto you, my brethren!" With these words John descended into the grave and gave up the ghost with joy. Such was the original close of the Leucian narrative; a later version of the legend made him not die, but either sleep in the grave, so that the earth was moved by his breath, or else be translated bodily to heaven, so that the grave was found empty.

From these edifying passages of the Acta Johannis we gain a much better impression of the real significance of the Gnostic religion, of its mystic fervour and ethical strength, than from the fantastic mythological systems of the schools which have been preserved by the reports of their ecclesiastical opponents, and on the basis of which histories of the Church, and of doctrine, are accustomed to give their colourless accounts of Gnosticism. The mythological features of the doctrine of the Æons obviously formed in popular Gnosticism merely the background, the transcendental scenery which imagination demanded; the religious interest did not depend on it, but concentrated itself wholly upon the one figure of the God and Saviour Christ, whose exaltation above all powers whether above the heavens, in the heavens, on the earth, or below the earth, is emphasised in the strongest possible fashion. With the historic Jesus of Nazareth He has indeed little in common but the name; of the Jewish Messiah every trace is eliminated; even the evangelical title of "Son of Man" is only one of many and various names which are used out of condescension for our poor powers of comprehension, without really corresponding to the nature of Christ. He is for the Gnostic nothing else than the "Saviour-God" (θεὸς σωτήρ) of the mystery-cults, the Lord of life in this world and the next, the victorious conqueror of all hostile demons, the pledge of salvation and continuance of life for those souls who have united themselves to Him by sacred ceremonies of initiation and the leading of a holy life. His work of salvation did not by any means first begin with the appearing of Jesus; from the very beginning of the world He has been the Saviour of all creatures, even of the animals. Among mankind He worked from the beginning as the manifestation of the Divine Logos, which tames the savagery of our souls, satisfies their thirst, lifts up those who are sunk in vileness and fleshliness; and this deliverance is effected as much by the communication of true knowledge regarding the special enemy of the soul as of knowledge regarding the true being of its Saviour. Since the soul sees in Him her Divine ideal or "law," she is filled with such love for Him that all her desire is directed only to Him, and in her conduct she endeavours to refrain from everything that is contrary to Him and would trouble or dishonour Him. The Gnostic belief in the deity of Christ was therefore not by any means a mere theoretic speculation; it was as far as possible from being a product of philosophy; it corresponded to and sprang from the yearning which underlay all the mystery-cults for a Divine friend, guide, and deliverer of the soul, with whom it could find itself closely united, by whom it could let itself be guided, and by whom it could feel itself saved in trouble and in death. The elements of nature-myth which belonged to Gnosticism in consequence of its originating, in common with the mystery-cults, from syncretistic nature-religion, never disappeared completely, and played, indeed, a considerable part in the doctrine and cultus of the Gnostic sects; but we cannot fail to recognise that in the Christian Gnostic circles from which the legends of the apostles were derived, nature-myth takes a very subordinate position in comparison with ethical feeling. The Gnostic belief in Christ and mystical love for Christ which are expressed in the prayers we have quoted, were a powerful source of ethical motive, the educative influence of which upon the Christianity of the time must not be underestimated. It is true it was an extreme ascetic ethic which was here preached. Its highest maxims were renunciation of the world and abstinence from sexual relations—but in that it only followed the prevailing tendency, which is found also in the Church communities from the first, though perhaps less stringently applied, and founded rather on eschatological hopes than on dualistic enmity to nature. But the motive which in early Christianity formed the basis of the ethical demand—the nearness of the world-catastrophe and the establishment of the Kingdom of God—was the less adequate the longer that catastrophe was delayed; in these circumstances the replacement of the early Christian apocalyptic motives by Gnostic mysticism and asceticism was in accordance with the needs of the time. It was precisely this practical side of Gnostic preaching which deeply impressed contemporary Christianity; even its ecclesiastical and dogmatic opponents were not able to escape this influence. We shall see later that Ignatius, the most passionate opponent of Gnostic docetism, completely shared the Gnostic mystical view of Christ and its ascetic contempt for the body. In this way of thinking and feeling the main tendencies of the time were harmoniously united: Oriental Gnosticism, the mystery-cultus which was common to East and West, Alexandrian Hellenism and Pauline Christianity. Only one factor did not seem to find its proper place therein: the early Christian tradition regarding Christ's life and death. What would have been the fate of Christianity if Gnosticism had succeeded in choking this main root of the faith of the Christian community under the accumulation of foreign elements which it introduced? It is certain that, for the permanence of Christianity, the preservation of this relatively realistic[1] historical tradition of the original Christian community was as indispensable as was, on the other hand, the adoption of the gnosis and mysticism which corresponded to the idealistic needs of the time. The great, the decisive question was whether these two streams, so different in their origin and character, could mingle and flow united through one channel. The solution of this problem was provided by the Church theology of the second century, especially the Johannine theology, which influenced all subsequent periods, and can only be understood in view of the situation of Christianity in the second century. As regards the relationship of the Gospel of John to the Leucian Acta Johannis, we may provisionally remark that

[1] As contrasted with mysticism and speculation. *Cf.* "idealistic" below, and see vol. i. p. 470 for a fuller development of the thought.—TRANSLATOR.

either Leucius did not know the Gospel of John at all,[1] or, if he did, did not regard it as Johannine or apostolic.

[1] This is the view of Corssen, *ut sup.*, 118–133. Hilgenfeld, too, considers it possible (*Z. f. wiss. Theol.*, 1900, Heft 1).

APOCRYPHAL ACTS AND GOSPELS

CHAPTER IX

THE ACTS OF THOMAS

THESE Acts are concerned with the missionary preaching, the miracles, and the martyrdom of Thomas in India. They have as little historical value as the Acts of John. There is indeed much to recommend the conjecture [1] that the Acts of Thomas are based on a Buddhist legend, the scene of which is laid in the Indo-Baktrian realm of the (historical) King Gundaphoros, and originated about the time of his conversion to Buddhism (the first century of our era): To transform a Buddhist missionary legend into a Christian one might easily occur to the Gnostic circles from which these apostolic Acts were derived, because the interest in marvellous stories of miracle, and in an ascetic sanctity which renounced marriage, was common to both. Although we possess the Acts of Thomas only in various ecclesiastical versions which correct the original to a greater or less extent, the original Gnostic character is still clearly visible even in the passages which have been much worked over. After the Acts of John, the Acts of Thomas, which are ascribed to the same author, Leucius Charinus, are the most valuable document of the popular

[1] *Cf.* Lipsius, *Apokr. Ap. Gesch.*, i. 281 ff.

Gnostic religion of the second century, its teachings, its worship, its liturgy and poetry. Leaving the rest of its contents out of account, I may confine my attention to these parts.

Of special value is the religious allegory about the soul, which, under the name of a "hymn," is inserted in the Syriac text of the Acts of Thomas.[1] This graceful story runs (slightly abridged) as follows: "When I was a child and dwelt in my kingdom in my Father's house, contented with the wealth and luxury of those who nurtured me, my parents equipped me and sent me forth from the place where my home was; they took from our treasury, and bound upon me, a rich but easily carried burden of gold, silver, and precious stones. They took off from me the splendid robe, the purple toga which in their love for me they had had made to my form. And they made an agreement with me, and wrote it in my heart that I might not forget it. 'If thou shalt go down unto Egypt and bring back the one pearl which is in the lake surrounded by the hissing serpent, thou shalt receive thy splendid robe again, and along with thy brother who stands next to us in dignity, thou shalt be heir in our kingdom.' I went forth from the East and came, accompanied by two attendants—for the way was long and dangerous—through the land of Babylon to Egypt. I came to where the serpent was, and abode

[1] Wright, *Apocr. Acts,* ii. 238 ff. ; Lipsius, i. 292 ff. According to a conjecture of Nöldeke, which Lipsius accepts, this hymn, which did not originally belong to the Acts of Thomas, has for its author the Valentinian Gnostic Bardesanes. This is also considered probable by A. A. Bevan, who has re-edited this hymn, with an English translation, in *Texts and Studies,* v. 3, 1897.

THE ACTS OF THOMAS

hard by its dwelling, waiting until it should be asleep that I might take my pearl from it. In my loneliness among strangers I found a fellow-countryman from the East, a free-born, handsome, and lovable youth, whom I made my friend and confidant, informed him of the errand on which I had come, and warned him not to associate with the unclean Egyptians. I adopted their garb that they might not be suspicious of me as a stranger and rouse the serpent against me. But they found out, nevertheless, that I was not one of their fellow-countrymen, and succeeded in worming their way into my confidence, and gave me their food to eat. Then I forgot my royal descent and entered the service of their kings, and under the burden of their oppression (or "under the magic influence of their food") I fell into a deep sleep. But my parents knew of·all that had befallen me, and they were troubled about me. Then they called together all the great ones of their kingdom and devised a plan for my return from Egypt, and wrote me a letter, signed by all these great men, to the following effect: 'From thy Father, the King of Kings, and thy Mother, the Queen of the East, and thy brother our second; unto thee our son in Egypt, greeting! Awake and rouse thyself from sleep, and give heed to the words of my letter! Remember that thou art the son of kings. Behold into what slavery thou hast fallen! Remember the pearl for the sake of which thou wast sent to Egypt. Think of thy robe, and remember the splendid toga which thou shouldst wear to adorn thee when thy name is read in the list of the worthy, and that thou, with thy brother, shalt reign as vice-king in our kingdom.' This letter, sealed by the King himself, flew like an eagle to me in Egypt, and was turned into speech. At its voice I woke up and roused myself from sleep; I kissed it, brake the seal, and read it, and its words agreed with that which was imprinted in my heart. I remembered that I was the son of royal parents, and my noble birth maintained its nature (or, "my free soul yearned after its natural condition"). I remembered the pearl for which I had been sent to Egypt, and I began to exercise magic upon the dreadful hissing serpent. I lulled it to sleep and charmed it to slumber, for I named the name of my Father over it, and the name of our second, and the name of my mother, the Queen of the East, and I took away the pearl and departed to go to my Father's house. I stripped off the foul garb of the Egyptians and left it there, and hurried forward upon the way to my home, the land of light. And my letter, my awakener, I found still on the road before me. As its voice had awakened me, so its bright splendour led me, and with its love did it drive me on. Passing Babel, I came to Maishan, the port upon the coast. Thither my parents had sent by faithful masters of the treasures the splendid robe and the toga which I had laid aside. When I received this garment, the form of which I no longer remembered, for I had put it off in my early childhood, it seemed to me to be a mirror of myself. I saw it wholly in me, and myself wholly in it; though distinct, we were yet wholly one, in one form. So, too, the two masters of the treasures who had brought it to me I saw as two, and yet again as one, of like form, for one writing of the King was inscribed upon them which restored

to me my pledge and my treasure, the splendid robe
with the precious stones, upon which, in all colours,
the King's likeness shimmered. And it seemed to me
as though I heard it speak, as though it sought to
force itself upon me; love urged me to it, I stretched
out my hand to take it, I grasped it and adorned
myself with its splendid colours. Then I went up to
the gate of greeting and reverence. I bowed my
head and worshipped 'the majesty of my Father,'
who had sent me forth, for I had fulfilled his command, and he had given me that which he had
promised. And at the gate of his princes I mixed
with his great men, for he rejoiced over me and took
me to him, and I was with him in his kingdom, and
he promised that I should also go in with him at the
gate of the King of Kings, and appear with my
offering and with my pearl before our King."

We can distinguish various strata in this narrative.
At its foundation lies a primeval nature-myth of the
same kind as in the stories which recur everywhere
of the removal of a treasure guarded by a dragon. In
Western Asia this became a localised legend of the son
of the Parthian king, who was sent to bring back from
the wonderland of Egypt the dragon-guarded pearl;
but there he was cast, by hostile magic, into a slumber
from which he was roused by some miracle or other.
This story, which has affinities with our "Dorn-
röschen" (Sleeping Beauty), was finally worked up
by a Gnostic into a religious allegory of the fate of
the human soul. The soul is sprung from the East,
the heavenly kingdom of light, and is of royal race.
"The father, the mother, and the brother," the
"second in esteem," are the highest divine beings of

the Syrian (Ophite) popular Gnosticism.[1] Egypt is the world of sense; here dwells the serpent, the hostile demon Ophiomorphos. The soul which has descended thither forgets its heavenly origin and its task, because, after putting off its heavenly garment of light, it is clothed in the foul garb of the stranger —the material body—passes into the service of the powers who rule in this realm, and is fed upon their food. The pearl which it has to win is the divine spark of light or spiritual part of its being, which is to be freed from the dominion of the powers of darkness. In order that this deliverance may be brought about, the slumbering recollection of its higher origin must be awakened in the soul. That is effected by the letter of the parents which is borne to it through the air; that is, the divine revelation, the words of which agree with the remembrance imprinted upon his heart, the natural God-consciousness of the *anima naturaliter Christiana*. Awakened, illuminated, and guided by this message from its divine home, the soul begins its return from the strange land of the world of sense to its father's house, and at the last stage of its journey receives back the splendid robe which formerly (in its pre-existent state) belonged to it—what is meant is the "heavenly body of light," which the pneumatic soul is to receive, and which, indeed, is so far different from it that the soul is mutable and sunk in the world of sense, but yet, on the other hand, is identical with it, inasmuch as

[1] *Cf.* above, p. 117 f. The complicated system, as it appears in Irenæus' account, was naturally simplified in popular Gnosticism into an idyllic family picture, just like the theological doctrine of the Trinity in popular Catholicism.

the soul also, in its true being, is pneumatic. The masters of the treasures who deliver over this heavenly garment to the soul are doubtless, like the escort upon its first journey, protecting angels, mediators and ministers of the divine revelation. Only the close of the narrative is obscure, according to which the return to the father, and the welcome to his kingdom and among his great ones, is not the last thing, the prospect of an appearance before the "King of Kings" being held out as something still higher. As this is not prepared for by any hint in what precedes, it must remain an open question whether this conclusion originally belonged to the story, and what the meaning of it is.[1] From among the numerous prayers and homilies scattered through the Acts of Thomas, which are distinguished for religious warmth, moral earnestness, and, in parts, poetic beauty, I select the following prayers of consecration[2] as especially characteristic of the Gnostic background of this work. (1) Before baptism: " Come, holy name of Christ, which is above every name! Come, power of the highest and perfect compassion! Come, highest gift of grace! Come, merciful mother! Come, consort of the male principle! (in the Syriac version catholicised into Communion of Blessing). Come, revealer of hidden secrets! Come, mother of the seven houses,

---

[1] On the assumption that the text is sound, Bevan conjectures (*ut sup.*, p. 40), in agreement with Nöldeke, that the " Majesty of the Father" who is greeted on the return is distinguished from the Father himself as a different person, and perhaps is identical with the "Next in Rank," a heavenly mediator who receives souls and guides them to the highest God, their Father.

[2] Tischendorf, *ut sup.*, pp. 213, 227; Wright, 166, 189; Lipsius, i. 311 f.

in order that there may be rest for thee in the eighth house (or, "whose rest was in the eighth house")! Come, messenger of the five members — reason, thought, understanding, reflection, judgment—impart Thyself to these newly converted ones! Come, Spirit of holiness, and purify their reins and hearts, and seal them in the name of the Father and of the Son and of the Holy Ghost!" Instead of the last verse there stands in the Syriac text, according to Wright's translation: "And he baptized them in the name of the Father and of the Son and of the Holy Ghost. And when they came out of the water there appeared unto them a youth with a burning torch, the brilliance of which was unbearable to their eyes." (2) Prayer of consecration before the Eucharist: "Come, gift of the Highest, perfect compassion! Come, Holy Spirit, consort of the male principle! Come, Thou who knowest the secrets of the Chosen One! Come, sharer in all the struggles of the noble warrior! Come, treasure of glory, favourite of the mercy of the Most High! Come, silent One, revealer of the mysteries of the Exalted, thou who disclosest that which is hidden and makest known what is secret! Come, Holy Dove, which hast borne the young twins! Come, hidden mother, who art manifest in Thy deeds, who givest joy and peace to those who follow Thee! Come and take part with us in this Eucharist which we celebrate in Thy name, and in the meal of love to which we are assembled at Thy call!" After these words, the account proceeds, Thomas cut upon the bread the sign of the cross, and brake it and began to distribute it. First he gave it to the woman, with the words: "May this be unto thee for forgiveness of sins and for deliverance from eternal transgressions (*i.e.* for deliverance from the eternal death incurred by transgression; therefore rightly paraphrased in the Syriac version, "and to eternal resurrection ")." Then he gave it also to the others who had received the seal (baptism), with the words: "May this Eucharist be unto you life and peace, and not for judgment and punishment!" (This is only in the Syriac text, and therefore is perhaps a Catholic addition.) In this celebration the absence of the cup is noteworthy; wine was entirely tabooed by the ascetic Gnostics, and therefore perhaps not permitted even at the Lord's Supper. The same was perhaps the case in regard to the sacred meals of the mysteries of Mithra (*sup.*, p. 108), of which we are also reminded by the sign of the cross cut upon the bread.

Whatever may be the interpretation of the two sacramental prayers which we have given, so much is certain, that the female principle appealed to in both as identical with the Spirit of holiness is the divine Sophia, the principle of revelation, redemption, and purification, who stands by the noble warrior in all his battles, and gives him a share in the eternal peace and joy of the kingdom of light. In the baptismal prayer the coming of this Spirit upon the candidate is besought as "the coming of the holy name of Christ, which is above every name," as, according to the Gnostics, the "name of Christ" descended upon him, with the Holy Spirit, at his baptism. We are transported into the circle of ideas of the Syrian popular Gnosticism when the redemptive principle is described as the "Merciful Mother" and Consort of the Male Principle, that is, of the divine Æon

Christ, with whom the Sophia in the Ophite Gnosis forms a syzygy; further, as Mother of the seven houses, who finds her rest in the eighth. This means the hebdomad of the world-ruling star-spirits or archons, exalted above whom thrones the Sophia, their mother and ruler. Of that lower Sophia which sank down into the material world, in contradistinction to her who rules above, which plays so important a part in the Valentinian system, there is in this popular Gnosticism no mention. If, on the other hand, the correct reading is: "Come, mother of the seven houses, that Thou mayest have rest in the eighth," we may find in this the significant thought that the true dwelling of the divine Sophia, wherein she shall find rest, is not in the transcendental world above the stars, but in the hearts of the pious—a thought which passes from mythological speculation to religious mysticism. Again, when the Sophia is described as the messenger, or envoy ($\pi\rho\epsilon\sigma\beta\epsilon\hat{v}\tau\iota s$) of the five members, reason, thought, understanding, reflection, and judgment, what is meant by these names are the Æons, which are elsewhere [1] enumerated in an exactly similar way, which went forth from the primal principle and form the content of the divine Pleroma, the powers of which the Sophia, as the mediator between the upper and lower world, is besought to communicate to the candidate. In the second prayer of consecration the Sophia is called "the Silent One" or "Silence and

[1] *Cf.* the three syzygies of the Simonians (p. 134), and the—according to Irenæus at any rate—five highest Æons of the Basilidean system (p. 145). Thilo, in his explanation of the Acts of Thomas (p. 194 f.), recalls the "five members" of the Manichæan "First Man," which again seem to be connected with the Buddhist psychology.

the revealer of the mysteries of the exalted one" (or, "of the entire greatness," *i.e.* of the Pleroma), inasmuch as she hides the divine truth from the world-powers and from sensuous men, but reveals it to pneumatic souls. Finally, when the Sophia is described as the "Holy Dove which bore the young twins," we may, indeed, recall [1] the doctrine of Bardesanes concerning the two daughters of the Holy Spirit; but whereas in that system the reference is to cosmogonic powers, we have in our prayer of consecration probably to find the interpretation in the immediately following strophe: "Come, hidden Mother, who art revealed in Thy deeds, who givest joy and peace to those who follow Thee." The "twin daughters" of the Holy Dove or the divine Sophia (the Holy Spirit) are nothing else than her deeds or influences, in which the (as to her essence) hidden Mother is revealed, namely, the joy and peace which she grants to her followers. Thus we have here, as above, a practical adaptation of the mythological speculations of the Gnostic schools to the religious mysticism of the Gnostic cultus-associations. The significance of these apocryphal works for the history of early Christianity consists precisely in the fact that it is in them that we first come to know Gnosticism in its strength as a religion and a cultus appealing to the masses, taking captive heart and imagination; for it was only in this way that it was possible for it to enter into competition with the Christianity of the Church.

As a further illustration of this we may give the parting prayer of Thomas,[2] which has many points

[1] So Thilo, *Thomasakten*, p. 190 f., and Lipsius, p. 319 f.
[2] Wright, p. 279 ff.; Lipsius, p. 329 f.

of contact with that of John (p. 183 f.): "My Lord and my God, my hope and my trust, my teacher and my consoler, be Thou with me until the end! Thou who from my youth upwards didst sow in me the seed of life and preserve me from being led astray; Thou who didst place me in the poverty of this world, and hast prepared me for Thy true riches; Thou who hast taught me that I am Thine, for which cause I have had no contact with woman, in order that Thou mightest find unstained that which Thou desirest to have. My mouth suffices not to praise Thee, nor my understanding to adore Thy goodness to me. Thou didst show me in a vision, when I was desirous of riches, that many come to harm through riches and possessions, and I believed Thee and remained in constant poverty, until Thou, the true wealth, didst reveal Thyself to me, and didst fill those who were worthy of Thee with Thy true riches, and delivered them from trouble and care and greed. Behold, I have fulfilled Thy will and completed Thy work. I have been poor and needy, a stranger and a slave, despised and imprisoned, hungry and thirsty, naked and weary, for Thy sake. Let not my trust be deceived nor my hope put to shame! I have planted Thy vine, put out Thy talent to usury, responded to Thine invitation to the Supper, have put on the wedding garment, have kept my lamp burning and my loins girded, and watched through the whole night: may I now come into Thy presence and worship before Thy holy beauty! The prisoner whom Thou hast committed to me (the sensuous man) I have smitten; the free man who is in me (the spiritual man) do Thou set free, and suffer not my soul to be disappointed of its hope! The inward have I made outward, and the outward inward: let Thy will be fulfilled in all my members! I have not turned myself back nor stretched myself forward: let me not become a wonder and a sign. The dead (the sensuous nature which is a prey to death) I have not made alive, and the living (the spiritual nature which is destined to life) I have not slain: grant that we may receive the crown of victory, O Thou Ruler of both worlds. May the (hostile) spiritual powers not perceive me (on my way to heaven), and the world-rulers not conspire against me, and the toll-keepers (at the gates of heaven) not oppress me; may the lower and the higher beings not withstand me, but flee and hide themselves because Thy victorious power surrounds me. So grant unto me now, O Lord, that I may pass through in quietness, that I may follow my path in peace and joy, and appear before the Judge (or, "before Thy glory"), and let not the slanderer (the Devil) look upon me, but let his eyes be blinded by Thy light, which Thou hast made to dwell in me, and let his lying mouth be dumb because he has found nothing against me!"

The preservation of the soul from the spiritual powers of darkness which threaten its life both here and above, lay wait for it upon its journey to heaven, bar the entry at the gates which lead to life, seek to injure it before its judge by their accusations; that is the pole about which all the imaginations and aspirations and hopes and fears of that time revolved, the one common centre in which the adherents of the mysteries of Mithra, of Sabazios, and of Isis, the Gnostics of East and West, heretical and orthodox

Christians, found a point of meeting. This one great preoccupation about the salvation and blessedness of the soul exercises a determining influence upon dogma and worship among the Gnostics as well as among the Christians of the Church. In order to save the soul from the evil spiritual powers, Christ must necessarily be a Saviour-God (θεὸς σωτήρ) whose origin is from heaven, like Mithra or any other of the gods of the mysteries. The belief in the divinity of Christ which first became prevalent in Gnostic circles was therefore based, not so much on historical knowledge and formulated judgment concerning the person of Jesus, as on the *a priori* demand of the same religious need which urged the adherents of the various mystery-cults to worship their several saviour-gods, and the subjects of Rome, especially in the East, to worship the Roman Emperor as the divine saviour of the world. But in order to guarantee the deliverance of the soul from the dark powers of death, the Saviour-God must not only draw his origin from heaven, the place of eternal life, but must also have attacked and conquered the demonic powers of darkness and death in their own home and stronghold, namely, in Hades. It is for this reason that we find, parallel to the myths of a descent to hell in the heathen mysteries, an exactly similar belief in the descent of Christ to hell, which first arose in Gnostic circles,[1] and for them had much the same significance as the belief in the bodily resurrection of Christ had for the Christian Churches—this being repugnant to the Gnostic docetism. From

---

[1] It is frequently mentioned in the Acts of Thomas. *Cf.* Lipsius, *ut sup.*, p. 326. "The thought of the descent to hell originated in Gnostic circles."

the Gnostics the "Descent into Hell" soon passed over into the faith of the Church, and was referred to the interval between the death and resurrection of Christ. In order, however, to secure and guarantee the fruits of the victory of Christ, the Prince of Life, over the powers of death, for those who believed in Him, a need was felt for mystical ceremonies of initiation, which by sensible yet super-sensible means, the "water of life and the bread of life," should establish a mystical communion between the soul and the conqueror of death. It is worth noticing that in the stories of conversion in the Acts of Thomas, in addition to the baptism with water, there is a further and, as it seems, more important "sealing" (ἐπισφράγισμα τῆς σφραγίδος), the anointing with oil, a usage of which there is also evidence in the case of other Gnostics, and which has a parallel in the cult of Mithra (*sup.*, p. 107). Even if, however, the anointing was held by the Gnostics to be the specific means of illumination and the communication of the Spirit, they by no means looked down on baptism with water,[1] but, on the contrary, ascribed to the consecrated water a miraculous power of bodily healing. In the Acts of Thomas, a young man has a withered hand restored by washing in the consecrated water, over which Thomas had pronounced the following prayer of consecration: "Come, Water of living waters, True Being sent down to us by Him who truly is, Spring which is sent to us from Quietness, Strength of Salvation, which comes down from that Power which conquers all things and subdues them to its will, come and dwell in these waters, that the gift

[1] *Cf.* Lipsius, *ut sup.*, p. 331 ff.

of the Holy Spirit may be perfectly consummated in them." We may see from this that ceremonial mysticism in these Gnostic circles—and much the same holds good of Church circles also—was by no means purely spiritual, but was based upon the crude supernaturalism of animistic magic.

APOCRYPHAL ACTS AND GOSPELS

CHAPTER X

THE ACTS OF PETER

EUSEBIUS, in his History of the Church, mentions (III. iii. 2) four apocryphal writings which bore the name of Peter—the Acts (πράξεις), the Gospel, the Preaching (κήρυγμα), and the Apocalypse of Peter, in regard to which he asserts that they had never been included among the Catholic (ecclesiastical-canonical) writings nor quoted by any ecclesiastical author. This is not, however, strictly accurate in the case of the three last-named. The Apocalypse of Peter will be treated at a later point in connection with the Epistles of Peter, and the "Preaching" will be discussed among the apologetic writings. In the present connection we have only to deal with the two Gnosticising apocrypha, the Acts and the Gospel of Peter.

The Acts of Peter[1] narrate that, after the departure of the Apostle Paul from Rome, Simon Magus came thither, and by his magical arts led many astray from

[1] Lipsius, *Apokr. Apostelgesch.*, ii. 1, where a complete philological apparatus is given relating to all the various manuscripts in which remains and fragments of these Acts are preserved. The statement of their contents given above is compiled from the text of the *Actus Vercellenses* (p. 174 ff.), and the Linus text of the *Passio Petri* (p. 91 ff.).

faith in Christ, and brought great trouble upon the Church there. Thereupon Peter was commanded by the Lord in a vision to journey to Rome. His voyage from Cæsarea, the conversion of the shipmaster, which took place on the way, and the reception of the Apostle by the Church at Rome are described, and then begins the detailed account of the struggle against, and victory over, Simon Magus by the superior miraculous powers of the Apostle. He causes the Magian to be challenged to the contest by a dog with a human voice, exorcises a possessed youth, makes a broken statue of the Emperor whole again by the use of consecrated water, makes a salt herring come to life, causes the imminent punishment of the Magian to be announced by an infant with the voice of a man, restores the sight of several blind widows, and then engages in a formal competition of miracle with his opponent. Whereas the Magian only succeeds in killing a young man by his magic and making a dead man stand upright for a moment, the Apostle, before the eyes of the people of Rome and the Prefect of the city, raises three dead men, one after another, to renewed life and health, and heals a great multitude of sick persons, so that the number of believers increases daily. But the Magian would not yet confess himself beaten, but declared that he would fly up to God before the eyes of the assembled people. He seemed, indeed, about to succeed in his attempted flight, when at the prayer of the Apostle he was hurled down from the sky, and died a few days later from the consequences of his fall. Now, when the time came for the Apostle to receive in heaven the reward of his work, Nero had him cast into prison. Several prominent Romans, whose wives had been persuaded by the Apostle's preaching to break off conjugal relations, had in their wrath at this sworn to compass his destruction. When the believers heard of this they urged the Apostle to escape. Against his will, he allowed himself to be persuaded, and started out, unhindered by his guards, whom he had converted. At the gate of the city, Christ met him. Peter asked, "Lord, whither goest Thou?" Christ replied, "To Rome, in order to be crucified a second time." Peter immediately turned back, and would no more allow himself to be influenced by any entreaties to avoid the death of a martyr. Sentenced by the Prefect to crucifixion for repudiating the gods of Rome, he besought that he might be crucified with his head down, since it would not be seemly for him to be crucified in exactly the same way as his Master. This is done, and he consoles the weeping Christians with the words: "Great and deep is the mystery of the cross, an ineffable and indivisible bond of love. Through the cross God has drawn all things to Himself. This is the tree of life, through which the dominion of death has been destroyed. This hast Thou revealed unto me, O Lord. Open also the eyes of all these that they may behold the consolation of eternal life." Then the mourners beheld angels standing with wreaths of roses and lilies, and the Apostle, in the strength of the cross which had been raised up, standing there and receiving a book from Christ, out of which he read the mystery of the cross. This longer discourse begins by saying that it was meet for Christ alone, as the ever upright and exalted, to be crucified upright; crucifixion with the head downwards was, on the other hand, a symbol of the birth of the seed of Adam, in whose case the divine order was reversed, so that the right appears as the left, and the left as right. This miserable creature had no movement of life;[1] therefore the higher power came in mercy into the world by means of a corporeal being, and restored the proper order, teaching men to recognise that which was accounted not good as really good, and that which was accounted injurious as really beneficial, as the Lord said in a mystery: " Unless ye make the right left and the left right, and the top the bottom and the front the back, ye shall not know the Kingdom of God." He who allows himself to be turned from error by this message, and strives to attain to the higher calling, shall become a partaker of perfection. The way which leads thereto is Christ. With Jesus Christ we must surmount the cross; He is ordained to us as the sole and only Word. Therefore, the Spirit saith, "Christ is Word and Voice" (Divine being in a human manifestation), but He is also the cross; as this consists of the beam and cross-piece and the nails which fasten the sufferer to it, so the human nature is attached to the Divine by the "nails of discipline," namely, through faith and penitence and good conduct. Finally, the discourse about the cross passes over into a parting

[1] *Cf.* above, p. 118 f., for the similar teaching of the Ophites regarding the miserable condition of men by nature, and how they were raised by the help of the heavenly Sophia to a higher place in the scale of life. In the place of this the popular Gnosticism of the Acts puts the revelation of the "higher power" through the appearing of Christ as man.

prayer addressed to Christ: "Thou, Lord, art my Father, [Mother], Brother, Friend, Creator and Perfector of Salvation, my Desire, my Consolation, my Satisfaction. Thou art everything to me, and everything is for me in Thee (or, "Thou art the All, and the All is in Thee; Thou art the truly existent, and there is nothing existent except Thee"). In Thee we live and move and have our being, therefore we must hold Thee to be the All. We pray Thee to give us that which Thou hast promised unto us, which no eye hath seen, and which hath entered into no heart of man. We thank Thee, weak mortals as we are, and praise Thee, for Thou art God [Lord] alone, and there is no other; Thine is the glory now and for ever! Amen." Thereupon the Apostle died, but afterwards he appeared several times to his disciples, and exhorted them to be faithful; he also appeared in a vision to the Emperor Nero, gave him a tremendous beating, and commanded him to leave the Christians in peace for the future, which he accordingly did.

The near relationship of these Acts of Peter with the Acts of Thomas and of John is obvious at the first glance. In all of them there is the same naïve delight in marvellous stories of miracle, the same zeal for an ascetic ideal of virtue (the turning away of wives from their husbands by the apostolic preaching is the constantly recurring cause of the martyrdom of the apostles); the same mystic symbolism of the cross, and docetic, in some cases monarchian, Christology. Of the latter, traces are discernible in spite of the Catholic working over of the text, as in the closing prayer which we have just given, the

Greek text of which describes Christ as "the sole God, the alone truly existent, the All," while the Latin text substitutes "Lord" for "God" and recasts the pantheistic phrases to make them morally edifying.[1] The docetic character of these Gnostic Acts is remarkably exemplified by the sermon which Peter delivered before the Roman Church on the Gospel story of the Transfiguration.[2] It begins with some general remarks on the possibility of knowing Christ: "That which we have comprehended through His mercy, we have written, even though it may appear weak to you, in such a way that what is delivered to you may be comprehensible to human flesh. The first thing is to know God's will and goodness. When the flesh (humanity) was formerly filled with error, and many thousands of men were cast into destruction, the Lord in His mercy showed Himself in another form and appeared in human shape, since no one is worthy to see Him as He is. Each one of us therefore saw Him as he was able to see Him, each according to his capacity." Then turning to the Gospel narrative, Peter describes his condition upon the mount of transfiguration, how he was robbed of his senses by the wonderful light and the indescribable voice, but the Lord raised him up, according to the word of the prophet: "He bears our sins and suffers for us; but we supposed that He was suffering pains and was smitten with wounds." Then follow some general Christological reflections: since "He is in the Father, and the Father in Him, He is Himself the fulness of majesty and has shown us all good. He ate and drank for our sakes, without feeling hunger

[1] Lipsius, ii. 1. 265 f.   [2] Lipsius, *ut sup.*, 183 f.

and thirst; He bore and suffered contumely for our sakes; He died and rose again on our behalf. He who, when I sinned, protected and strengthened me by His greatness will also comfort you, in order that ye may love Him—Him who is great and little, beautiful and ugly, youth and old man, appearing in time and wholly invisible in eternity, whom no hand of man can hold fast, and who yet is held by servants; whom no flesh has seen, and who is nevertheless now seen; whom no man has heard, and who yet is now known and heard; who once was The Word, and now appears as if He had undergone the utmost sufferings, who was never smitten but now is smitten; who *is* before the world was, and was known in time, the first and greatest of all powers, and yet given over to the powers; who is glorious, but among us was humble; who became visible from heaven, and was betrayed. This Jesus ye have, brethren, as door, light, way, bread, water, life, resurrection, refreshing, pearl, treasure, seed, satisfaction, grain of mustard-seed, vineyard, plough, grace, faith, word. He is all, and no other is greater than He. Praise be unto Him to all eternity!" The series of predicates is almost exactly the same as in the passage from the Acts of John quoted above (p. 175 f.); therefore either the Acts of Peter are dependent on the latter, or both had the same author.

CHAPTER XI

The Gospel of Peter

A FRAGMENT of this writing, along with another of the Apocalypse of Peter, was found in a grave at Akhmim and published in 1892 by the French scholar Bouriant. Since then it has been many times reprinted and discussed.[1] The fragment contains a narrative by Simon Peter of the passion and resurrection of Jesus, beginning with His condemnation, and breaking off with the return of the disciples to Galilee and the opening of a scene at the Lake of Galilee. The narrative follows in the main the type of the Synoptics, especially that of Matthew, but deviates in many points from all the canonical Gospels. I confine myself to noticing the more important divergences.

The condemnation of Jesus was due, according to the Gospel of Peter, not to Pilate, who vainly endeavoured to prevent it, but to King Herod. Joseph (of Arimathæa), who is introduced as "the friend of

[1] Especially by Harnack in his *Texte und Untersuchungen*, ix., Heft 2, and in the Report of the Proceedings (*Sitzungsbericht*) of the Berlin Academy, 1892, No. xliv. *Cf.* also Zahn's essay on the Gospel of Peter (1893), and that of Hilgenfeld in the *Zeitschr. f. wiss. Theol.*, 1893, Heft 2. (And Swete, *Gospel of Peter*, 1903.—TRANSLATOR.)

Pilate and of the Lord," begs, even before the crucifixion, for the body of the Lord. The bearing of the cross by Simon of Cyrene is not mentioned. During the crucifixion Jesus was silent, as though He felt no pain at all (ὡς μηδὲν πόνον ἔχων), just as, in the sermon of Peter which we have given above, it is said that He ate and drank only for our sakes, without Himself experiencing hunger or thirst, which obviously implies a docetic conception of the body of Jesus. Of one of the two malefactors we are told that he addressed to the enemies of Jesus the reproachful question, " What evil has this man done to you, who has been the Saviour of men ? " and that they, in their wrath at this, commanded that his (the thief's) legs should not be broken, in order that he might endure longer tortures. In spite of this echo of the Lucan episode of the penitent thief,[1] none of the words from the cross which Luke records are mentioned, nor is the psalm-quotation of the oldest tradition given in its canonical form, but with the curious alteration, " My strength, my strength, why hast thou left me ! " which can hardly mean merely the ebbing away of bodily strength, but is doubtless to be understood as meaning that the heavenly power of the Spirit of Christ departed from Jesus before His death—a conception which meets us frequently in Gnostic circles (cf. pp. 120 f., 145, 157, 161). And after these words He was taken up (ἀνελήφθη), namely, to heaven ; the

---

[1] It has nothing in common with John xix. 33, but, rather, contradicts the statement there (32) that the legs of both the thieves were broken. But even from the narrative in Luke the above account diverges so far that it may be doubted whether there is any direct reference.

narrator, therefore, takes the death of Jesus to be also the moment of His exaltation to heaven. That presupposes the same view as the statement in the Acts of John about the invisible Christ and the light-cross (*sup.*, p. 175). But this Gnostic docetic view contradicts the common Church tradition of the bodily resurrection of Jesus. In its inconsistent combination of these two conceptions, the Gospel of Peter shows itself designed to mediate between Gnosticism and the faith of the Church, just as the Gospel of John is intended to do. The earthquake which follows on the death of Jesus, or, to be more precise, is caused by the laying of His body upon the ground, aroused, according to the Gospel of Peter, universal alarm, so that not only (as in the canonical Gospels) the heathen centurion and his soldiers, but also the Jews, especially their elders and priests, perceived what a misfortune they had brought upon themselves, and began to lament, saying, "Woe to us for our sins! The judgment and the end of Jerusalem is at hand!" Yea, the whole Jewish people began to murmur against their rulers and to confess, with cries of lamentation, "Ye see how righteous a man he is!" Alarmed by this, the elders begged Pilate to allow the grave to be guarded for three days, in order to prevent the removal of the body of Jesus by His disciples, and the arising of a belief in the resurrection of Jesus among the people. The guarding of the grave by sentinels, and by sealing it, is described in even more detail than in Matthew. Then follows a very curious account of the occurrences of the Easter morning. "In the night in which the day of the Lord (Sunday) was breaking, while the soldiers were standing two and two at their posts, there rose a mighty cry in the heavens, and they (the soldiers) saw the heavens opened and two men descending in a beaming splendour of light and approaching the grave. The stone which was before the door rolled away, of itself, to one side, and the grave was opened, and the two young men went into it. When the soldiers saw that, they awakened the centurion and the elders (who had remained there with the guard), and while they were telling them what they had seen, they saw three men coming out of the grave, two of them supporting the other, and a cross following them. The heads of the two reached up to heaven, and that of the one whom they were supporting reached above the heavens; and they heard a voice from heaven which said, 'Thou hast preached obedience to them that sleep'; thereupon 'Yea' was heard coming from the cross. The watchers took counsel together, and decided to go away and report to Pilate what had happened. And while they were still taking counsel the heavens were seen opened again, and a man coming down and going into the grave." When Pilate heard the report, he declared, "I am pure from the blood of the Son of God ; ye were determined to have it so." At the desire of the Jewish rulers, who preferred to make themselves guilty of the most grievous sin against God rather than fall into the hands of the Jewish people and be stoned, Pilate commanded his soldiers to say nothing of what had happened—a version of the story which is simpler, more intelligible, and therefore, doubtless, older than the curious account in Matthew (xxviii. 11–15) of the bribing of the soldiers by the priests. It is then further narrated in the Gospel of Peter that on the Sunday morning Mary Magdalene, with her companions, came to the grave to make the usual lament for the dead, which had been omitted on the day of Jesus' death for fear of the Jews. (The mention of the customary lamentation for the dead only, instead of the embalming of the body, as the purpose of the women, is a departure from the older tradition of Mk. xvi. 1 = Lk. xxiv. 1, which can hardly be accidental). On their arrival at the grave the women found it open, and, sitting in the midst of it, a beautiful youth with bright gleaming garments, who asked them, " Why are ye come ? Whom seek ye ? The crucified ? He is risen and gone away. If ye believe it not, bend down and see the place where He lay, that He is no longer there. For He is risen and gone to the place whence He was sent forth." The women fled, filled with terror. It has also previously been mentioned, in regard to the " twelve disciples of the Lord," immediately after the crucifixion, that they were filled with mourning and fear, and hid themselves because they were being pursued " as evildoers who desired to burn the Temple." Now, after the close of the feast of unleavened bread, when all the passover-pilgrims were making their way homeward, they too returned, grieving over what had befallen, to their Galilæan homes. " But I Simon Peter and my brother Andrew took our gear (nets) and went to the sea (of Galilee), and there was with us Levi the son of Alphæus, whom the Lord . . ."

Here the fragment breaks off, and leaves us uncertain what happened to the three disciples at the Lake of Gennesareth. It is natural to conjecture that in the sequel an appearance of the risen Lord is narrated, which perhaps may have had some similarity with the narrative in John xxi., but the difference in the list of persons present is to be noted. The appearance to Peter and his two companions, which was probably narrated here, was in any case the first (*cf.* 1 Cor. xv. 5), and did not take place until after the return of the disciples to Galilee. With this the narratives of John and Luke of the appearances to the disciples in and near Jerusalem, and of Matthew about the appearance to the women at the grave, are all irreconcilable. On the other hand, verse 57 of the Gospel of Peter agrees so exactly with the genuine closing verse of Mark (xvi. 8), that there are grounds for the conjecture that there may have been some relationship between the lost close of Mark and the narrative which follows in the Gospel of Peter. In other cases also the Gospel of Peter has such close resemblances to the Gospel of Mark that, while its dependence upon the latter cannot be confidently asserted, it may with some probability be conjectured. On the other hand, dependence of the Gospel of Peter on any of the other three canonical gospels is not probable; its parallels with Luke and Matthew are all so incomplete, and show, alongside of the common elements, so much that is peculiar, that they can much more easily be explained as due to a common source in oral or written tradition (a primitive Aramaic Gospel?) than by direct dependence upon the canonical Gospels themselves. As regards the Gospel of John, the author of the Gospel of Peter differs so widely in his whole method of narration that any dependence is excluded, and even his acquaintance with it is not probable. On the other hand, it must not be overlooked that the Gospel of Peter has several characteristics in common with the Gospel of John, especially its uncompromising anti-Judaism, which it betrays not only in its whole manner of speaking of the Jews, but especially in removing all the blame of the death of Jesus from Pilate and fixing it upon the Jewish King Herod. Further, the mention of the "Garden of Joseph" (verse 24)—though as a designation for Joseph's grave, not in order to indicate its locality (as in Jn. xix. 41); the mention of the "not breaking the legs," though not with reference to Jesus (as in Jn. xix. 33), but of the penitent thief (in contradiction with Jn. xix. 32 ff.); the prominence given to Mary Magdalene in the resurrection-story, though she is accompanied by her friends, and Christ does not appear to her (*cf.* Jn. xx. 14 ff.); the dating of the crucifixion on the 14th Nisan, before the beginning of the Passover; finally—and this is the most important point—just as in the Gospel of Peter it is sometimes the death and sometimes the resurrection of Jesus which is thought of as the moment of His ascent to heaven (*vv.* 19 and 56), so in the Gospel of John His death is described as a "lifting up," "being glorified," "departure to the Father," and even though on the Easter morning He first says, "I am not yet ascended to my Father," He adds immediately, "Say unto my brethren, I ascend (now immediately) unto my Father and your Father, to my God and your God" (xx. 17). By thus placing the ascension so close after the resurrection, the writer of the Fourth Gospel has endeavoured, if not to remove, at least to soften, the contradiction between the ascension at the moment of death and the resurrection from the grave; we find the same contradiction in the Gospel of Peter, but here in its naked directness. For that is certainly the case when in one passage Jesus is exalted to heaven at the moment of His death, in another does not " return to the place from which He was sent forth " until the moment of the resurrection, and in a third is led forth from the grave by two angels, and needs to be supported by them like a man who is helpless (39); that is so far from being an exaltation to heavenly glory that it is much more a mere return to a very imperfect mode of earthly existence. It is, indeed, quite out of harmony with this when it is immediately added (40 ff.) that the head of Him who was led forth reached above the heavens, and that a voice from heaven addressed Him, saying, " Thou hast preached obedience to them that sleep," *i.e.* hast shown Thyself, as Lord and victor, to the under-world. Here we have the clear conception of the descent of Christ to hell in order to announce to the whole spiritual world its subjugation under His rule, a conception of which the Gnostic origin was clearly shown above (p. 204). Gnostic and docetic, too, is the figure of Christ which stretches above the heaven, and the walking cross which follows Him as He is led forth from the grave, and gives forth the voice of the (invisible) heavenly Christ. This whole series of fantastic conceptions only becomes comprehensible when we recall the mystery of the Gnostic cross of light from the Acts of Peter and John, where the cross as a mystical entity is more or less identified with the heavenly Æon Christ. But it is clear that this Gnostic Æon Christ, who reaches above the heavens, and raises himself to heaven, and descends into hell and announces to the world of spirits their subjugation, has little or nothing in common with the bodily resurrection of Jesus. We ought not to attempt to harmonise conceptions belonging to such different categories, but simply to let them remain contradictory, and interpret the contradiction as due to their diverse origin, one of them being derived from the Gnostic mystical philosophy, the other from the tradition believed in the Church. In the way in which it endeavours to combine these two, the Gospel of Peter supplies evidence of the same mediating ecclesiastical tendency which the Gospel of John also exemplifies, only that it is far inferior to the latter in theological depth and artistic skill; it also follows Church tradition more closely than the latter; to this extent it is correct to say that "it occupies an intermediate position between the Gospels and John."[1] Its author did not, like the fourth Evangelist, write in opposition to the Synoptic tradition, but took most of his material from it; at any rate it is drawn from the same stream of Church tradition from which the Synoptic Gospels are derived, only adding to it certain anti-Judaic and Gnostic-docetic views which prevailed in the author's environment, without his being conscious of any opposition between the source material and these added elements.

On these grounds we may conjecture that the Gospel of Peter is derived from Syria, the native home of Christian Gnosticism, and was composed in the first half of the second century, at a time

[1] Harnack, *Texte und Untersuchungen*, ix. 2 ff., p. 35, note.

THE GOSPEL OF PETER   223

when the evangelical tradition was still in a sufficiently fluid state to be capable of admitting variations and additions, and when, on the other hand, the Gnostic mythology was not yet consciously felt to be an incongruous element, and, more especially, the Gnostic docetism was not universally recognised as heretical. With this the external evidence is quite in harmony.[1] That Justin, in the middle of the second century, knew and used the Gospel of Peter is certain from his express mention of the Memorials of Peter ('Ἀπομνημονεύματα Πέτρου) in his *Dialogue with Trypho*, cap. cvi. He could not possibly have so described the Gospel of Mark, but only the Gospel of Peter, where Peter himself speaks in the first person; and moreover his quotation in *Apol.*, i. 35, is not found in Mark, or in any canonical Gospel, but only in the Gospel of Peter, verse 6 f. If we had the complete text of the Gospel of Peter, it is probable that the numerous other apocryphal or uncanonical quotations of Justin would find their simple explanation from his having used this Gospel, which he held to be the authentic memoirs of the chief apostolic authority. The same may be the case, too, in regard to several of the quotations of the Alexandrian Clement Also, in the Syrian document which underlies the *Apostolic Constitutions*, which dates from the beginning or middle of the third century, an extra-canonical Gospel was used, which Harnack has shown to be very probably no other than the Gospel of Peter. Finally, we should not fail to notice the statement of Eusebius in his *Church*

---

[1] *Cf.* Harnack, *ut sup.*, pp. 37–46; Hilgenfeld, *Zeitschr. für wiss. Theol.*, 1893, Heft 2.

History (VI. xii.), to the effect that the bishop Serapion of Antioch forbade to a church of his diocese the hitherto (*ca.* 200) unhindered use of the Gospel of Peter, because, although in the main it was in accordance with the true doctrine of the Saviour, it yet contained some additions which on close examination were found to involve docetic error and to be dangerous to orthodoxy. This quite agrees with the conclusion which we have come to above. The only remarkable thing is that a Gospel which diverged so much from the canonical Gospels, and contained so many Gnosticising additions, should have been allowed to pass unchallenged in ecclesiastical circles down to the end of the second century.

HELLENISM AND GNOSTICISM

CHAPTER XII

THE GOSPEL ACCORDING TO THE EGYPTIANS

THE εὐαγγέλιον κατ' Αἰγυπτίους is mentioned by Origen in his Homily on Luke i. 1 as the first of the extra-canonical Gospels used by the "heretics." From many quotations in Clement of Alexandria, it appears to have been used by the Egyptian Valentinians (Theodotus) and Encratites; and from Epiphanius (*Hær.*, lxxii. 2), also by the Sabellians, whose native home was in the Libyan Pentapolis. But it does not necessarily follow from this that it was originally a heretical Gospel. Against this is the way in which Clement still treats it as an authority which stands alongside of the four canonical Gospels (*Strom.*, III. xiii. 92), as well as the (at least probable, see below) fact that the author of the second Clementine Epistle, who was an ecclesiastically correct person, made use of it (*ca.* 170). We must remember, too, that both Encratites and Sabellians were not originally heretics, but represent a tendency of faith and life which in the second century had been very prevalent within the Church itself, and which had only been branded as heresy owing to the development of the Church as a whole having left it behind. There is thus good ground for the conjecture[1] that the Gospel of the Egyptians was originally the only Gospel in use among the Gentile Christians of Egypt, and was only gradually, in the course of the second century, forced into the background by the growing authority within the Church of the canonical Gospels, and that in such a way that it still for a considerable time remained in use among those communities in country places which had lagged behind the average rate of progress of the Church as a whole.

We have but scanty remnants of this Gospel, which have been preserved by patristic witnesses. Clement quotes several times (*Strom.*, III. ix. 63, 64, 66, xiii. 92, vi. 45; *Exc. ex Theodoto*, 67) a dialogue of Jesus with Salome. To her question, "How long shall death reign?" He replies, "So long as ye women bear children." She thereupon asks, "Had I done well, then, not to bear children?" To which He replies, "Eat every herb except that which has bitterness" (which, in spite of Clement's softening interpretation, must certainly be understood as an exhortation to abstain from marriage, which is compared to a bitter fruit). When Salome asks when that shall be made known about which she inquired, namely, the coming of the Kingdom of God, the Lord answered, "When ye shall trample on the garment of shame (the body?), and when the two shall be one, and the male with the female neither male nor female." Finally, on the same occasion, He said, "I am come to destroy the works of the woman," namely, as Clement adds in explanation, birth and death as having their roots in desire. A quotation of almost exactly similar wording,

[1] Harnack, *Chronologie*, i. 614.

which is probably, if not certainly, to be referred to the Gospel of the Egyptians, is found in the second Clementine Epistle (xii. 2). To someone who inquired concerning the coming of the Kingdom, the Lord answered, " When the two shall be one, and the outward as the inward, and the male with the female neither male nor female." In still another form we find the same thought in the citation from the Gnostic Naasenes (Hippolytus, *Philos.*, v. 7) : " There is neither female nor male, but a new creation, a new man which is both male and female." Similar, though more general, is the saying from the mystical discourse about the Cross in the Acts of Peter (*sup.*, p. 210) : " The Lord said in a mystery, ' Unless ye make the right as the left and the left as the right, and the top as the bottom and the front as the back, ye shall not know the Kingdom of God.' " Of the " modal " Christology of which we have found several instances in the Acts of Peter, Thomas, and John, we are reminded by the statement of Epiphanius (*Hær.*, lxxii. 2) that the Sabellians derived their error principally from the so-called Gospel of the Egyptians, where, among other mysterious utterances put into the mouth of the Redeemer, it was stated that He had declared to His disciples that " One and the same was the Father, the same the Son, and the same the Holy Ghost." Even if that is not a direct quotation, it must have had some sort of foundation in the discourses in the Gospel of the Egyptians.

From all this it may be concluded that the Gospel of the Egyptians, in regard both to its Christology and its ascetic morality, had close affinities with the Gnosticising tendency of the apocryphal Acts which we have discussed. It does not at all follow from this that it was originally the special property of a heretical sect; it may just as well have served for the edification of Gentile Christians within the Church, in Egypt and elsewhere, as was doubtless the case with the aforesaid Acts, and the Gnosticising "Gospel of Peter."

HELLENISM AND GNOSTICISM

CHAPTER XIII

THE GOSPEL ACCORDING TO THE HEBREWS AND
OTHER GOSPEL-FRAGMENTS

THE Gospel of the Hebrews (εὐαγγέλιον καθ' Ἑβραίους, or Ἑβραϊκόν, or Ἰουδαϊκόν) is chiefly known to us from the frequent quotations of Jerome, who found it in use as a book written in the Chaldæo-Syriac language, in Hebrew letters, among the Palestinian Jewish Christians or "Nazaræans" (and Ebionites?), and considered it so interesting that he translated it, so he tells us, into Greek and Latin. This was not, however, the first translation of it, for the Gospel of the Hebrews is frequently mentioned earlier by Clement, Origen, and Eusebius, and all of them mention it in the same way, as a book well known in the Church, like the Gospel of the Egyptians. What the latter was to the Gentile Christians in Egypt, that, probably, was the Gospel of the Hebrews to the Jewish Christians there,[1] having been brought thither from Palestine—namely, in earlier times the sole Gospel in use, until both alike were driven out by the canonical Gospels. Naturally, the book written in "Chaldæo-Syriac" must in Egypt have been translated, for the

[1] According to the very probable conjecture of Harnack, *Chronologie,* i. 638.

use of the Greek-speaking Jewish Christians, into Greek, and doubtless here first received the title of "Gospel of the Hebrews," which is its regular designation in the Fathers, in contradistinction to the Gentile-Christian Gospel of the Egyptians. In its native Palestine, on the other hand, it was preserved in the original Aramaic, and was held by most, as Jerome frequently remarks, to be the authentic work of the Apostle Matthew, and, therefore, the original of the canonical Gospel of Matthew. The real state of the case, in regard to their relation, is a difficult problem, in regard to which the judgment of scholars is still as unsettled as that of the learned Jerome of old seems to have been uncertain. I do not find myself able to agree either with those who attribute to the Gospel of the Hebrews, in its whole extent, a greater originality than to the canonical Matthew; nor, on the other hand, with those who hold it to be a secondary product entirely dependent on the latter. The view which most commends itself to me is, that the Gospel of the Hebrews, so far as we know it from the fragments that have come down to us, was a development of the Aramaic primitive Gospel independent of the canonical Gospels, in which some very early traditions are combined with legends and reflections of later origin. Since this embellishment and development of the primitive Gospel continued in Jewish circles throughout several generations, it is impossible to assign a definite time for the composition of the Gospel of the Hebrews. We may here collect the most important fragments.

There is no parallel to the canonical stories of the Childhood; these were doubtless lacking in the Gospel

THE GOSPEL OF THE HEBREWS 231

of the Hebrews, which seems to have begun with the baptism of Jesus.[1] That in itself shows independence of the canonical Gospels, for a later production dependent upon these would certainly not have omitted the stories of the Childhood, but have decked them out with further legends, as the *Protevangelium Jacobi* shows. The description of the Baptism is very peculiar. Jerome, *Adv. Pelag.*, iii. 2, reports: "In the Gospel according to the Hebrews, which is written in the Chaldæan and Syrian language, but in Hebrew letters, which is used by the Nazaræans to this day, (the Gospel) according to the Apostles or, as most say, according to Matthew, which the library at Cæsarea possesses, the story is thus told: ' Behold, the mother of the Lord and His brethren said to Him, "John the Baptist is baptizing for the forgiveness of sins; let us go and be baptized by him." Then said He unto them: "How have I sinned that I should go and cause myself to baptized? unless that which I have even now said be (a sin of) ignorance." ' " This denial by Jesus of His personal need for baptism is based upon an apologetic reflection, which is not derived either from the original tradition or from the canonical Gospels, but forms an independent parallel to the dialogue between Jesus and the Baptist in Matthew iii. 14 f., which is also inspired by an apologetic purpose. At the Baptism, the Gospel of the Hebrews probably narrated an appearance of fire in the Jordan; there is not, indeed, direct evidence of this, but there is a narrative of this kind in the

[1] *Cf.* Hilgenfeld, *Novum Testamentum extra Canonem Recept.*, iv. 19 f.; Handmann, *Das Hebräerevangelium*, 61 ff.; Harnack, *Chronologie*, i. 643 f. . Zahn takes a different view, *Gesch. des Kanons*, ii. 686 ff.

closely related Ebionite Gospel (see below); Justin, too, asserts that it was attested by "the apostles" (*Dial. c. Trypho*, lxxxviii.), and in the Cyprianic tractate *de Rebaptismate* the appearance of flames is mentioned in immediate connection with the above conversation between Jesus and His mother, which is only found in the Gospel of the Hebrews; therefore the appearance of flame was also probably narrated in it. Jerome, however, was silent in regard to that, because he suspected it of a Gnosticising tendency, which in his time was not considered so harmless as in the second century. Of the Baptism itself he found in this Gospel the following account: "But it came to pass that when the Lord was gone up out of the water, there descended upon Him the whole fountain of the Holy Spirit and rested upon Him, and spake to Him, saying, 'My Son, in all the prophets I was waiting for Thee that Thou shouldest come and I should rest in Thee; for Thou art my rest, Thou art my first-born Son, Thou art King for ever!'" Here the voice at the Baptism is not, as in Matthew, a statement in regard to Jesus, but an address to Him, as in Mark and Luke, and this is certainly the more original form; but, in contradistinction to both these, the Voice is not ascribed to God the Father, but to the Holy Spirit, who also, as the next fragment shows, is thought of as the Mother of Jesus. The disappearance of the incarnation of the Holy Spirit in the dove is connected with its being thought of as a personal Divine Being who in a measure dwelt in the prophets, looking forward to and preparing for His complete manifestation (as "the whole fountain of the Spirit") in Jesus as its first-born Son. That is an unmistakably Gnostic conception, closely connected with the Cerinthian doctrine of the descent of the heavenly Christ upon Jesus at baptism, and also with the Clementine doctrine of the continuous manifestation of the prophetic Spirit, but unconnected with the simpler form of the legend in the canonical story of the Baptism. Again, whereas in the canonical story of the Temptation Jesus is taken up by the Devil into a high mountain and to the pinnacle of the Temple, in the Gospel of the Hebrews the story runs: "My Mother, the Holy Ghost, took me by one of my hairs and carried me up to Mount Tabor," a passage of old-fashioned naïveté which is well attested by Jerome and Origen. In the fourth petition of the Lord's Prayer Jerome found, instead of the canonical ἐπιούσιον, the Aramaic *mahar* = "our bread for to-morrow." That is simpler than the canonical form, but does it follow that it is therefore more primitive? Is it not, rather, a correction of the obscure original? That is still a very doubtful point. In the story of the healing of the man with the withered hand (Mt. xii. 9 ff.), the Gospel of the Hebrews adds the interesting detail that the sick man was a mason, and lived by his trade, and therefore begged Jesus to restore his health in order that he might not be obliged to suffer the shame of begging. Is it possible that the canonical Gospels omitted that on account of the slur cast upon begging? Or was it for this very reason that the Gospel of the Hebrews adopted this addition? The saying about forgiveness runs in the Gospel of the Hebrews in part like Mt. xviii. 21 f., in part like Lk. xvii. 4: "If thy brother has sinned (against thee) in word, and has rendered thee satisfaction, thou shalt receive him seven times in the day." Simon Peter said: "Seven times in one day?" The Lord answered him: "Yea, I say unto thee, until seventy times seven! For even in the prophets, after they had been anointed with the Holy Spirit, there was found sinful speech" (how much more is it to be pardoned in ordinary men!). In the story of the rich young man (Mt. xix. 16 ff.), the Gospel of the Hebrews had (according to a statement of Origen in his commentary on Matthew) the peculiar addition: "The rich man, however, began to scratch his head, and it pleased him not (viz. the command to sell what he had and give to the poor). Then said the Lord unto him: 'How canst thou say, I have fulfilled the law and the prophets, seeing it is written in the law, "Thou shalt love thy neighbour as thyself"? And behold, many of thy brethren, sons of Abraham, are clothed in foul garments and perish of hunger, and thy house is full of many good things, and nothing cometh out of it to them.' And then, turning to Simon His disciple, who was sitting near Him, He said: 'Simon, son of John, it is easier for a camel to go through the eye of a needle than for a rich man to enter into the Kingdom of Heaven.'"

That this profound interpretation of the fulfilling of the law might be original is quite possible, but in that case it would be hard to understand why the canonical Gospels should have omitted it. "How the much more difficult account in the Synoptics could have arisen out of this plain narrative is unimaginable." Therefore we must see in this, rather, a "homiletic development and simplification," suggested by the desire " to make the original Gospel, the common source of the Greek Matthew and the Epistle to the Hebrews, as little offensive as possible to Jewish readers."[1] In Mt. xxiii. 35, Jerome found in "the Gospel of the Nazaræans" the reading, "Zachariah, the son of Jehoiadah," instead of "the son of Barachiah." As Zachariah the son of Jehoiadah appears from 2 Chron. xxiv. to have been, as a matter of fact, the last Old Testament martyr, the Gospel of the Hebrews seems to have here the more correct text; but, if this were original, how could the inaccurate statement in the canonical Matthew have been substituted for it? Is it not more probable that the canonical "Zachariah the son of Barachiah" was the more original (the reference being to the son of Baruch, the martyr whose story Josephus tells in *B.J.*, IV. v. 4), and that a Jew familiar with the Scriptures inserted in the Gospel of the Hebrews, instead of the name of a martyr unknown to him, as not being from the Old Testament, the familiar name from 2 Chron. xxiv.? The parable of the Talents, Mt. xxv. 14 ff., was, according to a statement of Eusebius, narrated in the Gospel of the Hebrews in the form that one of the three servants wasted his lord's substance with harlots and female flute-players, and was therefore thrown into prison; the second increased it, and was welcomed for so doing; the third hid it, and received blame for doing so, but not punishment. This

[1] Zahn, *Gesch. des Neutest. Kanons*, ii. 714, 715 f. A different conclusion is reached by Harnack, *Chronologie*, ii. 649; Handmann and Hilgenfeld, *ut sup.*

account is undoubtedly clearer to the popular understanding than the canonical, which so sharply distinguishes between faithful and unfaithful servants, without the admission of an intermediate class between. But for this very reason the latter has the better claim to originality. Moreover, the canonical account varies in Matthew and Luke; it is therefore probable that in the oldest tradition different versions existed side by side, and passed over independently into the various Gospels. In reference to Mt. xxvii. 51, Jerome remarks that in the Gospel of the Hebrews, instead of the veil of the Temple, it is the lintel of the door which is rent in twain—a variant of the legend which conveys the same symbolic meaning. The story of the Resurrection in the Gospel of the Hebrews appears to have been completely at variance with the canonical accounts. Jerome (*de Vir Illustr.*, 2 and 16) gives the following fragments:—" The Lord, after He had given the linen cloth to a servant of the priest (one of the guards at the grave?), went to James and appeared to him. James had taken an oath to eat no bread from the time when he partook of the cup of the Lord until he should see Him risen from among those that sleep. Then the Lord said to him, 'Bring a table and bread.' Thereupon He took the bread, blessed it, brake it, and gave it to James the Just with the words: 'My brother, eat thy bread, for the Son of man has arisen from among those that sleep.'" " And when He came to Simon Peter and those that were with him, He said unto them, 'Handle Me and see that I am not an incorporeal spirit ($\delta\alpha\iota\mu\acute{o}\nu\iota o\nu$)'; and immediately they touched Him and believed." Of these

THE GOSPEL OF THE HEBREWS 237

fragments, the first stands in direct contradiction with all the canonical accounts, and its only point of contact with the Gospel of Peter is that the servants of the priests are assumed, as it seems, to have formed part of the watch at the grave; the second has some resemblances to Lk. xxiv. 36 ff. and Jn. xx. 20, but of so free a character that dependence on the one side or the other is out of the question. Finally, the following sayings from the Gospel of the Hebrews, which have no canonical parallels, are attested by patristic evidence:—"Ye shall never be joyful except when ye have looked on your brethren in love" (Jerome *in Eph.* v.). "To grieve the spirit of one's brother is one of the greatest transgressions" (Jerome *in Ezech.* xviii.). "He that seeketh shall not rest until he finds; when he hath found, he shall be astonished; when he is astonished, he shall be lord (king); when he has become lord, he shall come to rest" (Clem. Alex., *Strom.*, V. xiv. 96; and—the two last clauses only—*Strom.*, II. ix. 45).

Anyone who makes an unprejudiced examination of these fragments will, I believe, come to the conclusion that, while the Gospel of the Hebrews has most affinity with that of Matthew, it is not dependent either upon it or upon any of the other canonical Gospels; on the other hand, that it is not distinguished from these by the greater originality of its text, and therefore, in the form at least in which it is known to us from patristic quotations, is not to be regarded as a source of the canonical Gospels. These facts can, it seems to me, be most simply explained by the supposition that the Gospel of the Hebrews represents an independent line of development, parallel to that of the Synoptic Gospels and the Gospels of the Egyptians and of Peter, which are all sprung from a common root, namely, the primitive Aramaic Gospel, in connection with which oral tradition, taking on various colourings due to local influences, worked as a differentiating factor.

The "Gospel of the Twelve Apostles according to Matthew," which was used by the heretical Jewish Christians or "Ebionites," seems to have been a further and freer development of the Gospel of the Hebrews. Epiphanius has given some fragments of it, and Origen and Jerome refer to it, but without distinctly differentiating it from the Gospel of the Hebrews. Its most striking peculiarity was not the absence of the story of the Childhood—which was doubtless also lacking in the Gospel of the Hebrews—but the fact that the Apostles spoke of themselves in it in the first person ("There came a man named Jesus, thirty years old, who chose us," Epiph., *Hær.*, xxx. 13).

The story of the Baptism, too, is different from that of the Gospel of the Hebrews, and is evidently an unskilful combination of canonical and apocryphal elements. The Spirit not only descends in the form of a dove, but enters into Jesus. The voice from heaven is thrice repeated: (1) "Thou art My beloved, in Thee I am well pleased" (*cf.* Mk. and Lk.); (2) "This day have I begotten Thee" (*cf.* Justin,[1] and Lk. acc. Cod. D); (3) "This is My Son, the beloved, in whom I am well pleased" (*cf.* Mt.). Between these there is mentioned the shining forth of a brilliant light (*cf.* Justin [1]), and the narrative ends by saying that John, alarmed at all this, fell at the feet

[1] *Dial. c. Tryph.*, lxxxviii.

of Jesus, with the words, "Lord, baptize Thou me." Jesus, however, refused, saying, "Let be, for so it is meet that all should be fulfilled" (following Mt., but here inappropriate, since Jesus had already been baptized). There are two other remarkable fragments, which point to vegetarian asceticism. In the account of the food used by John the Baptist, "locusts" are replaced by "oil-cakes," and before the Last Supper Jesus says: "I have not desired to eat meat at this passover with you" (Epiph., *Hær.*, xxx. 13, 22). Finally, a saying directed against the Jewish sacrificial system is put into the mouth of Jesus: "I am come to destroy (καταλῦσαι, *cf.* Mt. v. 17) the sacrifices, and if ye do not cease from sacrificing, the wrath (of God) will not cease from you" (Epiph., *Hær.*, xxx. 16). It does not seem to me possible, on the strength of these few quotations, to arrive at a definite opinion upon the special character of this Ebionite "Gospel of the Apostles according to Matthew"; from the fragments which have come down to us, we can as little affirm as deny that it had a Gnosticising, or anti-Pauline, or other heretical tendency. I cannot, therefore, understand why we should be required to assume the complete diversity of this "Ebionite" Gospel from the "Nazaræan" Gospel of the Hebrews, since it cannot be denied that the Fathers have constantly confounded and identified them. Among the quotations which have been given, apart from the story of the Baptism, which aims at harmonising canonical with non-canonical accounts, there is nothing which might not just as well have come from the Gospel of the Hebrews. As the Gospel of the Hebrews, which was common to all Jewish

Christians, was read in different places and in different languages, it may well have received, here and there, a slightly different form, sometimes shorter, sometimes longer, sometimes freer, sometimes more closely adapted to the canonical Gospels; and in order the more easily to maintain its authority against these, it may well have been in some circles brought under the name of the twelve Apostles, and have introduced these, or at any rate Matthew on their behalf, narrating in the first person, as Peter is made to do in the Gospel which bears his name. As, however, these were merely editorial alterations of form without essential change of content, it is quite intelligible that the Fathers did not pay much attention to these formal differences, but described one and the same Jewish Christian Gospel sometimes by one name and sometimes by another. To me, at any rate, it seems to be beyond doubt that when Origen, in his enumeration of the extra-ecclesiastical Gospels (Homily on Lk. i. 1), says nothing of the Gospel of the Hebrews, which was well known to him, but, on the other hand, speaks of a Gospel "with the title 'Of the Twelve'" (τὸ ἐπιγεγραμμένον τῶν δώδεκα εὐαγγ.), he means nothing else than the Gospel of the Hebrews.

In connection with these remnants of apocryphal Gospels there fall to be mentioned some detached sayings of Jesus which have been preserved by tradition without any mention of a source where they were originally reported, or of the connection in which they were spoken; under which circumstances the genuineness of the reported saying must of course remain doubtful. I arrange these sayings according to the age of the witnesses who attest them, and place at the end those whose attestation is anonymous.[1]

" To give is more blessed than to receive " (Acts xx. 35). When Jesus saw a man working on the Sabbath, He said unto him : " O man, if thou knowest what thou doest, thou art blessed ; but if thou knowest not, thou art accursed, and a transgressor of the law " (inserted, in Cod. D, between Lk. vi. 4 and 5 ; the thought is original, though it reminds us of Rom. xiv. 14, 23 ; "transgressor of the law " occurs only in Paul and James ; the genuineness of the saying is therefore questionable). " Be ye merciful, that ye may obtain mercy ! " (Clem. Rom., I. xiii. 2 ; Polycarp, *ad Phil.*, ii. 3 ; Clem. Al., *Strom.*, II. xviii. 91 ; *cf.* Mt. v. 7). " Behold, I make the last like the first " (Epistle of Barnabas vi. 13 ; *cf.* Mt. xx. 16, " The last shall be first, and the first last"; also Revelation xxi. 5, " Behold, I make all things new"). " Those who desire to see Me and to attain to My kingdom must receive Me amid trouble and suffering" (Barnabas vii. 11). "Wherein I meet you, therein I will judge you " (Justin, *Dial.*, xlvii., and Clem. Al., *Quis dives*, xl. Similarly in Cyprian, *de Mort.*, xvii., " According to what the Lord finds thee to be when He calls thee, as such does He judge thee "). " Even though ye have lain in My bosom, if ye do not My commandments, I will reject you and say unto you, I know not whence ye are, ye workers of iniquity " (2 Clem. iv. 5 ; *cf.* Lk. xiii. 26 f.

---

[1] *Cf.* James Hardy Ropes, *Die Sprüche Jesu* (Gebhardt und Harnack, *Texte und Untersuch.*, xiv. 2, 1896); Erwin Preuschen, *Antilegomena, Reste ausserkanonischen Evang.*, 1901 ; Harnack, *Die jüngst entdeckten Sprüche Jesu*, 1897.

and Mt. vii. 21 ff.). "Show yourselves approved money-changers, rejecting some, but retaining the good" (Clem. Al., *Strom.*, I. xxviii.; without the last two clauses, frequently in Origen, the Clementine Homilies, Basil, Jerome, etc.). "He who is married shall not put away (his wife), and he who is not married shall not marry. He who with the purpose of continence has vowed not to marry, shall remain unmarried" (Clem. Al., *Strom.*, III. xv. 97; *cf.* 1 Cor. vii. 10, where, however, Paul expressly disclaims the authority of the Lord for his opinion; therefore it is possible that, in the Encratite circles in which the Gospel of the Egyptians was current, this saying was manufactured out of the saying of Paul). "For not out of jealousy did the Lord in a gospel give the command, 'My mystery (keep) for Me and for the sons of My house'" (Clem. Al., *Strom.*, V. x. 64; *Clementine Homilies*, xix. 20; *cf.* Mt. vii. 6). "Pray for the great thing, and the small thing shall be added unto you; pray for the heavenly, and the earthly shall be added unto you" (Origen, *de Orat.*, ii. 2, and— without the second clause—Clem. Al., *Strom.*, I. xxiv.; *cf.* Mt. vii. 7 ff., vi. 19, 33). "He who is near Me is near the fire; he who is far from Me is far from the Kingdom" (Origen, *Hom. in Jerem.*, and Didymus *in Ps.* lxxxviii. 8). "For the sake of the weak I became weak (sick), and for the sake of the hungry I hungered, and for the sake of the thirsty I thirsted" (Origen, Commentary on Matthew; *cf.* Mt. xxv. 35 f., 2 Cor. viii. 9). "Grieve not the Holy Spirit which is in you, and quench not the light which is kindled in you" (Pseudo-Cyprian, *de Aleator.*, iv.; *cf.* Mt. vi. 22 f., Eph. iv. 30). "The weak shall be saved through the strong" (*Apostol. Constit.*, xxvi.). "Seek after faith and hope, by which is produced love to God and man, whereby eternal life is secured" (Macarius, *Homil.*, xxxvii. 1). "Why do ye wonder at the signs? I give you a great inheritance, such as the whole world has not" (Macarius, *Homil.*, xii. 17). "If ye do not fast from the world (renounce the world), ye shall not find the Kingdom of God; and if ye keep not the Sabbath (allegorical for the consecration of life?), ye shall not see the Father" (Egyptian papyrus fragment, ed. Grenfell and Hunt).[1] "I took my stand in the midst of the world, and appeared unto them in the flesh, and I found all men drunken, and none found I athirst among them, and my soul grieveth over the sons of men because they are blind in their hearts" (*ibid.*; *cf.* Jn. i. 5, 10 f., xii. 27, vii. 27; Mk. viii. 17 f.). "A prophet is not welcome in his own country, neither doth a physician work cures among them that know him" (*ibid.*; *cf.* Lk. iv. 24). "A city built upon the top of a high hill and stablished can neither fall nor be hidden" (*ibid.*; *cf.* Mt. v. 14 and vii. 24 ff.). "Wherever there is one alone I am with him. Raise the stone and there thou shalt find me, cleave the wood and there am I" (*ibid.*). The interpretation of this obscure saying as referring to the spiritual nearness of Christ (God) to the pious man who is free from worldliness, even in his daily work (Harnack) is very problematical; the parallel seems to me closer with the pantheism of the Gnostic "Gospel of Eve," where it is said: "I am thou and thou art I, and wheresoever thou art I also am, and in all things I am distributed, and wheresoever thou wilt thou

[1] *The Oxyrhynchus* "*Sayings*," Part I., 1.

gatherest me, and in gathering me thou gatherest thyself" (Epiph., *Hær.*, xxvi. 3).

It is evident that in this débris of apocryphal Gospels very various material has been thrown together. Alongside of bed-rock from the lowest strata of the primitive tradition, there are also curious conglomerates of late formation. But as literary monuments they have an incontestible significance.

HELLENISM AND GNOSTICISM

CHAPTER XIV

THE ACTS OF PAUL

THESE may appropriately be placed here, for in the estimation of the early Church· they held the highest place among the Apocrypha, standing quite close to the canonical Scriptures; Origen, *de Princ.*, I. ii. 3, cites them alongside of the Gospel of John. He either did not know, or did not care, that, according to a statement of Tertullian (*de Baptismo*, xvii.), a presbyter of Asia Minor was convicted of having invented these Acts to do honour to Paul. In spite of this and of certain features calculated to offend a strict ecclesiastical conscience, these Acts were long a favourite book of edification. Points likely to cause difficulty, such as the anecdote (known to Jerome, but nowhere to be found in the present text[1]) of the baptism of a lion, were eliminated, the long-winded narrative was abridged in many places (the gaping seams in the present Thecla-legend and in the Martyrdom of Paul are not to be overlooked, and the original text must have been different), and finally from the voluminous work a few specially valuable extracts were detached, such

[1] It is quite impossible to find a place for it in the scene where Thecla is exposed to the wild beasts in the theatre.

as the Thecla-legend, the correspondence of Paul with the Corinthians, and the martyrdom of the Apostle at Rome, which then, as independent wholes, were translated and preserved in the Churches of both East and West, while the bulk of the work was lost. With the disappearance of the work as a whole, the knowledge of the original connection of these various writings with the Acts of Paul was lost, and until recently it was not supposed that we possessed any part of it. This error has been lately (1897) removed by the discovery of Egyptian papyrus-fragments in which C. Schmidt detected the Coptic translation of the lost Acts of Paul, including the story of Thecla, the correspondence with the Corinthians, and the martyrdom at Rome, thus proving that these formed integral parts of the Acts of Paul.[1] Not until the difficult decipherment and translation of these Coptic papyrus-fragments has been completed and published can we hope to gain a clear idea of this apocryphal work, which was so highly prized in the ancient Church, and to arrive at a definite judgment in regard to some points on which the opinions of scholars are still at variance. In the meantime I may confine myself to the following extracts from the pretty Thecla-legend, which gives an excellent picture of the attitude of second-century Christianity.[2]

When Paul, so the Acts relate, fleeing from

[1] C. Schmidt, *Die Paulusakten: Eine wiedergefundene altchristliche Schrift des 2. Jahrhunderts* (in the new *Heidelberger Jahrbücher*, vii. p. 117 f. Also as a separate reprint.)

[2] Tischendorf, *Act. Apost. Apocr.*, 40 ff.; Wright, *Apocr. Acts*, 116 ff.; Lipsius, *Apokr. Apost.-Gesch.*, ii. 1. 424 ff.; Schlau, *Akten des P. und der Thekla und die ältere Theklalegende* (1877); Zahn, *Gesch. des N.T. Kanons*, ii. 865 ff.; Harnack, *Chronologie*, 491 ff.

Antioch, came to Iconium, he was accompanied by
the two smiths, Demas and Hermogenes, who made
pretence of great affection for him. He, on his part,
bearing in mind the goodness of Christ, did them
no harm, but was so full of love to them that he
instructed them in the words of the Lord, especially
in the doctrine of His birth and resurrection, and
recounted to them the wonderful acts of the Lord as
they had been revealed to him. Now, Onesiphorus,
hearing of his arrival, went to welcome him, and
recognised him from the description which Titus had
given of him: small stature, bald head, crooked legs,
knock-knees, big eyes, brows meeting in the middle,
long nose; full of charm, looking sometimes like a
man and sometimes like an angel. When the
Apostle was come into his house there was great joy,
prayer was offered on bended knee, and there was
breaking of bread and preaching "of the Divine word
concerning continence and the resurrection." Paul
said: "Blessed are they who have kept their flesh pure,
for they shall be the temple of God. Blessed are the
continent, for to them God will speak. Blessed are
those also who have renounced the world, for they
shall be well-pleasing to God. Blessed are they who
have wives as though they had them not, for they
shall have God for their portion. Blessed are the
God-fearing, for they shall become angels of God.
[Blessed are they who tremble at the word of God,
for them shall God call. Blessed are they who have
received the wisdom of Jesus the Messiah, for they
shall be called the sons of God.[1]] Blessed are they
who have preserved their baptism (baptismal grace),

---

[1] The bracketed clauses are only in the Syriac text.

for they shall rest with the Father and His beloved Son. [Blessed are they who have received the exhortation of the Messiah, for they shall be in great light. Blessed are they who for the love of God (or, " of Christ ") have forsaken this body (the martyrs), for they shall reap a harvest of eternal life and stand at the right hand of the Son of God.] Blessed are the merciful, for they shall obtain mercy, and shall not see the bitter day of judgment [and on the day of judgment receive the Kingdom]. Blessed are the bodies [and souls] of the virgins, for they shall be well-pleasing to God, and shall not lose the reward of their purity, for the promise of the Father shall be unto them for a saving power unto the day of His son, and they shall have rest in eternity." This sermon of Paul was heard from the window of the neighbouring house by Thecla, the daughter of Theocleia, and the promised bride of the distinguished youth Thamyris, and she was so much impressed by what she heard that it was impossible to induce her, day or night, to leave the seat at the window, her only desire being to listen to "the word of virginity and of prayer." Vain were the exhortations of her mother, vain the appeals of her promised husband when he was called to speak to her, and the grief of the whole household. Thecla would no longer listen to anything except the words of Paul. Thamyris hastened angrily into the street, found Demas and Hermogenes at the house were Paul was lodging, and inquired from them concerning the man who by his exhortation persuaded wives and virgins to reject married life. They denied their acquaintance with Paul, but admitted that he dissuaded young people from marrying, saying to them: "Ye shall not receive any resurrection unless ye remain chaste and keep your bodies undefiled." Then he invited them to a luxurious feast, and complained of his trouble about his promised bride. They advised him to accuse Paul before the governor as an adherent of the doctrine of Christ; he would then bring Paul to trial, and Thecla would become the wife of Thamyris. Moreover, they desired to teach him that the resurrection which Paul preached was (in reality) already past, inasmuch as we live again in our children and are (spiritually) raised to life through the knowledge of the true God.[1] Brought before the judgment-seat of the governor, Paul laid before him a solemn confession which contains nothing specifically Pauline, nor yet anything specifically Gnostic, but simply the general belief of the Church at that time: "The living God, the God of requital [Syr., who does not requite], the jealous God, the God who has need of nothing, who desires the salvation of men (*cf.* 1 Tim. ii. 4), hath sent me to deliver them from corruption and from impurity, and from all lust and from death, that they might not sin any more. Therefore hath God sent His Son (παῖδα), whom I preach, and upon whom I teach men to set their hopes, for He alone has had compassion on the erring world, that it might no more come into judgment, but have faith and the fear of God,

---

[1] This sentence is wanting in the Syriac text, and has no special appropriateness to the context. It is therefore presumably an addition of the Catholic redactor, who desires to characterise the opponents of the Apostle as Gnostics of the type referred to in 2 Tim. ii. 18. *Cf.* Lipsius, *ut sup.*, 453 f.

and knowledge of honour, and love of truth. If, then, I teach that which is revealed unto me by God, what wrong do I do in that?" Paul is then cast into prison, but Thecla, by bribing the jailor, gains access to him, in order to sit at his feet and hear of the great deeds of God. On the next morning she is sought by her friends, and when they find her in the prison with Paul she is brought before the governor along with him. The governor asks her why she acts contrary to the customs of the country. She answers never a word, but keeps gazing at Paul. Then her mother asks that she may be burnt, fool that she is, for a warning to all other women. The governor unwillingly yields to the pressure of the multitude, and orders Paul to be scourged and driven out of the city, but Thecla to be burned to death in the theatre. All the people flock thither to witness the spectacle. And as a lamb on the wide pasture looks round for its shepherd, so the eyes of Thecla ranged over the crowd in search of Paul. Then, suddenly, she sees the Lord Jesus Christ in the form of Paul standing beside her, and while her gaze is fastened on Him, He ascends up to heaven. The maids bring wood for the heap of faggots; Thecla is stripped and brought into the theatre; the governor weeps when he sees her, and admires her constancy. She mounts the pyre, stretching forth her arms in the form of the cross; the flames spring up, but they singe no hair of her head, for God causes the earth to rumble and a storm-cloud to pour down such a torrent of rain and hail that the fire is extinguished and the lives of many of the onlookers are endangered. (Here there seems to be a gap in the narrative, for

THE ACTS OF PAUL 251

nothing is said of the liberation of Thecla or of how she passed the next few days.) Six days later Thecla found Paul again, who in the meantime had continued fasting along with Onesiphorus and his family, and praying for her deliverance, in an open grave beside the road from Iconium to Daphne. Paul and his companions gave thanks for her deliverance, and then, from five loaves, some herbs, water and salt, they prepared a common meal, and rejoiced in "the pure works of Christ" (that means, in the pure, because vegetable, means of subsistence which Christ had created). Thecla then declared to Paul her resolve to cut off her hair and follow him everywhere. He reminded her of the dangers and temptations to which she would be exposed in this evil time, because of her beauty. She replied: " Give me but the sign of God [or, "the seal in Christ," *i.e.* baptism], and no temptation shall have any power over me more." He answered: " Have patience, Thecla, and thou shalt receive the water (of baptism)." Then he sent Onesiphorus and his family back to Iconium, and took Thecla by the hand and went with her to Antioch. Scarcely had they reached the town when a great man [the Syriarch], named Alexander, met them, and was immediately fired with such passion for Thecla that he offered the Apostle much money if he would give her to him. Paul answered that she did not belong to him, and that he did not know her. Alexander then tries to lay hold of her forcibly on the open street, but she defends herself, tears his robe, knocks the golden diadem [with the image of the Emperor[1]] from his head [and stamps it upon

[1] Omitted in some MSS. (perhaps from political expediency).

the ground]. Thereupon she is denounced to the governor and sentenced to fight with beasts in the arena. Thecla beseeches only that her virginity may be preserved, and is handed over to the protection of the rich princess Tryphæna, who had lost her daughter a short time before. Then when on a feast-day the wild beasts are exhibited, Thecla is bound upon the back of a lioness, which, to the astonishment of all the people, licks her feet. On the next day Thecla, accompanied by Tryphæna, who mourns for her, was brought into the theatre, where there arose a great tumult, some of the people demanding the death of the "sacrilegious woman" (ἱερόσυλος), others, especially the women, lamenting over this unrighteous sentence which should bring misfortune on the whole city. Thecla was then stripped, and, girded only with a loin-cloth, thrown into the arena, where she, feeling no fear of death, but only shame at her nakedness, took refuge in prayer, and, stretching out her arms cross-wise, awaited the onset of the beasts. A wild leopard and a lioness were first let loose upon her: the lioness lay down tamely at her feet, the leopard fell down dead. A powerful bear runs at her, but the lioness leaps upon him and tears him. Then draws near a lion trained to fight; him, too, the lioness attacks, and the two commence to tear each other. More beasts are loosed upon her, and Thecla awaits their onset, praying. Then, turning to one side, she sees a trench full of water, and, with the words, "On this, my last day, I shall be baptized in the name of the Lord Jesus Christ!" she leaps into the water. All the onlookers pity her, thinking that she will become the prey of the sea-lion; but the latter is killed by a flame which leaps out of the water, and at the same time envelops Thecla in such a cloud of light that her nakedness becomes invisible. (This self-baptism and the appearance of fire cannot originally have stood in connection with the fight of the beasts; a considerable portion has been left out, and things originally separate have been brought together.) Finally, they endeavoured to have Thecla torn in pieces by two bulls, by tying her between them and exciting the animals with hot irons; but the fire burnt the cords and freed her. At the sight of this Tryphæna fell into a swoon, and Thecla's enemy Alexander, fearing the anger of the Emperor, to whom Tryphæna was related, begged that Thecla might be released. She is brought before the governor, and confesses herself a servant of the living God, whose Son has even now aided her, the sole Way of Salvation and the Hope of Eternal Life, the Refuge and the Rest of all who are persecuted and oppressed. The governor then sets her free, and all the women in the theatre praise with one voice the God of Thecla as the one true God. Tryphæna takes her back to her house, and, along with her servants, is converted by Thecla's instructions to belief in Christ. After some days Thecla learns that Paul is sojourning at Myra in Lycia, whereupon she puts on men's clothing and, accompanied by youths and maidens, sets out to go to him. She finds him occupied in preaching the Word. His anxiety lest she may have fallen into some new temptation is quieted by her confession that she has received the bath of water: " For He who gave thee strength for the Gospel, also gave me strength for the water (of baptism)." Paul has no objection to offer. He takes her into the house of Hermæus (Hermes), where she tells the believers her wonderful adventures; then at her desire he sends her back to Iconium with the charge, "Teach the Word of God!" Arrived there, she visited first the house of Onesiphorus, and, falling on her knees at the spot where Paul had formerly sat and taught, she offered, with tears, a prayer of thanksgiving for her deliverance from her many troubles. Then she saw her mother again, and tried in vain to convert her. Afterwards she journeyed on to Seleucia, where she dwelt in a cave for seventy-two years, living upon water and herbs, and enlightened many with the Word of God.

As regards the theological standpoint of these Acts, it is, in the first place, certain that in their present shape—what their original form was we do not know—their theology has a thoroughly Catholic character, without definite tendency, either Gnostic or anti-Gnostic. "The doctrinal element is very much in the background; what may be inferred as to the doctrinal opinions of the author from incidental indications, points to a very simple theology. In particular, the Christological formulas of the Nicene period are entirely lacking" (Lipsius). But if we were simply to place this writing among the documents of orthodox Gentile Christianity, and even ascribe to it an anti-Gnostic tendency, we should be overlooking the fact that the ethical standpoint of these Acts is precisely that which is vigorously attacked by the orthodox author of the first Epistle to Timothy as a characteristic of Gnostic heresy. The ascetic ideal of life was no doubt common to the whole of contemporary Christendom, but that "ethical enthusiasm" which aimed at making the ascetic ideal of a continent and celibate life into an absolute and universal duty was rejected by the orthodoxy of the Church as a heretical error. The first Epistle to Timothy attacks (iv. 2 f.), as hypocritical and misleading teachers, those who forbid to marry and command to abstain from meats which God hath created (*i.e.* flesh-food); nay, he even commands the younger women to marry (v. 14), and speaks of child-bearing as a means of salvation for women (ii. 15), while, on the other hand, he directly forbids women to teach (ii. 12). Of all this the Acts of Paul inculcate, as certainly as the Acts of John, of Peter, of Andrew, of Philip, the direct contrary. Perfect virginity is everywhere praised as the highest Christian virtue; indeed, in Paul's sermon (see above) it is even described as the condition of the resurrection and of blessedness. It is precisely as a virgin Christian and confessor that Thecla is counted worthy of the high favour of being permitted to see Christ in visible appearance under the form of Paul, as a delivering and protecting spirit, similar to the Christophanies under the form of apostles which frequently occur in the other Acts. In addition to continence, another point which is emphasised is abstinence from flesh and wine, which is several times expressly enforced by the example of Paul and Thecla; and this also is in harmony with the known characteristics of Gnostic asceticism, and contrary to 1 Tim. iv. 3 ff. Finally, it is quite contrary to 1 Tim. ii. 12 that Thecla is formally and solemnly commissioned by Paul to teach the

Word, and continues to do so as an anchorite for seventy-two years. That she also baptized is not, indeed, expressly said, in our text at least, but it is probably to be assumed; indeed, it may be conjectured that in the original text it was directly asserted, as it would otherwise be impossible to understand how Tertullian (*de Bapt.*, xvii.) could speak of persons who defended the claim of women to teach and baptize by appealing to the example of Thecla. It is with a view to depriving them of this weapon that Tertullian in the same passage relates the deposition of the Asiatic presbyter who was convicted of being the author of these Acts. As Tertullian, when he wrote that, was still in his pre-Montanist Catholic period, it may be conjectured that it was precisely this teaching and baptizing by a woman which, in conjunction with the extreme asceticism, was the chief ground of offence found by Catholic Christians in these (as in the other) apocryphal Acts. As, however, they were found to be otherwise edifying and entertaining, recourse was had to a Church revision of them, which rejected the features most open to objection, but did not remove all traces of their original character, which plainly betrays its origin from a Gnostic manner of thought and feeling[1] such as was current among the people generally, and indeed, to a considerable extent, within the Church itself.

[1] *Cf.* on this point the detailed discussion in the thorough work of Lipsius, ii. 1. 443–467. Zahn, Schlau, and Harnack take a different view.

DOCTRINAL AND HORTATORY WRITINGS OF
THE CHURCH

CHAPTER XV

THE RELATIONS OF THE CHURCH WITH GNOSTICISM

THE main task of the Church in the second century was to define its own position in regard to Gnosticism, to attack its dangerous extravagances, but at the same time to adopt such of its ideas as were valuable, and to connect them with the Messianic beliefs of the primitive community. In the course of these struggles, and mutual adjustments, of the most diverse elements, Christianity developed into a world-religion which was able to overcome all other religions, for the very reason that it had adopted what was best in them all, and so assimilated its borrowings to its own distinctive principle that, without losing its unity and distinctiveness, it yet presented the most various aspects, and succeeded in satisfying the most manifold needs of human nature.

Gnosticism originally arose neither from Christianity nor from Greek philosophy, but was a religious movement which sprang from the heathen-Jewish syncretism of the East. Its fundamental motive was not the theoretical desire of understanding the world, of knowledge for knowledge' sake, but the practical religious desire for the salvation of the soul from the powers of death and for the securing of a blessed life in the world to come. This was the final end of all its speculation as well as of all its mystic rites. In order to establish the possibility of a future life of the soul, it was necessary to ascribe to it some kind of relationship to the immortal divine life, either by supposing the soul to have come down to earth from heaven, the region of the divine life, as the Babylonians and Persians, and, among the Greeks, the Pythagoreans, believed, or by supposing that there was implanted in it by the higher powers a spark of life, "a seed" of divine essence and life, as the various schools of Gnostics taught, in harmony with the Orphic theosophy. Because of this divine essence and origin, the soul feels itself confined in this world as in a prison, or, at any rate, in a foreign country far from its higher home, feels its body to be a weight which holds it down, a fetter, even a sepulchre. Will the prisoner be freed by the death of the body? Or will it not then become more than ever the prey of the destroying powers which lie in wait for it upon its way to the upper world, bar the gates of heaven against it, and cast it down to the abyss of darkness, or even devour it? That was the anxious question to which men hoped to find a reassuring answer in the secret teaching of "those who know" (the Gnostics) and in the secret worship of the initiate (*i.e.* the Mysteries). For the solution of these pressing questions, myths that came down from a hoary antiquity offered welcome suggestions. Especially appropriate was the legend which appeared almost everywhere, in various forms, of a divine or semi-divine being who descended into the kingdom of the dead, tasted all the terrors of hell, and yet through his divine power, or through the help of a messenger of God who was sent to his aid, was brought back again, safe and victorious, to the upper world of life and light. All these legends—of the descent to hell of Ishtar, of the Mandæan Hibil Ziva, of Hercules, of Orpheus, of the rape and recovery of Persephone—have as their common characteristic the teaching that the might of death has, after all, been overcome by superior divine strength, and the prison-house of Hades opened. To this element in the legends the speculations regarding the other world which were embodied in the mysteries attached themselves, making the resurrection of the mythical conqueror of death a type and pledge of the victory of all those to whom the mysteries of the other world have been revealed, and who through sacred rites of initiation have entered into a relationship with the Lord of Life, the "Saviour-God," which should endure beyond the boundary of death. The Mysteries of Mithra, Sabazios, Isis, and Demeter all aimed at communicating to those who were initiated into them a share in the life of their divinity, by means of which they might feel themselves "born again for ever," that is, assured of a blessed life in the other world.

Gnosticism being thus essentially and in its origin an eschatological belief in redemption based upon mythical traditions and mystical usages, had points of contact with the Christian belief in redemption, as understood and preached by the Apostle Paul, so close that the one could not fail to influence the other. In the Pauline Christ, the Son of God, who came down from heaven and suffered death, but at the same time, through His mystical offering of Himself, overcame death, and by His resurrection became Lord of living and dead and pledge of life to His followers, to whom, by mystical ceremonies, He communicated His Spirit, as the earnest of their future possession of life, there was found, in higher potency and with greater power of carrying conviction, all that the yearning of pious souls had sought in Gnosticism and the Mysteries. In place of the god or hero who in ages long ago had burst the gates of death and opened up to souls a way of ascent to heaven, there was here the clearly outlined figure of a historical Redeemer, who in the fulness of time had appeared among men and had completed before their eyes the sacrifice of Himself in death, and then, as victor over death and prince of life, had manifested Himself by revelations and visions, by signs and wonders of all kinds, and continued still to manifest Himself. It was quite natural that the Gnostics and Mystics soon began to appropriate the Christian Redeemer, and to refer to Him all that they had hitherto asserted concerning the saviour-gods (θεοὶ σωτῆρες) of the myths and mysteries. Thus the human Messiah of the primitive community and the Heavenly Man and Son of God of the Pauline teaching now passed into the metaphysical Divine Being of the Gnostic "Sotēr Conception," the object both of transcendental theological and cosmogonic speculations, and of a mystical worship, in which exactly the same significance was attributed to the new Saviour-God, Christ, as previously to the mythical saviour-gods, and He therefore took for the religious consciousness of the faithful the place of the Deity in an absolute sense. This apotheosis, as it originated among the Gnostics, of Jesus, the historical founder of the Christian community, was not, therefore, based on any "value-judgment" of the ethical eminence or achievements of Jesus, but simply on the fact that they transferred to the Jesus of the Gospel message the ideas which had long ago been postulated by the religious consciousness, and long ago elaborated by the religious imagination, of a divine saviour, conqueror of death and bestower of life. And there had been an effective preparation for this transference, first in the Messianic passages of the Jewish apocalyptic writings, and then, more especially, in the Pauline theology. But this Christianising of the heathen syncretistic Gnosis by its adoption of the evangelical figure of the Redeemer could not fail to have an important reflex influence on the Christian Church. How was it possible for the Christians to remain behind the Gnostics in veneration for the Redeemer? If the latter had made Jesus a Divine Being, a manifestation of the Divine Sotēr, the Church must follow them on this path, and it did so from the first with the less hesitation because it had the same interest in seeing in its Redeemer the conqueror over all demonic powers, whether in this world or in the world to come; and how could He be that if He were not a superhuman Divine Being? This also explains the fact, which from the modern standpoint is paradoxical, that the Church-teachers of the second century had no controversy with the heretical Gnostics as to whether Christ was a God—that was a presupposition which was common to both: the one point at issue was whether the God Christ had really become man in Jesus, or whether the humanity of Jesus was merely apparent. This conception of the "seeming manhood" of the Redeemer (docetism) would naturally never have arisen merely on the basis of the evangelical tradition, which, in spite of all the narratives of miracle, certainly describes the life of Jesus as a thoroughly human life. The simple explanation is that the Gnostic doctrine of Christ did not originate from the evangelical tradition, but from the attachment of the mythico-mystical idea, which had long been in existence, of a saviour-god, to the Person of Jesus. As the Gnostic Christ was essentially and in origin an ideal religious figure, the character of his temporal manifestation—whether in a real or only in a seeming man—might appear indifferent, or the latter might appear a mode of manifestation more worthy of a heavenly Divine Being, at least to the taste of the Gnostics, who laid all stress on the spiritual, and despised everything material. But the Church with sure insight saw in this docetic doctrine of Christ a serious danger to her faith, which, had this view been adopted, would have been loosed from its historical foundations, and, becoming the plaything of fantastic speculations, might have been emptied of its ethical content. But as, on the other hand, the Church was unwilling to be behind the Gnostics in recognising the Deity of the Redeemer, the task set for it was so to adjust the ideal and historical points of view that the Divine and human sides might each come to their rights in the one Divine-human Person of Christ. We shall see later how this problem of reconciling deity and humanity already presses, in all its definiteness, upon Ignatius, and how in John it received, by the force of his religious genius, a temporarily definitive solution.

The docetism of the Gnostic Christology is connected, as was remarked before, with the dualistic manner of thought which, in other respects also, led to collisions with the faith of the Church. The Gnostic contempt for material existence was not derived, any more than their Gnosis in general, from philosophical speculation; it was a subsidiary phenomenon of the same attitude of mind which expressed itself in the earnest preoccupation with the things of the other life: the introspective attitude, the higher valuation of spiritual goods, the deepening of the personal self-consciousness, and the individualisation of religion. This tone of mind had, for centuries past, led many away from the official national religions, in which it found no satisfaction, to the mystery-cults. It had first found a half-mythical, half-philosophical expression in the Orphic "wisdom"; then it had found a theoretic basis in the idealistic philosophy of Plato, and, through the influence of the later Stoics, Cynics, and Neo-Pythagoreans, had become a widely diffused system of thought and conduct. This idealistic turning-away from the things of sense to the higher spiritual world is the counterpart of the Jewish apocalyptic turning-away from the present world and looking to the world to come, a world, not indeed purely spiritual, but still thought of as the antithesis of the present, a wondrous world from heaven. Thus, it was easy for these two antitheses of the present, the apocalyptic and the idealistic - philosophic, to become combined into a metaphysico-religious dualism of flesh and spirit, visible and invisible, eternal and transient, such as we find in Philo and in Paul. In the case of these two thinkers this dualism was not able to break down the monotheistic foundation of their religious consciousness. But it was so natural an inference that the two contrasted spheres of existence had a different origin, that it is not to be wondered at if many Jews of the Oriental and Hellenistic Diaspora actually drew this inference, and ascribed the creation of the material world to another author than the highest, purely spiritual God. This is the explanation of the distinction which appears from the first in the Jewish-syncretistic Gnosis between the subordinate creator-god, or, in some cases, creative spiritual powers, and the Supreme God, who is far removed from the material world. This distinction, which first originated from, and corresponded to, a practical religious attitude, afterwards gave rise to reflection upon the relationship between the subordinate powers and the Supreme God. Suggestions were derived in part from the heathen (Babylonian) myths relating to theogony and cosmogony, in part from the Greek philosophumena regarding the Demiurge, the World-God, the creative powers of the Cosmic Logos, and the like. From the manifold combinations of these various elements there grew up the fantastic speculations of the Gnostics concerning the divine beings who sprang from the primal Deity (Archons, Æons, Syzygies), which had almost the same relation to the Gnostic religion as the Church dogmas of the Trinity and the Two Natures of Christ had to the Christian religion. The Church, however, with sure insight, saw in these Gnostic speculations not mere extravagances of imagination, but a serious danger to monotheism, that foundation-stone of Biblical Christianity, rejected them with decision as a relapse into heathen polytheism, and set up as a cardinal tenet of faith the unity of the Creator with the Father of Jesus Christ. On the other hand, the Church recognised a certain germ of truth in the Gnostic doctrine of God, in so far as it softened the hard transcendentalism of the Jewish monotheism, and related the revelation of God in the world and in man to the supramundane Father-God as equally essential "moments" in the one Deity. The Logos, or Son of God, and the Spirit represent, in a simplified form, the same profound thought as the Æons of the Gnostic Pleroma, namely, that the Divine in history and in the hearts of men is the same in essence as the God who is enthroned above the world and time.

In ethics, also, and in eschatology, the Church took up an intermediate position between the abstract dualism of the Gnostics and the crude realism of the Jewish-Christian primitive community. To the spiritualism which despised the corporeal as worthless and unclean it set certain limitations, appropriate to the conditions of human life. It is true that in this regard the teachers of the Church found themselves in a difficult position, inasmuch as they shared in essence the dualistic point of view. The world-renouncing temper, the enthusiastic expectation of the end of the age, and ascetic hostility to the things of sense and the charms of the world, fill the Church literature of the first centuries; and the edifying romances of the Gnostics (Acts of the Apostles) possessed a great attraction for Christians within the Church, just because they went to an extreme in asceticism and contempt for the world. But high as was their estimate of asceticism in general and continence in particular, they disapproved of the condemnation of married life which was customary among the Gnostics, and held firmly to the view of Paul that marriage was both permissible and advisable for Christians in general, while celibacy was more advantageous in the case of persons who had received a special measure of grace—a mediating view which led by a natural consequence to the Catholic doctrine of the dual standard of morality and the evangelical counsels of perfection. Again, while the Gnostic dualism expressed itself in the rejection of the bodily resurrection, for which it substituted a spiritual resurrection to the knowledge of truth, yet the Church, however much it might depreciate the bodily life, would not suffer itself to be deprived of the hope of a future resurrection of the body, any more than of a belief in the bodily resurrection of Christ. Indeed, the struggle against the Gnostic denial of the resurrection led the Church into the opposite extreme of maintaining a resurrection of the flesh. It may be admitted that, in face of a one-sided spiritualism, the Church represented in this the sound religious thought that the body as the instrument of the spirit has, by Divine appointment, a positive value. But on the other hand it cannot be denied that the Church, by the crudely realistic form which it gave to the belief in the resurrection, came into conflict not only with the eschatology of the Apostle Paul

(1 Cor. xv.), but also with its own, since—not indeed in the primitive period, but from the third century onward—it rejected the expectation of an earthly kingdom of Christ (called "Chiliasm," from Apoc. xx. 3-7) as a Jewish error, and held that the final end of the world would follow immediately upon the Parousia of Christ, and the permanent conditions of blessedness in heaven and damnation in hell would begin. How the resurrection of the flesh is to be reconciled with this, it is difficult to say. In fact, the Church eschatology (as may be observed even in the Gospel of John) is only to be understood as an artificial accommodation, a compromise full of contradictions, between the Jewish apocalyptic hopes of the primitive community and the spiritualised idea "of eternal life" for which Paul prepared the way and which became the rule in Gnostic circles. In no other point was the influence of Gnosticism, enlightened by Hellenism, carried through with such important consequences as in the victory of this ethical and mystical idea of eternal life over the earthly, eudæmonistic Messianic dreams of early Christianity. And that in this the higher right, and historical progress, were on the side of Gnosticism must be admitted by anyone who compares the crude, sensuous chiliastic hopes which a Papias and an Irenæus still cherished with the fine saying from a sermon of Valentinus which has been preserved to us by Clement of Alexandria (*Strom.*, IV. xiii. 89): "From the beginning ye are immortal and children of eternal life, and ye desired to take death upon you to the end that ye might drain it to the dregs and make an end of it, that death might die in you and

through you; for if ye destroy the world without being yourselves destroyed, ye are lords of creation and of all that is transient." That is the Hellenistic (Platonic-Stoic-Philonic) thought of the inner "pneumatic" deliverance from the bonds of the world and of death, which is often expressed in the Gospel of John, too (iii. 36, v. 24 f., xi. 25 f.); only that there a concession is made to the popular Church belief, in so far that to the present spiritual resurrection is added a future bodily resurrection, for which Gnosticism substituted the entrance of souls, which even here are immortal, into the heavenly world of light. In this ethico-mystical Gnostic doctrine of salvation we ought not to see a "secularisation" of Christianity, but rather a development, a purification of its at first thoroughly worldly and sensuous hopes of salvation and dreams of a Messianic age, by the transference of these hopes to the spiritual and supramundane region. If, then, to-day many seem to complain that by this Hellenistic Gnostic idealism Christianity was estranged from the "healthy realism" of its views regarding salvation and the Kingdom as destined to be historically realised upon the earth, it ought to be taken into consideration that the apocalyptic transcendental dreams of the Parousia and of the earthly kingdom of the Messiah were widely enough removed from a healthy ethico-historical realism; further, that Christianity could hardly have survived the disappointment of its childish illusions by the weary delay of the fulfilment of its hopes, had not its thoughts of salvation risen above the earthly and taken refuge in the heavenly, the kingdom of the spirit and of truth; finally, that the transcendent loftiness of the ethical ideal was, then as ever, not a hindrance to, but rather a source, an accumulator, of that unconquerable power of inspiring men to do and to suffer by which it moves the world.

Another controversial point on which the Church similarly took up an intermediate position between Gnosticism and the Jewish-Christian belief of the primitive community was the estimate of the Old Testament. Since Gnosticism, as we saw before, began as a Jewish-syncretistic heresy, it is readily intelligible that from the first it applied a more or less thorough-going criticism to the Old Testament, and, in particular, rejected the ritual law as an irrational ordinance of subordinate powers which was a hindrance to the ethical life. This formed a special point of contact and connection between Jewish Gnosticism and the Pauline Gentile Christianity. While strict legalistic Jewish Christianity took such grievous offence at the Pauline antinomianism that it identified Paul simply and completely with the arch-heretic and charlatan Simon Magus, the Gnostics of almost all schools (with the exception of the Ebionites and Elkesaites) felt themselves sympathetically attracted by the Pauline non-legalistic religion of redemption. But just as they amalgamated his doctrine of Christ with heathen mythology, so they exaggerated his antinomianism into a complete contempt for the Old Testament. That, the Church could not approve, since she recognised in the Old Testament a Divine revelation and the basis of her own faith. On the other hand, the influence of Gnosticism had so intensified her consciousness of the distinction between the Mosaic and the Christian religion, that she could no longer think of simply recognising the Old Testament in all its parts as an absolute authority. The Church therefore took the *via media* of regarding the Old Testament as a preparatory revelation of the pre-existent Christ, which must be understood from the point of view of its fulfilment in the Gospel. Whatever harmonised with the latter retained its authority as revealed truth; the remainder was partly dropped, partly adapted to be understood in a Christian sense by means of allegorical interpretation.

Thus the Church opposed Gnosticism at every point where it threatened to undermine the Christian faith by attacking its evangelical foundation; but at the same time she so far learned from the Gnostics that her consciousness of the novelty and unparalleled loftiness of the Christian religion, in comparison with all earlier religions, was deepened and clarified, her range of vision widened, and her capacity to conquer the heathen world and its culture was strengthened. It would therefore not be correct to condemn Gnosticism as an influence wholly opposed to, and destructive of, the essence of Christianity. On the contrary, it exercised the most potent influence in the development of Christianity; by it was brought about the unfolding of the new principle into a comprehensive system, rich in thoughts and interests of the most various kinds, and thus the formation of a universal Church was rendered possible. That, however, the mutual adjustment of elements so diverse as the primitive Messianic belief, Paulinism, the Gnostic syncretistic religion, and Hellenistic popular philosophy, did not at once succeed; that old and new, Jewish, Oriental, and Hellenistic, could not be welded into a harmonious unity without some resistance and some inconsistencies, may be readily understood. Various tendencies persisted side by side within the Church. From the combination of Paulinism and Gnosticism there grew up a religion of redemption at once speculative and mystical; from the Jewish-Christian Messianic belief there grew up an apocalyptic chiliastic religion of recompense; from the combination of the Gospel with Græco-Roman Hellenism, a theistic ethical religion; but the link of connection which held together all these various tendencies was always the central Person of Jesus Christ, although He might be variously regarded, by some as Divine-human Redeemer, by others as the Messianic King and Judge of the world, by others a God-sent Teacher and Law-giver of pure morality. It is by this very plurality of its forms of development that the nature of Christianity is manifested, according to the fulness of the mercy and truth which are contained in it.

CHAPTER XVI

THE EPISTLE TO THE HEBREWS

THIS Epistle falls into three parts. The introductory portion (i.-iv.) demonstrates the superiority of Christianity to the Old Dispensation by a general exposition of the superiority of Christ to the angels and to Moses, as the Son of God to His servants, and attaches to this an exhortation (iii. 7–iv. 13) to Christians not to prove themselves unworthy of the rest promised to the people of God, as the unbelievers of the old covenant did, by hardness of heart and disloyalty. The second portion (iv. 14–x. 18) states the main thesis of the theological argument: Christ is the true High-priest, come from God, perfected as man, exalted to heaven; and has become the author of eternal salvation. Before entering on the details of this argument, the author reproaches his readers with being unripe for this difficult doctrine, on which he could have said so much (v. 11), but that they were still at the standpoint of infants, for whom the milk of elementary teaching is appropriate, not the strong meat of the perfect, whose power of judgment is developed; yea, they are still in need of a warning against apostasy, which would lead to irrevocable destruction. Nevertheless, he hoped, concerning them, that with the help of God they would again exhibit their former zeal, and thereby attain and hold fast unto the end the full certainty of blessed hope, which, resting upon unfailing promises, attaches our souls as though by a sure anchor to the heavenly world, into which Christ has preceded us as our High-priest (vi. 9–20). From this he returns again to the main theme, the argument being developed in the following chapters (vii.–x.). In the first place, Psalm cx. being taken as the starting-point, it is shown that Christ, as the antitype of the priest Melchizedek, is a High-priest of a new and higher order than the Aaronic, for whereas the Law makes priests of men having infirmity, stained with sin, and subject to death, the word of the oath, which is subsequent to the Law, made the Son High-priest, who is perfect for ever, sinless, not subject to death, and exalted above the heaven. And to this personal superiority of the High-priest of the new covenant corresponds also that of his office. Under the old covenant there was an earthly sanctuary made with hands, a mere copy and shadow of its heavenly prototype; under the new covenant, the true tabernacle made by God, in which the heavenly High-priest Christ fulfils His ministry (viii.). Then, again, the sacrifices are contrasted. There, an offering of beasts daily repeated, which could not purify the conscience or make perfect the offerer, but was only, like the ordinances concerning meats and purifications, a material symbol of the coming time when the true order of things should be established; here, on the other hand, the sacrifice, offered once for all, of the unstained life of Christ, who by an eternal spirit offered Himself to God, and through His own blood entered into the heavenly sanctuary, where He now administers the blessings of the world to come. Thereby He has obtained eternal redemption, which purifies the consciences of men from dead works and prepares them for the priestly service of a pure heart and life. So, too, the high-priestly self-offering of Christ has brought about the "perfection" which in the Old Testament worship was only symbolically represented and never really attained; and by this is fulfilled the promise in Jeremiah of a future covenant when God's law should be written in the heart, and sins should be no more remembered (ix. 1–x. 18). The third part (x. 19–xiii. 21) draws out the practical consequences of the superiority of Christianity to Judaism which has been established in the preceding portions. A warning is given against the apostasy which in some cases has already begun, which will be attended with punishments so much the heavier as the blessings of the new covenant are greater in comparison with the old. The readers are exhorted to hold fast their faith and hope, and reminded, in that connection, both of their own former steadfastness amid persecutions and of the multitude of Old Testament examples of faith, and also, finally, of the pattern of the Author and Perfecter of their faith, who, having endured the shame of the cross, was exalted to heavenly joy. So now, too, the readers are to regard their sufferings as a wholesome chastening by God, and hold fast to the grace by which they have obtained a share in the kingdom of the heavenly Jerusalem which cannot be shaken, the kingdom of the angels, of the Church of the first-born and of just men made perfect. The Epistle closes with a series of ethical exhortations relating to special duties, among them one enjoining especially submission to the leaders of the Church, and with an injunction, based on a brief recapitulation of the argument, to follow Jesus faithfully upon the path of shame and suffering (xiii. 10–14). It is fitly described in its own phrase as "a word of exhortation" (xiii. 22).

As to the readers to whom this Epistle was originally addressed, no conclusion can be drawn from the title, which is certainly a later addition, suggested by the contents. It cannot have been intended for Jewish Christians in general, since quite definite circumstances of the community to which it is addressed are frequently mentioned. The Church at Jerusalem has been suggested, on account of its relation to the Jewish sacrificial and priestly worship, but that is on many grounds impossible. A letter which is not a translation from the Hebrew, but was evidently originally written in Greek and in a good Greek style, cannot have been addressed to the Aramaic-speaking Christian community of Jerusalem; and for men who read the Old Testament in the original, an argument based on the Septuagint version, such as prevails throughout the Epistle to the Hebrews, would be very ill-adapted. And how could it be said of a Church in which, in the sixties, there were still doubtless many eye-witnesses of the events of the Gospel history (*cf.* 1 Cor. xv. 6) that the Gospel had come to "us" (the readers) through those that heard it (ii. 3). How could it be said of the poor Jerusalem Church, which itself needed to be supported by collections among the Gentile Christians, that it had ministered, and still ministered, to the saints by its gifts of love (vi. 10)? The references to the Jewish sacrificial and sacerdotal systems are, indeed, of a kind which makes against, much more than favours, the supposition of its being addressed to Jerusalem, for it is not the real Temple that is spoken of, but the ideal sanctuary which the author constructed for himself in imagination from the Mosaic description of the Tabernacle, and he makes, moreover, historical errors in regard, for example, to the altar of incense, the ark of the covenant, and the "daily" offering of the high-priest, which would surely be impossible in a letter addressed to the Jerusalem Church by one of its own members (*e.g.* Barnabas the Levite). It would be more natural to think of the Church at Alexandria, since this would at least understand a Greek letter and was in the habit of using the Septuagint, and because the contents of the letter show evidence of Alexandrian culture. But the latter circumstance only, after all, implies the Alexandrian education of the author of the letter, not necessarily that his readers lived at Alexandria. Why should Alexandrian readers be specially greeted by the Christians from Italy (xiii. 24)? This passage points most probably to readers in Italy; and on that ground alone the conjecture of Holtzmann, that the letter to the Hebrews was directed to the Roman Church, has far the greatest probability of any of the conjectures which have been suggested. A further, confirmatory point is that the first trace of the existence of the Epistle to the Hebrews is found in the first Epistle of Clement, which was written from

Rome; the author appears to have taken as his model the typological method of using Scripture which we find in the Epistle to the Hebrews, and in places makes verbatim extracts from it.

The content and aim of the Epistle to the Hebrews are quite suitable to the Roman Church. No doubt, if the usual opinion were right, according to which this letter was addressed to a Jewish Church in order to warn it against reverting to Judaism, that would not be appropriate to the Roman Church, which, as we saw above, was even at the time of Paul's letter to the Romans an essentially Gentile-Christian Church, in which there was present only a minority of Jewish Christians. There is, however, nothing in the Epistle to the Hebrews which necessitates the supposition that the whole community to which it was addressed was inclined to apostasy; on the contrary, it is "certain persons" only who are said to have forsaken the Christian assembly (x. 25). Thus, even on the presupposition that only Jewish Christians were in view, the situation implied in the Epistle is appropriate enough to the circumstances which we have found reason to assume to have been present in the Church at Rome. But this presupposition itself is by no means beyond doubt, for it has been rightly remarked[1] that apostasy "from the living God" (iii. 12) cannot refer merely to a reversion to Judaism, but to a falling back into heathenism; and, further, that the elements of Christian doctrine to which it is said that the readers ought no longer to be limited

---

[1] Von Soden, *Jahrb. für prot. Theol.*, 1884, 453 ff., and introduction to the commentary in the *Hand-Komm. z. N.T.*, iii. 2; Weizsäcker, *Ap. Z.*, 492.

(vi. 2) are described in such a way that it is much more natural to think of Gentile proselytes to Judaism than of born Jews, for the "penitent turning away from dead works" cannot refer to the abandoning of the ceremonial law, observance of which could not, after all, be for a Jew a subject of repentance; but what is meant must be evil heathen ways of life, which are called "dead" because they separate men from the living God, and because they incur sentence of death; moreover, faith in God, in the resurrection of the dead and eternal judgment, could hardly be called, for Jews, the beginning of Christian instruction, since these were already objects of belief to them, but these doctrines, together with the religious ceremonies of washings and laying on of hands, doubtless formed the first stage of instruction in the faith for those proselytes who, through Judaism, passed over to Christianity. Similarly, the warning in xiii. 9 not to allow themselves to be led astray by manifold and *strange* (foreign) teachings, as, for example, regarding meats, which did not profit those who occupied themselves therewith, suggests less a reversion of Jewish Christians to Jewish legalism, which would not be for them a "foreign teaching," than a syncretistic tendency to combine the Christian means of grace with various other ascetic and mystical means of salvation, such as were at that time offered to the world by numberless sects and teachers of mysticism. What it more especially suggests is a comparison with the Gnostic syncretism of the false teachers at Colosse, who desired to supplement the redemptive work of Christ by an ascetic and mystical worship of angels and spiritual powers, whom they placed as mediators of salvation beside and above Christ. We may assume a similar Gnostic spiritualism, which placed the historical Saviour in an inferior position as compared with angels or spiritual powers who do not take upon them flesh and blood, and whose service consists in mystical purifications and ascetic abstinences, in the case of those to whom this Epistle was addressed. To this points also the strong emphasis laid, upon the one side, on the exaltation of Christ as the Son of God above the angels, and, upon the other, on the necessity of His temporary humiliation to a lower position than the angels, through His assumption of human corporeity for the purpose of His redemptive suffering and death; these two together form the natural and constantly recurring antithesis in Church writers to the Gnostic myths regarding spiritual powers (or angels, or æons). This syncretism was sufficiently wide and indefinite to include pagans, Jews, and Christians among its adherents. It might thus easily happen that in times of persecution, when the name of Christian became a danger, the weaker spirits were tempted to sever themselves from the Church and join one or other of the syncretistic associations, of which the saviour-gods and mystical ascetic practices seemed to offer a substitute for the Christian doctrine of salvation. That was not a falling back into Judaism, but an apostasy into heathen syncretism, which in its professed higher wisdom not only lost from beneath its feet the historical foundation of the Gospel of Jesus, but also the elements of Biblical monotheism, as vi. 1 f. distinctly indicates. To infer from the fact that the Christians are described in the

Epistle (ii. 16, iv. 9) as "the seed of Abraham" and "the people of God" that we must assume its readers to have been Jewish Christians is an over-hasty conclusion, seeing that Paul himself describes Christians as the true sons of Abraham, and as the Israel of God (Gal. iii. 29, vi. 16), and the Epistle of Barnabas, which has such close affinities with the Epistle to the Hebrews, speaks (iii. 6) of Christians as the people (λαός) which God has prepared in His Beloved.

As regards the time when the Epistle was composed, it can at least be asserted with probability that it belongs to the post-apostolic age. The author shows acquaintance with several of the Pauline letters, so that they must have been before him in a collection, which would hardly be possible until some time after the death of Paul. Then, too, in xiii. 7 the termination of the "walk" of their teachers is mentioned, and they are held up as models of faith to the Church. Probably the meaning is that they had died martyr-deaths; in any case, the passage shows that the time of the apostles and first witnesses was already past. It is implied, too, in v. 11 that the beginnings of this Church had been a sufficiently long time ago for a ripe understanding of Christian truth to be fairly expected from its members. Finally, the Church addressed is not only at present suffering conflict and persecution (xii. 1-13), but had also at an earlier time faithfully borne grievous persecution, with contumely and affliction, imprisonment and loss of property. If we refer this earlier suffering to the Neronian persecution, of which the "making of a shameful spectacle" of the Christians

($\theta\epsilon\alpha\tau\rho\iota\zeta\acute{o}\mu\epsilon\nu\text{o}\iota$) reminds us, the "present" persecution must be in the time of Domitian. The reign of Domitian is therefore the earliest possible *terminus a quo* for the writing of Hebrews, but the possibility is not excluded that it was written in the time of Trajan, in which case the earlier persecution was that under Domitian. Thus, the only limits that can be assigned to the possible time of composition are from 95 to 115. If it is urged against this that the sacrificial system is spoken of in the Epistle as still in being, in a way which implies that the Temple had not yet been destroyed, that is to make the same mistake as when it is argued that the typological treatment of the Jewish cultus warrants the conclusion that the readers were resident in the neighbourhood of the Temple. Since the author speaks, not of the Temple, but of an ideal place of worship, the Tabernacle, the present tense in which the sacrificial system is described does not refer to the actual subsistence of the levitical worship, the significance of which was for the allegorist a timeless idea which has nothing to do with actual fact. The sacrificial system is frequently spoken of in this way in Jewish and Christian literature [1] in the present tense, long after Jerusalem had been destroyed. That the destruction of Jerusalem is not mentioned, would no doubt be surprising if the Epistle had been written soon after 70 A.D. to a Jewish-Christian Church, but there is nothing strange in it on our hypothesis that the Epistle was addressed to a Gentile-Christian Church at Rome towards the end of the first or beginning of the second century.

[1] *Cf.* Barnabas vii. f. ; 1 Clem. xl. f. ; Justin, *Dial.*, cvii.

Who the author was, can only, in the absence of certain tradition, be a subject of conjecture. That he was not a native of Palestine, or in any way connected with Jerusalem, is, in any case, certain; for, had he been so, he could not have written elegant Greek and cited the Old Testament only in the Greek version, and he would not have fallen into the above-mentioned errors in regard to matters connected with the priests and the Temple. Among the various conjectures, the happiest is Luther's guess that it was Apollos, the learned Alexandrian, who, after being a follower of the school of John the Baptist,[1] was converted to Christianity and confuted the Jews by proving from the Scriptures that Jesus was the Messiah, but also was able to make such an impression on the Greeks at Corinth that they formed a special party under his name, and who, therefore, in spite of his friendly relations with Paul, must have retained an independent way of teaching, based upon his Alexandrian education. If Apollos was not the author—a point which, in the absence of distinct evidence, must remain undecided—the author was certainly a man exactly of the type of Apollos: influenced by Paul, but freely working up and recasting his ideas in the spirit of Alexandrian Hellenism.

The Hellenistic basis of the Epistle to the Hebrews, its dependence in thought and word upon the Book of Wisdom, and especially upon Philo, is so

---

[1] It is possible that there is an allusion to the practices of this school in the "washings and laying on of hands" which are mentioned among the elementary lessons which ought to be left behind, vi. 2 (*cf.* Acts xviii. 24–xix. 7).

obvious that there is not the smallest room for doubt upon the matter.¹ The allegorical treatment of the Old Testament Scriptures; the view of Christ as the great and sinless High-priest, not sprung from among men, both the mediator of creation and the sustainer of the universe; the view of the ritual sacrifices as means, not for the forgiveness of sins, but for reminding us of them, all are Philonic. The author shares with Philo (*De legg.*, xxiii.) the mistake regarding the daily offering of the high-priest; in agreement with Philo (*Confus. ling.*, xxxiii.), a passage is cited in a form which is nowhere found in the Old Testament; in agreement with Philo, and not with Paul, Abraham's obedience of faith is found in the fact that he started out to go to the Land of Promise which as yet he knew not (xi. 18). Finally, the fundamental thought of the Philonian system, the antithesis between the higher prototypal world of the "Ideas" (κόσμος νοητός, ἐκ τῶν ἰδεῶν συσταθείς) and the earthly, sensible, antitypal world is made by the author of the Epistle to the Hebrews the basis of his Christian speculation, and applied to the relationship of Christianity to Judaism; he sees,² that is, in the earthly sanctuary of the Jewish worship the copy and antitype of the true and heavenly sanctuary, which, preceding the former as a supersensuous reality, has come to historical revelation in Christianity, and forms, partly the object of Christian experience through faith, partly of Christian hope. From this

---

[1] *Cf.* Siegfried, *Philo*, pp. 321–330.
[2] viii. 5, ὑπόδειγμα καὶ σκιὰ τῶν ἐπουρανίων; ix. 23 ff., τὰ ὑποδείγματα τῶν ἐν τοῖς οὐρανοῖς, ἀντίτυπα τῶν ἀληθινῶν. *Cf.* with this Wisd. ix. 8, μίμημα σκηνῆς ἁγίας ἣν προητοίμασας ἀπ' ἀρχῆς.

identification of Christianity with the higher spiritual world, which, because it will only be manifested in the future, is the world " to come," results the paradox that Christianity appears as belonging to the future world. We must not, however, conclude from this that the Christian belief of the author had wholly passed into eschatological hopes; the explanation of the paradox is simply that the future world is at the same time the higher world of heaven, which even in the present exists, nay, indeed, existed from the beginning as the unseen reality; which even now has not come to full manifestation, but with which Christians are brought by Christ, the heavenly Highpriest, into such a relation that they are able to taste its powers and have already received its first-fruits (vi. 4 f.).

The mediator between the two worlds is in Philo the Logos, as the first-born, or eldest Son, of God. He mediates both the creation and the upholding of the world, as well as the religious relation between God and men, since, as envoy, interpreter, and prophet of God, He reveals Him to men, and as the High-priest and representative of men He reconciles them with God. All these characteristics of the Philonian Logos, though without this special designation, are transferred by the author of the Epistle to the Hebrews to Christ. Christ is the Son of God, the Son absolutely in a unique sense, essentially distinguished from the prophets, from Moses, and also from the angels, by the fact that through Him God made the world, and thereby constituted Him the heir, that is, the Lord and administrator of all things (i. 2). The Son is of like being with the Father, for He is called "the effulgence of His glory and the express image of His being, upholding all things by the word of His power" (i. 3)—predicates which are partly taken from the Book of Wisdom, where they are used with reference to the personified wisdom of God (Wisd. vii. 25 f.), partly from Philo, who speaks of the Logos as the "image of God," and of the spirit of man, made after the image of the Logos, as "the effulgence of the glory and the impress of the Divine power," while of the Logos he also says that he "upholds existence and produces all that is." And just as Philo describes the Logos, in spite of his dependence upon the sole primal God, as a (second) God, so the Epistle to the Hebrews, in the quotation from Ps. xlv. 7, makes God Himself address the Son as " God " (i. 8 f.). The apotheosis of Christ which was thus introduced into the theology of the Church was therefore of Alexandrian origin, and the motive which underlies this further development can easily be recognised from Heb. i. ; it is the justifiable desire to express, in the exaltation of the Person of Christ above all other intermediate beings, the exaltation of the Christian religion, as the most perfect revelation of God, above all earlier forms of religion. If the author, under the influence of Philo, goes beyond the Pauline conception of Christ as the Heavenly Man, he follows in Paul's footsteps not only in thinking of the Son from the first as wholly subordinate to the Father, by whom He is made the heir of all things and appointed High-priest, and to whom He owes obedience (i. 2, v. 5, 8), but also, especially, in laying the emphasis, not on the metaphysical mediatorship of the (pre-existent) Son, but on what He has become to us, and achieved for us, by His incarnation as the historical Saviour Jesus, and on the exaltation which He has thereby earned, to be the heavenly High-priest in His post-existence. Herein lies the essential distinction between the Church's belief in Christ, on the one hand, and the Gnostic spiritualism and the Philonian Logos-speculation, on the other. It is true, Philo saw something in the nature of human manifestations of the Divine Logos in some of the great figures of religious history, especially in Moses, but also in the patriarchs and in the ceremonial mediatorship of the high-priest; but it was quite a different thing when the Christian Alexandrian taught that the Divine Son and Creator of the world, exalted above the angels, had taken human flesh and blood and, in Jesus, had become our brother. Philo had also called the Divine Logos the great High-priest, who, like Melchizedek, the king of peace, had the truly existent (God) for his portion, was a partaker in no sin, and as the unblemished had immortal and unstained parents, God for His Father and Wisdom for his mother, and who, as the representative of men before God, turns the Divine mercy towards them;[1] but in Philo this remained an abstract theory, the mediatorship was rather metaphysical than religious, and contained no religious warmth or power. It was only when the Christian Alexandrian identified this heavenly High-priest of speculation with Jesus, the Son of Man, the Saviour of sinners, who had lived upon earth, that the antithesis between the two worlds, whose division Philo had not been

[1] Philo, *De somn.*, i. 37, 38; *De profug.*, 20; *Leg. alleg.*, 26; *Quis rer. div. hær.*, 42.

able to bridge, was overcome—that free access to the throne of grace was opened up to the religious consciousness which longed for fellowship with God (Heb. iv. 14–16).

It is not, indeed, quite clear how the author connects the two equally important sides of his Christology, how he conceives of the incarnation in Jesus of the pre-existent Son of God. He speaks, it is true, of the assumption of human flesh and blood by which the Son, who is exalted above the angels, takes for a time, as an earthly man, a lower place than they (ii. 9, 14); but just how this is accomplished remains obscure, since the indications point in two different directions. According to one passage (vii. 14), Jesus sprang from the tribe of Judah, and is therefore in His earthly manifestation a son of Israel, which implies human parentage. According to the other, however (vii. 3), He is, like His prototype Melchizedek, king of peace, without father or mother or descent, or beginning of days or end of life. According to this, it appears as if the author thought of the incarnation as apart from any natural mediation, not merely of an earthly father, but even of an earthly mother, and this perhaps is also pointed to in the words —a misquotation of Ps. xl. 9—which he puts into the mouth of Christ: "A body hast thou prepared for Me" (x. 5). A similar purely supernatural view of the incarnation seems to have been held by Barnabas, since he does not acknowledge Jesus to be the Son of Man (*Ep.* xii. 10); the docetic Christology was already in the air, but it was not yet recognised as heretical; it was still in its harmless and inoffensive beginnings.

It was not merely by the assumption of a human

body that the Son of God became like us, but also by His submission to the suffering, weakness, and temptation which belong to the common lot of man. As sufferings serve us as an ethical discipline and give the occasion for the exercise of obedience, so Christ also "learnt obedience by that which He suffered," and "was made perfect by suffering," being exalted to heavenly dignity and joy as the reward of His humiliation and patience (v. 8 f., ii. 9 f., xii. 2). How this human subjection to temptation and learning of obedience is to be reconciled with His heavenly origin and Divine creative power has not, however, been thought out in detail by the author. There remains, therefore, in this Christology an "unreconciled dualism of metaphysics and history, an unbridged gap between the speculative construction which starts from above and deals with the pre-existent world-creating Son, and the historical, which starts from below and deals with the life of Jesus" (Holtzmann). To a certain extent that was already the case with Paul, as indeed it is the inevitable and universal consequence of the mythical conception of the manifestation of a personal super-earthly being in an earthly human life; but in the Epistle to the Hebrews (and in John) the "hiatus" is much more striking than in Paul, because on the one hand the metaphysical background of the Person of Christ is exalted above humanity into essential deity, and, on the other, His earthly human life (not merely death), and the moral value attaching to it, are much more strongly emphasised than by Paul. And this constitutes a decided advance in the Epistle to the Hebrews; in it begins what was carried out by

THE EPISTLE TO THE HEBREWS 289

the Gospel of John, the completion of the Pauline Christology by connecting the historical picture of the life of Jesus with the speculative ideal figure of the heavenly Christ—a completion which was necessary in order to avoid the dangers of a one-sided transcendental speculative doctrine of Christ such as was represented by Gnosticism, and to preserve for the Christian faith, along with its historical foundation, its ethical content and value.

As the Son of God become man, Christ was, according to Heb. iii. 1, " the Apostle and High-priest of our confession," by whom we have been made partakers of the heavenly calling. As the messenger of God, he has revealed to us the Divine will for our salvation, which has destined us to be partakers of the heavenly world; as the High-priest who forms the subject of our confession, He was the forerunner and opener of the way, who has opened up to us access to that world, or to the heavenly Temple, and is the administrator of its eternal blessings. The means, however, by which He Himself was made perfect, and became for us the author of salvation, was suffering and death. This is in the Epistle to the Hebrews, as in Paul, the keystone of Christ's work. It was for this purpose that, according to ii. 14, the Son of God took flesh and blood, "that through death He might destroy the strength of Him who had the power of death, that is, the devil, and deliver those who through the fear of death were all their lifetime bondmen"; and, according to x. 5–10, God prepared for His Son a (human) body, in order that by offering up His body once for all He might make an end of animal sacrifices and consecrate us to the fellowship of God. But the point of view from which the Epistle to the Hebrews regards the death of Christ is different from that of Paul. Whereas in Paul's teaching Christ as the representative and substitute of guilty humanity expiates and removes the curse of the law by passively suffering its sentence of death to be carried out upon Him, this fundamental idea of the Pauline doctrine of salvation is absent in Hebrews; here Christ is the active sacrificing Priest who offers His holy life to God in obedience and endurance, as a costly offering which possesses the power to purify men's hearts and consecrate them to the fullest fellowship with God.

Thus, instead of an expiatory act of God carried out in Christ for the satisfaction of the law, there is here substituted Christ's own ethical act, which, as a gift of the highest value, well-pleasing to God, surpasses and supersedes all earlier offerings, and initiates a new worship of God "in spirit and in truth." Whereas in Paul the juridical theory of expiation and imputation, derived from the Pharisaic theology, formed the starting-point of his doctrine of redemption, the Epistle to the Hebrews finds the starting-point for its theory in the sacrificial ritual of the Old Testament, which it ingeniously interprets as a symbolical prototype of the higher ethical and spiritual sacrifice of Christ. The High-priest of the Old Testament went every year anew with the blood of the sacrifice into the Holy of Holies, the seat of the revealed presence of God, in order, by sprinkling the blood, to make atonement for the sins of the people, that is, to do away with, somehow or other, their power to pollute and to separate us from God. How this was effected, what was the atoning power of the blood, the author has not thought out for himself, but has adopted the conception as a datum and applied it to his own purpose. The very fact of the constant repetition of the sacrifice shows, so runs his argument, that the means were insufficient, because animal sacrifices could not purify the conscience or "make perfect," that is, place us in an ethico-religious position corresponding to our destiny (ix. 9, 13, x. 1–4). There was therefore needed, to effect this purpose, a better sacrifice and a better priest. This is Christ, the heavenly Son of God, whom God, even before the institution of the levitical priesthood, appointed, under the figure of Melchizedek, an eternal High-priest of a higher order. He does not need, like a human high-priest, to offer first for his own sins, since, in spite of all the weakness and exposure to temptation which He shared with us men, He is, as the superhuman Son of God, holy, unstained by sin, separate from sinners, and exalted above the heavens. Therefore, too, He was able to offer a better sacrifice than those of the levitical priests. He offered Himself to God as the unblemished sacrifice by means of the eternal, immutably perfect Spirit which forms His heavenly being (ix. 14). To this higher priesthood and better sacrifice there corresponds, finally, the more perfect effect of His work. The High-priest by his sprinkling of the blood in the earthly holy place was only able to produce a "purifying of the flesh," *i.e.* an external, merely ritual purification, which was so far from a real removal of sin that it signified, on the contrary, only a yearly remembrance of the sins which were not done away (ix. 13, x. 3 f.). Christ, on the other hand, entered into the true Temple once for all with His own blood and obtained eternal redemption, namely, the true removal of sin by the full forgiveness of it, the purification of our conscience from the polluting guilt of dead works, that is, works which cause death, and obtained for us at the same time power and consecration for the service of the living God (ix. 14, 26, x. 10, 18). The removal of the consciousness of guilt which separates us from God, and transference into a position, analogous to Christ's own condition of perfection, of perfect godliness (holiness) and of the pure service of God—this is the saving work of Christ, which is based upon His offering once for all upon the cross, while its permanent power rests upon His eternal ministry as High-priest in the heavenly sanctuary.

Thus, in content, the saving work of Christ comes to essentially the same thing as in Paul's teaching, but whereas in the latter its effects are directly connected with the death of Christ for the satisfaction of the law, or of the Divine righteousness, this essential link in Paul's chain of thought is wanting in Hebrews, and the death of Christ is here immediately connected with the subjective consciousness of men, upon which it works as an ethical sacrifice of pious obedience, bringing atonement and perfection. " The terminology of atonement which is developed in such detail serves ultimately only as a pictorial form of expression for the perfect fellowship with God into which Christ introduces us, and for the possibility of a pure life which is enjoyed by His followers, who are freed from a sense of guilt in the same measure in which that possibility is realised" (Holtzmann).

At the same time the Epistle to the Hebrews has also a substitute for the objective side of the Pauline doctrine of redemption—the removal of the curse of the law—in the thought, expressed though it is only once, that Christ by His death overcame him that had the power of death, the devil, and freed those who through the fear of death were all their lives in bondage (ii. 14 f.). Inasmuch as the devil is here the personal representative of death as the punishment of sin, which Paul thought of as the effect of the judging and slaying curse of the law, the overcoming of the devil by Christ's death is very much the same thing which Paul describes as our redemption from the curse of the law by Christ's suffering in our stead. The difficulty under which the Pauline theory labours—that the death of Christ is the rendering of a satisfaction due to the law, as if the law was an independent ruler alongside of God, whose demand for punishment God Himself was obliged to recognise and satisfy—is got rid of in the Epistle to the Hebrews by the substitution, for the abstract idea of the law, of the popular conception of the devil, who however has not to be satisfied with a redemption price, but is simply defeated by the ethical act of the sacrificial death of Christ.

In the doctrine of the Christian condition of salvation the Epistle to the Hebrews diverges from the Pauline teaching even more widely than in the doctrines of Christ and of redemption. It is true the writer speaks often and emphatically of faith, but he understands by faith something different from what is meant by Paul. Faith is not for him the ardent mystical union with Christ in which Christ's death and resurrection are appropriated and inwardly reproduced; Christ is not so much its object as its pattern. It was by His faithful endurance of suffering, looking to the heavenly joy, that Christ showed us the way of faith and its victorious end, and is become "the author and finisher of faith." The object of faith is much more general than with Paul; it is the confident direction of thought and feeling towards the blessings of the unseen and future world (xi. 1). Since these blessings are already present in the heavenly world which has been opened up by the heavenly High-priest Christ, and in which He bears rule, and a foretaste of its powers has already been experienced by Christians in the possession of the Holy Spirit (vi. 4), faith is not mere hope in a future good, but also a partial inward possession of it in the present (x. 34). But in so far as these blessings of the higher world are only to be fully manifested and communicated in the future world, in so far faith is still essentially hope of this splendid future, and must manifest itself in faithful, trustful endurance and patience amid the fightings and sufferings of the temporal life. Endurance and patience are the manifestations of the obedience of faith, and therefore the condition of the obtaining of salvation, of the inheritance of the promise (vi. 11 ff., x. 36 ff.). It is not only the final deliverance which Hebrews makes dependent upon the ethical proving of faith, in obedience to the will of God amid opposition and suffering—that would be so far quite Pauline—it connects the present righteousness of the believer with this practical effect of faith, and thus gives to the Pauline doctrine of redemption, which it has in view throughout, a different turn. " Righteousness " is not here, as in Paul, the gift of God to be received by faith, and consisting in an acquittal of the believing sinner on the ground of Christ's atoning death; it is the pious attitude of mind manifesting itself in obedience, in doing and suffering, which is the essence of faith. Faith does not first receive the righteousness of God ; it is recognised, "testified to," by God, in virtue of what it is in itself, as the right condition of man; indeed, the man himself " works " righteousness by his own faith, righteousness here meaning the being recognised by God as righteous.[1] Even where the Epistle to the Hebrews takes over verbally the characteristic phrases of Paul, as in the quotation of Hab. ii. 4 (x. 38), it gives them a different sense. In Paul the force of the quotation was: He who is just by faith (justified) shall live; in Hebrews: the righteous (pious) man shall preserve his life in consequence of his faith, *i.e.* of his confident endurance, which is the antithesis of timorous drawing back or apostasy, by which all would be lost again. It is easily understood that in this conception of faith and its righteousness the old Pauline antithesis between faith and works, faith and law, disappears, for, as faith itself is the direction of the will in accordance with the will of God, it necessarily includes within

[1] The place of the Pauline formulas δικαιοῦσθαι and λογίζεσθαι δικαιοσύνην is taken by the formulas μαρτυρεῖσθαι δίκαιον εἶναι or, more shortly, μαρτυρεῖσθαι διὰ πίστεως (xi. 4, v. 39) and ἐργάζεσθαι διὰ πίστεως δικαιοσύνην (xi. 33).

itself works and the ethical fulfilment of the law. Now, it is true this element of moral power is not foreign to the Pauline conception of faith—faith displaying itself in love and serving as a source of actual righteousness of life, but for Paul this aspect of ethical activity is not the fundamental essence of faith; that lies rather in religious receptivity, in the surrender of the heart to Christ, to be personally united with Him. This mystical side of the Pauline faith in Christ is absent from the Epistle to the Hebrews; its place is taken in part by the fervent hope in the promised blessings of the future world, in part by the ethical energy of obedience, endurance, and patience; these together form the attitude of mind, well-pleasing to God, in which the righteousness of man consists, and which therefore was essentially the same in the Old Testament saints as in Christians (xi.).

While it is certain that this is not the old Pauline doctrine, it is equally certain that it would be a mistake to regard it as Jewish-Christian or primitive Christian doctrine. Rather, it is a peculiar development, under the influence of Alexandrianism, of the Pauline theology. What the Epistle to the Hebrews has in common with Paul is its view of the absolute superiority of Christianity to Judaism; what is different is the theory by which this view is supported. Paul conceived of Judaism under the aspect of the law which demands and judges, and therefore placed it in contrast with the Gospel; the former works wrath and causes death, the latter reconciles and makes alive; on the one side, curse, on the other, blessing. The Epistle to the Hebrews, on the other hand, looks at Judaism from the point of view of the cultus, the central point of which was the ritual of atonement, and therefore places it in a positive relation to Christianity as a symbolical preparation for it. As a consequence of this it sees the Christian system of salvation under the forms of the Old Testament ritual: Christ is the High-priest, His saving work is the priestly sacrifice of atonement, which purifies and consecrates the sinful people, faith is a priestly service, its fruit is an offering well-pleasing to God, the final perfection is a sabbatic rest, Christians are the people of the Lord, their consciousness of salvation is free access to the heavenly sanctuary. But this is so far from meaning that Christianity is merely a higher form of Judaism, that, on the contrary, Judaism is boldly explained to be the insubstantial, shadowy symbol, Christianity the eternal substance of religion. This thought is worked out in the Epistle in all its possible variations. It is not Christianity that is a copy of Judaism, but Judaism that is a shadow of the heavenly sanctuary which in Christianity has been made manifest, *i.e.* Christianity, although it appeared later, is in idea the earlier, the eternal, in comparison with which Judaism is only of temporary, preparatory significance. For this reason the promises and hopes of pious Israel were from the first directed to a goal which lay beyond the Israelitish theocracy, to the Sabbath rest in the heavenly kingdom, not merely in Canaan. Abraham himself, when he followed in faith the call of God, looked forward to the heavenly fatherland; looking to the reproach of Christ (in order to take an anticipatory share in it), Moses despised the riches of Egypt; to Christ, the High-priest, represented by Melchizedek, the patriarchs themselves did homage. Just as Philo endeavoured to Hellenise the Old Testament by allegorising its historical figures into symbols of the ideal world, so the author of Hebrews endeavoured by the same method of type and allegory to Christianise the Old Testament. And this way of looking at it was found by the consciousness of the Church much more illuminative than the Pauline antithesis of law and Gospel, because it made possible a practical use of the Old Testament in the interests of the faith and morals of the Church, without a slavish bondage to the outward form—that of the national history—into which its teachings had been cast. The old conflict of Paul with the Judaisers was for the author of Hebrews entirely a thing of the past, and he could therefore the more freely apply the whole law, and more especially its ritual portion, as an allegory of the Christian way of salvation. For the very reason that the old covenant, with its sacerdotal and sacrificial system, was merely a prototype of the new covenant which had been established in Christ, the former has now lost all significance, the shadow gives way before the substance. That had not been perceived by Philo, who, by a curious limitation, desired to see the literal sense of the law maintained alongside of the allegorical spiritualisation. It was the pupil of that apostle who saw in Christ the end of the law for Jews and Greeks alike (Rom. x. 4) who was the first to draw from Philo's allegorical interpretation the decisive practical inference that the outward forms of the ritual law had lost all significance and value since its spiritual sense had been revealed in the new covenant. The Pauline criticism of the

THE EPISTLE TO THE HEBREWS 299

law was a necessary preliminary before the true consequences of the Philonian allegorisation of the law could be perceived. Conversely, this consequence of the allegorical view served the followers of Paul as a means of supplementing the Pauline criticism of the law on its positive side, and of so far softening the antithesis between law and Gospel, that the thought of a development and fulfilment of the legal religion in the religion of the spirit took the place of that of a breach with the legal religion. That remained henceforth the point of view of the Church in regard to the Old Testament and the Mosaic law.

WRITINGS OF THE PAULINE SCHOOL

CHAPTER XVII

THE EPISTLES TO THE EPHESIANS AND COLOSSIANS

THE Epistle to the Ephesians, traditionally ascribed to Paul, falls into two parts, the doctrinal portion, i.–iii., and the practical, iv.–vi. It begins with a long ascription of praise to God for the readers' state of grace, in which the pre-temporal decree of their election in Christ has been brought to pass. Then follows the prayer that God may give them the spirit of wisdom and revelation, that they may know the whole fulness of the glory of the inheritance which is the object of their hope, and of the exceeding greatness of the might of God in the resurrection and exaltation of Christ, who has been appointed Head over all spiritual powers, as well as of the Church, which is His body, the fulness of Him that filleth all in all (i. 3–23).

This is the statement of the main theme of this doctrinal and hortatory epistle, which is then further developed, first in regard to the relation of the Gentiles and the Jews to Christianity. Both have been raised up by God, with Christ, from their earlier death in sin and transferred into the heavenly world; the Gentiles, in especial, who had previously been in a state of alienation from God, have been brought nigh by the blood of Christ. In His death, the dividing wall of the Jewish law has been done away with, and peace restored, between Jews and Greeks, and also between them both and God, so that now even those who aforetime were heathen are built together upon the foundation of the prophets and apostles into one holy temple of God (ii.). This destination of the Christian salvation for all is the mystery which was earlier hidden, but now has been revealed to the holy apostles and prophets, especially to Paul, and, by the Church, is made known also to the heavenly spiritual powers. May the readers therefore, firmly founded in faith and love, be enabled ever more fully to grasp the whole extent of the love of Christ! (iii.). Then follows in the second part (iv. 1 ff.) the exhortation to walk worthy of their calling, to keep the unity of the Spirit in the bond of peace, not to allow themselves to be carried away by false doctrine, but by truth and love to grow into ever more complete union with Christ, the Head, by whom the whole body is held together and built up. Therefore they must lay aside the old man with his heathen lusts, and put on the new man who, after God, is created in righteousness and holiness of truth, and show themselves, especially by brotherly love, purity, temperance, and wisdom, the children of light. The social relationships, too, between husbands and wives, parents and children, masters and servants, are to be sanctified by the Christian spirit. The ethical section closes with a reference to the keen conflict against spiritual powers, which can only be sustained by the help of the armour of the Spirit (vi.

10-18); a sentence or two of personal matter follow, and a liturgical benediction forms the conclusion.

This writing, with its doctrine and exhortations, cannot in any case be a letter of Paul to the Ephesian Church, for in such a letter the absence of all personal references and greetings would be quite unintelligible. But the address is uncertain even from the point of view of textual criticism; the words "in Ephesus" do not seem to have stood in the original superscription; in both the Sinaiticus and Vaticanus they have been added subsequently; they were not read by Origen and Basil; in Marcion the address ran, "to the Laodiceans" (Tert., *Adv. Marc.*, v. 11). Upon these textual facts various theories have been built up— the letter was originally addressed to no definite circle of readers, but "to the saints who are also believers," *i.e.* Christians in general (but how does that suit vi. 21 f.); or it was a circular letter, the address of which was left blank in order to be filled in with the names of the different communities of recipients. For this last hypothesis some have thought they found a point of support in Col. iv. 16, where the Colossians are directed to see that their letter is read in Laodicea, and the letter sent thither read among them. The conclusion proposed to be drawn from this is that our canonical Epistle to the Ephesians was this encyclical, originally directed to several churches in Asia Minor, including Laodicea and Colosse. All these ingenious hypotheses[1] become worthless if Paul was not the author of the Epistle, and the epistolatory form only serves to embody a Church homily designed to emphasise the

[1] *Cf.* von Soden, *Hand-Kommentar*, iii. 1. 85 f.

THE EPISTLE TO THE EPHESIANS 303

unity of the universal Church which is built upon the foundation of the apostles, as against the centrifugal tendencies of heretical Gnosis. That this is the fact is an inevitable inference from the style of the Epistle to the Ephesians, which, both in construction and vocabulary, is quite un-Pauline,[1] and also from the peculiarity of the contents of the letter, which imply an ecclesiastical situation and a theological mode of thought which have advanced far beyond those of the time of Paul, and at the same time stand in such close dependence upon the Epistle to the Colossians—which is probably itself interpolated—that it may be considered as in the main a variation on the same themes which appear there.

The author, a Jew by birth, and probably from Asia Minor, addresses in the name of Paul, with whose Epistles he has made himself thoroughly familiar, those Gentile Christians who cherished libertine principles and, misled by Gnosticism, desired to separate themselves from the Church, especially the Jewish-Christian portion of the Church. For this tendency they found support in a Gnostic theory which separated the Christ of speculation from the Jesus of the evangelical tradition,[2] and thus robbed Christianity of its historical foundation and its ethical content—a heresy of much the same kind

[1] The details will be found in any Introduction.
[2] To this points unmistakably the passage in iv. 20 f. : "Ye did not so learn Christ, if so be that ye heard of Him, and were taught in Him, how He is the truth in Jesus." The commentaries of Klöpper (p. 142 ff.) and von Soden (*Hand-Kommentar*, iii. 1. 136) agree in substance with the above interpretation, though they do not draw the same inference in regard to the character of the false doctrine which is opposed.

as that which is opposed in the Ignatian and Johannine Epistles. This opposition to a libertine and docetic Gnosticism explains all the peculiarities of the Epistle to the Ephesians: its insistence on a practical Christianity manifesting itself in moral purity and love, its doctrine of Christ as the sole Head both of the whole spiritual world, and also of the Church which He founded by His pattern deed of love, its doctrine of the eternal election of the Church in Christ, of the union of Jews and Gentiles in the Church into a new organisation of mankind, of its constant growth from Christ and into Him as the means of the fulfilment of the all-embracing world-plan of God. All this goes beyond the standpoint of Paul. He had had to contend for the equal rights of Gentile Christians against Jewish particularism; now the condition of affairs was that it was much more necessary to oppose the arrogance and unlovingness of the (Gnostically inclined) Gentile Christians by reminding them of their former exclusion from, and present admission to, participation in the promises and the inheritance of Israel, which, as being an undeserved grace on the part of God, they were bound to prize the more gratefully and hold fast the more firmly. In this we ought not to see an un-Pauline concession to Judaism; for the author, indeed, all that is specifically Jewish—the law, circumcision, descent from Abraham—is worthless and nugatory, and the Jews are "by nature children of wrath even as others" (ii. 3). *i.e.* they are, by reason of the inborn sinfulness of the flesh, as liable to the Divine judgment, and therefore as much in need of salvation, as the heathen (*cf.* Rom. iii. 9–20). Their original advantage was only that they were the recipients of the promises, and that the pre-existent Christ worked among them as a prophetic Spirit of revelation; whereas the Gentiles, because alien from the theocracy and the promises of Israel, and therefore still without relation to Christ, were consequently without hope and without God (ii. 12). According to this, the Old Testament religion, being a prophecy of Christ, is itself a revelation of the pre-existent Christ, a Christianity before Jesus, only obscured and fettered by national limitations, which were first removed by the revelation in Christ, and more especially in His death. That became in the post-apostolic period the usual way of Christianising the Old Testament, and thus annexing it to the use of the Church.

That Christianity, although it appeared later, was the eternal religion, superior to both Judaism and heathenism, is expressed in an adaptation of the Pauline doctrine of election which is peculiar to the Epistle to the Ephesians, and takes the form that the Christian Church was the object of a pre-mundane Divine election in Christ (i. 4 f.). As Christ was "the Beloved" (i. 6) or the "Son of God's love" (Col. i. 13) in a special sense, so from the beginning all who were to belong to Him as members of His body were taken up along with Him into God's will of love. Christ is therefore not properly speaking a mere individual person, but in a certain sense the "intelligible abode" or "epitome" of the totality of the elect, the cosmic principle of unity which, according to the Divine appointment, is to unite in itself as Head not only the Church, but even the universe, to pervade all things and fill all things (i. 10, 23, ii. 21). In view of this eternal election of Christians in Christ, the Pauline doctrine of the pre-existence of Christ is extended to include the pre-existence of the Church as an ideal unity contained in Him, and thus the idea of this Christological conception is brought to its most definite expression; it is the supra-temporal or eternal truth of the religion of redemption, which is based on the conception both of the personal pre-existent Redeemer and of the ideally pre-existent or predeterminate community of the redeemed.

The doctrine of Christ's person and work in the Epistle to the Ephesians is so closely connected with that of the Epistle to the Colossians that it appears advisable to take the latter, since it is the more definitely outlined, as the point of departure, and then compare it with the other. Common to both is the endeavour to oppose to the false and subversive Gnosis which obscured the value of the Christian redemption, the true ecclesiastically edifying "Gnosis" concerning Christ and His work of salvation. This anti-Gnostic polemic is itself based on a Gnostic foundation, and makes use of the ideas and phrases customary in the religious speculation of the time in a sense acceptable to the common consciousness of the Church. When, in Colossians i. 15, Christ is called "the image of the invisible God," that recalls the Pauline phrase, "the image of God" (2 Cor. iv. 4); but the addition of "the invisible God" points to the Philonic thought that God, who is in Himself invisible, is manifested only in the Logos, and that the latter is the mediator in all the relations of God to the world. Again, when Christ is further described as "the first-born of all creation," that recalls the Pauline ideas of the "first-born among many brethren" and "first-born from the dead"; but it has its nearest analogue in the Philonic statement about the Logos, that he, in distinction from the world, is the first-born or eldest Son of God. Further, in i. 16 ff. it is said that in Christ, and through Him, and unto Him, all things in heaven and earth, all things visible and invisible, and, especially, all spiritual powers, have been created, and that He is before all things, and in Him all things have their being. Now, even if Paul, in 1 Cor. viii. 6, described Christ as the instrument in creation, this goes much beyond his thought, for here Christ is not only the means but also the end of creation, while, for Paul, only God is that, and finally, indeed, God shall be so exclusively and absolutely the end of all things that Christ surrenders His lordship into the hand of God (Rom. xi. 36; 1 Cor. xv. 28). But, as He in whom all things have their being, Christ is exalted to be the bearer of the omnipotence which upholds the world, the immanent cosmic principle—an idea foreign to the Pauline conception of Christ as the prototypal Head of humanity, while it is quite in harmony with the metaphysical significance of the Logos, in regard to whom Philo taught that the incorporeal world was founded in him and that he sustained and exercised his power throughout the whole universe.[1] In verse 18 a transition is made from

[1] Philo, De mundi opif., x.: ὁ ἀσώματος κόσμος ... ἱδρυθεὶς ἐν τῷ θείῳ λόγῳ. De profug., xx.: ὁ τοῦ Ὄντος λόγος δεσμὸς ὢν τῶν ἁπάντων συνέχει τὰ πάντα μέρη καὶ σφίγγει καὶ κωλύει αὐτὰ διαλύεσθαι. De vita Mosis, iii. 14: τοῦ συνέχοντος καὶ διοικοῦντος λόγου τὸ σύμπαν. De somniis, i. 11: ὃν ἐκπεπλήρωκεν ὅλον δι' ὅλων ἀσωμάτοις δυνάμεσιν αὐτὸς ὁ θεός.

the cosmic mediatorship of Christ to His historical mediatorship as the Saviour: He is the head of the Church, His body, because He is its beginning (its founder and author) as the first-born from the dead; He is in all things (in the cosmos and in the Church) to have the pre-eminence, because all the fulness (of the Godhead, ii. 9) was pleased to dwell in Him, and by Him to reconcile all things unto Him. No parallels to these statements are to be found in Paul; in Philo the same thought is found, in so far as his Logos is wholly filled with supersensuous powers which, going forth from him, communicate themselves to the world; but he has not the conception of the Pleroma itself. On the other hand, we have seen above what a prominent rôle the Pleroma played in the Ophite and Valentinian Gnosis, as the sum of the spiritual powers which go forth from the transcendent divine Being and are the organs of His relation to the world. That it is from this quarter that the conception of the Pleroma passed into the Epistle to the Colossians may be inferred with the greater probability in view of the abrupt fashion in which it is here introduced, which is only intelligible on the presupposition that it was a current idea with the false teachers who are here attacked. There was no simpler way in which the Church teacher could meet the Gnostic syncretism which made Christ one of the many spiritual beings (Æons) of the Pleroma than by emphatically insisting that the whole Pleroma dwelt in Christ, and dwelt in Him bodily (i. 19, ii. 9), *i.e.* that the Person of the historical Saviour was the embodiment, the epitome, the sole bearer and mediator from the beginning, of all the Divine life-giving and saving powers. The author, doubtless, did not think of any definite point of time at which the divine Pleroma took up its abode in Christ; certainly he did not date its commencement from the resurrection, since it precedes His atoning death (verse 20), and contains the reason why it was possible for Christ's death to have an influence coextensive with the whole spiritual world. This doctrine, too, of the cosmic influence of the atoning death of Christ is intimately connected with the gnosticising Christology of this Epistle, while it is entirely foreign to the original Pauline doctrine, which, indeed, has no room for it. For in conformity with Paul's doctrines the atoning death of Christ could only have reference to mankind, with whom Christ, as the prototypal Head of the race and by the assumption of a human body, is united by such bonds of solidarity that it was possible for Him to die for them as their representative (2 Cor. v. 19 ff.; Rom. viii. 3), whereas He was not connected in any such way with the world of spirits. On the other hand, it is a characteristically Gnostic idea that through the fall of certain spiritual beings a cleft, a division, has been made in the divine Pleroma, the consequences of which are felt upon earth, so that the redemption of men through the divine saviour can only take place simultaneously with the restoration of the cosmic harmony, with the reconciliation or overcoming of spiritual powers who are opposed to God. We find the same thought also in the Epistle to the Colossians, and in the twofold form which we have indicated: according to i. 20, all things in heaven and earth have been reconciled again through and to Christ;

according to ii. 14 f., God "has blotted out the handwriting in ordinances which was against us (the condemning law), put it away and nailed it to the cross, and having spoiled principalities and powers, He made a show of them, leading them in triumph." In this we recognise the Church's transformation of the Gnostic myth of the spiritual powers or archons who rule the different world-spheres, and who are overcome and robbed of their destructive power by the saviour-god. The victory over the hostile spiritual powers is found by this Church gnostic to be accomplished in the death of Christ, since the bond of the law which kept sinful humanity in their thrall is annulled by the atoning death—a combination of the Pauline (Gal. iii. 13) with the Gnostic doctrine of redemption, such as is already hinted at in Heb. ii. 15, and subsequently became the rule in the patristic theology. Under this mythical veil we may discern the true thought that the religious principles of the pre-Christian world (that is, the spiritual powers) have been transcended in Christianity and raised to a higher unity ("reconciled").

If we turn again to the Epistle to the Ephesians, we find there the same gnosticising development of the Pauline Christology and soteriology, only that the metaphysical speculation is less elaborated and the relation of Christ to the Church, with its results for practical religion, comes more into the foreground. But just as the latter is not lacking in Colossians, so in Ephesians there is not lacking the cosmic background and frame for the plan of salvation which is historically realised in the Christian Church. It is true that in Ephesians nothing is said directly of the creation of the world through Christ (in iii. 9 God alone is described as the Creator, since the words "through Jesus Christ" are not genuine), but we find it indirectly implied in the thought, to which we have referred above, of the election of the Church in Christ before the beginning of the world (i. 4). As, according to Col. i. 16 f., Christ was not only the mediator but also the end of the creation, in whom all things have their being, so it is said also in Eph. i. 10 that all things, both heavenly and earthly, are destined to be brought into unity in Christ, and in i. 23 that He "fills all in all." Thus, here also, Christ is a cosmic principle of unity; the only difference is that it is not expressly said that He was so from the first, in virtue of His metaphysical essence; the whole stress lies on the thought that He, having become the Head of the Church in consequence of His redeeming work, shall finally become, in virtue of the saving process which is realised in and through the Church, the Head of the universe, who filleth all in all. That is especially clear in iv. 8 f., where, with a free application of Ps. lxviii. 19, it is said of Christ: "He hath gone up on high; He hath taken captivity (*i.e.* captives) as his spoil, and given gifts unto men. Now that He hath ascended, what is it but that He also descended into the lower parts of the earth? He that descended is the same who hath ascended above the heavens in order that He might fill all things." This passage is undoubtedly based on the same Gnostic myth of the victorious descent to hell and ascent to heaven of the saviour-god to which allusion is also made in Col. ii. 15. Christ has descended from His heavenly home not only to the earth, but also into the regions that lie beneath the earth, that is, into Hades, and from thence has mounted up victoriously through all the heavenly regions, making prisoners, on His way, of all the heavenly powers ("disarmed them and led them in triumph," Col. ii. 15), and has thus subjected all things—heaven, earth, and the under-world—to His authority and filled them with His living power, out of which He now bestows heavenly gifts upon His followers.[1] With this ruling and "filling" of the world by Christ, which is based on historical rather than metaphysical grounds, is connected the peculiar turn which is here given to the conception of the Pleroma. Whereas in Col. i. 19, ii. 9 it is the fulness of the Godhead, of the Divine life-giving powers which have been deposited in Christ as their bearer and epitome, in Ephesians i. 23 the Pleroma is the Christian Church, which is related to Christ as the body to the head, and which therefore is His completion in the sense that it is only in and through it that He becomes in reality what before He was only by vocation—the Head over all things. Christ and the Church thus mutually condition one another: while it is only in connection with Him that the Church is able to fulfil its eternal destiny, so He needs the Church in order, through His fulfilment in her, to become wholly that whereto the love of the Father has destined Him. That which is set up by the Divine decree as the end and

---

[1] With this interpretation of the passage as a reference to the descent to hell, ascent to heaven, and victory over the spiritual powers agrees Klöpper, *Commentary*, p. 127 f. If it is accepted, the Gnostic origin of the conception, which was recognised by Baur and Hilgenfeld, can scarcely be disputed.

goal of providential administration is not Christ alone, but Christ in His organic unity with the Church, or, to say the same thing in another way, the end is the Church as the body of Christ, to which He is the Head which binds together and directs the whole. It is true Christ is called in Colossians also the Head of the Church, which can only grow as God wills by holding fast to Him (i. 18, ii. 19); while, conversely, in Eph. iii. 19 it is the destiny of the Church to be filled with the whole fulness of God, or to grow up to the full manhood of the fulness of Christ (iv. 13), that is, to mature into a perfect organism in which the whole saving power of Christ and of God may come to a fully developed manifestation. There is thus no real opposition between the two schemes of thought, and in both the Gnostic term Pleroma is made use of in a special sense acceptable to the Church; but in one case the application is more doctrinal and Christological (Col.), in the other more practical and soteriological (Eph.).[1]

The saving work of Christ upon earth was that of a peacemaker and messenger of peace, in the double sense that He made peace between the two portions of mankind, who were separated from one another by the dividing wall of the Law, Jews and Gentiles, and also between God and mankind, who were alienated from God by sin. It is to the removal of this twofold enmity that the atonement made by Christ is referred (ii. 11–22). Here, too, the writer follows closely the statements of Colossians (i. 20 ff., ii. 14 ff.), but at the same time he amplifies them from his new point of view—the death of Christ has

[1] *Cf.* Holtzmann, *N.T. Theol.*, ii. 240 ff.

not only made peace between man and God by doing away with the Law and its condemnation, but has also made peace between Jew and Gentile by doing away with the social wall of partition formed by the ritual law, and has thus created by the union of these two parts a new humanity, a new social organism, the mystical body of Christ, or the Church, in which the heathen who were formerly afar off have now access to the Father in *one* spirit, as fellow-citizens of the saints and fellow-members of the household of God. Christianity is therefore, according to our author, the removal of the barriers of the national and ceremonial particularism of Judaism, and the reception of the Gentiles into the covenant relationship of the Old Testament people of God—in short, the universalisation of the Old Testament religion, set free from its national and legal limitations. That was precisely the constant and fundamental view of Christian Hellenism, in which the practical results of Paulinism were preserved, while the arguments of his polemical theology were abandoned, and the relation of Christianity to the Old Testament religion was conceived more simply and more definitely than by Paul. But this deutero-Paulinism is still very far from being Judaistic; even the author of the Epistle to the Ephesians, although a born Jew, will not hear of any special privileges of the Jewish people in the Kingdom of Christ, or of the maintenance of the Jewish ceremonial law, any more than the author of the Epistle to the Hebrews, or the Epistle of Barnabas, or the Gospel of John; he is so far beyond all this that he only speaks of a "so-called circumcision, in the flesh, made with hands," as of something obsolete about which no one troubles himself any more (ii. 11). Like Paul, too, he is quite convinced that our salvation does not come of our own efforts, is not a consequence of our works, but is a gift of God, the work of His grace through faith (ii. 8 f.). Yet he does not speak of justification by faith, and does not make faith the antithesis of works, as Paul had done. It is not, however, because his thinking is more Judaistic than Paul's that he departs from the Pauline conception of justification, but, on the contrary, because this specifically Jewish conception was as foreign to his Hellenistic mode of thought as was the idea, which went along with it, of representative atonement. He sees in Christ's death no longer the expiation of the curse of the Law, but the sacrifice of love, well-pleasing unto God, which He offered, and in which He dedicated Himself for the sake of the Church, in order to consecrate it as His own and God's peculiar possession (v. 2, 25 f.); exactly the same conception will meet us again in the Gospel of John. And just as the saving value of the death of Christ does not rest upon the representative expiation but upon the Saviour's ethical act of love, so its effect is not mediated by the forensic act of imputing righteousness, or pronouncing just, but consists directly in the removal of the polluting consciousness of guilt which separates us from God, in purification, forgiveness of sins, the giving of life to the spiritually dead, the raising up and transference of them to the heavenly world with Christ—in short, in the opening up of free access to the Father for all, for those who before were "afar off" as well as for those who were "nigh," for Gentiles as well as Jews. All these expressions, especially the last, the "drawing nigh and having access to the presence of God," are found in Hebrews also as descriptions of the saving work of Christ.

The appropriation of redemption is effected, according to Ephesians, quite in accordance with Paul, by faith and baptism. Baptism is described in v. 26 as a "washing of water with the word" whereby Christ purifies the Church; the word (of the Gospel) is to be thought of here as the effective power in the purification and consecration, to which the "washing of water" is related as the sacramental means, as in Jn. iii. 5 water and Spirit are associated as the means to the new birth. Faith is the acceptance of the word of truth when heard, of the gospel of salvation. It is the means whereby grace works savingly, since it receives the promised Holy Spirit as the seal of the truth of the Gospel and as an earnest of our inheritance (i. 13 f., ii. 8). Through faith, Christ makes His dwelling in our hearts (iii. 17; *cf.* Jn. xiv. 23), so that we can rejoice in confident access to God (iii. 12; *cf.* Heb. iii. 6, iv. 16, etc.). Of works it is said, indeed, that our deliverance does not come from them, that no man may glory, but alongside of that their great importance is emphasised by the statement that "to walk therein" is the end and aim of our Divine vocation and new creation in Christ (ii. 9 f.). Faith is therefore the fundamental means of salvation, but not the whole, and not the highest end, which is to walk in good works, or in love (v. 2). Therefore the author desires for his readers love with faith, as the most excellent Christian virtues (vi. 23), a combination which is not found in this form in Paul, but which is quite in the spirit of the deutero-Pauline Church theology. Only if Christians are rooted and grounded in love are they able, together with all the saints, to comprehend Christian truth in its full extent, and to know the love of Christ in its full significance, which outstrips intellectual knowledge, and so to attain to complete possession of the fulness of God's salvation (iii. 18 f.). Important, therefore, as is the place which knowledge holds in Christianity, yet its ecclesiastical value is conditioned by the fact that the endeavour after knowledge, and discourse concerning truth, are subordinated to the rule of love, which is concerned to maintain the unity of the Spirit by the bond of peace, in order that all may attain to unity of faith and knowledge of Christ, to the full maturity of manhood which befits the Church as the body of Christ—no longer, like children, allowing themselves to be carried to and fro by every wind of delusive human teaching, but, in constant union with Christ the Head, growing up into Him in all things (iv. 2–16). Thus there is here opposed to the centrifugal tendencies of a subjective Gnosis which tends to split up into many sects, a knowledge and love of truth which finds its bond of peace in the unity of Christian faith and in the Church's loving consciousness of fellowship. And while that deceptive Gnosis was allied with heathen unchastity, and served especially as a cloak for the dark deeds of the orgiastic mystery-cults,[1] our author exhorts his

[1] The connection of v. 6 with the preceding and following warnings against debauchery and shameful deeds of darkness certainly suggests this conjecture. *Cf.*, on this point, E. Pfleiderer, " Heraklitische Spuren in der altchristlichen Literatur," in *Jahrb.*

Christian readers to put off the old man of their former heathen life, and to be renewed in the Spirit of their minds, putting on the new man who after God is created in righteousness and holiness of truth; to have nothing more to do with the unfruitful works of darkness, but to walk as children of light, whose fruit consists in every sort of kindness and righteousness and truth; no longer to indulge in shameful revelries and drunkenness, but to seek inspiration in the united praise and prayer of the Church; and in all things conscientiously to fulfil the obligations of their relation to the community and of their calling. For this he gives more detailed directions in a further elaboration of the list of domestic duties in Colossians, and describes with special care the ideal of Christian marriage, the prototype of which is the union of Christ with the Church, that great and holy Christian mystery which forms the antithesis to the shameful deeds of darkness of the heathen mysteries (iv. 17–vi. 9). In conclusion, he warns them, in an image based on that of 1 Thess. v. 8, to fight the good fight of Christian virtue, which is the more strenuous because we have to contend not merely with flesh and blood, but with the powers of darkness, the evil spirits beneath the heaven (vi. 10–16). This last is a thought peculiar to our Epistle, and differentiates it strikingly from Colossians, in which the fight with the demons is not the permanent duty of Christians, but was victoriously completed in Christ's death: Colossians seeks to overcome the fear of the demons

f. prot. Theol., xiii. 213. The further suggestions made there as to Heracleitic influence in the Epistle to the Ephesians I must leave an open question.

cherished by anxious ascetics; Ephesians, on the other hand, exhorts careless libertines to an earnest and circumspect practice of virtue.

What high significance is attached in our Epistle to the Church we have seen above in the doctrine of Christ, with whom the Church is as closely united as the body with the head, or a wife with a husband, or a building with its foundation-stone and corner-stone. These three images are no doubt derived from Paul, but they acquire an extended significance in Ephesians from the fact that it is no longer, as it usually is in Paul, the individual church, but the Church as a whole, which is in view. But there are also several points of detail in which the thought which underlies these images differs from that of Paul. Whereas in 1 Cor. iii. 11 it is Christ alone who is the foundation of the edifice of the Church, in Eph. ii. 20 ff. the Church has for its foundation the apostles and the (Christian) prophets, while Christ is the cornerstone which binds the whole together. Whereas in 1 Cor. xii. the Church is the body of Christ in the sense that He is thought of as the animating soul of the whole, according to Ephesians and Colossians the Church forms the body dependent on Christ as Head, but at the same time necessary to Him, as the body is necessary to the head to form a complete organism; from the head it receives its unity and the strength and capacity for growth which are ministered to it through all kinds of connective materials, but it also grows up into Him again, and serves, by its increase of strength to the full maturity of manhood, to fulfil, or fully to display, the higher life which dwells in Christ as the Son of God (iv. 12–16).

The figure of marriage suggests that the Church stands to Christ in the voluntary mutual obligations of a union of love. As man and wife become in marriage one flesh, so the Church in conjunction with Christ forms the one "new man" who is created "according to God"; as Christ loved the Church and gave Himself for it, in order to consecrate it for Himself as His pure possession, so the Church must walk in love, as befits the followers and beloved children of God. Next to the purity of the ethical life of all its members, the unity of the fellowship of the Church is to be guarded and furthered; for the Church is one body and one Spirit, it has one Lord, one faith, one baptism, one God. Only by the unbroken unity of all the members with one another and with Christ the Head can the edification of the whole be furthered. To this end serve the various gifts and offices which have been bestowed upon the Church by the exalted Christ: those of apostles, prophets, evangelists, pastors, and teachers (iv. 11). We see here already the beginnings of a fuller organisation of the Christian community, but as yet without strict distinctions of status and clerical authority, such as we meet with a little later in the Pastoral Epistles. Especially noteworthy is the high importance assigned to the prophets in the Church. They appear alongside of the apostles as the foundation of the Church, and as organs of the spirit of revelation, to whom the mystery of the Divine saving purpose, which was hidden from the foundation of the world, is now revealed (ii. 20, iii. 5). They are therefore the continuators of the apostles' work and the agents of a constant immediate Divine revelation in the Church, a view which unmistakably points to the temporal and local nearness of Montanism. Another thing which equally suggests the latter part of the post-apostolic period is the way in which it is asserted of "the holy apostles" that the mystery of the universality of salvation, as designed for Gentiles as well as Jews, was revealed to them as a body, though it is implied, of course, that Paul had a special insight into it. It is obvious that in the apostolic period no one could have spoken in this way of the "holy apostles," least of all Paul himself, who did not ascribe either to himself or to the earlier apostles a specially sacred character in virtue of their office, and who could not possibly have appealed to the whole body of apostles as consentient witnesses for the universal destiny of salvation, and who, finally, though he described himself as the least of the apostles (1 Cor. xv. 9), would not have described himself as less than the least of all Christians, as the author of Ephesians, with the exaggeration of an imitator, has done (Eph. iii. 8). This kind of language was natural only to a Pauline Christian of the second century, for whom the historical relation of Paul to the original apostles was already obscured, and by whom the apostles as a whole were regarded as a harmonious body of a specifically sacred character in virtue of their office.

In view of all these considerations, the Epistle to the Ephesians is to be regarded as a deutero-Pauline writing whose author was similarly circumstanced both as regards time and place to the redactor of the Epistle to the Colossians, which he so closely follows. That he was the same person, as Holtzmann conjectures, is not indeed impossible, since the differences which have been pointed out between them are not too great to be explained by the different character of the false teachers who are opposed in the two cases —Gnostic ascetics in Colossians, Gnostic libertines in Ephesians—but I cannot regard this conjecture as possessing any very great probability. However, little importance attaches to it; the main point is that both Epistles, Colossians in its present form[1] as well as Ephesians, exhibit Christianity in contact with Gnosticism and in process of adjusting its relation thereto, strongly influenced on the one hand by Gnostic speculation, on the other strongly opposing its errors and subversive tendencies from the point of view of the common faith of the Church, and in the name of the Apostle Paul. In their combination of these two sides, as doctrinal and polemic writings at once gnosticising and anti-gnostic, they are very closely related with the Ignatian and Johannine literature, which also probably originated at about the same time and place; while, on the other hand, in the Pastoral Epistles the popularised Church Paulinism wages war against heretical Gnosis, no longer with the weapons of gnosticising theology, but only with those of organised ecclesiastical authority.

[1] See vol. i. for further discussion of the Epistle to the Colossians. —TRANSLATOR.

WRITINGS OF THE PAULINE SCHOOL

CHAPTER XVIII

THE IGNATIAN LETTERS

UNDER the name of Ignatius, Bishop of Antioch, there have come down to us seven letters, addressed respectively to the churches of Ephesus, Magnesia, Tralles, Rome, Philadelphia, Smyrna, and to Polycarp, bishop of Smyrna. Eusebius knew these letters and cited them (*H.E.*, iii. 36) in the above order, which is due to the fact that the first four were written from Smyrna, where the Antiochian bishop made a halt on his way to Rome as a prisoner, the last three, somewhat later, from Troas. In the fourth century these seven letters were interpolated, and the collection was also extended by the addition of six others (to the Antiochians, Tarsians, Philippians, to Hero, an Antiochian deacon, and to a certain Maria of Kassobola, with her letter to Ignatius), making thirteen letters in all, which have been preserved in Greek, Latin, and Armenian. To these were added finally four other letters which are only preserved in Latin—two addressed to the Apostle John and one to the Virgin Mary, with an answer from her. The spuriousness of these last four letters was of course always held by Protestant theologians to be beyond doubt; and there has been unanimity also in regard to the other six letters, not contained in the Eusebian collection, since the scholars Ussher and Voss discovered the Latin (in 1644) and the Greek (in 1646) text of the original collection which was known to Eusebius. Only the letter to the Romans was wanting in these manuscripts, but this was discovered later (1689) in the Antiochian Acts of the Martyrs. Since then, therefore, we have known the Greek original, and a faithful Latin translation, of the seven Epistles which are brought together under the name of Ignatius in Eusebius. Whether these seven, which are in any case the earliest of the "Ignatian" letters, are genuine, or are forgeries like the six, or ten, letters added later, has been, since the famous critical work of Johannes Dallæus (Daillé) (1666) and the reply in defence of the genuineness of the letters by Pearson (1672), the subject of endless controversies. A new impulse to critical investigation was given by Cureton's publication (1846) of the Syriac text of three Ignatian letters, those to Polycarp, the Ephesians, and the Romans (the last-named including a fragment of the Epistle to the Trallians). Bunsen was followed by several other writers in the opinion that in this shortest Syriac collection the genuine original Ignatian letters had been found; it was, however, soon proved beyond a doubt that it was really an excerpt from the "intermediate" collection of seven letters. It is with these, as is now universally acknowledged, that the question of genuineness has to do. Even yet, it is true, no unanimity has been arrived at upon the point, but the majority of scholars are decidedly inclined to recognise the genuineness of these seven letters. I myself, although I previously, in common with the Tübingen critics, contested their genuineness, have been convinced by the very thorough argument of Lightfoot (*Apostolic Fathers*, Pt. II., vol. i., 2nd ed., 1889), and will endeavour here, as briefly as possible, to lay before the reader, that he may examine them for himself, the most decisive reasons in favour of the genuineness of the letters, referring here, once for all, to the relevant section of Lightfoot's work (i. pp. 328-430).

In regard to the external evidence, it cannot be denied that it is so decidedly in favour of genuineness that only the most cogent internal grounds for doubt could stand against it. Most important of all, in this respect, is the letter of Polycarp to the Philippians, which—assuming its genuineness—was written only a few weeks after the journey of Ignatius through Smyrna and Troas, whence his letters are dated, and thus ranks as the evidence of a contemporary and eye-witness. In this letter there are not merely a number of reminiscences of, and allusions to, the Ignatian letters, but also the following direct mention of them (xiii.): "We have sent you, according to your request, the letters of Ignatius to us (viz. those to Polycarp and to the church at Smyrna), along with all the others which we have by us; they accompany the present letter. Ye will be able to profit much by them, for they contain faith and patience and every kind of edification relating to our Lord. Whatsoever ye have yourselves heard concerning Ignatius and his companions we beg you to communicate to us." Polycarp therefore possessed, in addition to the two letters of Ignatius addressed to himself and his church, several others in addition, probably the four which Ignatius had written from Smyrna to the Ephesians, Magnesians, Trallians, and Romans, of which it would seem that the Smyrnæans had taken copies before they were despatched. Of all these letters echoes are found in Polycarp's letter, but not of the letter to the Philadelphians; which may be naturally explained from the fact that this letter, written from Troas, would not be known to Polycarp like the six others. It is also noteworthy that Polycarp, in the same chapter (xiii.) promises the Philippians that he will, in accordance with their wish and that of Ignatius, deliver their letter to Syria, either in person or by a messenger. What this letter of the Philippians was, we are not told here, but we learn from the letters of Ignatius to Polycarp (viii.) and to the Smyrnæans (xi.), in which these, and all churches, are directed to send by envoys or letters to the Antiochian church congratulations on the restoration of peace there. Thus an incidental and in itself obscure reference in the Epistle of Polycarp finds its explanation in the Ignatian letters; that tells undoubtedly not in favour of forgery, but of genuineness. But in other respects also the simple letter of Polycarp, which has also the testimony of Irenæus in its favour, is far from making the impression of a pseudonymous "tendency-writing"; it would, indeed, be difficult to say in the interest of what tendency it could have been forged. Could it have been to authenticate the forged Ignatian letters? But in that case it must have been written by the same hand as these, and that is impossible, since the style in the two cases is entirely different; of the bold originality of the Ignatian letters, the simple letter of Polycarp shows not a trace.

Further patristic evidence in favour of the Ignatian letters is found in Irenæus and Origen. The former quotes (*Adv. Hær.*, V. xxviii. 4) the passage from *Rom.* iv.: "As one of our men said when he was condemned for confessing God to be thrown to the wild beasts, 'I am the wheat of Christ, and shall be ground by the teeth of the wild beasts, that I may be found to be pure bread.'" This saying is too characteristically Ignatian to have been derived from any other source than the Ignatian Epistle to the Romans. Why Irenæus only speaks of "one of our men" and does not name Ignatius, we do not know; and it is equally impossible to explain why, in his polemic against the heretics, he never appealed directly to Ignatius, even where he has very close analogies with the thoughts and words of the latter. (*Cf.*, *e.g.*, the comparison of heresy with a sweet-tasting poison in *Trall.* vi. with Iren., *Adv. Hær.*, I. xxvii 4; regarding the difficulty of converting heretics, *Smyrn.* iv., *cf.* Iren., III. ii. 3; regarding the "insubstantiality" of the Docetics, *Smyrn.* ii. and *Trall.* x. with Iren., IV. xxxiii. 5). In Origen we find two quotations from the Ignatian letter to the Romans: (1) in his treatise on prayer, in cap. xx.: "'Nothing that is visible is good' (*Rom.* iii.), since it has only seeming and not true being"; (2) in his preface to the Song of Solomon: "I remember that one of the saints, named Ignatius, said of Christ, 'My love is crucified' (*Rom.* vii.), and I cannot blame him for the word." Origen's interpretation of this saying as a reference to Christ does not correspond to the sense of the original,[1] where the reference is to the slaying of earthly passion in Ignatius, but this misunderstanding, which in a quotation made from memory is easily intelligible, cannot overthrow the fact that it is a quotation from the Ignatian letter to the Romans. There is a quotation, too, from the Ignatian letter to the Ephesians in Origen's homily on Luke: "Excellently is it written in a letter of one of the martyrs (I mean Ignatius, who in succession to the blessed Peter was second bishop of Antioch, and who in the persecution fought with beasts at Rome): 'And the virginity of Mary remained hidden from the prince of this world' (Eph. xix.)." In regard to Eusebius it has been remarked above that he cites our seven Ignatian letters in chronological order (*H.E.*, iii. 36); in the same passage there are verbal quotations from the letters to the Romans and Smyrnæans, and from Polycarp's letter to the Philippians. In spite of the preference which is undoubtedly given in these patristic quotations to the letter to the Romans, it is impossible to separate it from the other six as the only genuine one, as Renan wished to do; and still more impossible to deny genuineness to it alone (Völter, Bruston); according to external testimony, not less than inner criteria, all seven letters belong together so inseparably that they must stand or fall together.

Besides the direct patristic evidence, we have to notice an indirect testimony from profane literature. The satirist Lucian, a Syrian by birth, who about the middle of the second century lived at Antioch in the

---

[1] It has been defended in recent times, notably by Dr C. Bigg.
—TRANSLATOR.

practice of his profession as a lawyer, and made many journeys both in the east and west of the Empire, describes in his writing *De Morte Peregrini* the career of a religious enthusiast who first became a Christian, afterwards a Cynic, and finally, from fanaticism and thirst for glory, at the Olympian games (in the year 165) solemnly burnt himself to death before all the people. How much historical matter underlies this satirical romance may be left an open question; but in any case many traits in this biography are based on actual customs and occurrences which Lucian must have observed among the Cynics and Christians of his time.[1] Among them are several which apply so exactly to Ignatius of Antioch and his experiences and actions during his captivity that it may be inferred with much probability that Lucian was acquainted with the Ignatian letters. He tells of Peregrinus that as a Christian he had taken a prominent position as prophet and " president of the synagogue" in the church to which he belonged, had expounded its sacred Scriptures and made many new ones himself, and, by those who believed in him, had been honoured "as a god" (Ignatius was named Theophorus, *i.e.* bearer of God) and lawgiver and leader. When on account of his Christianity he was thrown into prison in Syria, the Christians left no means of freeing him untried, or at least, when it became evident that this was impossible, of mitigating his condition as much as possible.

[1] *Cf.* Zeller's essay, "Alexander und Peregrinus. Ein Betrüger und ein Schwärmer" (a Deceiver and an Enthusiast), in *Vorträge und Abhandl.*, ii. 173-187. Also Bernays, *Lucian und die Cyniker*, 1879.

From early morning the old women who were called "widows," were to be seen waiting at the doors of his prison, accompanied by orphan children; nay more, the office-bearers of the church had obtained permission, by bribing the jailors, to spend the whole night with the prisoner, in order at the common meal to speak their holy words. In addition to this, from various cities of Asia deputies of the Christian churches had been sent to support the prisoner with consolation and counsel. When he was set free again he travelled about, always accompanied by a troop of believers as by a bodyguard, who provided abundantly for all his needs. Later on, Peregrinus, in consequence of coming into conflict with the dietary laws of the Christians, broke with them and became a Cynic. In this character he sailed from Troas to Italy, and immediately on landing publicly delivered invectives against all and sundry, but especially against the Emperor, from whose well-known clemency he had no punishment to fear except that of being excluded from the city. His efforts to obtain the glory of martyrdom having thus come to nothing, Peregrinus, when all other means of attracting attention failed, publicly announced that at the next Olympic festival he would have himself burnt alive, in order, like a second Hercules, to teach men by his example contempt of death. Before carrying out this self-immolation with a view to apotheosis, Peregrinus, so the story goes, sent missives to almost all the famous cities, containing his last will ("testaments"), with exhortations and directions, and appointed some of his companions to the duty of delivering them, whom he called "ambassadors of death" and "couriers of Hades." Now this historical romance unmistakably presents several points of analogy with the situation implied in the Ignatian letters: the hero takes a high position as a leader among his fellow-believers and is honoured like a god; he is thrown into prison in Syria on account of his faith; the believers crowd into the presence of the prisoner, bribing the guards; the churches in the various cities of Asia send envoys to greet and support him; he travels about surrounded by a whole bodyguard of friends; he journeys from Troas to Italy; he displays his courage as a confessor in the presence of the Emperor; he covets the martyr's crown; he desires, by a free-will offering of himself, to imitate his saviour-god and set up a standard of virtue for men; he sends before his death missives containing his last wishes and exhortations to various cities; he appoints for this purpose special messengers, to whom he gives the names "ambassadors of death" and "couriers of Hades" (an obvious parody on the "ambassadors of God" and "couriers of God" who, according to *ad Polyc.* vii. and *Smyrn.* xi., were to be sent as deputies of the churches to Syria). It is hardly possible to suppose that such numerous and striking analogies are accidental. If, however, they are based on the acquaintance of Lucian with Ignatius, his fellow-countryman, this is an evidence of the genuineness of the Ignatian letters which is of equal weight with that of Polycarp's letter, and the consonance of the two is the more weighty since they are wholly independent of one another. To invalidate external testimony of this strength, only the strongest internal grounds of doubt would be sufficient. Are there really such grounds? Will those which are alleged stand a close scrutiny?

The critical doubts which, from the time of Dallæus up to the present, have been raised regarding the genuineness of these letters, refer partly to the external situation in which these letters are supposed to have been written, partly to the polemic against false teachers which they contain, partly to the organisation of Church life which they recommend, and partly to the character and language of the author. A discussion of these four points will suffice to characterise the Ignatian letters, so that we may spare ourselves the wearisome analysis of the contents of each individual letter.

(1) *The Situation of the Writer.*—Ignatius, condemned at Antioch to fight with beasts in the arena, is sent as a prisoner, under the guard of ten soldiers, to Rome. The journey is made overland through Asia Minor, and a rather long halt is made at Smyrna, and again at Troas. In Smyrna, Ignatius meets the deputies of the church of Ephesus (its bishop, Onesimus, with four companions), of Magnesia (its bishop, Damas, with two presbyters and one deacon), and of Tralles (the bishop, Polybius), who came to convey to the martyr the sympathy of their churches. In gratitude for their greeting he wrote from Smyrna to thank the churches in question, warning them in his letters against being misled by itinerant teachers of error, and exhorting them to unanimity and obedience to the bishops and presbyters. From Smyrna, too, he wrote his letter to the Romans, in order to inform them of his approaching arrival and

THE IGNATIAN LETTERS 333

to warn them not to rob him by their intercession of the martyrdom which he coveted. He then proceeded on his journey to Troas, where another halt was made. This respite the prisoner made use of to write three further letters, to the churches of Philadelphia and Smyrna, and to the bishop of the latter, Polycarp. The occasion for these letters was furnished by the news, which had in the meantime reached Ignatius, of the favourable turn which matters had taken at Antioch. Whereas in the four earlier letters he had begged those addressed to intercede for his orphaned church, he now urges the Philippians and Smyrnæans to send to Antioch, by envoys and letters, their congratulations on the restoration of peace (this probably refers to the cessation of the persecution). How Ignatius had received news of the restoration of peace at Antioch we nowhere learn directly. It may, however, be supposed that the news was brought by the deacons Philo of Cilicia and Rheius Agathopus from Syria, who had followed Ignatius by way of Philadelphia and Smyrna (*cf. Phil.* xi. and *Smyrn.* x.), but had only overtaken him in Troas.

In taking a general view of all these circumstances, we certainly do not receive the impression of artificial invention; and none of the particulars give solid grounds for critical difficulty. That Christians were condemned to fight with beasts, and that such condemned persons were brought from the provinces to Rome, is a well-known fact; and that a prisoner might on the journey enjoy so much freedom as to receive his friends without hindrance and to write letters, will not strike us as improbable if we recall the freedom permitted to Paul in Rome (Acts xxviii.

31), or the description in the apocryphal Acts of Paul of the uninterrupted intercourse of the Christians with the imprisoned Apostle, or the later Acts of Martyrs, such as those of Perpetua and Felicitas, or Lucian's account of the imprisonment of Peregrinus, to whom his Christian admirers procured access both by day and night by bribing the jailors (*cf.* with this the indication in *Rom.* v. that the guards, in spite of the fees they received, became more and more harsh). As regards the route of travel, overland through Asia Minor, I may refer to the arguments of Zahn (*Ignazius von Antiochia*, pp. 250–294) and Lightfoot (*ut sup.*, p. 361 ff.), who not only furnish a satisfactory solution of the difficulties which are raised in regard to this point, but also show how from a multitude of minute unconscious indications a consistent picture of the situation may be obtained, which could never be the case if we were dealing with an artificial invention.

(2) *Polemic against Heretics.*—In all the other Ignatian letters except those to Polycarp and the Romans, opposition to dangerous heretics forms a principal portion of the contents. The error combated consists partly of Gnostic docetism, partly, it would seem, of Judaism. In this connection the difficult question arises whether these were two separate heresies, or whether a single heresy is in view which united these two errors. Lightfoot defends the latter view with arguments which deserve the most careful attention. In general, he truly remarks, the language remains essentially the same in all the various passages which deal with the false teachers, even if in some cases it is their Docetism which is

more prominent, or, as in the letters to the Magnesians and Philadelphians, it is the Judaism which is chiefly in view. This is in itself decidedly in favour of the assumption of one and the same heresy, and this impression is strengthened if we examine more closely the attacks which are specially directed against Judaism.

Ignatius exhorts the Magnesians (viii. ff.) not to allow themselves to be led astray by false opinions and useless ancient myths, for if they still continued to live in Judaism they were denying the grace (of Christ). " The prophets themselves lived according to the faith in Christ Jesus, and were persecuted on that account, because they were inspired by His grace, that the unbelieving might be convinced that there is one God, who hath revealed Himself through Jesus Christ His Son, who is His Logos, proceeding forth out of silence, who was well-pleasing in all things unto Him who had sent Him. But if those who had grown up in ancient (Jewish) things came to newness of hope (to the Christian hope of salvation), so that they no longer kept the Sabbath, but lived according to the standard of the Lord's Day, on which our life dawned through Him and His death, which some deny—this mystery of our faith for the sake of which we suffer, in order to prove ourselves the disciples of our sole Master Jesus Christ—how could *we* live without Him? For the prophets themselves were His disciples in the spirit, inasmuch as they expected Him as their teacher, wherefore He on whom they justly hoped has, on His coming, raised them from the dead. Let us therefore not be insensible to His goodness; for if He should treat us as we (in our despising of His grace) treat Him, there would be an end of us at once! Therefore, seeing we have once become His disciples, let us learn to live in accordance with Christianity. For he who calls himself by any other name than this, is not of God. Therefore put away the evil leaven, which is old and perished, and turn to the new leaven, which is Christ! It is foolish to take the name of Jesus Christ into the mouth and yet play the Jew. Christianity has not come to believe in Judaism, but Judaism to believe in Christianity!" All this he says to his readers, not with the idea that some of them are already on this false way, but in order to warn them against the snares of error. They must be firmly convinced of the birth and suffering and resurrection (of Jesus) under Pontius Pilate, as of certain and indubitable facts. From this close of the polemic it is clear that the same false teachers whom Ignatius charges, on account of their addiction to Jewish fables, with living as Jews, were also Docetics, who as Gnostics (that is the other name which they preferred to the name of Christians) denied the reality of the birth, suffering, and resurrection of Jesus. It cannot, therefore, be simple Judaisers of the old kind, who were anxious to maintain the Mosaic law, that are here in view; the reference is obviously to those Gnostics whose teaching consisted chiefly of Jewish "myths," that is to say, of a syncretistic allegorical interpretation of the Old Testament, and who had, therefore, been Jewish heretics before they became Christian heretics, as was very often the case with the earlier Syrian Gnostics. Ignatius contrasts their mythico-allegorical misinterpretation of the Old

THE IGNATIAN LETTERS

Testament with the Christian interpretation, according to which the ancient prophets were inspired by the grace of Christ and looked to Him as the coming deliverer; therefore they serve as witnesses of the oneness of God, who has revealed Himself by His Son, the Logos who proceeded forth out of silence, *i.e.* the sole mediator of revelation; they serve, therefore, to refute the false teachers who, by their myths about a host of intermediate beings, endanger both the oneness of God and the unique significance of the revelation in Christ.

The same conclusion is suggested by the polemic in the letter to the Philadelphians, among whom, while matters had not come to a split in the church, there had been "a sifting" (by the expulsion of certain false teachers). "Be not deceived," cries Ignatius (iii.), "he who follows a schismatic ($\sigma\chi i\zeta o\nu\tau\iota$) shall not inherit the Kingdom of God; he who follows a false belief is not in accord with the sufferings of Christ (rejects their religious significance). Therefore all must hold fast to the one eucharist, since it is the one and uniting flesh and blood of Christ"; as Ignatius himself had taken refuge in the Gospel as the flesh of Christ, and in the apostles as the presbytery of the Church. "And the prophets moreover we love because they too looked forward to the Gospel in their preaching, and hoped in Him; in whom also they believed and were saved, in union with Jesus Christ. But if anyone offers you Jewish stuff, do not listen to him. For it is better to hear Christianity from a circumcised man than Judaism from one who is uncircumcised. But if both speak not of Jesus Christ, they are merely tombstones on which are inscribed the names of men. . . . I trust in the grace of Jesus Christ, who shall set you free from every fetter. But I warn you, do nothing from party spirit, but according to the teaching of Christ. I have heard some of you saying, 'If I find it not in the archives (ἀρχείοις = authoritative writings, especially those of the Old Testament), I believe it not in the Gospel.' And when I said to them, 'It is written,' they answered, 'That is just the question.' But Jesus Christ is for me the archives; the unassailable archives are His cross and His death and His resurrection, and the faith which He founded; it is in them that I desire to find my justification. Good indeed are the (Old Testament) priests, but better is the (Christian) High-priest, to whom has been committed the Holy of Holies, the mysteries of God. He alone is the door of the Father through which enter in Abraham and Isaac and Jacob, the prophets and apostles, and the whole Church; all these come into the unity of God. But the Gospel has something better than the rest—the coming of the Saviour, our Lord Jesus Christ, His passion and resurrection. For the prophets who are dear unto us prophesied of Him, but the Gospel brings the fulfilment, even life incorruptible." This passage is very instructive as an indication of the character of these heretics. There were among them persons who were not circumcised, and who nevertheless offered in their discourses Jewish matter. These cannot possibly have been genuine Jews, zealous for the law, for circumcision and the rest; but yet the matter of their discourses appeared Judaistic to Ignatius, inasmuch as it rested upon an allegorical interpretation of the Old Testament

Scriptures, and had the effect of depotentiating Christ and His death and resurrection. Whether this Jewish Gnosticism was set forth by a Jew or a Gentile, Ignatius cared not; his concern was whether they taught Christ or not. In the latter case all these proud Gnostics were in his eyes mere tombstones which bore as their inscriptions only the empty names of the dead. Their appeal to the decisive authority of venerable "archives"—by which, along with the Old Testament, they may have meant apocryphal writings, such as the apocalypses and Justin's "Gnosis of Baruch," etc.—made no impression upon Ignatius. Highly as he esteemed the Old Testament—its patriarchs and prophets were included for him in the one Church of God, which through Christ has obtained redemption and eternal life—it has its significance for him only as a prediction of Christ which was fulfilled in the Gospel. In the Old Testament, so understood, he found every tenet of his Christian faith "written," *i.e.* witnessed beforehand by holy oracles. If, however, his Gnostic opponents would not admit this use of the Old Testament, if they interpreted the passages in which he found his faith written differently—namely, on the lines of their Gnostic mythology—Ignatius, as a practical follower of Paul, abandoned the letter of the "archives" to the strife of exegetes and allegorists, and held to Christ alone, whose death and resurrection were for him the "unassailable archives" which he placed in contrast with all the myths, allegories, and shadowy figures of the Jewish-Christian Gnostics as the sole truth.

If we have thus established that the heretical

teachers attacked by Ignatius did not belong to two different sects, but were adherents of one and the same heresy, namely Jewish Gnostics, for whom, however, Judaism did not consist, as in the case of the earlier Judaisers, in the strict observance of the law, but in deriving their myths from the allegorical interpretation of the Old Testament Scriptures, the way is now prepared for the attempt to determine more exactly from the indications in the remaining letters their historical position. The letter to the Smyrnæans begins by placing emphatically in the forefront the Christological confession that our Lord was truly of David's race according to the flesh, and the Son of God according to the Divine will and power (*cf.* Rom. i. 3 f.), truly born of the virgin, baptized by John in order to fulfil all righteousness, truly crucified for us under Pontius Pilate, in order by His resurrection to set up His cross as an ensign for His united Church, which was to be formed out of both Jews and Gentiles. "All these sufferings He endured for our sakes, and He truly endured them, as also He truly raised Himself up;[1] it is not true, as some unbelievers affirm, that His sufferings were mere appearance (τὸ δοκεῖν), it is they who are mere appearance, and according to their opinions so it shall happen unto them, they will be incorporeal phantoms (οὖσιν ἀσωμάτοις καὶ δαιμονικοῖς). For I know and believe in Him as having after His resurrection

---

[1] ἀνέστησεν ἑαυτόν, a formula which is not found in the New Testament, and is at variance with the Pauline conception of the resurrection as a mighty deed wrought upon Christ, but which is in material agreement with Jn. v. 26, x. 18. *Cf.* also the usual formula in cap. vi.

existed in the flesh; as a corporeal man He ate and drank after His resurrection with His disciples, although He was spiritually united with the Father. Therefore I would fain warn you against beasts in human form; receive them not; avoid if possible every meeting with them; only pray for them, if perchance they may be converted; difficult as that is, it is within the power of Jesus Christ, our true life. If it was only in appearance that these things were done to our Lord, then I am only fettered in appearance; wherefore then have I delivered myself over to death? I can do all things because He, the perfect man, makes me strong. Some deny Him in ignorance, or rather are denied by Him, for they are advocates of death rather than of truth; they have not allowed themselves to be convinced by prophecy nor by the law of Moses, nor, up till now, even by the Gospel, nor by our manifold sufferings. What profits it if a man praises me but slanders my Lord, not confessing Him as having borne our flesh (σαρκοφόρον); such an one has wholly denied Him and is a corpse-bearer (νεκροφόρος). Their unbelieving names I have not thought fit even to write, and I will remember them no more until they have been converted to the sufferings (of Christ), which are our resurrection. Let no man deceive himself. Even the heavenly beings and the glory of the angels and the principalities, both visible and invisible, if they believe not in the blood of the God Christ, only judgment awaits them. He that can receive it, let him receive it! Let none be puffed up because of his office. Faith and love are everything, there is nothing better than these. Mark those who think falsely in regard to the grace of Jesus Christ, how they are (also in practice) opposed to the will of God; they take no thought for brotherly love nor about widows, orphans, the oppressed, the imprisoned, the hungry and thirsty; they hold aloof from the eucharist and from (united) prayer, because they do not acknowledge that the eucharist is the flesh of our Saviour Jesus Christ, which flesh suffered for our sins, and was raised up by the Father through His goodness" (vi.). This polemic against Gnostic docetism is found also in the letter to the Trallians ix. and x., and in some passages of the letter to the Ephesians, *e.g.* cap. vii., where the readers are warned against those who bear the Christian name in base deceit, doing deeds unworthy of God, and, like mad dogs, are hard to cure. Wherein their error consisted is clear from the Christological confession which Ignatius opposes to them: "One is the physician (saviour), who is fleshly and spiritual, born and unborn, God who has appeared in man (or, "in the flesh"), true life in death, (born) of Mary as well as of God, first suffering,[1] then impassible, Jesus Christ our Lord."

From all these passages it is clear that Ignatius was not opposing mere general tendencies but definite persons, whose names he could have named (*Symrn.* v.), whose heretical opinions and schismatic conduct he knew exactly and hated thoroughly. He cannot have acquired this knowledge in his short sojourns in

[1] *Cf.* Polycarp iii., τὸν ἄχρονον, τὸν ἀόρατον, τὸν δι' ἡμᾶς ὁρατόν, τὸν ἀψηλάφητον, τὸν ἀπαθῆ, τὸν δι' ἡμᾶς παθητόν. The different position of the human predicates in the passage above may be explained from its anti-docetic purpose.

a few churches of Asia Minor during his imprisonment, but only during his former official activity as bishop at Antioch; it is there, in the chief city of Syria, which had long been the headquarters of the Gnostic syncretism, that we must seek the home of the heretics whom Ignatius attacks. That was the home of the Ophites or Naasenes, an originally Jewish-heathen Gnostic sect, whose teaching first came into contact and rivalry with Christianity through the Simonians. But parallel with, or shortly after, the libertine Simonians, there flourished at Antioch the important school of Menander, represented by the two influential teachers Saturninus and Basilides. Both[1] were, according to Irenæus' account, docetics, Saturninus the more decidedly so, since he held the deliverer, Christ, to be an unborn, incorporeal, formless divine being, who had only seemingly ($\delta o\kappa\acute{\eta}\sigma\epsilon\iota$) appeared as man, and so could not really suffer and rise again. But according to Basilides, too, the heavenly Christ-spirit who appeared on earth in the form of Jesus had no part in the sufferings; they were borne by Simon of Cyrene, who was magically substituted for him. Thus both these Gnostic teachers denied the reality of the bodily humanity, of the birth, the death, and the resurrection of the divine deliverer Christ; both rejected the belief in a crucified redeemer and the hope of a bodily resurrection of the faithful. Where, then, we find that Ignatius expressly emphasises the thought that the Redeemer is as truly spiritual as corporeal, as truly born as unborn, God manifested in man, and especially that he truly suffered and died,

[1] *Cf.* the description given above (p. 143 ff.); and see Kreyenbühl, *Das Evangelium der Wahrheit*, i. 331 ff.

truly rose again, and after the resurrection was still in the flesh; finally, when he threatens those who denied this bodily humanity of the Redeemer with the fate of becoming themselves incorporeal demons, that is, ghostly phantoms such as they held Christ to be, the direct reference to the heresy of these Antiochian Gnostics is not to be mistaken. No other Gnostic teachers, except perhaps Marcion (who is out of the question from considerations of date and place), taught such decided docetism as these two Antiochians, Saturninus and Basilides; in the Valentinian schools, and still more by Carpocrates and Cerinthus, this docetism was materially limited. Lightfoot (*Ap. F.*, II. i. 382, ed. 2) truly observes that "the strongly marked type of docetism assailed in the Ignatian letters, so far from being a difficulty, is rather an indication of early date, since the tendency in docetism was to become less pronounced as time went on."

A further clear allusion to the Basilidean Gnosis is found in the letter to the Trallians, where (v.) Ignatius says that he could well have written to them of heavenly things, but he fears that they are not yet mature enough to bear them; they would be choked by such strong food. Then he continues: "For I am not a disciple (of Christ) because I am in bonds and because I am able to understand heavenly things and the spatial order of the angels and the hosts of the powers that rule the world. For we are still far from being secure of not losing God." Now this theory of the heavenly principalities and their spatial distribution over the 365 heavenly regions is a peculiar doctrine of the earlier Basilidean system as described by Irenæus,[1] and the reference to it here by Ignatius can therefore scarcely be denied. It is found also in the passage cited above from *Smyrn.* vi., in which the heavenly beings and the glory of the angels and the visible and invisible principalities are threatened with judgment, if they do not believe in the blood of the God Christ. These Gnostic spiritual powers have for Christian faith so little independent existence that they on their part need redemption, and can only obtain it in the same way as the Church, namely, by faith in the blood of Christ, the atoning power of which extends throughout the whole cosmic spiritual realm, because it is the blood of the self-offering of a God who has appeared in the flesh—a view which has its nearest parallels in the Gnostic Christology of Colossians. In both cases it is a proof of the extent to which the orthodox opponents of the heretical Gnosis were themselves under the influence of Gnosticising conceptions.

What Ignatius says, too, regarding the moral conduct of the false teachers whom he attacks, as well as what he does not say, agrees very well with what we know from other sources regarding the Antiochian Gnostics of the time of Hadrian. Had they been libertine Simonians, or Valentinians, or Carpocratians, their orthodox opponent would certainly not have neglected to hold up to reprobation an exhaustive catalogue of their crimes. Instead of that, the worst he can say of them is that they are

[1] Kreyenbühl (*ut sup.*, p. 336) calls attention to the fact that in the Latin translation of Irenæus, I. xxiv. 7, the exact linguistic equivalent of τοποθεσίαι ἀγγελικαί is found, viz. *cœlorum locales positiones.*

lacking in zeal in the philanthropic activities of the Church, and that they hold aloof from the eucharist because they do not believe in the sacramental presence of the flesh and blood of Christ (*Smyrn.* vi.). That is intelligible enough in the case of a docetic sect which was excessively pleased with itself for its esoteric Gnosis (and magic), shut itself off in its secret organisation from the body of the Church, and did not wish to be considered either Jewish or Christian,[1] exactly as is reported of the Basilideans. As regards Saturninus, however, he enjoyed the reputation of a peculiarly ascetic sanctity, because he counted sexual intercourse and the use of flesh meat as among the works of the devil, from which the redeemed must abstain, a strictness which, according to Irenæus, made such an impression upon his contemporaries that many were won to him by it. Now, it lies in the nature of things, and has repeatedly been experienced in practice, that the *nimbus* of the ascetics constitutes a danger to the authority of the regular ecclesiastical offices. Ignatius, as bishop of Antioch, seems to have had an experience of this kind with his contemporary and fellow-countryman, Saturninus: an inference which is warranted by a remark in the letter to Polycarp (v.): "If any is able to continue steadfast in chastity to the honour of the Lord's flesh (*i.e.* dedicating his body in virgin purity to the Lord; *cf.* 1 Cor. vi. 15 and vii. 34), let him persevere therein without glorying overmuch. If he glory in it, he is lost; and if he stands in higher respect than the bishop, he is

---

[1] An allusion to the fact that the heretics gave themselves a distinctive name, viz. that of "Gnostics," is found in *Magn.* x.

destroyed!"[1] We see from this that to the champion of ecclesiastical order the ascetic reputation of his Gnostic opponents was almost as fatal a crime as their dogmatic extravagances; moreover, these two characteristics, the ethical mortification of the flesh and the dogmatic denial of the reality of the flesh of Christ, were very closely connected, and it must be admitted that, in this, simple logical consistency was rather on the side of the heretics than on that of the Church, which, both in theory and in practice, was confronted with the difficult task of reconciling contradictions by ingenious compromises.

Ignatius himself, indeed, was too little of a theologian and too much of a Churchman by temperament to trouble much about the conceptual unity of the opposite sides of his Christian belief, both of which were valued and indispensable postulates of his religious feeling. On the one hand, he shared with the Gnosticism and mysticism of his time the presupposition that Christ was a superhuman and supratemporal divine being of the same kind as the saviour-gods of the various cultus-associations, each of whom was held by his adherents to be the most effectual mediator of the divine power and pledge of imperishable life. On the other side, however, it was equally certain and important to him that the God Christ had revealed Himself in the truly human life and death and bodily resurrection of the Jesus of the Gospel record. He therefore simply

[1] This interpretation of the words ἐὰν γνωσθῇ πλέον τοῦ ἐπισκόπου I hold with Zahn (against Lightfoot) to be the only possible. (Lightfoot interprets: "If his vow be made known to others besides the bishop."—TRANSLATOR.)

combined the two sides as antithetic predicates of one and the same subject: flesh and spirit, God and man, supra-temporal and temporal, unborn and born, impassible and suffering. In this the elements of the Church dogma of the "God-man" were doubtless already given, the problem was set for theology, but Ignatius himself had not yet apprehended it as such; he had not reflected on the difficulty of the intellectual reconciliation of the two sides, but grasped them by a bold synthesis in an image of the intuitive imagination. He was thus able to use with perfect freedom formulæ which at a later date were challenged as heretical; he could speak as innocently of "one God Jesus Christ," of the birth, suffering, or blood of "the God Christ"[1] as of the "perfect, or the new, man, Jesus Christ,"[2] without being conscious of any Monarchian, Patripassian, or Ebonite implications. With the same freedom he often uses Gnostic technical terms, which later fell under suspicion as watchwords of certain heretical systems, whereas in Ignatius' time they were still without dangerous associations and were the common property of all circles. Of this kind is the much-canvassed passage in *Magn.* viii.: "The sole God has revealed Himself through Jesus Christ His Son, who is His Logos, proceeding forth out of silence, who in all things was well-pleasing to Him who sent Him."[3] In this, its original, form the

[1] *Eph., Inscr.* vii., xv., xviii.; *Rom., Inscr.,* iii., vi.; *Smyrn.* i.; *ad Polyc.* viii.

[2] *Smyrn.* iv.; *Eph.* xx.

[3] According to the genuine reading, ὅς ἐστιν αὐτοῦ λόγος <ἀΐδιος, οὐκ> ἀπὸ σιγῆς προελθών. The words in brackets are a later interpolation. See Lightfoot, ii. 126.

phrase is not a polemical allusion to the Valentinian doctrine of the Æons, and does not refer at all to the transcendental origin of the Logos, but only expresses the idea that the revelation of God through His Son as His personal word or organ of revelation for the world, followed upon the Divine "silence" or "quietude," *i.e.* absence of revelation. The "Sigē" is therefore not yet here, as in the Valentinian system, a personified Æon, but it might be said that we see here the first movement in the direction of the personification of that conception. Of this kind, too, is the passage in *Eph.* xix. : "And there was hidden from the Prince of this world the virginity of Mary and her child-bearing, as well as the death of the Lord, three mysteries to be cried aloud (lit. "mysteries of crying," μυστήρια κραυγῆς) which were accomplished in the stillness of God. How, then, have they been revealed to the Æons? A star shone in heaven above all the stars, and its light was ineffable, and its newness aroused surprise; the other stars along with the sun and moon formed a chorus about this star; it surpassed them all in its light, and men were alarmed at this new appearance. From that time all magic was destroyed, and every bond of evil disappeared, ignorance was done away with, the ancient empire fell in ruins, when God was made manifest as man, unto newness of eternal life, and that which was prepared by God had its beginning." This whole passage has a "Gnostic colouring" (Lightfoot); the Æons to which the mystery of the supernatural birth is made known by the miraculous star, are at least nearer to the Gnostic signification than to the ordinary sense of the term; like the Sigē, they are on the way to their Gnostic personification. The description of the miraculous star for which all the other stars, with the sun and moon, formed a chorus, sounds like a Gnostic myth, which is probably related to the narrative in Mt. ii. as the source rather than the elaboration of the latter. The appearance of the destruction of magic in conjunction with that of ignorance, as consequences of the Incarnation, is very characteristic of the position, at once Gnosticising and anti-Gnostic, of the Antiochian bishop, who recognised, indeed, that the light of true knowledge of divine things had dawned in Christianity, while condemning the caricature of Christian knowledge in unethical magic, such as was practised especially by the Basilideans, as a remnant of the disappearing heathenism, of the falling kingdom of Satan. We are also reminded of the Gnostic manner of speech by the expression Pleroma, which, however, in the superscriptions of the letters to the Ephesians and Trallians is translated, so to speak, from the Gnostic into a popular sense. Lightfoot well remarks, in regard to these and similar expressions (*ut sup.*, i. 388): "Ignatius could use this language and indulge these thoughts because they had not yet, at least in any marked way, been abused to heretical ends. And we may perhaps even go a step further. Will not the suspicion cross our minds that Ignatius may have moved more or less in the same circles from which Valentinianism sprung?" As Valentinianism was derived from the popular Gnosticism of the Ophites, which had its headquarters in Syria, this conjecture is doubtless well founded.

The heretics attacked by Ignatius did not, therefore,

belong to the great fully-developed schools which in the middle of the second century flourished in Egypt and in Rome (Valentinians and Marcionites), but to the earlier Antiochian Gnostic sects, of which the principal representatives were Saturninus and Basilides. That gives us sure grounds for determining the time of composition of the Ignatian letters. According to a statement of Clement of Alexandria (*Strom.*, VII. xvii. 106), the founders of the heresies, among whom he gives a prominent position to Basilides, the fellow-student of the Antiochian Saturninus, first appeared in the time of the Emperor Hadrian. Now, as the Ignatian letters show us a development of the heresy which had proceeded to the stage of schism, it can scarcely be supposed that they date from the early years of the reign of Hadrian (117–138); we must rather place their composition in the latter part of this period. This brings us to the date formerly assigned by Harnack (towards 130 A.D.), which I prefer to that which he has assigned more recently [1] (110–117, or perhaps 117–125). After Harnack had himself demonstrated how entirely untrustworthy the chronology of Eusebius is in regard to the Antiochian succession of bishops, and the consequent uncertainty of the ascription of the martyrdom of Ignatius to the reign of Trajan—a demonstration which, in its main results, is not contested from any side—there was no remaining reason, so far as I can see, for placing the composition of the Ignatian letters in the time of Trajan, since their characterisation of the heretical teachers points unmistakably to the Antiochian Gnostics Saturninus and Basilides, who, according

[1] *Chronologie der altchristlichen Literatur*, i. 405 f.

to the uncontested statement of Clement of Alexandria, first appeared in the time of Hadrian.

(3) *Church Order.*—Ignatius sees the principal protection against heresy in the close and harmonious relation of every church with the bishop who forms the centre of its organisation. For this reason all his letters are full of exhortations to obedience towards the bishop and the presbyters as the surest means of preserving the unity of the church in faith and love. He calls the Ephesians happy (v.) because they are as closely united with their bishop as the Church is with Christ, and Christ with the Father, that all may be in harmony and unity. "Let no man be deceived. If anyone abide not within the precinct of the altar, he is deprived of the bread of God. For if the prayer of even one or two has so great power, how much more that of the bishop with the whole church! Let us give heed, therefore, not to oppose the bishop, that we may be obedient to God. For we must receive everyone whom the Lord sends into His household as Him who hath sent him. Clearly, then, we must look upon the bishop as the Lord." Again, in chapter xx. : " Come ye together, every man of you, in the grace that is common to all, in one faith and in Jesus Christ the Son of Man and Son of God, that ye may obey the bishop and the presbytery with undistracted mind, breaking one bread which is the medicine of immortality, the antidote against death unto eternal life in Jesus." *Magn.* iii. : " He who obeys the bishop obeys not him only, but the Father of Jesus Christ, the Bishop of all; conversely, he who acts hypocritically towards the bishop seeks to deceive not only the visible bishop but the invisible." Chapter xiii. :

"Submit to the bishop and to one another as Christ submitted to the Father, and the apostles to Christ and the Father, that there may be unity in flesh and spirit" (outward and inward; cf. Eph. (N.T.) iv. 4). *Trall.* ii.: "If ye are submissive to the bishop, as to Jesus Christ, ye seem to me to live, not according to men, but according to Christ. It is therefore needful that ye should do nothing without the bishop; but be submissive also to the presbytery as to the apostles of Jesus Christ." Chapter iii.: "Similarly, all shall honour the deacons as Jesus Christ, and the bishop as an image (τύπον) of the Father, and the presbyters as the Sanhedrin of God and as the college of the apostles. Without these (three offices) there is no church worthy of the name" (ἐκκλησία οὐ καλεῖται). Chapter vii.: "He that is within the precinct of the altar is pure, which means that anyone who does anything (in Church matters) apart from the bishop and the presbytery and the deacon is not pure in his conscience." *Philad.* iii.: "All who are of God and of Jesus Christ hold with the bishop." Chapter iv.: "There is one eucharist, one flesh of Christ, and one cup of His blood unto union, and one altar, as there is one bishop, together with the presbytery and the deacons." Chapter vii.: "The Spirit cried, saying: 'Do nothing without the bishop, keep your flesh as the temple of God, love unity, flee divisions, be imitators of Christ as He was of the Father." Chapter viii.: "The Lord forgives all who repent, if they are converted to the unity of God and the Sanhedrin of the bishop." *Smyrn.* viii.: "Do ye all follow the bishop as Jesus Christ followed the Father, and follow the presbytery as the apostles, but honour the deacons as the law of

God. Let no man do aught relating to the Church without the bishop. Only that eucharist shall be counted valid which is held under the authority of the bishop, or of one whom he commissions. Wherever the bishop appears, there let the people (of the church) be, as wherever Christ Jesus is, there is the Church catholic. It is not permissible either to baptize or to hold a love-feast apart from the bishop; only what he approves is well-pleasing also to God, that all things may be secure and settled (above caprice and contention)." Chapter ix.: "It is good to know God and the bishop; he who honours the bishop will be honoured by God; he who does anything behind the back of the bishop is serving the devil." *Ad Polyc.* iv.: "Nothing shall be done without thy (the bishop's) approval, and do thou nothing without the approval of God." Chapter v.: "It is fitting also that those who desire to marry should enter upon their union with the approval of the bishop, that their marriage may be according to the Lord and not according to lust." Chapter vi.: "Give heed to the bishop, that God may give heed unto you. I offer myself for those who submit to the bishop, the presbyters, and the deacons. May it be mine to have my part with them in God!"

It is quite intelligible that this array of passages should have given rise to the impression that we were here in presence of the complete hierarchy of the Catholic Church, and that they consequently could not have been written by Ignatius at the beginning of the second century, since in the Acts of the Apostles, which dates from the same period, bishops and presbyters are identical, and therefore a monarchical episcopate is not implied. Yet this argument was not sound, for it overlooked several important points. In the first place, it is especially to be noticed that the Ignatian idea of the episcopate is very different from the hierarchic conception which arose later (from the end of the second century onwards). The bishop has not yet acquired for Ignatius, as he has for Cyprian, the character of a priestly mediator between God and the people; nor even, as in Irenæus, of the successor of the apostles and the depositary of sound tradition. He is here simply the centre of the organisation and the guarantor of the unity of the church; his authority rests upon the practical utility and necessity of a regular organisation of the church, with a personal head as the representative of unity, to whom all can be, and ought to be, united, in order to resist subversion by heresy and schism. No definite theory is set up as to the grounds on which the bishop lays claim to this authority; it is simply assumed as a recognised fact in all the churches where this organisation of the offices is already established. That this was not universally the case in the time of Ignatius is shown by his letter to the Romans, in which no bishop is mentioned. It is also very instructive that Polycarp, in his letter to the Philippians, while he clearly distinguishes himself as bishop from the presbyters who are associated with him, exhorts those whom he is addressing to submit to "the presbyters and deacons" (*Phil.* v.), evidently because these were the only officers in Philippi at the time when he wrote, there being as yet no monarchical episcopate. If Ignatius had written to the Philippians, he would doubtless have done the same; but as he was writing to churches in which the organisation had developed into a regular episcopate, he enjoins upon them submission to the bishop. Furthermore, this "monarchical" episcopate is by no means to be thought of as an autocracy; the bishop was the president of the college of presbyters, who formed his "Sanhedrin," his "spiritual garland," and are compared with the apostles, as the bishop is compared with Christ or God. We must not press these figures too closely; they vary considerably (in one case it is the deacons who are compared to Christ while the bishop is described as the representative of God, while in other passages he, as the head of the individual church, is paralleled with Christ as the Head of the Church universal); they are not intended to embody dogmatic or ecclesiastical definitions, but serve to commend Church-order to popular respect as a copy of the heavenly order. As in the latter all disharmony is excluded, so the offices in the church should harmonise with one another "like the strings of the lyre" (*Eph.* iv.). "In this earliest form of Church organisation the bishop has neither a sacerdotal nor a Catholic character; he is the spiritual and moral leader of his people, comparable rather with the pastor of a pietistic church than with a bishop in the modern sense of the term."[1]

A further indication of conditions which are still primitive is the fact that the bishop's administrative sphere is still limited to his local church; the bishop and the presbyters are the officers of the church in

[1] Reville, "Études sur les origines de l'épiscopat," in the *Revue de l'histoire des religions*, xxii. 276.

a particular city; of a diocese extending beyond that there is no trace, not even in *Rom.* ii., where the "bishop of (belonging to) Syria" is designated, not from his sphere of office, but from his place of residence, as the context clearly shows. There is, in fact, in Ignatius no trace at all of an organisation going beyond the individual churches and uniting together them or their bishops in one great Church. The latter does not yet exist as a unity articulated and represented by priests, but only as the sum of the individual churches, which have their ideal unity in Christ their Head, just as each separate church has its centre in its bishop. In this sense it is said in *Smyrn.* viii.: "Where Jesus Christ is, there is the Church catholic." The word has here still its original sense, the universal Church in contradistinction to the separate local churches (*cf. Magn.* iii., "God the Bishop of all"); it was only later that it acquired the technical dogmatic sense—the orthodox Church resting on the apostolic succession of the bishops and the apostolic doctrinal tradition, in contradistinction to the heretical sects. This technical and confessional sense of the word "Catholic" only became fixed in the second half of the second century, in the course of the struggle with the Gnostics and Montanists. When once the word Catholic had acquired this later sense (= apostolic and orthodox), it was hardly possible to use it, without risk of misunderstanding, in its earlier sense of "universal" in contradistinction to particular local churches. Since Ignatius uses it in the earlier sense, this is an argument, not against, but in favour of the early composition of the letters.[1]

[1] Lightfoot, *ut sup.*, i. 415, and ii. 310 ff.

As a matter of fact, Ignatius' position is the same in regard to ecclesiastical organisation as in regard to dogmatic theology; in both cases there are strong tendencies in the direction of later developments, but there is no attempt to carry them to their logical issue, either in the sphere of dogma or of Church politics. With the same directness and simplicity with which Ignatius put forward his bold synthesis, "God and man, timeless and born, impassible and dying," without even suspecting the tremendous difficulties involved in an intellectual adjustment of these antitheses, he set up his parallels between the bishop and Christ, and the bishop and God, without suspecting that the hierarchic organisation of a theocratic church represented by an infallible Pope might ultimately grow out of them. It is true this development is not the direct continuation in the same line of the ideas of Ignatius, inasmuch as it is based on the presupposition that the episcopate was founded by the apostles, and that the bishops are the successors of the apostles and the depositaries of the tradition of their true teaching; and precisely this thought, which is of fundamental importance to the Catholic idea of the episcopate, is completely lacking in Ignatius, who never compares the bishops with the apostles, but only the presbyters. This, however, is connected with the fact that Ignatius' ideal of ecclesiastical unity has not gone beyond the individual church, the thorough organisation of which under its clergy seemed to him a sufficient protection against the storms of heresy. He never considered the possibility of the falling away into heresy of a whole church, along with its bishops and presbyters, and the necessity, in order

THE IGNATIAN LETTERS 359

to guard against such dangers, against which the individual church was undefended, of establishing a more comprehensive ecclesiastical organisation. A so narrowly limited horizon would not have been possible after the middle of the second century. Accordingly, the ecclesiastical conditions, as well as the anti-Gnostic polemic, point to the composition of the Ignatian letters before the middle of the second century.[1] They must have been written at a time when the danger of a lapse into heresy was still confined to individuals, so that it was possible to hope to find in the organisation of the individual church a sufficient protection against it—that is, before the great extension of heresy in the powerful Gnostic schools after the middle of the second century.

(4) *The Character of Ignatius.*—When the contents of letters or other writings point to peculiar traits of character in their author, there are two cases, and two only, in which these give ground for doubt regarding the genuineness of the writings: the cases are those in which either these traits are in contradiction with what is known with certainty from other sources regarding the character of the writer in question, or where they diverge too greatly from what, on grounds of analogy, might be expected from a man of the period and environment, social position and occupation, secular and religious education, of the supposed writer. The first case does not here concern us, since we have no further information regarding Ignatius, and must form our picture of his character entirely from his letters. The only question,

[1] *Cf.* Harnack, *Chronologie*, p. 394 f.

therefore, which we have to ask is whether this picture is of such a kind as to be incompatible with what, on grounds of analogy, is probable or conceivable in the case of a Syrian Christian bishop of the beginning of the second century. I do not think we have any right to answer this question in the affirmative; on the contrary, it seems to me that in every case where reasons for doubting the genuineness of the Ignatian letters have been based on the character of the author, the critic has not sufficiently distinguished between his own taste, or the prevailing mode of thought in his own period and environment, and the wholly different conditions under which the author of these letters lived and wrote. If we place ourselves unprejudicedly in his time and circumstances, no trait in the personal character which is here drawn for us will appear impossible, and while some of them may perhaps be unsympathetic, the whole character will appear impressive and worthy of respect.

Some have found an inconsistency between Ignatius' hierarchical imperiousness and his expressions of exaggerated humility and self-abasement. As bishop, he would take the place of Christ and of God in the church, and claims the unconditional submission of all its members to his will. On the other hand, he declares that he will not only (as is reasonable) not compare himself with the apostles, but that he will not set himself up at all as a teacher of others; nay, that he does not even regard himself as being, as yet, a true disciple, but will only be so when he has attained the martyr crown (*Eph.* i., iii.; *Rom.* iv., v.; *Trall.* v.; *Polyc.* vii.). Nay, more, he calls himself the last of the Antiochian Christians, not worthy of belonging to them (*Eph.* xxi.; *Magn.* xiv.; *Trall.* xiii.). These are certainly exaggerated utterances which are not to everyone's taste, but why should they suggest spuriousness? Have there not been at all periods Christians, and especially clerics, who clothed their self-consciousness in the form of unmeasured self-abasement? And is it probable that a forger, whose general aim would, after all, be to exalt his hero in the eyes of his readers, would have made the celebrated martyr Ignatius speak of himself in such a fashion?

As for the charge of hierarchic imperiousness, there is not so much basis for it as some, on the ground of certain passages, have thought. When Ignatius commands that nothing shall be done in the churches without the approval of the bishop, he adds immediately that the bishop shall do nothing without the approval of God (*Polyc.* iv.). The authority which the bishop claims, rests, for Ignatius, neither on sacramental ordination nor on legitimate succession, but on the fact that the bishop is the personal representative of the Divine will and the Christian spirit in the churches. Excellent rules and exhortations for the conduct of the episcopal office are contained in the letter to Polycarp, chapter i.: He is to fulfil his office by caring in every possible way for the bodily and spiritual well-being of the members of his church. Especially shall he give heed to the unity of the church, which is more important than all else. He shall bear with all men and receive all in love, watch and pray without ceasing, speak to each member of the church personally, bear the infirmities of all as a perfect athlete, imitating God's (merciful) spirit. The more the toil, the greater the gain. (ii.) If he loves only the good disciples, that is no credit to him; rather, he shall gently urge the worse to obedience. Not every wound is benefited by the same salve. Be, therefore, wise as a serpent and harmless as a dove. " The time needs you as a pilot needs the wind, and those endangered by the storm need a haven" (? *i.e.* needs sometimes from you driving power, sometimes refreshing rest). (iii.) In face of false teachers, the bishop must stand fast like an anvil, as a strong athlete who takes blows and yet comes off victor. He must ever increase in zeal, learn to understand the times, and wait for the Lord who is above time. (iv.) He must not neglect the widows, for, after the Lord, he is their provider. He should cause meetings of the church to be held more frequently, and should seek out all the members personally. He is not to despise slaves, but he must restrain their pride, that so they may better serve the honour of God, and thus obtain from God a better freedom, and not demand to have their freedom purchased out of the common funds. (v.) He is to shun the evil arts (of heresy and magic —often associated together, especially in the case of the Basilideans) and speak against them openly. He shall exhort husbands and wives to mutual faithfulness and love. The continent are not to boast, and, especially, are not to exalt themselves above the bishop, which would be their moral ruin. Marriages are to be concluded with the approval of the bishop, that they may be made in a Christian spirit and not in fleshly lust. In looking through these pastoral rules, we must admit that the bishop, in the view of

Ignatius, is to be the spiritual father and counsellor of his people. "There is nothing in these instructions which might not have stood in an apostolic epistle, or which betrays a clerical ecclesiasticism. In many phrases we catch a distinct echo of the exhortations of Paul. Ignatius claims no disciplinary power for the bishop; he confines himself to moral remedies—preaching and the cure of souls. Nor does he, in directing his exhortations to Polycarp, exclude the other members of the church; he addresses him only because, in his capacity as bishop, he is to set an example in the practice of all the Christian virtues."[1] And it certainly cannot be denied that it is a genuinely Christian ideal of virtue which is here drawn in the portrait of the pattern bishop.

Offence has especially been taken at the eagerness for martyrdom which is expressed in some of the Ignatian letters — most passionately in Romans. Some of these utterances certainly make the impression of a fanaticism which is something other than sound piety. But are they necessarily on that account proofs of spuriousness? Does not Church history tell us that in the Church of the early centuries the desire for martyrdom at times became epidemic? Why should it be impossible that even an apostolic father and pious bishop should have succumbed to this aberration? This becomes the more intelligible when we reflect that the error is only an exaggeration of pious zeal, an excess of self-sacrifice, and that to such excess the Syrian Ignatius must have been especially predisposed by his pas-

[1] Reville, *ut sup.*, p. 278.

sionate temperament. Attention has lately been called, and justly so, to this innate tendency in the Syrian to what is passionate, eccentric, and orgiastic as an explanation of what is peculiar in the personality and language of Ignatius;[1] only, in my opinion, this "hereditary bias" should not be made a ground for condemning his character, but rather for excusing the personal and literary weaknesses of one who is, withal, a man of mark. Beyond question, Ignatius remained, even as a Christian, a passionate Syrian; his Christian faith was not free from the superstitious elements of that very Gnosticism and mysticism which he so zealously opposed, and his intense love to Christ had as its reverse side the passionate hatred against all those who ventured to differ from his opinions. But despite all this he was a heroic personality; he understood his time, he recognised the dangers which threatened Christianity from the devastating floods of heresy, and recognised the necessity for finding a bulwark against them in the episcopate as the representative of Church unity. Into the effort to realise this idea he flung himself with all the passionate energy of his soul and the uncompromising intensity inspired by his consciousness of his mission. His style corresponds: rough, incorrect, often obscure or bombastic, but at the same time original, lively, vigorous, the true expression of his impulsive nature.

[1] *Cf.* Kreyenbühl, *Evang. der Wahrheit*, p. 285 ff.

WRITINGS OF THE PAULINE SCHOOL

CHAPTER XIX

THE LETTER OF POLYCARP TO THE PHILIPPIANS

THIS stands or falls with the Ignatian letters, to which it refers both directly and indirectly (*sup.*, p. 325 f.), and from which, at the same time, it is so fundamentally different in form and content that the hypothesis of its being from the same hand, and written with the purpose of facilitating the acceptance of these, must be rejected as wholly impossible. It is supported by the evidence of Polycarp's disciple Irenæus, who recommends it (*Adv. Hær.*, III. iii. 4), as an excellent record of the faith and preaching of Polycarp, to all Christians who are concerned about their salvation. It is mentioned by Eusebius too (*H.E.*, iii. 36) in connection with the Ignatian letters, and he makes two verbal quotations from chapters ix. and xiii. The letter of Polycarp offers no internal difficulties; if its testimony to the Ignatian letters had not supplied a reason for attacking it, its genuineness would never have been called in question. It would be difficult to say with what object a later writer could have composed it and ascribed it to Polycarp, since no definite tendency, whether of a dogmatic or ecclesiastical character, can be discovered in it. It is just the absence of striking thoughts which distinguishes Polycarp's letter from that of Ignatius. Its significance consists in the fact that it is a simple expression of the average Church belief, of which Polycarp is a representative, in the first half of the second century.

The occasion of the letter was supplied by a letter of the Philippians to Polycarp, in which they told of their reception of Ignatius on his journey through Philippi with his companions and fellow-prisoners, Rufus and Zosimus (of whom nothing further is known), and also begged Polycarp to make arrangements for the transmission of their letter to Antioch,[1] and to communicate to them the letters of Ignatius which were in his (Polycarp's) hands. It also probably told of a scandal which had occurred in the church—the offence of a presbyter named Valens and his wife, who seem to have acted dishonestly in regard to some church property. The writers had also expressed a wish to receive from the highly respected teacher Polycarp a letter which might serve to their instruction and edification. Polycarp met their wishes in a way as dignified as it was modest. He says (iii.) that he would not have ventured to write to them "regarding righteousness" (Christian piety) if they had not requested him to do so; he well knew that neither he nor anyone like him could venture to compare themselves with the "blessed and glorious" Apostle Paul, who had first in person accurately and thoroughly instructed the Philippians

[1] It was clearly a letter of congratulation such as, by the desire of Ignatius, was also sent by Polycarp, and from other churches, to the church at Antioch on the occasion of the restoration of peace there. See above, p. 326.

in the word of truth, and then when absent from them had written letters[1] to them, by the study of which they might receive edification in the faith "which is the mother of us all" and is followed by hope, while love takes the first place of all (*i.e.*, in value, in the sense of 1 Cor. xiii. 13). (Ignatius, speaking from another point of view, says in *Eph.* xiv. : "The beginning is faith, the end is love, these two united are God.") At the very beginning Polycarp had expressed his joy at the fair, steadfast, and fruitful religious condition of the Philippians, which had been manifested afresh in the loving reception of the Christian prisoners (Ignatius and his comrades) on their journey through. He then adds a short description of the object of Christian faith: Jesus Christ, who suffered for our sins, was raised up by God and set upon the throne at His right hand, to whom is subjected everything in heaven and earth, whom all things that have breath worship, who comes as the Judge of living and dead, whose blood God will avenge on the disobedient. On these things is based the hope that God, who raised up Christ, shall also raise us up, if we do His will, and love that which He loved, and shun all unrighteousness. Faith and hope are thus made the incentives to love and holiness; this is the theme which Polycarp is constantly developing, in different connections, in a simple and edifying way.

The polemic against heretics, which occupies so large a space in the Ignatian letters, is only once

---

[1] If ἐπιστολάς is to be understood as plural in meaning (which is, however, not certain), Polycarp seems to have supposed that more than one letter was written by Paul to the Philippians, but can hardly have spoken with knowledge (*cf.* Lightfoot, *ut sup.*, iii. 327).

lightly touched on by Polycarp. He exhorts the Philippians so to serve the Lord as He Himself and the apostles and prophets have ordained, avoiding offences and the false brethren who bear the name of the Lord in hypocritical fashion, and lead astray foolish men; and then he characterises these false teachers in three sentences (vii.): "Everyone who doth not confess that Christ is come in the flesh is an antichrist; and he who doth not confess the testimony of the cross, is of the devil; and he who distorts the words of the Lord to his own lusts, and asserts that there is neither resurrection nor judgment, is the first-born of Satan." This epithet was also applied by Polycarp, according to a statement of Irenæus (*Hær.*, III. iii. 4), to Marcion, on the occasion of a personal encounter with him, and on that ground it has been suggested that it is against the Marcionite Gnosis that this polemic is here directed. But this is quite improbable. The heretics attacked here are evidently the same docetics as in the Ignatian letters, and these we have recognised as the earlier Antiochian Gnostics, Menander, Saturninus, and Basilides; and to these applies also the characteristic here mentioned of denying the resurrection and the judgment. When it is added to this that they pervert the words of the Lord according to their lusts, that points to a libertine Gnosis such as the Simonians and Basilideans were charged with teaching, but would not be appropriate to Saturninus, and, certainly, not to Marcion, who was a strict ascetic. Equally inappropriate to the latter, as an admirer of Paul, is the charge of denying "the testimony of the cross," whether this means the testimony of the

Church to the crucifixion of the redeemer (Zahn), or the testimony of the death on the cross to the true humanity of the redeemer, as against the docetics (Lightfoot); in either case the reference can only be to Gnostics who expressly denied the crucifixion of the redeemer; as both Basilides and Cerinthus did. According to both, the Christ-Spirit had no part in the death, which was undergone only by the man Jesus (so Cerinthus), or by Simon of Cyrene, who was substituted for him (so Basilides). Of Basilides it is expressly asserted that he taught that all who have this knowledge are freed from the spiritual powers and do not need to acknowledge the crucified; whoever acknowledges him is still the servant of those powers; whoever denies him is free, because he knows the ordinance of the Father; his soul shall be saved, while his body has not to look forward to any resurrection (*cf.* above, p. 145 f.). It seems to me that Polycarp's condemnation quoted above applies excellently to this teaching of Basilides. If we take into account also that, in an attack on Marcion, some mention of his scandalous error in separating the good God of Christ from the unkind or "righteous" God of the Old Testament would necessarily be expected, we are certainly justified in concluding that a reference in the above passage of Polycarp's letter to the Marcionite Gnosis is very improbable, and that, on the other hand, it confirms the results which we arrived at above regarding the heretics of the Ignatian letters. This conclusion will stand, whatever be the relation of the passage to Irenæus' statement about the invective which Polycarp hurled at Marcion: "Thou art the first-born of Satan." It is possible that this is a legend based only on the passage in the letter; but it is also possible that Polycarp really repeated the same reproach which he had first, while fresh from the influence of Ignatius, directed against the earlier Antiochian Gnostics, on the occasion of a personal encounter with Marcion, the pupil of the Syrian Cerdon, who, since the middle of the second century, had been the most dreaded heresiarch.

But while Ignatius had opposed his docetic antagonists by uniting in a bold synthesis the God-Christ, to whom he also firmly held, with the man Jesus, the unborn and impassible spirit with the flesh which underwent birth and death, of the one Person of the Redeemer, and so laid the foundation of the Church doctrine of Christ, it was not the way of the practically disposed Polycarp to indulge in half-Gnostic, half-orthodox speculations of that kind. He simply recommended his readers to avoid the empty teachers of error, and to hold to the word which was delivered unto us from the first, to fast unto prayer, and to pray God not to bring us into temptation, and, for the rest, to hold fast unwaveringly to the hope and earnest of our righteousness, Jesus Christ, who through His suffering for our sins gave us a pattern of faithfulness and patience (vii., viii.). Here the appeal is to the traditional faith of the church as the established authority, against the innovations of the Gnostics; and the ethical and practical manifestation of this faith is enjoined upon the reader; in this there is a close analogy with the first Epistle of Peter, which has a similar purpose, and from which Polycarp frequently quotes. He speaks of Christ by preference as "our Lord"; once, like Hebrews, as "the eternal

High-priest"; once or twice as "God,"[1] a proof that the conception of the redeemer as a Divine Being, which was derived from the Gnostic mysticism (not from philosophy), had found its way even into circles of the faithful who stood quite aloof from speculation. But Ignatius' favourite formula of "the blood and passion of our God" is not found in Polycarp; it would be too extravagant for him; similarly, the doctrine, characteristic of the Ignatian mysticism, of the real presence of the flesh and blood of Christ in the eucharist as a sensible, yet super-sensible, means of salvation which ensures immortality, is not found in Polycarp. Whereas in Ignatius we find the mystical "Gnostic" side of Paulinism developed, under the influence of the heretical Gnosis, in the direction of the Catholic dogma, Polycarp held to the practical side of Paulinism, and popularised it in the direction of ecclesiastical morality, like the first Epistle of Peter and the Pastoral Epistles.

In relation to Church order, also, Polycarp stands nearer to the latter than to Ignatius. Of Ignatius' insistance on submission to the bishop as the representative of God and Christ in the Church, we find no trace in Polycarp. He exhorts (v.) the younger members of the Church to be in subjection to the presbyters and deacons as to God and Christ, seeing that they are servants of God and Christ, not merely of men; and he exhorts them to fulfil their office worthily and selflessly, according to the truth of the Lord, who became the servant of all; the presbyters

---

[1] In xii. 2 we should read ὁ αἰώνιος ἀρχιερεύς, θεὸς Ἰησοῦς Χριστός . . . εἰς τὸν κύριον ἡμῶν καὶ θεὸν Ι͞υ Χ͞υ—the latter probably, at least.

are especially to show themselves merciful towards all, and to turn again those who have wandered from the way, to take under their protection all the weak, especially widows, orphans, and the poor, to refrain from avarice, faction, and passionateness, not to be harsh in their judgments, but to remember that none of us are free from sin and guilt (vi.). In all this there is no mention of a bishop over the presbyters; probably there was no bishop as yet in the church at Philippi, and Polycarp, though himself bishop of Smyrna, did not feel himself called to insist, on principle, upon the centralisation of the organisation in a bishop in a place where this had not come about spontaneously. In this, as in his doctrine, he was not, like Ignatius, the enthusiastic herald and pioneer of new ecclesiastical developments, but the mild and conservative representative of the traditions of apostolic times, an "Apostolic Father" in the fullest sense of the term.

WRITINGS OF THE PAULINE SCHOOL

CHAPTER XX

THE PASTORAL EPISTLES

THIS is the name given to the letters to Timothy and Titus ascribed by Church tradition to the Apostle Paul, their contents being mainly exhortations and prescriptions about the pastoral work in the churches, in view, especially, of the danger to which they were exposed from false teachers. To this extent the three letters are very closely connected, but they are distinguished by the fact that both the polemic against the false teachers and the prescriptions regarding Church order in 2 Timothy and Titus show an earlier stage of development than 1 Timothy, which thus appears to be the latest of these letters. An orderly arrangement of the contents is hardly to be discovered in any of the three letters.

1 Timothy.—After a brief salutation, Paul exhorts Timothy, whom he has left behind in Ephesus as his representative, to beware of false teachers, in characterising whom he adds an excursus on the right use of the (Old Testament) law, followed by a reminder of his own personal experience, after which he returns to the heretics and excommunicates two of them by name (chap. i.). Then follow directions regarding the worship of the Church, interrupted by incidental remarks (ii. 4-6) regarding the Divine purpose of salvation and the apostolic office of Paul, and rules for the conduct of bishops and deacons (iii. 1-13), concluding with a eulogy on the Church and its (liturgically formulated) confession (iii. 14-16). Then further remarks concerning the false teachers (iv. 1 ff.), and personal exhortations to Timothy, reminding him of his consecration to office by the laying on of the hands of the presbytery (iv. 11-16). To this are attached in chapter v. directions regarding his conduct towards old and young in the Church, and towards widows and presbyters, along with exhortations to masters and servants. Then come (vi. 3 ff.) reiterated warnings against heretics and against worldly-minded and avaricious persons. In contrast to these, Timothy is to practise diligently all the Christian virtues and fight the good fight of faith, holding fast to the confession and keeping the Christian commandment blamelessly, until the appearing of the Lord Christ, to the glory of God, the Lord of lords. Then follows (vi. 17 ff.) a special exhortation to the rich to show Christian conduct, and finally (20 f.), yet another warning to Timothy against Gnosis falsely so called.

2 Timothy begins with an exhortation to Timothy to follow the example of his mother and grandmother, and of the imprisoned Apostle himself (i. 3-14). Remarks concerning his personal opponents and friends (i. 15 ff.). Further exhortations to steadfastness amid sufferings, following the examples of Jesus and of Paul (ii. 1-13). Then follows a warning against false teachers, whose empty logomachies

THE PASTORAL EPISTLES 375

Timothy is to avoid, whose pursuit of "knowledge" is associated with immorality, whose folly shall be evident to all men; a servant of God must rebuke them with mildness, hoping for their conversion to the knowledge of the truth (ii. 14–iii. 9). Then follows a second warning to be faithful amid sufferings, which fall to the lot of all true Christians, to hold fast the sound doctrine learned from the Apostle and confirmed by the holy Scriptures, which must be the more zealously preached by Timothy the more the false teachers turn away from truth to fables (iii. 10–iv. 5). In view of his imminent martyrdom, the Apostle then exhorts Timothy to come to him speedily in his loneliness, and to bring Mark with him, and closes with some personal references and greetings (iv. 6–22).

Titus.—After an extended introduction (i. 1–4), there follow directions for the appointment in every town in Crete of presbyters and bishops, for whom it is the more necessary that their moral character should be blameless, in view of the fact that the churches are exposed to the machinations of tempters who profess to know God, and deny Him by their deeds (i. 5–16). In opposition to them, Titus is to impress upon all, young and old, men and women, masters and servants, both by word and example, the sound doctrine accordant with the grace of God, which is destined for all, for their salvation and ethical education, in the hope of the appearing of our great God and Saviour Jesus Christ, who, by His offering of Himself, has redeemed us and purified us to be His peculiar people (ii. 1–15). Especially is he to exhort Christians to obedience to the civil government, and to a peaceable life, mindful of the mercy of God which has delivered us, by the laver of regeneration. To this faithful saying Titus shall testify, that believers may be diligent in maintaining good works; on the other hand, he is to shun foolish debatings about genealogies and questions about the law, and after warning a heretic once or twice, he is to have nothing more to do with him, since such an one has pronounced his own condemnation (iii. 1–11). Then the Apostle urges Titus to meet him at Nicopolis, where he intends to winter, and closes with personal references and greetings (iii. 12–15).

Since Schleiermacher, in his study of 1 Timothy (1807), raised critical objections to its genuineness, which were soon extended by Eichhorn to the other Pastoral Epistles, doubts regarding the Pauline origin of these letters have been freely expressed. The decisive contribution to the problem was made by Baur's essay (1835), which supplemented the negative grounds of doubt by the positive historical demonstration that these three letters are only to be understood in connection with the struggles of the Church against the Gnostic movement of the second century. That has since become the generally prevailing conviction of critical theology,[1] and it is not likely to be reversed even by the recent reactionary movement in favour of the acceptance of tradition. The spuriousness of these letters is proved beyond doubt by the concurrence of various lines of proof, each of

[1] All the relevant matter will be found most satisfactorily set forth in Holtzmann's monograph on the Pastoral Epistles, as also in his *New Testament Introduction* and *New Testament Theology*, to which I may give a general reference for what follows.

THE PASTORAL EPISTLES 377

which singly would suffice to establish it, viz.: (1) by the historical impossibility of the situation implied in each of the letters; (2) by the character of the false teachers who are opposed; (3) by the peculiarity of the doctrine and language; and (4) by the conditions of Church order and life which they imply.

(1) *The Impossibility of the Historical Situation.*— 1 Timothy professes to be written, according to i. 3 f., during a short separation of the Apostle Paul from Timothy, whom he, when proceeding to Macedonia, had left behind at Ephesus, with the task of opposing the false teachers who were active there. For the intervening period, therefore, before his early return to Ephesus (which is contemplated in iii. 14 and iv. 13), Paul gives Timothy rules of conduct, and a detailed description of the false teachers, whom Timothy, who had been with Paul in Ephesus, must have known as well as he did. But, further, there is no room in the life of Paul, as known to us, for this whole situation; for in the only case in which Paul travelled from Ephesus to Macedonia, and on to Corinth (Acts xx. 1 f.), Timothy was among his travelling companions (*ib.*, 4; *cf.* 2 Cor. i. 1); and, moreover, according to Acts xx. 16, Paul by no means contemplated an early return to Ephesus. The situation implied in the Epistle to Titus is that Paul and Titus have been together in Crete, and that Paul, after his departure, gives Titus, who has remained behind in Crete, directions for the full organisation of the churches, and the appointment of presbyters in every town. But at the same time he directs Titus to come to him in the near future at Nicopolis, where he intends to spend the winter (iii. 12). Now, there is no

trace either in Acts or in the Pauline letters of his having ever laboured for a considerable period in Crete, and founded churches there, or of his having wintered at Nicopolis. Only as a prisoner on his voyage to Rome did Paul touch at Crete (Acts xxvii. 7–13), and at that time there can have been no Christian churches there, for if there had been, we should have been told of his greeting them. But if Paul, during his short stay there, had preached and founded churches, the time between this and the composition of the letter to Titus would have been too short for the circumstances which it implies (intrigues of heretics and formation of sects) to have arisen there. Moreover, Titus was not in the company of Paul on his journey as a prisoner, recorded in Acts xxvii., and therefore could not be left behind in Crete. Nicopolis must be the city founded by Augustus in Epirus, in celebration of his victory; it cannot have been the Thracian Nicopolis, which was only founded by Trajan. Why Paul should have wintered in Epirus is not clear; the last winter before his imprisonment (59–60 A.D.) he spent in Corinth.

In 2 Timothy the situation is apparently simpler. Paul had been shortly beforehand in Corinth, where he had left Erastus behind him; then in Troas, where he left books and a cloak; and in Miletus, where Trophimus was left behind ill (iv. 12 and 20). Timothy is now urged to come to the imprisoned Apostle soon, before the beginning of winter, all others, with the exception of Luke, having left him; he is also to bring with him Mark and the things left behind by Paul (iv. 9 ff. and 21). Paul is thus to be thought of as a prisoner in Rome, where he has come through

THE PASTORAL EPISTLES 379

his first trial safely and been delivered from the jaws of the lion (i. 17; iv. 16). The situation is nearly related to that in Philippians, especially in the oscillation between hope of the favourable issue of the trial and fear of its ending badly, though the joyous martyr tone, as in iv. 6 ff., greatly predominates, which might seem to indicate a rather later period than that of Philippians. But during the composition of Philippians Timothy was in the company of Paul (Phil. i. 1), and therefore must have had personal knowledge of the first trial, which is spoken of in Phil. i. 7; why, then, should news of it be given to him here? According to Phil. ii. 19, 23, Timothy was not to leave until Paul was assured as to the result of his trial, and then to go to Philippi, not to Asia Minor, where he is represented as being in 2 Tim. i. 15 and iv. 12. It is also strange that Paul, writing from Rome, should now remind Timothy of the circumstances of that journey which he had made three years earlier, from Corinth by way of Troas and Miletus to Jerusalem (Acts xx. 3 ff.), circumstances which could not be unknown to Timothy, who was then his travelling companion, so that it is difficult to understand why Paul should be speaking of them here as though he was communicating things unfamiliar to Timothy. These various echoes of Acts and Philippians, which yet never exactly agree with them, make the impression that a later writer has invented the situation as a frame for his letter, whether simply with the help of his reminiscences of those writings, or perhaps using genuine fragments of Pauline letters, or short notes which may have been sent at various times to addressees unknown to us. 2 Timothy iv. 9-21, for example, may well be a note of Paul dating from the beginning of the Cæsarean imprisonment, and i. 15-18 a similar one from the Roman imprisonment. However, hypotheses of this kind may be left an open question, since they do not affect our criticism of the Pastoral Epistles as a whole.

In addition to the special difficulties which are involved in the situation of the writer in each case, there is a further difficulty which affects all three letters, namely, the curious relationship of Paul to his two former disciples, Timothy and Titus. Although they are supposed to be only separated from him for a short interval, Paul is represented as giving them rules for the conduct of their office, the carrying out of which would require an independent activity of some years' duration. Although they have been hitherto working alongside of Paul, he now communicates to them these detailed descriptions of the circumstances and dangers of the churches in question, which they must have known just as well as he did himself. And then, how curious seems the personal relation of Paul to these two helpers of his! He feels constrained to assure Timothy, his trusted friend and fellow-worker through many years, with solemn asseveration that he knows himself to be called to be a herald and apostle of the Gospel and teacher of the heathen (i. 2, 7); and this friend, who has long been tested in the work of the mission, he is made to treat like an unripe youth, to warn him against youthful aberrations, and to exhort him to faithfulness and zeal (1 Tim. iv. 11-16, v. 22 ff., vi. 11 ff.; 2 Tim. i. 5 ff., ii. 1 f., 7 ff., 15, 22, iii. 14, iv. 5). That is not the way in which Paul himself would write to Timothy, but a later writer might well put exhortations of that kind, intended for the teachers and leaders of the churches of his own time, into the mouth of Paul.

These latter difficulties, which concern the relation of the traditional author to the addressees, would retain their weight even if it were possible to lighten the difficulties of the supposed situation by the hypothesis of a second imprisonment of Paul, by means of which room could be found for the situation of 1 Timothy and Titus in the interval between the first and second imprisonments, and for 2 Timothy during the second; but this hypothesis of a second imprisonment is highly precarious. The first trace of the legend regarding it occurs in the Gnostic Acts of Peter, where it is clearly connected with the Roman legend about Peter; and to the same source is doubtless to be referred the statement of the Corinthian bishop Dionysius which is reported by Eusebius (*H.E.*, II. xxv. 8), according to which Paul and Peter travelled together from Corinth to Antioch to die the martyr-death there together, which would naturally imply the liberation of Paul from his first imprisonment at Rome; but the completely unhistorical character of this legend is evident from the fact that it makes Peter and Paul co-founders of the Corinthian Church. This equation of Peter and Paul is a product of the Catholic ecclesiastical formation of legends at Rome, and has no historical value. On the same grounds is to be explained the statement in the Muratorian canon that the martyrdom of Peter in Rome and the journey of Paul to Spain are no longer told at the close of Acts.

The fact is, this story is only known to the Roman legend, and has left no trace in genuine history. Acts is not only completely silent in regard to it, but also allows it to be clearly seen, by the farewell discourse which Paul is made to deliver to the Ephesian elders at Miletus, that it regarded the journey of Paul to Jerusalem and to Rome as a progress to death, and therefore was far from thinking of a liberation from this first imprisonment and a return to his old sphere of missionary activity. The Fathers, too, of the second and third centuries know nothing of all this. Eusebius (*H.E.*, II. xxii. 2) and Jerome (on Isa. xi. 14) are the first to mention definitely this second imprisonment, and in neither case on the ground of an independent source, but basing their conclusion on 2 Tim. iv. 16 ("first examination") and on Rom. xv. 24, 38 (Paul's intention of visiting Spain; *cf.*, on this point, i. 246 *sup.*). How weak these grounds are is obvious. From then till now the supposition of a second imprisonment of Paul has been based only on the desire to save the genuineness of the Pastoral Epistles by finding a place for them— since room is not to be found in the known life of Paul—in an unknown extension of it. As, however, the two Epistles to Timothy contain unmistakable though not exact analogies to earlier circumstances in the life of Paul (the two journeys from Ephesus to Macedonia, and from Corinth by way of Troas and Miletus to Jerusalem, Acts xx., *cf.* also the Epistle to the Philippians), these earlier situations must have repeated themselves in a remarkably similar fashion in the hypothetical new period—a supposition of the highest improbability! If, however, we drop this obviously forced hypothesis of the second imprisonment of Paul, which owes its existence only to the wish to save the genuineness of the Pastoral Epistles —which is on other grounds untenable—we cannot avoid the conclusion that the situation implied in each of these letters is historically impossible, and, therefore, invented.

(2) *The False Teachers against whom the Polemic is directed.* — That these were second-century Gnostics was recognised even by Irenæus and Tertullian, who found in individual traits of the false teachers who are here described the Gnostics of their own time. When Timothy is exhorted (1 Tim. vi. 20) to avoid empty babblings and the "antitheses of gnosis falsely so called," that can only be understood as a direct allusion to the famous work of Marcion which bore the title "Antitheses," and enjoyed in Gnostic circles the position of a canonical book.[1] According to Tit. i. 16, they were people "who profess to know God, but by their works deny Him," that is, who boasted of possessing a special "Gnosis," a claim to which their conduct did not correspond. In reference to the latter, various charges are made which are not all suitable to the same heresy. According to 1 Tim. iv. 3, the heretics were ascetics who forbade marriage and the use of certain foods (flesh-meat), and denied that "every creature of God is good, and nothing is to be rejected if it be received with thanksgiving," and that "to the pure all things are pure; but to them that are defiled and unbelieving nothing is

[1] Harnack, *Dogmengeschichte*, iii. 1. 257, who refers to Tertullian, *Adv. Marc.*, I. xix.

pure; but both their mind and their conscience are defiled" (Tit. i. 15). According to this, their asceticism cannot have consisted in a Jewish legalistic scrupulosity, but rested evidently upon a metaphysical dualism which held the sensuous world not to be a creation of the good God. This was precisely the character of the stern asceticism which Marcion shared with the Syrians Saturninus and Cerdon; of the former (*sup.*, p. 144) it is distinctly asserted that he held marriage and the use of flesh-meat to be works of Satan, from which the redeemed must abstain; Marcion is, moreover, sarcastically described by Tertullian [1] as "the most holy teacher" who "imposes holiness on the flesh"—that is, abstinence from marriage and from certain foods. Marcion's well-known enmity to the law is referred to in 1 Tim. i. 6–11: "They desire to be teachers of the law, but know not what they say nor whereof they dispute. But we know that the law is good, if a man use it lawfully, knowing, that is, that the law is not intended for the righteous but for the lawless and unruly, for the ungodly and sinners . . . according to the gospel of the glory of the blessed God which was committed to me." Ambiguous as this description of the false teachers as those who desire to be "teachers of the law" certainly is in itself, the antithesis makes it quite clear that it is not a case of Jewish legalism, but of ultra-Pauline antinomianism which opposed to the Old Testament, as the law of the merely righteous God, the Gospel of the good God in a dualistic antithesis, and denied that the former had any significance for Christians. To this

[1] *De Præscrip.*, xxx.; *Adv. Marc.*, I. xiv., xxviii., xxix., etc.

Marcionite radicalism, the Church Paulinist opposes the conservative view regarding the right use of the law as a means for the correction of sinners, and expressly refers, in support of this view, to the "Gospel of Paul," in order to enforce, against this Marcionite ultra-Paulinism, the authority of Paul as rightly interpreted by Church tradition. While the anti-legalism of Marcion was associated with strict asceticism, it led in other Gnostic schools to the opposite, libertine practice. It had been so earlier in the case of some of the Syrian Gnostics (Cainites and Simonians), and it was so again in a part of the Valentinian school, which flourished at Rome contemporaneously with Marcion, especially in the branch of it which was represented by Marcus. To this section would apply the charges of avarice and self-indulgence brought against the false teachers in 1 Tim. vi. 4 f. and 2 Tim. iii. 2-7, and the charge of impure zeal in the conversion of women, the latter especially being a dark feature in the picture of the Marcosians drawn elsewhere by the writers on heresy. To the Valentinian heresy, too, must be referred what is said about the preoccupation of the false teachers with myths and endless genealogies (1 Tim. i. 4). We have not to think here either of Jewish genealogies or Essene classes of angels, but, as Tertullian long ago recognised, of the series of æons and syzygies of the Valentinians, who arranged their mythological personifications in a genealogical system which naturally admitted of being spun out *ad infinitum*, and of which the presentation differed considerably in the various schools. The boasting of a deeper knowledge of God, which was not in accordance with their moral conduct (Tit. i. 10-16), is also appropriate to the Valentinians, who combined with lax morality an intellectual arrogance which expressed itself in their self-designation of "pneumatics," in contradistinction to the "psychics." This intellectual arrogance, however, was not a characteristic confined to the Valentinians, but was common to all the Gnostics from the first; so far as this goes, the polemic of the Epistle to Titus would apply equally well to the earlier Syrian Gnostics; and as the Jewish syncretistic mythology played a larger rôle in their teaching than in the later Hellenised systems, the reference to "Jewish myths" and the prominence of false teachers who are "of the circumcision" (Tit. i. 10, 14) would be quite appropriate. There is no reason to think of a Judaising heresy distinct from the Gnosticism elsewhere in view, any more than in the quite analogous case of the false teachers opposed by Ignatius in his letters to the Philippians and Magnesians (*sup.*, p. 334 f.). In both cases there are not two kinds of heretics, but one and the same Jewish-Gnostic sect, who mingled, in their fantastic speculations, Old Testament stories and names with Oriental myths, and substituted for the Mosaic law their own arbitrary ascetic ordinances ("commandments of men"). It is, however, possible that the special emphasis laid upon the Jewish origin of this heresy is connected with the fact that the author wrote in the character of Paul, whose opponents had been "chiefly they of the circumcision." The statements, couched in somewhat general terms, of Titus and 2 Timothy do not suffice to define the sect of Gnostic heretics who are in view more closely; even the heresy which is specially mentioned in 2 Tim. i. 18, of teaching that the resurrection was already past—in the sense of a spiritual resurrection through the knowledge of the truth[1]—applies to almost all the Gnostic systems, to the earlier Syrian as well as to the later Western schools. If, now, we notice that in 2 Tim. ii. 25 the false teachers are censured with less severity than was usual on the part of the Church teachers in later times, and a hope is still held out of their conversion, while even the Epistle to Titus (iii. 10 f.) recommends that short work should be made of them, while 1 Tim. utterly condemns them as apostate from faith and fallen under the power of Satan (i. 6, 20, iv. 1 f., v. 15, vi. 20 f.), the conjecture naturally suggests itself that in the former two letters we must assume an earlier stage of development of the Gnostic heresy, which points to the time of Hadrian, whereas in 1 Tim. the attack is doubtless directed against the fully developed Gnosticism of the time of the Antonines.

(3) *Peculiarities of Doctrine and Language.*—In face of the heretical subjectivism which rejected the Old Testament and took its stand upon an esoteric tradition, the Church's attitude was to hold fast to the holy Scripture, as being in all its parts inspired by God (θεόπνευστος), and, as such, profitable for teaching, for reproof, for correction, for instruction in righteousness (2 Tim. iii. 16). On this view, even the Old Testament law does not stand in antithesis to the Gospel as a purely negative preparation for the Christian salvation, but in its ethical portion, if

---

[1] *Cf.* Iren., *Adv. Hær.*, II. xxxi. 2 : "esse resurrectionem a mortuis agnitionem veritatis"; and Tertull., *De Præscrip.*, xxxiii.

understood and used in the right way, as purified by Christianity, and disengaged from the ceremonial law, which was of purely temporary application, it is a valuable part of inspired Scripture and a permanently valid norm of Christian conduct. Therefore, instead of the original Pauline deliverance from the law (Gal. iv. 5; Rom. x. 4), it is now deliverance "from all lawlessness" which is described as the purpose of the coming of our great God and Saviour Jesus Christ (Tit. ii. 14). Therefore it is not surprising that the Christian piety of Paul and of Timothy appears as the continuation, on the same lines, of the Jewish piety of their ancestors (2 Tim. i. 3, 5).

Of still higher importance is the doctrine of God; that He is one, living, eternal, incorruptible, invisible, almighty, blessed, truthful, faithful, merciful, good and gracious (1 Tim. i. 11, 17, ii. 5, iii. 15, iv. 10, vi. 13, 15 f.; 2 Tim. ii. 13; Tit. i. 2). It is especially noticeable as a peculiarity of the language of our epistle that it uses the title Saviour ($\sigma\omega\tau\acute{\eta}\rho$), which is elsewhere applied only to Christ, quite as frequently of God, indeed in 1 Tim. exclusively of God. This emphasising of Christian monotheism is not to be explained merely on the general ground of opposition to heathen polytheism—for, after all, in the language of the heathen mystery-cults the phrase "saviour-god" ($\theta\epsilon\grave{o}s$ $\sigma\omega\tau\acute{\eta}\rho$) was in constant use—it is the specifically Gnostic antithesis between the good God of redemption and the "not-good" God of creation and the law which the Church teacher has in view in emphasising the unity of God as the sole Lord of lords and Author of all salvation.

Christianity is the revelation of the Divine mercy

by the "appearing" (ἐπιφάνεια) of the Saviour Jesus Christ (2 Tim. i. 10). This expression is derived from the Gnostic terminology, in which it betokened the sudden becoming visible of the spiritual Being, Christ, who had previously belonged to the heavenly world. But in face of the Gnostic docetism the "great mystery of godliness," that is, the Church's faith in Christ, is thus formulated, 1 Tim. iii. 16: "who was manifest in the flesh, justified in the spirit, seen of angels, preached among the nations, believed on in the world, received up into glory"—a liturgical confession of the incarnation of Christ and His exaltation to the spirit-world by the resurrection (which is His justification; that is, the proof that He was a supramundane being); and also of His manifestation in the heavenly world of the angels, and in the earthly universal Church. It is thus a combination of the two aspects of Christ's being, human and superhuman, similar to the juxtaposition of the two aspects in the Ignatian formulas, *e.g. Eph.* vii. (p. 342). Here as there, and also in John's Gospel, the higher nature and origin of Christ forms the unquestioned presupposition: He has been manifested in the flesh, has come into the world (1 Tim. i. 15); therefore He did not take His origin from the world. But since it was not this but the reality of the incarnation which was the point of controversy, it is natural that the chief stress should be laid upon His true humanity, 1 Tim. ii. 5: "There is one God, and one mediator between God and man, the *Man* Christ Jesus" (the antithesis to the manifold divine principles and intermediate beings in the Gnostic mythology is obvious). In 2 Tim. ii. 8 the origin of Christ from David's seed is mentioned, and supported by an appeal to the Pauline Gospel (*cf.* Rom. i. 3). On the other hand, in Tit. ii. 13 there is mention of the "appearing of the glory of our great God and Saviour Christ Jesus," in which the great preponderance of probability is in favour of understanding by "the great God" Christ Himself.[1] Surprising as this designation would be in the mouth of Paul himself, it does not greatly astonish us in a "deutero-Pauline," a contemporary of the Syrian Gnostics and of Ignatius, for all of whom the deity of Christ was a common and unquestioned presupposition. But just as Ignatius boldly took over this presupposition from the Gnostic ideas of the time, without reflecting on the relation of the deity of Christ to that of the Father or to the humanity of Jesus, so in the Pastoral Epistles there is no attempt to adjust the heterogeneous Christological statements; in particular, the Johannine doctrine of the Logos is as foreign to them as to Ignatius.

The aim of Christ's work is described as that of destroying death and bringing life and immortality to light (2 Tim. i. 10), an association of life and light which recalls Jn. i. 4. The specifically Pauline doctrine of the significance of the death of Christ as an expiation, for the wiping out of the guilt of sin, a ransom to redeem from the curse of the law, is only once touched on, in the statement that Christ "gave

[1] That the whole phrase τοῦ μεγάλου θεοῦ καὶ σωτῆρος ἡμῶν qualifies Χοῦ Ἰοῦ is probable both on grammatical grounds—since otherwise the article would be repeated before σωτῆρος—and also on material grounds, since the expected "appearing in glory" refers to the *parousia* of Christ, which is never thought of as at the same time a *parousia* of God the Father. *Cf.* von Soden, *Hand-Komm.*, iii. 1. 211 f.

Himself as a ransom-price (ἀντίλυτρον—not a Pauline term) for all" (1 Tim. ii. 6). Elsewhere it is always the ethical side of the Pauline thoughts regarding redemption which is uppermost. Christ " gave Himself for us, that He might redeem us from all lawlessness, and purify us as a people for His own possession, zealous of good works " (Tit. ii. 14). It is therefore not, as in Paul, from the law (Gal. iv. 5), its curse and bondage, but from lawlessness, *i.e.* immorality, that Christ has delivered us, and has won for Himself as a possession an ethically pure people, diligent in good works; the place of the religious redemption has been taken by the moral renewing and building up of the Church, though the exact way in which this result is brought about by the death of Christ is not made clear. In any case, the doctrine of redemption in the Pastoral Epistles stands nearer to the deutero-Pauline Epistle to the Ephesians (*cf.* especially Eph. v. 25 f.) than to the original Pauline teaching. Yet, instead of the limitation of the Divine will of mercy to the Church, which is peculiar to Ephesians, the Pastoral Epistles—in opposition to the sectarian arrogance of the Gnostics—expressly teach the universality of the Divine purpose of salvation : Tit. ii. 11, " The grace of God hath appeared, bringing salvation to all men, educating us to the end that, denying ungodliness and worldly lusts, we might live soberly and righteously and godly in this present world "; 1 Tim. ii. 4, " It is the will of God that all men should be saved, and come to the knowledge of the truth," and, verse 6, " Christ gave Himself a ransom for all." If, in 2 Tim. ii. 19, " The Lord knoweth them that are His," there is an allusion to the Pauline doctrine of predestination, it is immediately counterbalanced by the hortatory application, "Let every one that nameth the name of the Lord depart from unrighteousness." The author is well aware that there are still in the Church impure members, who as "unrighteous" cannot belong to God's "possession"; but the decisive point, as regards belonging to it, is not a predeterminate decree, but the moral conduct of the individual.

The appropriation of salvation is associated, still more definitely than by Paul, with baptism. Tit. iii. 5: "Not by works which we have done in righteousness, but according to His mercy hath God saved us, by the washing of regeneration, and the renewing of the Holy Spirit, which He has poured out upon us richly, through Jesus Christ our Saviour, that we, being justified by His grace, might become heirs according to the hope of eternal life." As, according to Eph. v. 26, the washing of baptism is the sacramental means for the purification of the Church, so here it is the means to regeneration and (synonymous with this) the "renewal" which is wrought by the Spirit, the end of which is justification and inheritance of life. In Paul's teaching, too, the communication of the Spirit and newness of life is associated with baptism (Rom. vi.); but according to Rom. xii. 2 renewal in the spirit of the mind is the continuous ethical task (sanctification) which has justification, not for its end, but as its presupposition. Faith is named in two places only (1 Tim. i. 16 and 2 Tim. iii. 15) as the means of appropriating salvation; elsewhere in the Pastoral Epistles πίστις is sometimes faithfulness, sometimes orthodox belief, sometimes even the truth which is believed (*fides quæ creditur*). Being thus weakened to theoretical correctness of belief, faith naturally needs to be supplemented on the practical side, and is therefore frequently combined with love, or with love and patience, as cardinal virtues of Christianity; just as in the Ignatian letters, so here, faith and love associated are the alpha and omega of all true Christianity (1 Tim. i. 14, ii. 15, iv. 12, vi. 11; 2 Tim. i. 13, ii. 22, iii. 10; Tit. ii. 2). Faith bears the objective sense of the Church's doctrine and rule of faith in passages like 1 Tim. iv. 1, "Some shall fall away from the faith"; iv. 6, "the words of the faith and sound doctrine"; vi. 10 and 21, "to err from the faith."

The general expression for the whole of the Christian life is in the Pastoral Epistles the term—peculiar to them—"piety" ($εὐσέβεια$—A.V. "godliness"). It betokens the theoretical and practical right conduct of the Church Christian, his holding fast to the common faith of the Church, as also to the scheme of conduct which the Church approves. In this sense the doctrine and knowledge which are "according to piety" are spoken of in 1 Tim. vi. 3 and Tit. i. 1; in 1 Tim. iii. 16, the "great mystery of piety" is equivalent to the main contents of the Church's faith. The practical side is prominent in passages like 1 Tim. ii. 2: Christians are to lead a tranquil and quiet life in all piety and gravity; iv. 7: Timothy is to exercise himself unto piety, which is profitable for all things, and hath the promise of the life that now is as well as of that which is to come; vi. 5: piety with contentment is the true riches; 2 Tim. iii. 5: the Church is the (fruitful) power of piety, while heretics have only the empty form. To asceticism the writer does not deny all value (1 Tim. iv. 8), but he opposes to the excessive Gnostic dualistic asceticism the sound conviction that every creature of God is good, and nothing is to be rejected which is received with thanksgiving, since it is consecrated by God's word and by prayer (iv. 4 f.), and that to the pure all things are pure, but to the impure and unbelieving (the two are simply identified) nothing is pure; their mind and conscience are defiled (Tit. i. 15 ff.). Great stress is laid upon the practice of good works. As in Eph. ii. 10 God has foreordained us to walk in good works, so in Tit. ii. 14 the purpose of salvation is that the people who are God's possession shall be zealous unto good works. It is true that in 2 Tim. i. 9 and Tit. iii. 5 the merit (desert) of "works done in righteousness" is denied, but Christians are nevertheless to give diligence to live in good works, since these are "good and profitable unto men" (Tit. iii. 8), *i.e.* have valuable consequences both for the doer and the community. 1 Timothy goes even further, ascribing to good works a religious value as a foundation for the certainty of salvation, for that is doubtless the sense of vi. 18—the rich by their beneficence lay up in store for themselves a good foundation for the future, that they may lay hold on the true life. If even this goes somewhat outside the lines of the original Pauline teaching, much more surprising is the statement in 1 Tim. ii. 15 that woman is to be saved by childbearing. Here, in opposition to the Gnostic rejection of marriage,[1] the writer formu-

---

[1] Also, doubtless, to the enthusiasm of prophetesses and other women who came forward to teach, whom the writer in 1 Tim. ii. 11 f. (perhaps also in the interpolation in 1 Cor. xiv. 34 f.) directs

lates the sound principle of practical morality that woman best fulfils her vocation in the married life; but how widely different that is from the view of Paul in 1 Cor. vii.! The strong emphasis laid upon reward as the motive of Christian morality is, however, as much in accordance with the early Christian view as with the requirements of the Church—now on its way to become a universal Church—for the ethical education of its people, and is thus quite naturally connected with the practical and ecclesiastical attitude of the Pastoral Epistles. In general, it cannot be denied that the Christianity here recommended, consisting of a simple practical piety which avoids empty verbal debates and the exaggerated asceticism of the heretics, deserves to be called a "sound teaching," and was, and is, from the ecclesiastical point of view, more useful than the more idealistic original Paulinism, with its very numerous theoretical and practical difficulties.

The Church is spoken of in 1 Tim. iii. 15 as "the pillar and ground of the truth, the firm foundation of God." It is therefore the basis upon which the truth of the Christian faith is supported and sustained, and the place where alone it is to be found. He who teaches otherwise than the Church, has not the truth, and cannot therefore, according to our Church teacher, have morality either. We have here the full antithesis between orthodoxy and heterodoxy, coupled with the prejudice which persisted thenceforward that heterodoxy and immorality always go together. That can only be explained at a time when the

to keep silence, because they were inconvenient and disturbing to the growing organisation of the Church.

Church, in fierce conflict with dangerous heresies, is roused to intense self-assertion and exclusiveness. It is no longer Jesus Christ alone (as in 1 Cor. iii. 11), nor Christ together with the apostles and (Christian) prophets (as in Eph. ii. 20), but simply the Church, which is now the firm foundation of truth, or of God. As such it bears the two mottoes: "The Lord knoweth them that are His," and, " Let him who nameth the name of the Lord depart from unrighteousness" (2 Tim. ii. 19). The Divine election is, therefore, the pledge of their steadfastness; but not all the members who belong to the outward Church are really among the elect, but only those who hold aloof from unrighteousness. Thus, alongside of the ideal conception of the Church we have already the empirical, the *ecclesia visibilis* which contains within its membership both good and evil. The organised Church is, however, as the authoritative teacher, also an object of faith ; "in short, we have here the whole of Catholicism *in nuce*!" (Holtzmann).

(4) *Church Order.*—The directions given in Titus and 1 Timothy regarding the establishment of grades of office in the Church carry us far beyond the apostolic period. Paul knew of no organised office, but only of voluntary service to the Church, based upon the charismatic endowment of individuals; and among these were "overseers" ($\pi\rho o\ddot{\imath}\sigma\tau\acute{a}\mu\epsilon\nu o\iota$), for whom the respect of the Churches is claimed (1 Thess. v. 12 f. ; 1 Cor. xvi. 15 f. ; Rom. xii. 8). But, according to Tit. i. 5, Titus is to appoint presbyters in every city, as the Apostle had charged him to do ; and according to 1 Tim. iv. 14, the presbyters already form a close college, the "presbytery," which

in virtue of its prophetic inspiration communicates by the laying on of hands the charism of the grace of office. The relation of the presbyters to the bishops is not quite clear; it is, however, clearly to be recognised that in the circles from which these epistles emanated the episcopate had not, as in the Ignatian letters (with the exception of Ignatius' letter to the Romans), taken the form of a monarchical authority over the presbyters; presbyter and bishop are not yet designations of definitely distinguished grades of office in the Church.[1] Yet the two are not simply identical. Probably we are to understand by presbyters the "elders" who, in virtue of their age or their long association with the church, naturally occupied a position of respect and honour, while the "episcopoi" were the actual overseers of the church, who were charged with the direction and oversight of the common affairs. In so far as these overseers belonged to the "notables" they were also "presbyters"; but all presbyters were not necessarily "episcopoi." The bishops were not yet above the presbytery, but formed part of it, as those members of it who were especially charged with the outward affairs of the church.[2] While the constitution of

[1] The qualifications required from the bishop in 1 Tim. iii. 1 ff. are exactly the same as those demanded of the presbyter in Tit. i. 5; and as in the former passage only bishops and deacons are mentioned, in the latter presbyters only, ἐπίσκοπος and πρεσβύτερος seem to be used as interchangeable terms.

[2] They are therefore called in 1 Tim. v. 17 οἱ προεστῶτες πρεσβύτεροι, who are therefore worthy of double honour (honourable maintenance), especially in cases where they also "labour in word and doctrine." That was not therefore universally the case, but was counted an especial advantage.

the Church was at this time rather aristocratic than monarchical, yet the position which Timothy and Titus occupy in these letters—primarily, it is true, as representatives of the Apostle on a visitation-journey, but also as holding permanent disciplinary and teaching authority—already indicates the tendency to the formation of an episcopal primacy, which naturally grew up in times of difficulty out of the teaching and disciplinary functions of the bishop. "The Pastoral Epistles show us, in this point also, a transition; they set over the presbyters and episcopoi of the former order of things, as a model for future times, the envoys of the Apostle, who, as such, have a higher authority" (Weizsäcker).

The fact that in the Pastoral Epistles the episcopate appears in a less developed condition than in the Ignatian letters does not warrant us in immediately concluding that they are of earlier date. As regards 1 Timothy, at any rate, this conclusion is negatived by the fact which we have observed, that the heretics who are here opposed seem to belong to a later form of Gnosticism than those of the Ignatian letters. It must not be overlooked that Church organisation developed more slowly in the West than in the East, which is connected with the fact that the conflict with heresy arose later in the West than in the East. Lightfoot (*Apostolic Fathers*, Pt. II. vol. i. p. 398 f.) refers in this connection to the Epistle of Clement of Rome and the *Shepherd* of Hermas, neither of which shows any trace of episcopal organisation in the Roman Church, and remarks that this difference of circumstances between the Roman Church and those of Asia Minor (as exhibited in the Ignatian letters) is easy to explain: "The episcopal government was matured as a safeguard against heresy and schism. As such it appears in the Ignatian letters. But Asia Minor was the hotbed of false doctrine and heretical teachers. Hence the early and rapid adoption of episcopacy there. On the other hand, Rome was at that time remarkably free from such troubles. It was not till the middle of the second century that the heresiarchs found it worth their while to make Rome the centre of their operations. . . . Hence the episcopate, though it doubtless existed in some form or other in Rome, had not the same sharp and well-defined monarchical character with which we are confronted in the Eastern Churches." There is, therefore, nothing against the supposition[1] that the Pastoral Epistles, which owe their origin to the Western Church, in spite of the less developed Church order which they imply, arose partly contemporaneously with, partly later than, the Ignatian letters.

[1] To find in Polyc., *Phil.* iv., "We know that, as we brought nothing into this world, so we can take nothing out of it," a quotation from 1 Tim. vi. 7 is a quite arbitrary assumption. The same thought is found in almost the same words in Seneca, *Ep.* cii. 25, and was therefore evidently a popular proverb with which everybody was familiar.

THE JOHANNINE WRITINGS

CHAPTER XXI

THE APOCALYPSE

THIS book is still the most obscure in the whole New Testament, although on certain points a measure of agreement has been reached. There are now scarcely any representatives of the traditional opinion, according to which it consists of inspired predictions regarding the course of the world's history, part of which have already been fulfilled, while part are still to be fulfilled in the future. Scientific criticism has, since the time of Lücke (1832), come to see that the Apocalypse of John belongs to that class of literature, current among the Jews from the Maccabean period onward, which uses prophetic visions as a conventional literary form in which to embody, for the consolation and edification of the writer's contemporaries, the religious hope of a speedy relief from the time of oppression, and of the final victory of the people of God over the hostile world-powers. The Book of Daniel was the earliest of these apocalypses, and set the pattern for the whole series (*cf.* above, on the apocalypses of Enoch, 2 Esdras, and Baruch, pp. 75–96). When a key to the interpretation of the visions of Daniel had been found in the circumstances of the Jewish war in the time of Antiochus Epiphanes, it was rightly concluded that the Johannine Apocalypse was to be explained from the circumstances of its own time.

Accordingly, when the mystical number 666 in xiii. 18 had been interpreted almost simultaneously by several scholars (Benary, Hitzig, and Reuss), from the numerical value of the Hebrew letters, as a reference to the Emperor Nero, the conclusion was drawn from a comparison of chapters xiii. and xvii. that the Apocalypse originated soon after the death of Nero in the year 68. This long remained the prevailing view, especially in the earlier Tübingen school, which, on the presupposition, to which it still held firmly, of the composition of the book by the Apostle John, supposed that the key to the whole book was to be found in the party-conflict between Judaisers and adherents of Paul—an interpretation which could not be carried through in detail without great arbitrariness (especially conspicuous in Volkmar). A new impulse towards the more thorough investigation of the problem was given in 1882 by a pupil of Weizsäcker, Daniel Völter, who formulated the hypothesis of a repeated revision and extension of a primary document by various authors between 66 and 170 (fixing, later, 140 as the lower limit). The method of documentary criticism here applied underwent in the next fifteen years the most manifold variations: Vischer assumed a Jewish document as the basis, which had been worked over by a Christian editor; Sabatier and Schön, on the other hand, assumed an original Christian document into which Jewish materials had been interpolated; Weyland distinguished two Jewish sources, dating from the times of Nero and Titus, and a Christian editor of the time of Trajan ; Spitta distinguished a Christian primary document of the year 60 A.D., two Jewish sources of 63 B.C. and 40 A.D., and a Christian redactor of the time of Trajan ; Schmidt, three Jewish sources and two Christian redactors; Völter (in a second work in 1893), an original apocalypse of the year 62, and four revisions under Titus, Domitian, Trajan, and Hadrian. The consequence of all these mutually opposed and more and more complicated hypotheses was, finally, that " the uninitiated received the impression that nothing is certain and nothing impossible in the field of New Testament criticism " (Jülicher, *Introd.*, p. 287). A wholesome reaction against the exaggeration of these literary and historical methods was initiated in 1895 by Gunkel's able book, *Schöpfung und Chaos*, where the arbitrariness of many of the interpretations of references to the history of the time was shown, and the explanation of most of the problems of the Apocalypse on the basis of earlier apocalyptic tradition and also from primitive mythology was defended. This religious-historical method is in any case to be welcomed as a valuable corrective and supplement to the literary-historical method, and may no doubt, as Jülicher holds, " be destined to mark an epoch in the interpretation of the Apocalypse "—provided that it does not, in its turn, fall a victim to the usual fate of good ideas, that of being ridden to death through one-sidedness and want of moderation. It has already been applied in the commentary of Bousset (1896), which, with that of Holtzmann (1893), offers the most valuable aid to the understanding of the Johannine Apocalypse.

The conclusions that seem to me[1] to be firmly established by the diligent research of the last two centuries is as follows. The Apocalypse of John did not arise gradually as the result of numerous revisions and combinations of documents, but appears from the homogeneity of its language and tone, and also from a certain harmony in its dramatic structure, to be the work of a Christian writer at the end of the first or beginning of the second century, and to be designed to serve a definite religious purpose. But this author has embodied in his work apocalyptic material of various kinds, both from oral and written tradition, differing in its character, origin, and age, and has welded it together in a sometimes more, sometimes less felicitous fashion into a single whole. Whence he derived these foreign elements, whether they were originally Jewish or even (in part) heathen, and to what extent he recast them in working them up, is a question which must be considered anew in each individual case, and the solution of which is still so difficult—and may well, indeed, remain so permanently—that the greatest care and caution is everywhere necessary. And this we shall be the better able to exercise if we bear in mind that these questions regarding the origin and character of the various elements which are here combined, however interesting they may be as problems of the history of religion, are, after all, of subordinate importance for the understanding of the whole work, and its significance in the history of early Christianity. The task of the exegete consists primarily in ascertaining

[1] In essential agreement with the views of Weizsäcker, Sabatier, Holtzmann, Jülicher, and Bousset.

approximately, so far as is possible, the meaning which the writer himself attached to his visions and images; what sense they may have borne in their original form is certainly a question of less importance, since the writer himself can scarcely have had any definite knowledge regarding it.

The Apocalypse begins with a superscription, i. 1–3, which announces the contents, origin, and purpose of the book: "The revelation of Jesus Christ which God gave unto Him, to show unto His servants the things which should shortly come to pass, and He (Christ) made it known by His angel to His servant John, who bare witness of the word of God and of the testimony of Jesus Christ, even of all things that he saw. Blessed is he that readeth and they who hear the words of the prophecy, and keep that which is written therein, for the time (of the final fulfilment) is at hand." This revelation therefore is ultimately ascribed to God; proximately to Christ and His angels. The conception of the communication of higher revelations through angels belongs, from Dan. viii. 16 onwards, to the standing features of apocalyptic literature, and is thence adopted here, and again at the close, xxii. 16, although in the course of the work no special angel appears as the mediator of revelation. As, according to i. 10, the seer beheld his vision while in a condition of being filled with the Spirit, and as, according to xix. 10, the spirit of prophecy is identical with the testimony of Jesus, it would be more natural to expect that the revelation of Jesus would be made through the Spirit rather than through the angel. But we should hardly be justified in basing upon that an objection to the genuineness of this superscription.

THE APOCALYPSE 405

The angel of revelation appears again not only at the close (xxii. 16), but also several times in the course of the work, and stands in no contradiction with the spirit of revelation, because "angel" and "spirit" are never definitely distinguished by the writer, as will frequently appear.

In verses 4-8 the writer salutes the Seven Churches of Asia, to which he is charged to write in the vision that follows. To the Pauline greeting, "Grace be unto you, and peace!" he makes the peculiar addition, "from Him who is, and was, and is to come, and from the seven angels which are before His throne, and from Jesus Christ, the true witness, the first-born from the dead and the ruler of the kings of the earth." The paraphrastic description of God is an expansion of a Rabbinic interpretation of the name Jahwe, which is found in the Targum of Jerusalem, in the explanation of Ex. iii. 14, in the form *qui fuit, est, et erit*. The seven spirits which are before the throne of God appear again in iv. 5 under the figure of seven candles, and in v. 6 under that of the seven eyes of the Lamb, and are doubtless to be identified with the seven stars in the hand of the Son of Man, i. 16, which, in verse 20, are interpreted as the angels of the seven churches, and are identified also with the seven angels who stand before God (viii. 2). In the book of Enoch (xx.) the six or (according to another reading) seven archangels are enumerated by name; as to the origin of this Jewish tradition there can be no doubt;[1] even the uncertainty regarding the number points to the Persian doctrine of six, or, if

[1] *Cf.* Beer on Enoch xx. (in Kautzsch's *Pseudepigr. des A.T's.*, p. 251), and Bousset, *Kommentar*, p. 216 f.

Ahura Mazda is counted in, seven Amesha Spentas ("immortal holy ones"), who are connected with the seven Babylonian star-gods (sun, moon, and the five planets). From the same source comes the Gnostic hebdomad of world-ruling spiritual powers or archons, who in their systems are placed in a position of more or less direct antagonism to the supreme Deity. For the Christian apocalyptist they are, of course, only subordinate instruments of God; but the fact that they are named immediately after God and before Christ is very instructive as regards the strong influence of the syncretistic mythology of the East upon the Jewish-Christian apocalyptic, which arose parallel with the beginnings of Gnosticism. Later, when, in face of the developed Gnostic systems, the dangerous character of this doctrine of spirits was recognised by the Church, and it was felt to be opposed to the unity of God and the unique mediatorial position of the Divine Saviour, a Christian teacher in Asia Minor could scarcely have written as our author does in Apoc. i. 4, where the position of the spirits indicates that Christ is thought of as essentially similar to them, as the chief among them, as indeed is also the case in the Roman apocalypse of Hermas. Christ is described in i. 5 as the "true witness," the revelation of God, the "first-born from the dead and ruler of all the kings of the earth"; in writing this, the author must have had in mind, besides the Pauline formulas of Col. i. 18 and 1 Cor. xv. 20, Psalm lxxxix. 28, where God gives to the Davidic King the promise: "He shall be my first-born, the highest of the kings of the earth." This Jewish Messianic conception is followed immediately in i. 5 ff.

THE APOCALYPSE 407

by an expression of the Christian consciousness of salvation which recalls 1 Pet. i. 19, ii. 9, iv. 11: " who hath loved us and redeemed (or, with another reading, " washed ") us from our sins, and hath made us a kingdom, priests (*i.e.* a royal priesthood) unto God His Father: to Him be the glory and dominion for ever!" After this ascription of praise comes the main point of all the apocalyptic hopes of the Christians, stated in a solemn liturgical formula, i. 7 : " Behold, He cometh in the clouds, and every eye shall see Him, and they which pierced Him, and all the tribes of the earth shall mourn over Him." This formula is a combination of Dan. vii. 13 and Zech. xii. 10 ; the latter passage is referred to also in Jn. xix. 37, where the Evangelist follows the apocalyptic writer ; the same is doubtless the case in Mt. xxiv. 30, where the divergence from the two other Synoptists is most simply to be explained by dependence upon the Apocalypse,[1] which is also to be noticed in some other passages of Matthew. The closing formula in i. 7 : " Yea and Amen," and the self-witness of God as the Eternal and Almighty in verse 8, clearly exhibit the elevated language of early Christian liturgy. Whether this formula in 7 was inserted by the writer himself for use in the public reading of the Apocalypse, or, with the same purpose, by one of the earliest copyists, I do not know.

In verses 9-20 the seer describes how on the island of Patmos, where he was "for the word of God and the testimony of Jesus," being on the Lord's day in a spiritual rapture, he was commanded by a mighty voice to write the letters to the Seven Churches (chaps. ii.

[1] *Cf.* Bousset, *Kommentar*, p. 220.

and iii.), and thereupon saw, standing amid the seven candlesticks, "one like unto a son of man," with eyes like flame, feet like glowing brass, a voice like the voice of many waters, holding in His right hand seven stars, while out of His mouth proceeded a sharp sword; and His countenance was like the sun shining in its strength. Then he fell as though dead (for fear). And the One like unto a son of man laid His right hand on him and said: " Fear not, I am the First and the Last and the Living One. I was dead, and behold I am alive again for evermore, and I have the keys of death and Hades. Write now what thou hast seen, and what is, and what is to come; the mystery of the seven stars which thou sawest in my right hand and the seven golden candlesticks: the seven stars are the angels of the Seven Churches, and the seven candlesticks are the Seven Churches." The description of this Christophany is modelled on the theophanies of Ezek. i., Dan. vii. 10, Enoch xlvi.; the loftiness of God, the awful Ruler of the world, is transferred by the Christian seer to the exalted Christ, whom he describes, following verbally Dan. vii. 13, as "one like unto a son of man," not according to the Gospel formula as "the Son of Man." This very dependence on literary predecessors is in itself a proof that the vision was not really seen in this form by the author, but is the reflective product of an imagination filled with Oriental imagery. How incapable of visual realisation is the sword proceeding forth from the mouth of the Son of Man!—or the seven stars in His right hand, which He nevertheless lays upon the seer! And in putting the interpretation of the stars and lamps into the mouth of the Son of Man Himself (v. 20 f.), the writer exchanges the rôle of seer for that of an apocalyptic mystagogue. He certainly did not himself invent these two mystical symbols, but took them over from the common material of apocalyptic tradition, the roots of which reach back to the Babylonian myth of the seven higher star-gods. As Daniel made the heathen spiritual powers into angel-princes over the nations (Persians, Greeks, and Jews, Dan. x.), so the apocalyptist John makes them the guardian angels or spirits of the individual Christian churches. In this way he is able to represent what Christ charges him to say to the churches as addressed to the angels which represent them, though in this the circumstance that these seven angels are previously represented as surrounding Christ, and that there is therefore no reason why they should need to receive the revelation of Christ through the intermediary of the seer, is overlooked. The difficulty of this somewhat awkward conception is simply to be explained by the fact that the apocalyptist has to reckon, in the first place, with a traditional mythical conception according to which the star-spirits belonged to the immediate entourage of God (like the Persian Amshaspands), and that he then gives to this myth the new form that these star-gods are the guardian-spirits and representatives of the Christian churches, for which the word of God is communicated to them through the prophet. There is, similarly, another Christian adaptation of an ancient myth in verse 18, where Christ says of Himself that He has been dead, and is now alive for evermore, and has the keys of death and Hades. This power of the keys of death belongs, according to Jewish ideas, only to God; here it is ascribed to the Son of Man as having Himself been dead, therefore in Hades, but having become alive again—that is, having thence returned victorious. We are reminded of the Babylonian-Gnostic myths of the conquest of the powers of death by a divine hero who descended into the under-world, broke through its gates, seized the keys of it, and, as victor over death and hell, returned to the world of life and light to be the saviour and the pledge of life to his own.

In chaps. ii. and iii. are given the seven letters which have been already announced. First comes that to the church of Ephesus, as the principal city of the province, and perhaps also the native place of the writer. Christ, who proclaims Himself as the Lord of the stars and lamps—that is, of the churches—praises the Ephesian Christians for their conduct towards evil men, the pseudo-apostles and Nicolaitans, whom they refuse to tolerate, and for their patience in the bearing of afflictions, but blames them because the fervour of their first love has cooled, and exhorts them to return to their first works, that is, to the first enthusiasm of their brotherly love, which expressed itself in abundant works of beneficence, and finally promises to "him that overcometh" that he shall eat of the tree of life in the Paradise of God. The false apostles in verse 2 are men who, under a cloak of Christianity, penetrate into the churches as emissaries of the Nicolaitans (verse 6), who are identified with the Balaamites (verse 14 f.) and the followers of the false prophetess Jezebel (verse 20 ff.), and were therefore a libertine Gnostic sect similar to the Simonians and Cainites. They did not originally spring from the Christian Church, but were Jewish-pagan syncretists, of whom there were many in the Jewish-Hellenistic Diaspora; it was natural, however, that they should seek to propagate their libertine heathen principles and orgiastic mysteries in the Gentile-Christian or mixed churches, with which they had in common antinomianism, in the sense of a rejection of legalistic orthodox Judaism. These Jewish-pagan syncretists had originally had nothing whatever in common with the Apostle Paul and his Christian disciples, although at a later period their hero, Simon Magus, was made by Jewish malignity a caricature of Paul. Their agitation can hardly have got a foothold in the Christian churches much before the end of the first century, for the polemic in the letters to the Seven Churches in the Apocalypse gives the impression that its appearance was then quite recent, and that the danger was consequently the greater for the churches, which were still unused to this mode of attack by agitators disguised as Christian apostles. An instance of wandering heretical preachers of this kind coming from Syria to Ephesus is found in the letter of Ignatius to the Ephesians, chap. ix.; but these men were disseminating a Gnostic docetism of the same kind as Saturninus, Basilides, and Cerinthus. Nothing of that kind, however, is mentioned in the case of the Nicolaitans in the Apocalypse; they obviously represent an earlier stage of Gnosticism, when it still consisted of Jewish-heathen syncretism and libertinism, and did not concern itself with Christian doctrine. With this agrees the statement of Irenæus, who in III. xi. 1 remarks concerning the Nicolaitans that, though they grew from the same root as Cerinthus (the popular syncretistic Jewish-Syrian Gnosis), they appeared "much earlier"—a statement which carries with it important consequences for the chronology of the Johannine Apocalypse on the one hand, and of the Johannine Gospel and Epistles on the other.

The church at Smyrna is exhorted to faithfulness under the persecution which is already to some extent in progress, but which threatens to be more severe in the future. With this persecution appears to be connected in some way as its cause, the slanders of those who call themselves Jews, but are in reality a synagogue of Satan. To the faithful is promised the victor's crown of (eternal) life and immunity from the second (eternal) death. The persons who call themselves Jews (verse 9) are certainly not a party in the Christian church, but are real Jews who are hostile to the church, and are concerned in the persecution, either as instigating or encouraging it. The only question that remains is whether they were ordinary orthodox Jews, in which case they are not to be identified with the Nicolaitans and Balaamites, or whether they were identical with these, and therefore heretical Gnostic Jews. Either is possible; a consideration which tells somewhat in favour of the second alternative is that the description of them as a synagogue of Satan, who wrongfully arrogated to themselves the name of Jews, seems to be more appropriate if they had really, by adopting a semi-pagan heresy and by rejection of the law, put themselves outside the pale of orthodox Judaism, than if they were strict Jews to whom the name of Jews is refused only because of their hostility to Christianity; we do not, so far as I know, find any instances of this elsewhere. On the other side it may be urged that slander and persecution of the Christians on the part of heretical Gnostic Jews, who were in the habit of endeavouring to propagate their opinions among the Christians, is less probable than on the part of orthodox Jews, who hated Christians as their rivals in the propaganda of monotheism. A half-century after the time of the Apocalypse the Jewish colony in Smyrna played a very odious part at the trial and martyrdom of the bishop Polycarp; if their attitude towards the Christians at the time when the Apocalypse was written was one of equally intense hostility, it is not difficult to understand that they might be described by a writer who was himself a Jewish Christian as a synagogue of Satan and unworthy of the Jewish name.

The church at Pergamos is praised for its loyalty to the faith, which it had preserved in a time of severe persecution and at a difficult post, "where Satan's throne is," but is also blamed for having in its midst some adherents of the doctrine of Balaam, who of old taught the Israelites to eat things offered to idols and to commit fornication. They have also some who hold the teaching of the Nicolaitans (verses 14 and 15). This raises the question whether those who held the doctrine of Balaam and those who held the doctrine of the Nicolaitans were two different though closely related sects, or one only under two different names. In favour of the latter alternative, appeal may be made to the similar significance of the names Balaam and Nicolaus (subduer of the people), though not of course in the sense that the writer of the

Apocalypse had himself given the name of Nicolaitans to this sect, on account of the word-play on Balaam —no one would have understood that—but that the sect itself, in its native Syria, had been named from Balaam, and then when it penetrated into Hellenistic regions the corresponding Greek name had been substituted for the Semitic (the relation between the names being the same as in the case of "Naasenes" and "Ophites"). A sect which took the name of Balaam, the heathen seer and magician who suggested the temptation of Israel to take part in heathen idolatry and licentiousness, is exactly parallel with the sect of the Simonians, who made Simon the magician and pander their hero, and of the Cainites, who honoured Cain, Esau, Korah, the Sodomites, and Judas, as their patrons, and declared indulgence in all shameless practices and the dissolution of all order to be the perfect Gnosis (Iren., I. xxxi.; Epiphan., xxxviii. 3). It is quite intelligible that the abandonment of the Mosaic law by sceptical Jews, who had come under heathen influence, led to a "naturalistic" manner of thought and life which gloried in the practice of just those things which were most strictly forbidden to the Jews, such as participation in heathen sacrificial feasts and licentious orgies; only a mistaken prejudice in favour of the view that the reference is to a party which owed its origin to Pauline Christianity could have induced the exegetes to attempt to read artificial metaphorical meanings into the word πορνεῦσαι. It is also to be noticed that the Nicolaitan teaching had found an entrance to the churches of Pergamos and Thyatira only, and even here only in the case of individuals;

the great majority of the Christians had from the first resolutely rejected this crude heathen-syncretistic naturalism. Gnosticism did not become really dangerous until later, when it had moderated its youthful wildness, filled out its myths with Hellenistic and Christian ideas, and substituted for this licentious libertinism a strict ascetic self-discipline (Saturninus); it was only then that it began to make an imposing impression on Christians, and exercised such a power of attraction that the simple faith of the Church seemed to be threatened in its very foundations. That is the situation in the Ignatian and Johannine Epistles, which for that very reason must be considerably later than the Letters to the Churches in the Apocalypse. What the writer meant by the "throne of Satan" in Pergamos (verse 13) we do not know. Since it stands in some kind of connection with the persecution of the church there, it can hardly refer to some mere show-place of the city, such as the temple of Æsculapius or of Zeus, but must be some institution connected with the politico-religious world-power of Rome, whether as the seat of proconsular administration or the centre of the organisation of the worship of the Emperor by the priests of the temple "of Augustus and Rome" which was at Pergamos. The promise at the close of this letter is also enigmatic —what is the meaning of the "hidden manna," or of the "white stone" with the "new name thereon which no one knoweth but he that receiveth it"? I do not undertake to solve this enigma, but my impression is that those interpreters are on the right lines who do not think in this connection of purely spiritual blessings, but take account of the apocalyptic realism which, as we see in Baruch xxix. 8, expected in the Messianic period a repetition of the rain of manna for the benefit of the faithful; and also of the widely diffused conviction—not less among the Christians of the Church than among pagans and Gnostics—of the magic power of secret formulæ and names, by the possession of which a man could lay even the spirits of the lower world under a spell.[1]

The church at Thyatira is praised for its growing zeal in works of love, its faith and patience, but blamed for its toleration of serious errors, since a woman named Jezebel, who called herself a prophetess, had tempted some members of the church to eat idol-sacrifices and commit fornication, in punishment for which she herself is threatened with sickness, her companions in guilt with severe affliction, and her children with (premature) death. To the remaining members of the church, however, who did not, like these deceived deceivers, boast of themselves that they "had known the deep things of Satan," it is declared that Christ will lay on them no further burden (of observances); but that which they now had (in the way of Christian morality), they must hold fast until He should come again. To those who should be faithful and overcome is promised a share in the Messianic reign (described in the language of Psalm ii. 8 ff.), and also that Christ will give them "the morning star" (ii. 28). What is meant by this is still quite obscure; perhaps some explanation will be forthcoming from the Babylonian-Gnostic astrology.

[1] *Cf.* Enoch lxix. 14 ff., and see Beer thereon in Kautzsch's *Pseudepigr.*, p. 276. Also Bousset's *Kommentar*, p. 251. In regard to the magical formulæ in general, see Dieterich, *Abraxas*.

On the other hand, what is said of the teaching and conduct of the prophetess Jezebel is easily understood in the light of what is said previously about the Nicolaitans and Balaamites. We may leave it an open question whether the name Jezebel was the real name of the woman, or an allegorical nickname; she herself, however, was doubtless no allegory, but a real person belonging to that class of women in whom religious and erotic exaltation is combined, of which the religious history of all times furnishes so many examples. As the adherent of one of the libertine Gnostic sects, such as the Nicolaitans of verse 14 f., she propagated its principles by oracles uttered in a state of ecstasy and by shameless orgies, and justified her conduct by professing that this was the only way to attain to the knowledge (Gnosis) of the ultimate mysteries, "the deeps of Satan." These words (verse 24) are not to be taken as an ironic phrase of the writer of the Apocalypse, which would not be in harmony with the stern seriousness which he shows elsewhere, but are doubtless simply a literal quotation of the watchword of these curious enthusiasts. This agrees so well with the picture that Irenæus draws of those " Gnostics " who desired to know "the depths," and of the Cainites, who held that acquaintance with all experience, and absolute freedom from moral scruples, was the way of salvation, that I see no reason to trouble about other ingenious but artificial attempts to explain it. The assurance given to the faithful (verse 25) that no other burden will be laid upon them, beyond the observance of traditional Church morality, which means especially (according to verse 20) abstinence from meats offered to idols and unchastity, reminds us of the prescriptions of the apostolic decree in Acts xv. 28 f., but naturally has no direct reference to this passage, for that is chronologically impossible, since Acts is later than the Apocalypse. It would be more justifiable to find in Apoc. i. 25 evidence that the apostolic decree has some kind of historical basis (*cf.* above, vol. ii. 235).

The churches of Sardis and Laodicea (iii. 1-6, 14-22) are sharply censured for their religious lukewarmness and moral laxity. There are only a few in Sardis who have not defiled their garments (by immorality); to them it is promised that they shall be clothed with white raiment (as partakers in the Messianic marriage-feast; *cf.* xix. 8), and that their names shall not be blotted out of the Lamb's book of life, but Christ will recognise them as His before His Father and the angels (iii. 5)—this last being the Gospel formula for inclusion in the Messianic Kingdom, and practically equivalent to that which, from Daniel (xii. 1) onwards, became the standing formula of Apocalyptic—" to be enrolled in the Book of Life." The church of Laodicea is warned against the dangers of self-deception, and exhorted to look within and reform itself, because Christ stands before the door and enters in to whomsoever will open to Him, and will sup with him—this, too, being a current figure of Jewish Apocalyptic (*cf.* Enoch lxii. 14 ff.: " The Lord of spirits will dwell above the elect, and they shall eat with the Son of Man, and shall continually sit down and rise up with Him. They shall be clothed with the garment of splendour, and that shall be a garment of life, and their raiment shall not grow old, and their splendour shall not fade ").[1]

The church of Philadelphia receives the highest testimony of any of the seven (iii. 7-13). Christ, who is described (as in Isa. xxii. 22) as the bearer of the key of David, *i.e.* as Lord of the theocracy, declares to this church, which has kept His word and not denied His name, that He has set before it an open door which no man can shut, and that He will cause the hostile Jews to come and worship before the church's feet, and acknowledge that Christ has loved it. Probably this does not mean a conversion of the Jews by the missionary efforts of the Philadelphian church; it is an eschatological promise that the church, having remained faithful in face of a persecution directed against it by the Jews, shall share in the Messianic reign of Christ (ii. 26 ff.)—the "open door" is to the heavenly theocracy, verse 8 compared with 7—and that their present oppressors will then be at their feet as conquered foes, and acknowledge the rule of the Christians who are beloved by the Messiah. "These letters are still under the influence of a thoroughly Jewish eschatology and a realistic conception of the future" (Bousset). At the close the victor is promised that he shall be made a pillar in the temple of God, and shall never leave it again, and upon him shall be written the name of God and of

---

[1] Beer (Commentary on Enoch in Kautzsch's *Pseudepigr.*, 272) remarks that the conception of the heavenly garments of the blessed was derived from Persia. It was current also in the Gnostic poetry; *cf.* the hymn of the soul in the Acts of Thomas, *sup.*, p. 192 ff.

the New Jerusalem which cometh down from heaven, and the new name of Christ (verse 12), figures which recall Isa. lvi. 5, lxxii. 6, and are intended to indicate inseparable connection with the Kingdom of Messiah which should be victoriously established upon earth (the New Jerusalem which comes down from heaven).

After the revelation announced in the first vision (i. 9–20) regarding the present ($ἅ$ $εἰσὶν$) has been completed in the seven letters dictated to the seer by Christ, there begins in chap. iv. the revelation of the future, introduced by a new vision. The seer beholds a door opened in heaven, and hears again the same voice as in the former vision, which now commands him to "come up hither" (to heaven), in order that there may be shewed to him all things which shall occur hereafter (iv. 1, $ἅ$ $δεῖ$ $γενέσθαι$ $μετὰ$ $ταῦτα$; cf. i. 19, $ἅ$ $μέλλει$ $γίνεσθαι$ $μετὰ$ $ταῦτα$). Thereupon he fell again into a spiritual ecstasy, as he had done before at the time of the first vision, i. 10. (The close of this trance is naturally understood to take place immediately after the dictation of the letters, and the recurrence of the enthusiastic state is therefore clearly indicated here.) In this condition he beheld in the first place the heavenly visions of chaps. iv. and v., which precede the opening of the book of fate, just as in chap. i. 12–20 a similar scene precedes the letters. He beholds in heaven the Divine Majesty seated upon a throne, glorious as precious stones or as the rainbow, surrounded by four-and-twenty elders in white raiment, wearing golden crowns, also seated upon thrones. What the seer understood by this vision is doubtful. Some have supposed that there is an allusion to the twenty-four priests of the Jewish cultus; but it is questionable on what grounds the representatives of these could receive the honour of sitting upon heavenly thrones, with crowns on their heads, round about God. Much more probable is the conjecture of Gunkel[1] that these twenty-four elders were originally twenty-four Babylonian star-gods, who, divided equally between north and south, were thought of as performing the functions of judges of the living and the dead (according to Diodorus Siculus, ed. Becker, ii. 31); these Babylonian gods became in Judaism great angels and members of the heavenly council, a pendant to the seven, or six, archangels who sprang from the Babylonian star-gods or Persian Amshaspands (see above, on i. 4). The apocalyptist makes use in the description of this heavenly vision of conceptions long current in tradition, without reflecting on their origin; it is not probable, therefore, that he has in view the judicial functions of the twenty-four Babylonian elders, and intended to signify by their appearance the beginning of the judgment of the world; what happens in the sequel is much more an act of worship than of judgment.[2] The seven lamps before the throne are interpreted by the writer of the Apocalypse himself as "the seven spirits of God" (iv. 5), which he had already introduced (i. 4) as in

[1] *Schöpfung und Chaos*, p. 303 ff.
[2] *Cf.* Bousset, *Kommentar*, p. 291: "That the apocalyptic writer has only half understood the old traditional figure is shown by the fact that he gives to the elders priestly functions. It was customary to represent God's majesty and state under this figure, and the original significance of the πρεσβύτεροι was lost sight of."

immediate attendance upon God; the astrological origin of these angel-spirits is here confirmed by the figure of the burning torches. What the seer meant by the glassy sea before the throne is obscure. Again, it is so impossible to realise visually the position of the four marvellous creatures "in the midst of, and round about, the throne," that we are forced to recognise that these things were not really seen in vision, but composed by learned reflection from traditional conceptions. The "living creatures" who had respectively the forms of a lion, an ox, a man, and an eagle, and had each six wings, and a multitude of eyes round about and within, are a combination of the cherubim in Ezek. i. 10 (where, however, the four faces are found together in each) and the seraphim of Isa. vi. 2; their animal forms or attributes betray their origin from nature-myth. In Judaism they become angels of the highest rank (*cf.* Enoch lxi. 10 f., lxxi. 6 f., xxxix. 12; in the last passage there is ascribed to them, as here, the unceasing praise of the thrice holy God).

The worship offered to God by the four "living creatures" and the four-and-twenty elders prepares the way for the great scene which follows this vision. In this God holds in His right hand the book of fate, written within and on the back, and sealed with seven seals, of which no one in heaven or earth or in the under-world is able to loose the seals except the "Lion of the tribe of Judah, the Root of David," who has won the victory (over Death and Hell) in such wise as to be able to open the book. Christ being thus introduced, the seer immediately beholds Him standing in the midst of the heavenly assembly, "a Lamb as

THE APOCALYPSE 423

though it had been slain, which had seven horns and seven eyes." This Lamb received from the hand of God the book of fate; and thereupon there sound forth in His praise the hymns of the elders and of the myriads of angels (v. 9 ff.). This representation of Christ under the two figures of a victorious lion and a slain lamb is characteristic of the Apocalypse; it undeniably corresponds to the two aspects of the conception of Christ in the mind of the Church, which united victorious, heroic courage with patient humility. It may, however, be doubted whether this alone suffices to explain the twofold image, and especially the expression, peculiar to the Apocalypse, but there much in favour, "the slain lamb" (τὸ ἀρνίον τὸ ἐσφαγμένον). Neither the paschal lamb nor the lamb (ἀμνός) of Isa. liii. (1 Pet. i. 19) furnishes a parallel to this apocalyptic lamb with its seven horns and seven eyes, which also stand for the seven spirits which go out into the whole earth (v. 6). These spirits are obviously the same which are associated in iii. 1 with the seven stars; as they are here associated with the seven eyes of the lamb, the conclusion suggests itself that there was an original connection between these eyes and the stars, and that the lamb is therefore an originally mythological figure.[1] If, further, we consider that this "lamb" has seven horns, and is therefore represented as more like a ram than an actual lamb, the conjecture is perhaps not too bold that the picture of this lamb which represents Christ in the Apocalypse is based upon the sign of the ram

[1] The suggestion is made by Gunkel, *ut sup.*, p. 299 note, and worked out on the same lines as above by Havet, *Origines du Christianisme*, iv. 327 ff.

in the zodiac,[1] and the lion upon the sign "Leo." Both these signs have reference to the sun, the former as beginning the spring, the latter as marking the period of his victorious strength in midsummer. Now, the sun-god, in the various forms which he takes in his yearly progress through the signs of the zodiac, was the central point of the nature-religions of Asia Minor, and consequently of the religion of Mithra, on whose cultus-monuments the circle of the zodiac, with the sun-god mounting or descending, is often found. It was therefore quite natural for a writer as familiar with the imagery of mythology and apocalyptic as the seer of the Apocalypse is, to set over against the heathen sun-god, who is sometimes a young and weak ram, sometimes a strong lion, the Son of Man, whose "countenance is as the sun that shineth in its strength" (i. 16), and who, similarly, is both a strong lion and a weak sacrificial lamb which seems "as though it had been slain" (ὡς ἐσφαγμένον). This further trait might also, if we adopt the suggestion of a reference to the cultus of the sun-god in Western Asia, find a point of connection in the mystical sacrifices of rams and bulls (Kriobolium and Taurobolium) in the Mithra-cult, in which the animal was always "slaughtered," and the blood as it streamed freely down was held to be a means of purification and the gaining of life (*cf.* v. 9, vii. 14). In view of the fact that the actual manner

[1] It is to be noted that the word ἀρνίον, which is only used in the Apocalypse, is connected with ἀρνειός, which in Homer signifies "ram"; also that among the Persians the zodiacal sign in question was designated by a word which also means "lamb"; finally, that the ἀρνίον in xiii. 11 corresponds to the "ram" in Dan. viii. 2 f.

of Jesus' death upon the cross was not a "slaughter" causing an abundant flow of blood, the strong emphasis upon the "slaughter" and the forth-pouring of blood in the case of the apocalyptic "lamb" have so little historical motive that it is allowable to look round for suggestions elsewhere, and of these the purifying blood of the ram and ox in the Phrygian and Mithra mysteries the more readily suggests itself because the parallel images of the ram (= lamb) and the lion also point to this sun-worship. This is, it must be admitted, only a possible hypothesis, of which it is at present difficult to estimate the probability, and the validity of which I am not prepared to champion.

In chapter vi. the seer describes the opening of the first six seals of the book of fate. As each is opened there takes place before the eyes of the seer a symbolic action typifying the earthly events which each book contains. At the opening of each of the first four seals there appears a rider, the first upon a white horse, the second upon a red, the third upon a black, and the fourth upon a pale horse. The last personifies death, who destroys men by sword, hunger, pestilence, and wild beasts; the other three refer to great judgments upon the peoples by war and famine. We are not, however, to think of definite historical occurrences; the apocalyptist is painting the terrors of the future in the symbolic representations of great calamities which had long been current: the four horses are from Zech. i. 8; war, famine, and pestilence from Jer. xiv. 12, xv. 2, xxiv. 10, etc. It is possible, indeed, that war is represented by both the first and second riders, in the twofold form of a Parthian and a Roman invasion, the former symbolised by the bow, the latter by the sword, but this does not appear to me to be necessarily the case. We must allow some freedom of imagination to the apocalyptist, and not suspect in every petty detail of the image which presents itself to him intentional allegory and historical allusion. It is only at the opening of the fifth seal that the seer unrolls a new and striking picture; he hears the souls of the martyrs (naturally not only those of the Neronian persecution) from their resting-place—which he locates, following a traditional conception, under the heavenly altar—crying to God for a final vengeance for their blood. In this he gives expression to a feeling which is so human and universal that it is found among the Christians of his time and of later times (*cf.* Tertullian) as well as among Jews. But their desire for judgment and recompense cannot immediately be fulfilled; they receive for the present only white raiment as a pledge of their future glory, and are exhorted to wait yet a little time until the number of the martyrs shall be filled up. A similar thought, though couched in more general terms, is found in 2 Esdras iv. 35 and Enoch xlvii.: the reward of righteous souls and the answer of their prayers shall only be given when the number of the righteous has been completed. There is hardly sufficient reason to assume a definite literary relationship. This belief was obviously part of the common stock of ideas of the pious circles which found their solace in apocalypses among both Jews and Christians; it was closely connected with their predestinarian view of providence and their pessimistic judgment of the actual conditions. Things must become steadily worse in this present world-era until the deliverance of the new age shall dawn. At the breaking of the sixth seal there occur the awful earthquakes and signs in heaven which, according to the scheme of the apocalyptic drama, formed the woes immediately preceding the end ; all the inhabitants of earth, and especially (note the still clearly audible echo of the early Christian tone) the rulers, the mighty and the rich, fall into great fear and seek to hide themselves from the face of the Judge of the world and from the wrath of the Lamb, for "the great day of their wrath is come, and who is able to stand?"

This would lead us to expect that at the opening of the seventh seal the judgment will begin. But with chapter vii. commences the first of those interpolations between the announcement and the catastrophe, of which there are several subsequent examples. In all these cases, the purpose is the same, that, namely, of putting back the clock of history and retarding the end, of allaying impatience and damping apocalyptic ardour. With this purpose our author takes from the rich storehouse of apocalyptic tradition now this and now that group of conceptions, and inserts them as interludes, which suspend the action at the most exciting parts of his eschatological drama, without troubling particularly about the connection of these interpolated scenes with their context. An interlude of this kind is chapter vii., the first half of which is taken over from Jewish Apocalyptic (whether by way of oral or written tradition we do not know). Four angels who stand at the four corners of the world, and rule over the winds (*cf.* Enoch lx. 12, lxix. 12), are commanded by an angel who arises in the east to hold back the winds that damage land and sea until the servants of God have been sealed upon the forehead, *i.e.* (as in Ezek. ix. 4) marked out as to be spared in the judgment. Accordingly, one hundred and forty-four thousand men are sealed, twelve thousand of each tribe, though in the enumeration both Joseph and his son Manasseh are counted and Dan is left out; perhaps because, according to Jewish tradition, Antichrist was to come of this tribe (*cf.* Iren., V. xxx. 2). These one hundred and forty-four thousand who are sealed must originally, since there is no reference whatever to Christ, have been Jews, the chosen remnant of the theocratic people who, according to ancient promise, should survive the sifting judgment (Rom. xi. 1–7, ix. 27 ff.; Isa. x. 20 ff.). This conception of the sealing of one hundred and forty-four thousand servants of God must, therefore, have been taken over from the Jewish apocalyptic tradition, but this does not, of course, exclude the possibility that the Christian apocalyptist, on his part, thought of these sealed men as the chosen of Israel who believed in Christ, in whom he saw the kernel of the new people of God. But they are only the kernel, for far from restricting the Christian Church to these one hundred and forty-four thousand Jews (or Jewish-Christians), he represents as attached to it a great multitude which no man could number of all tribes and nations, who, clothed in white robes and with palms in their hands, sing praises to God and to the Lamb (vii. 9 f.). When the seer asks who these are, he is told : "These are they who have come out of great tribulation, and have washed their robes and made them white by the blood of the Lamb—therefore are they before the throne of God and serve Him day and night in His temple, and He that sitteth upon the throne shall spread His tabernacle over them ; they shall not hunger any more, neither thirst any more, neither shall the sun light on them nor any heat, for the Lamb which is in the midst of the throne shall shepherd them, and shall lead them unto the fountains of the waters of life, and God shall wipe away all tears from their eyes" (vii. 14–17). The question whether the seer thought here only of the Christian martyrs, or of the Gentile Christians in general, seems to me to be of no great consequence, since he certainly sees at hand a time of universal severe testing (iii. 10), in which all those who hold out faithfully must be to a greater or less extent martyrs. The very fact that they have endured this great tribulation and, trusting in the sacrificial blood of the Lamb,[1] have submitted to the blood-baptism of suffering, has in the eyes of the seer purified them from all heathen defilement of sin, and made them capable of a priestly service of God, in the same immediate fellowship with Christ and perfect bliss as the chosen of the ancient people of God. That gives us an interesting glimpse of the progress of thought by which so decided a Jewish-Christian as our seer is,

[1] This I hold, with Bousset (*Commentary*, 334 f.), to be the meaning of ἐν τῷ αἵματι τοῦ ἀρνίου, v. 14, for "to make their garments white in the blood of the Lamb" would be an impossible conception. Christ's sacrificial death is thought of as the ultimate cause, while their own blood-baptism of martyrdom is thought of as the proximate cause of their purification. In this, too, the analogy with the mystical blood-baptism of the Taurobolium and Kriobolium remains unmistakable, and therefore the possibility of an allusion to it is undeniable.

and remains, was enabled to rise to the most unrestricted Christian universalism, by a method other than the Pauline dialectic—for him the common experience of suffering, the blood-baptism in which, in a sense, Christ's sacrificial blood ever flows anew, was the effectual means of purification which consecrated the heathen brethren to an equal dignity of priestly service with the ancient people of God. That is the higher, Christian, ethical version of the idea which underlay the heathen mystery-cults—for example, the religion of Mithra—in which the ascent to each successive grade of consecration could only be attained by severe tests of endurance and courage, and the white garment of the priests was conferred upon those who had purified themselves by the blood-baptism of the Kriobolium or Taurobolium, and for those who had thus been "born again" all earlier distinctions of nation and rank disappeared in the common brotherhood.

In chapter viii. the seer returns to the vision of the seals. The seventh seal is opened, a silence of strained expectation falls in heaven; but the end is not yet. It is postponed by two new pictures which simultaneously, and merging into one another like dissolving views, enter the seer's field of vision —that of the seven angels with trumpets, and that of the angel with the censer at the altar of incense (of the heavenly Temple, which served as the model of the earthly). The latter vision again has two developments. The smoke of the incense as it rises aids the prayers of the saints, and the fire which is taken from the altar and cast upon the earth produces there thunder, lightning, and earthquake.

THE APOCALYPSE 431

This was perhaps to prepare the way for a vision of seven thunders, which is also touched on incidentally in x. 3, but allowed to drop again. The figure of the angel with the censer soon disappears, to make room for the seven angels with trumpets who have already been seen (verse 6). The soundings of the trumpets which then follow announce for the most part those catastrophes of nature which form the standing repertory of apocalyptic prodigies, the original suggestion of which is found in the Egyptian plagues. More unusual are the scenes which are ushered in by the fifth and sixth trumpets (ix. 1 ff.). There falls from heaven a star which seems to take on human shape (as a spiritual existence it can, of course, change itself at any time into an animal or a man; *cf.* Enoch lxxxvi., lxxxviii., xc.) and receives the keys of the pit of the abyss. When he opens this there comes up a smoke which darkens the sun, and from which hellish swarms of locusts come forth, having a shape which combines scorpion, horse, and man, and owning as their king Abaddon, the angel of destruction; and these for a period of five months torment all who are not sealed. This picture, which defies all natural or historical interpretation, is simply a piece of popular mythology similar to the myths of the centaurs, harpies, and the like. Our author did not, of course, invent it himself, but took it over from folk-lore and used it as valuable material for the elaboration of his vision of the seven trumpets. The same applies to the vision which appears at the sixth trumpet (ix. 13 ff.). It has been thought, indeed, that because the fabulous horsemen are sent forth from the direction of the Euphrates in order to destroy a third of the human race, that this must mean the armies of the Parthians; but formidable as these warriors were, their horses had not, after all, the heads of lions and tails of serpents, each with a head of its own, nor did they spit forth fire and brimstone. Horses of that kind belong not to history but to mythology; they are fire-spitting [1] dragons whose home is placed by legend in the East, a reminiscence of the fact that they have their origin in the Babylonian cosmology and astrology.

As the sixth trumpet introduced the second, or next to last, woe (ix. 12, xi. 14), we now naturally expect the commencement of the third and last woe which brings the end; but, as after the sixth seal, this is deferred by the insertion of a new interlude. But whereas the former interpolation (vii.) was unexplained, the author this time feels obliged to justify himself to his readers by alleging a direct divine command, given to him, he asserts, in a special vision (chap. x.). He sees another angel coming down from heaven, almost as gloriously equipped with the attributes of divine majesty as the Son of Man in chap. i., but not identical with Him. He has in his hand a little book, open; at his voice, which resembled the roaring of a lion, the "seven thunders" (? of viii. 5) lifted up their voices; and the seer desired to write down what they uttered, but was prevented by a heavenly voice, because at the seventh trumpet, which was now about to sound, the mystery of God should be accomplished. However, he is commanded

---

[1] Holtzmann gives a useful reference (*Kommentar*, p. 335) to the giants on the Pergamene altar, which, instead of feet, have snakes with heads.

by the angel to eat the book which the angel had brought from heaven, which shall be sweeter than honey to the taste but bitter in the belly. This comes to pass, and then he is told that he must again prophesy over nations and kings. The difficulty which has been found in this chapter is due to the fact that interpreters have sought in it something much deeper than is really there. It seems to me to be merely a reflection of the writer, couched in apocalyptic imagery, on the further course of his book; he is undecided whether to develop further the vision of the thunders which has been in his mind for some time, or to describe the end forthwith. At a command from above he abandons the former plan, but is not permitted immediately to hasten on to the end; he must first appropriate the contents of a new source of revelation in order to draw from thence new prophecies with a definite reference to the fate of nations and rulers. That is a clear announcement in advance of the subject of the following chapters, xi.–xiv. and xvii.–xix., which are notably distinguished from the rest of the stereotyped apocalyptic material by their reference to definite historical events, hopes, and fears. Whence comes this difference? That, the author himself explains: he has drawn the material for the following prophecies from a new source—namely, "the little book," the varied contents of which call forth mixed feelings in him (and, he assumes, in his readers), a fact which he suggests by a figure borrowed from Ezek. iii. 1. The first of the materials from this new source of revelation is the fragment relating to the fate of Jerusalem and the Temple, xi. 1–13, which is so unconnected with what precedes and follows that a definite meaning can scarcely be extracted from it. The first two verses, indeed, are intelligible enough—the measuring off of the temple and its inner forecourt signifies its immunity from profanation by enemies, while the remainder of the holy city (Jerusalem) is abandoned to them for forty-two months. Wholly obscure, however, is what is said of the two witnesses: they are (1) to preach for 1260 days, in a garment of penitence; (2) they are the two olive trees and candlesticks of the Lord (the same image which is used with reference to Joshua and Zerubbabel in Zech. iv.); (3) they are great wonder-workers, fire goes forth from their mouths for the destruction of their enemies, they hold back the rain, change water into blood, smite the land with plagues (partly resembling Moses and partly Elijah); (4) nevertheless they are overcome by the beast which comes up from the abyss, and are slain and lie unburied (like the priests Ananias and Jesus, who were killed during the Jewish war) upon the streets of the great city "which spiritually is called Sodom and Egypt," where also their King was crucified; (5) the downfall of these two prophets is hailed with rejoicing by the inhabitants of the earth, to whom they had been a torment; (6) after three and a half days they are raised up again by the divine spirit of life, and mount up before the eyes of their enemies in a cloud to heaven (as in the stories of Enoch and Elijah); (7) in that hour there comes a great earthquake which destroys a tenth of the city and slays 7000 men. No interpretation of these enigmatical two witnesses has been found which will harmonise all these various and inconsistent statements; perhaps the author himself did not know the interpretation of this oracle which he took from his little book of revelations. It seems as though mythological traditions were here intertwined with historical events into a knot, the loosing of which has been found impossible by others before ourselves. Regarding the time or environment in which this fragment, or the source from which it was taken, originated, nothing definite is known to us; we may conclude, however, from xi. 1 f., 8, 13, that it must have originated prior to the destruction of Jerusalem and in a circle of which the members could not believe in a profanation or destruction of the Temple. As this would be surprising in the case of Christians, to whom the prophecy of Jesus in Mk. xiii. 2 must have been known, it is possible to infer the Jewish character of this fragment, or of the source from which it was taken; but this conclusion is not imperative, since it was just in the region of apocalyptic that the boundaries between what is Jewish and what is Jewish-Christian were least clearly defined.

In xi. 14 ff. the author takes up again the thread, interrupted at ix. 21, of the trumpet vision, so that x. 1–xi. 13 has the same position as an interlude between the sixth and seventh trumpets as chapter vii. between the sixth and seventh seals. And just as in viii. 1, at the opening of the seventh seal, instead of the expected end two new visions force their way in, the same thing repeats itself at the seventh trumpet, which at the third woe (verse 15) seems about to bring in the end. It is true the hymn of the heavenly voices, to which the four-and-twenty elders respond, clearly celebrates the dawning of the eternal

Kingdom of God, accompanied by judgment upon the enemies of God and reward to His servants (15, 17 f.), but before this comes to pass terrible and decisive battles must take place in heaven and upon earth. To the eye of the seer the heavenly temple is opened and the prototypal ark of the covenant is made visible; lightning and thunder and storm and earthquake go before, presaging the decisive moment. Then appears (xii. 1) a great sign in heaven: a woman arrayed with the sun, and with the moon at her feet, and upon her head a crown of twelve stars; and she was in travail. And before her there rose up a great fiery dragon with seven heads adorned with diadems, and ten horns, who, with his tail, casts down a third part of the stars from heaven to earth, and who is ready to devour the child of the woman as soon as it is born. But the man-child, who is destined to rule all nations with a rod of iron, is caught away to the throne of God; and his mother flees into the wilderness, where she is to be nourished for 1260 days in a place of refuge prepared for her by God. Thereupon there was war in heaven between the Archangel Michael and his angels and the dragon with his hosts; the latter were defeated, and also the great dragon, the old serpent "who is called the devil and Satan," the deceiver of the whole world, was cast down to the earth with his angels, whereupon there arose in heaven a song of victory, announcing the coming of the Kingdom of God and the reign of His Christ. But the battle, decided in heaven, now raged in all its fury upon earth. The dragon persecuted the mother of the man-child, who was carried away upon the wings of a great eagle into the wilderness, where she was kept safe from the serpent for "a time and times and half a time." And the serpent cast up out of his mouth after her a river of water, to carry her away with its flood, but the earth swallowed it up. But the dragon, in his wrath at the escape of the woman, "went away to make war upon the rest of her seed which keep the commandments of God and hold the testimony of Jesus." This curious vision cannot be satisfactorily interpreted either from the Christian or from the Jewish point of view, for it has its ultimate roots in heathen mythology. However much the original myth has been worked over by Jewish and Christian hands, this foundation is visible underneath all these later additions. The woman clothed with the sun and standing upon the moon, wearing a crown of stars and borne upon eagles' pinions, is certainly neither a historical person nor a religious allegory; she is, rather, a heavenly light-goddess. Similarly her enemy and the enemy of her son, the fiery dragon, who smites down to the earth with his tail a third part of the stars of heaven, who wages war against the angels and is cast out of heaven, then pursues the woman as she flees upon the wings of the eagle and casts forth from his mouth after her a flood of water, is obviously a mythical being such as is found not only in the Babylonian cosmogony in the form of the water-monster Tiamat, but in numerous other stories of hostile dragons. A very striking parallel to this myth has been pointed out by Dieterich (*Abraxas*, p. 117 ff.). When Leto was about to bring forth Apollo, the son of Zeus, she was persecuted by the earth-dragon, the Python, who strove to destroy her expected son, at whose hands, according to an oracle, he was to meet with disaster. Leto, however, was carried away by the wind-god Boreas and brought to Poseidon, who prepared for her a refuge upon the island of Ortygia, while he hid her with the waves of the sea from the eyes of her pursuer. Here Leto brought forth Apollo, who, on the fourth day after his birth, had grown so strong that he slew the hostile dragon upon Parnassus. Thus, in both stories we have the persecution of a divine mother (and a light-goddess) by a dragon which seeks to destroy her son, the flight of the mother on the wings of the wind (or of an eagle), retirement to a hidden place of refuge, water floods—which play, however, a different part in the two stories; finally, a combat in heaven between the light-god and the dragon, in which the former is victorious. The main difference in the two myths is that in the Apocalypse the persecution of the mother by the dragon does not begin until after the birth of her son and his being carried away to God, and after the defeat of the dragon in the heavenly war; but as this stultifies the persecution, which was originally directed only against the son, we are justified in conjecturing that we have here a variation, due to interests of a different character, of an originally simpler story more like that of the Greek myth. That this Greek myth was current as a popular legend in Western Asia may be conjectured from the fact that the flight of Leto is often depicted upon the coins of those regions. Now it is well known that in the history of religions there is nothing more common than the transference of popular legends from one religion to another, but in the process of assimilation the legend is so transformed that its foreign

THE APOCALYPSE 439

origin is often lost sight of by the religious consciousness. How many German Christians are there who have any idea what a mass of Germanic heathenism clings to their popular legends and customs? It was doubtless much the same with the Hellenistic Jews of the Diaspora in their adoption of heathen legends. They saw in them ancient mystical traditions, and interpreted them in their own way, without stopping to ask whether they were of Babylonian or Greek or Egyptian origin. Egyptian mythology also offers an interesting parallel to Apoc. xii., to which Bousset directs attention in his *Commentary* (p. 410). Hathor, the mother of the young sun-god Horus, flees from the persecution of the dragon, Typhon, who had slain her consort, Osiris, to a lonely place where she brought up her child in concealment, until he grew strong and by means of magical arts overcame the dragon. The close affinity of this myth with the Greek Leto-Apollo-Python legend is obvious. They are merely different variations of the fundamental representation of the battle of the light-god with the powers of darkness, which found a natural place in every religion of sun-worship.

It is, therefore, quite useless to debate whether the mythical background of which we get glimpses here and there in the Apocalypse comes from one popular legend or the other. It is much more important to notice what kind of modifications the mythical material has undergone in the course of being worked over — perhaps several times — in the apocalyptic literature. As the author probably draws this vision from the same source as chap. xi., namely, the little book of revelations mentioned in x. 9, he found the myth before him in an already monotheistic version, whether as a Jewish prophecy of the birth and translation of the future Messiah, or as a Christian allegory of the birth and deliverance (ascension?) of Jesus. That the young sun-god should become for the writer of the Apocalypse the Messianic child is entirely natural; it is more difficult to see what signification was given to the mother, the goddess of the myth. Was she understood to represent the ideal Israel, and did the crown with the twelve stars (of the zodiac) signify the Twelve Tribes? The sun and moon and the flying on eagles' wings would not, it is true, in this case have any very definite significance, but who can demand that in the transformation of a sun-myth into a Messianic apocalypse everything in the original should find its exact place in the adaptation? The transformation of the dragon—which in the myth signifies the earth-spirit or the heaven-storming monster of the abyss—into the enemy of the moral order, "the devil who deceives the earth," is simple, but what was to be made of the principal trait in the myth, the persecution of the mother of the sun-god by the dragon, the birth of her son in concealment, and the victory of the hero, when but two or three days old, over the enemy? The last point could not be retained, for the rôle of conqueror of Satan could not well be given to the Messianic child, and the only course open was to represent him as caught away from the pursuit of the dragon and removed to the presence of God, there to remain until his victorious appearance as Messianic hero (xix. 11 ff.). Accordingly the overcoming of the dragon, which as an essential feature of the myth could not be allowed to fall away, must be assigned to the Archangel Michael, who as the traditional guardian-angel of Israel could easily take the place of the Messiah in the decisive battle in heaven. With the translation of the Messianic child and the victory of Michael over the devil-dragon the story should really come to an end, since there is no longer any visible reason for the persecution of the woman; but this was an essential feature of the myth, and must be introduced in some way. In order to effect this, the bold expedient was adopted of representing the dragon, after being cast down from heaven, as beginning his devilish work upon earth again by persecuting the mother of the Messiah (the Church either of the Old or of the New Covenant), and, though he was not able to destroy her, waging a bloody war with her children. This served to explain how it was that, in spite of the defeat of the devil-dragon by the heavenly powers, the power of Satan upon earth should still continue to manifest itself in the suffering of the saints (whether Jews or Christians). Thus the difficulties of Apoc. xii. find a relatively simple solution if we assume that we have here a Messianic adaptation of a heathen sun-myth. In accepting this suggestion I have left it an open question whether this Messianic adaptation was originally made from the point of view of the Jewish Messianic hope and was later interpreted in a Christian sense by John, the writer of the Apocalypse, or whether in his source the Messianic child was already interpreted in a Christian sense—that is, of Christ Jesus. This question can hardly be answered with certainty, for the objection which may be brought against the latter view—that in this case the life and death of Christ Jesus between His birth and translation, *i.e.* ascension, is passed over in silence—is weakened by the consideration that in the adaptation of a heathen myth to set forth Christian beliefs some imperfect junctures and historical inconsistencies or lacunæ could hardly be avoided. Yet the preponderant probability seems to me in favour of supposing that in the apocalyptic source from which our author took this vision the Messianic child signified only the future Jewish Messiah, and therefore his translation to heaven had nothing to do with the ascension of Jesus, but is connected with the Jewish tradition that the Messiah should be kept in the presence of God in heaven until the time of His victorious appearance upon earth. In that case only the heavenly hymn of victory, *vv.* 10 ff., is a Christian addition of our author, who here repeats the thoughts of vii. 14 ff., the Christian character of this addition standing in striking contrast to the mythical victory over Satan in what precedes (*v.* 7 f.).

Chapter xiii. describes the instruments made use of by the devil-dragon in his conflict with the saints, namely, two fearful beasts, one of which rises out of the sea and one out of the land (*vv.* 1 and 11). The first has, like the dragon (xii. 3), seven heads and ten horns, and upon these horns ten diadems (in the earlier passage there are seven diadems upon the heads), and upon its heads names of blasphemy; it is like a leopard, a bear, and a lion; one of the heads looks as if it had been smitten unto death and its deadly wound healed again; and there was amazement at the beast throughout the whole earth, and men worshipped the dragon and the beast, to which he had given authority to continue for forty-two months to blaspheme the name of God, and His dwelling-place, and them that dwell in heaven, and to wage war against the saints and to overcome them. This vision of the beast from the sea is modelled, with the exception of the single matter of the deadly wound, upon the vision in Daniel vii. 2 ff. of the four beasts which rise up out of the sea, the lion, the bear, the leopard, and a fourth frightful monster, which together have seven heads and ten horns, to which is added an eleventh horn which has eyes and a mouth speaking great things, and wages war with the saints of the Most High and overcomes them; in verses 24 ff. these ten, or eleven, horns are interpreted as signifying kings, the last of whom shall speak defiant words against the Most High, ill-treat His saints, and abolish the law, until after a time and times and half a time judgment comes upon him. As is well known, the author of this earlier Apocalypse understood by this eleventh horn the Syrian king, Antiochus Epiphanes, and by the four beasts the great empires which succeeded one another as rulers of Western Asia; but underlying these images, which he interprets with reference to the history of the time, there are probably ancient mythical traditions which go back to the Babylonian cosmogony,[1] traces of which have also been preserved in the apocalyptic tradition of the sea-monster Leviathan and the land-monster Behemoth (Enoch lx. 7 f.; Baruch xxix. 4). Undeniable as this mythical basis may be in the Apocalypse of Daniel, and, consequently, in all the later ones, we must avoid attributing

[1] Gunkel, *Schöpfung und Chaos*, p. 360 ff.

too much importance to it in the interpretation of the Johannine Apocalypse. We cannot tell in what form the mythical traditions were known to the writer of the Apocalypse of Daniel, and therefore we do not know how far he modified them in the interests of his application of them to the history of the time, or how much he may have added to them —whether, for example, the grotesque images of the $3 + 4$ heads and $10 + 1$ horns, and the horn with eyes and a mouth that speaks, are to be referred to the traditional myth, or were freely invented by the apocalyptist as an allegory of the history of the time, or whether they are a mixture of mythical tradition and allegorical composition. But if we cannot be sure of this in regard to the first Apocalypse (that of Daniel), we certainly cannot be so in regard to the later imitation, especially as in Apoc. xiii. we have not this at first hand, for this chapter doubtless belongs, like the preceding one, to the "little book of revelations" which our author, according to x. 9 ff., adapted to his own use. Whether the first author of the vision of the two beasts used other mythical material in addition to his Daniel model must be left an open question; in any case Daniel was his main source, in which the mythological material had already been transformed into a historical allegory. But the imitators of Daniel did not, of course, keep to his particular allegory, but understood the figures of the ancient seer as eschatological prophecies, and sought by the addition of new traits to adapt it to the circumstances of their own time. These considerations suggest the rule by which Apoc. xiii. (and xvii.) are to be interpreted: in so far as the Johannine pictures exactly or partially resemble those of Daniel, the possibility of mythical tradition is to be kept in view, and a historical interpretation is in some places not applicable at all, in others only with the greatest caution; where, on the other hand, the Johannine vision has peculiar traits which are not in that of Daniel, it is based on free allegorical composition, whether by our author or his predecessor (the author of the "little book of revelations"), the explanation of which is to be found, not in mythical traditions, but in historical references. Here too, of course, the greatest caution is necessary, because there is always a possibility that the same pictures mean something different for the later author than for his predecessor.

I can accordingly deal briefly with Apoc. xiii., passing over arbitrary interpretations and leaving doubtful matters in suspense. The beast's rising from the sea (verse 1) comes from Dan. vii. 3, and rests upon an ancient myth; its likeness to a leopard, bear, and lion makes it a combination of the beasts in Daniel, which were perhaps derived from some mythical creature of mixed characteristics, like the cherubim, which Daniel has resolved into its elements in order to typify in this way the various world-empires. Our Apocalypse, on the other hand, again combines them into a unity, not because of the ancient myth, but because all other hostile powers had long since been resolved into the one awful world-power of the Roman Empire. The seven heads and ten horns are also found in Daniel,[1] and may with the more

[1] The seven heads are not, indeed, expressly seven, being only arrived at by an addition of the 3 + 4 heads of the four beasts. But whence this curious addition, if not suggested by some mythical tradi-

certainty be referred to the mythical tradition because in xii. 3 they are also ascribed to the dragon, the mythical origin of which is beyond doubt. The fact that the diadems which, in xii. 3, crown the seven heads of the dragon, are placed upon the ten horns in the vision of the beast in xiii. 1, is only a reminiscence of the interpretation, given in Dan. vii. 24, of the ten horns as ten kings; since, therefore, the ten kings are taken from Daniel, it is not necessary to find therein a special historical reference, *e.g.* to ten Roman emperors. The ten kings are mentioned again in xvii. 12, but with a somewhat artificial interpretation which makes it clear that the author has no special purpose in naming this number, but simply retained it because it was traditional. The "names of blasphemy" inscribed on the heads of the beast are not found in Daniel, and may perhaps be an allusion to certain titles of the Roman emperors which appeared to ascribe divinity to them ("Augustus," "Divus"). The "lofty things" spoken against God by the mouth of the beast are several times mentioned in Daniel (vii. 8, xi. 25); our Apocalypse adds the "blaspheming of the name of God and of His dwelling-place and of them that dwell in heaven" (verse 6); in this we may perhaps find an allusion to the profanation of the Temple at Jerusalem which was planned by the Emperor Gaius. It is true that the "blasphemy against those that dwell in heaven" has no special

tion which told of a seven-headed monster? This is confirmed by Apoc. xii. 3, where seven heads are ascribed to the mythical dragon. Here there can certainly be no historical motive for this number seven; it is therefore not essential in xiii. 1 either.

appropriateness in this connection, but this may be simply explained as derived from Dan. vii. 25 and viii. 10. Another trait which is literally taken over from Dan. vii. 21 is that the beast "makes war upon the saints and overcomes them"; the continuance of this state of things for forty-two months (verse 5) is certainly also a paraphrase of the oracle there, according to which the saints are to be delivered over to the power of the enemy for "three and a half times" ($=\frac{7}{2}$ years). In the case of all these details the fact that they belong to the apocalyptic tradition from Daniel onwards dispenses us from seeking any historical explanation of them; it is sufficient to know that the author has adapted the prophecies of Daniel to the circumstances of a later time, that of the conflict with the Roman Empire. A trait which is wholly peculiar to the Johannine vision of the beast is found, however, in verse 3, "and (I saw) one of the heads of the beast as though it had been smitten to death, and its deadly wound healed again." This can only point to Nero, who died by a sword-stroke (v. 14, $\pi\lambda\eta\gamma\dot{\eta}$ $\tau\hat{\eta}s$ $\mu\alpha\chi\alpha\iota\rho\eta s$), and concerning whom a legend arose among the people that he was not dead, but had recovered from his wound and was living somewhere in hiding, and would return to terrify the world. This return of Nero is not spoken of more precisely till chapter xvii. In xiii. 3 the legend is only touched on, and that quite incidentally, without exercising any influence on the remaining contents of the chapter, which deals only with the God-opposing power of the Roman Empire, given to it by the devil-dragon, and with the worship of the Emperor, which is brought about by demonic influence. The latter is dealt with especially in the second half of the chapter, from verse 11 on, in which the seer beholds a second beast rising from the land, having two horns like a lamb and speaking like a dragon; which, being charged with the power of the first beast, causes all the inhabitants of the earth to worship the first beast (the Imperial power). This second beast, too, has probably a mythical basis in the fabulous Behemoth, the terrestrial counterpart to the sea-monster Leviathan; but whether the writer of the Apocalypse was thinking of this mythological background is very doubtful. He was at any rate more closely in touch with the vision in Dan. viii. of the two-horned ram, which stood beside the river and pushed with his horns towards all quarters of the world, and was so strong that no beast could stand before him, nor was there any that could deliver out of his power. This image of Daniel (viii. 2 ff., with the interpretation in 20–25) was adopted by the later apocalyptist, and further developed with allusion to the circumstances of his time. He describes how the second beast exercises in the service of the first all kinds of magical arts, causes fire to fall from heaven, makes statues come to life and speak, in order to move the inhabitants of the earth to pray to the first beast (13 ff.); he also compels people of all ranks, if they wish to carry on any business, to bear his name or his number upon their hands or foreheads (verse 16 f.). No satisfactory explanation is ever likely to be given of this vision, since there are mingled in it historical traits and fables of mythical origin, intertwined and entangled in such a way that they cannot be loosed. We may think of the priesthood of the Imperial cultus, which was officially organised ("Asiarchs") to promote by moral and political pressure the worship of the Emperor, then especially flourishing in Asia; on the other hand, the persuasion of the multitude by magical arts recalls the numerous sorcerers of the time, such as Simon Magus, Apollonius of Tyana, and the like. But none of these historical interpretations suffices to explain everything, and the mythical explanation leaves the whole matter still involved in obscurity. Here it is the part of wisdom to confess ignorance. Even regarding the number of the beast, 666 (verse 18), we can no longer at the present day give a single interpretation as the sole possible and absolutely certain. The reference to the "Emperor Nero" as indicated by the numerical value of the Hebrew letters of the name has still the preponderant probability in its favour, but a reference to the Emperor Gaius, based on the numerical value of the Greek letters, deserves careful consideration, provided that the reading which it implies, 616, can be critically justified—a point on which opinions differ. We have also to take into account the possibility that while the original author of this vision meant this enigmatic number to stand for the Emperor Gaius, the later redactor changed the reference to the Emperor Nero and, with this end in view, interpolated verse 3 and the further references in verses 12 and 14 in a context with which, on strict examination, they do not appear to agree very well; for what has Nero's deadly wound to do with the blasphemous self-deification of the beast, *i.e.* of the Imperial Power, and with the propaganda for the setting up of images of the Emperor and the worshipping of the Emperor? These things, which form the subjects of the rest of the chapter, seem to point rather to the Emperor Gaius, whose mad freak of self-deification excited the Jews so terribly, than to Nero, who did not molest them in this way.[1] Later, however, when the wrath aroused among the Jews by Gaius was forgotten, and in its stead the bugbear of the return of Nero possessed the popular imagination, a Christian redactor of this vision could see the incarnation of the devilish beast of the Imperial power only in Nero, whose mysterious death and expected return seemed to make him the exact counterpart of the slaughtered and yet living lamb of the Christians. Finally it is to be remarked that to the hand of the Christian redactor are probably due, in addition to the backward-pointing references in verses 12 and 14, both the words "the slain lamb" in verse 8, and verse 9 f., which contains a warning of violent opposition and an exhortation to patience and faith, a theme which runs throughout the Johannine Apocalypse from beginning to end.

In chapter xiv. 1–5, the seer beholds the Lamb standing upon Mount Zion, with one hundred and forty-four thousand of the redeemed, who bear His name and the name of His Father upon their foreheads, and sing a new song which is known only to them. They have been redeemed from among sinful mankind, as a first-fruits to God and the Lamb,

[1] This is no doubt the kernel of truth in Spitta's hypothesis, which may be retained without adopting his impossible interpretation of verse 3 as a reference to the illness of the Emperor Gaius. That this verse comes, not from the first author but from a later redactor, perhaps from John, is rendered probable by the remarkable echo of ὡς ἐσφαγμένον, v. 6, in the ὡς ἐσφαγμένην of xiii. 3.

because they are virgin, and follow the Lamb everywhere, and there is no lie found in their mouth (no denial of their faith), in short, because they are in every respect blameless (*vv*. 1–6). In effective contrast with the worshippers of the beast, who are spoken of before, and whose punishment is described immediately after (*vv*. 6 ff.), the writer of the Apocalypse here sees a foreshadowing of the victorious perfection of the chosen band who own allegiance to the Lamb, and have proved it by the strictness of their ascetic continence and the faithfulness of their confession even amid sufferings. These élite of the Christian ascetics and martyrs are naturally not identical with the one hundred and forty-four thousand who were sealed of the twelve tribes of Israel, vii. 2–8, who do not consist of the élite of the Christians, but of the chosen remnant of the theocratic people, and are derived from Jewish apocalyptic tradition. To these chosen of Israel, the redeemed of mankind form the fitting counterpart (xiv. 4), the definite number being no doubt taken over from the former, where alone it is appropriate, because it has there a natural explanation. In other respects the whole picture in xiv. 1–5 is so thoroughly in the style of the author of the Apocalypse (*cf*. chaps. iv. and v., vii. 9 ff.) as to justify the conjecture that he himself designed it, and placed it as a contrasted picture before the following dark scenes of judgment.

These are introduced (*vv*. 6–11) by the appearance of three angels in heaven, the first of whom[1] has " an

---

[1] If in *v*. 6 ἄλλον is to be read (as is probably the case, in view of the repetition in *v*. 8 f.), this can only refer back to x. 2; to the angel there, with the little book of revelation, there corresponds

eternal gospel" to proclaim to the inhabitants of the earth, an exhortation, namely, to pray to and fear the sole God and Creator of the world, because the hour of judgment is come nigh; a proclamation which has nothing in common with the Christian message of salvation, except that it points to the fulfilment of the secret counsel of God (x. 7). The second angel announces the fall of Babylon the Great, which has made drunk all nations with the wine of wrath of her fornications, *i.e.* has infected all men with her vices and brought them under the sentence of the Divine wrath. The third angel threatens all worshippers of the beast, that they shall drink of the wine of the wrath of God, and be tortured in fire and brimstone day and night without cessation. To this threatening of vengeance, taken from his source, our author adds, out of his Christian consciousness, the exhortation (verse 12), "Here is the patience of the saints who keep the commandments of God and the faith of Jesus," with which may be compared the similar formulæ in xiii. 10 and xii. 17, in each case added by the hand of the author to his traditional material as a stereotyped *ceterum censeo*. Then comes a voice from heaven with the promise: "Blessed are the dead which die in the Lord from henceforth" (that is, in loyalty to their faith in Him, even amid the sufferings which await them), to which the spirit of the seer replies in confirmation: "Yea, they shall rest from their labours, for their works do follow them" (*i.e.* the reward of their works and sufferings

here the angel with the "eternal gospel"; which indicates that the following picture of judgment is derived from the same source as xi.-xiii., or at least a similar one.

awaits them). This promise of a blessed rest for the faithful forms an effective contrast to the unceasing torment of the worshippers of the beast (verse 11) and the following scenes of judgment (14–20). In imitation of Dan. vii. 13 there appears, sitting upon a white cloud, "one like unto a son of man" (here, as in i. 13, without the definite article), with a golden crown upon His head, and a sickle in His hand. This means the Messiah; who, as the agent in the judgment of the world, seems to stand on the same footing as the other angels of judgment, since He is commanded by "another angel," who comes forth from the (heavenly) temple, to put in the sickle, for the hour of the harvest is come. The consummation of the judgment is represented under the two figures of harvest and vintage, as in Joel iii. 18; its awfulness is made vivid by the violent image of a wine-press of God, from which the blood poured forth in streams that reached sixteen hundred furlongs and rose to the bridles of the horses, a representation which recalls Enoch c. 3, and therefore belongs to Jewish apocalyptic tradition, as does this whole picture of judgment in chap. xiv., with the exception of *vv.* 1–5 and 12 f. which were added by the author.

Although the judgment pictured in xiv. 14–20 probably formed the conclusion in the source from which our author derived it, it was not his intention to make it the final end. To postpone this still further he uses the same device as once or twice before—he extends the course of the drama by inserting further *entr'actes*, and preludes of the final catastrophe, drawn from the storehouse of apocalyptic tradition. The same service as is rendered to him in this respect in viii. 6 by the vision of the seven trumpets, is now (chaps. xv. and xvi.) performed by the vision of the seven bowls, filled with the wrath of God, which are poured out one after another by seven angels and cause all sorts of plagues in nature and among men, not markedly distinguished from the analogous plagues in the earlier visions. At the pouring out of the sixth bowl the river Euphrates is dried up in order to make ready a way for the kings of the East. After that there come forth from the mouth of the dragon and of the beast and of the false prophet (the last-named stands for the second beast of xiii. 11) unclean spirits in the form of frogs, wonder-working demonic spirits, which go forth unto the kings of the whole world and gather them together to the great decisive day of battle which shall take place in Armageddon (xv. 12–16). This strange picture is difficult to interpret. Whether it is an allusion to the dreaded invasion of the Parthians seems to me as doubtful as in the allied vision of the sixth trumpet (ix. 14 ff.). Just as the riders and their horses are there drawn as mythical figures, so here, the frog-like wonder-working spirits point to an ancient folk-tale, to which the name Har-Magedon also doubtless belongs; for that this refers to a mountain near Megiddo (which is non-existent) is not very probable. Gunkel (*ut sup.*, p. 388, note 2) points to an analogous legend. According to Enoch vi. 5, the conspiracy of the fallen angels in Gen. vi. takes place upon the top of Hermon. A geographical locality for the mythical decisive battle of Har-Magedon is as little to be sought as in the case of the high mountain on which the Messiah was tempted by Satan. We are here upon entirely mythical ground, and as we do not know the folk-tales to which the seer alluded, we must simply be content to do without a more definite interpretation. Noteworthy is the parenthetic insertion in this mythical picture of a warning spoken by Christ, which reminds us of iii. 18. At the outpouring of the seventh bowl the prodigies of the seven trumpets are repeated—thunder, lightning, hail, and earthquake, the only addition being that, in consequence of the earthquake, the cities of the heathen fall down, especially the great city of Babylon (Rome), to which God "remembered to give the cup of the wine of His wrath." This is therefore a prelude to the judgment upon Rome which follows.

This is introduced in chapter xvii. One of the angels with the bowls carries away the seer in the spirit into the wilderness, in order there to show him "the judgment upon the great harlot that sitteth upon many waters, with whom the kings of the earth have committed fornication; and they that dwell in the earth were made drunk with the wine of her fornications." This means the city of Rome, which was not, indeed, like its prototype, the real Babylon, seated upon many waters, but the customary designation of Babylon (Jer. li. 13) is retained as an allegory, which is interpreted later (verse 15). This woman is now beheld by the seer sitting upon a scarlet-coloured beast which is full of names of blasphemy and has seven heads and ten horns, the standing attributes of the devil-dragon (xii. 3), and of the beast to which he has committed authority over the earth (xiii. 1 ff.), namely, the Roman Empire, upon whose world-power rests the luxurious splendour of Rome, the metropolis of the world. This is portrayed in verse 4: the woman is arrayed in purple and scarlet and decked with gold, precious stones and pearls, and holds in her hand a golden cup full of the abominations and unclean things of her fornications. Upon her forehead is inscribed a mysterious name, "Babylon the Great, the mother of the harlots and abominations of the earth"; and she is drunk with the blood of the saints and of the witnesses of Jesus. The interpretation of this vision which is given (*vv.* 7 ff.) by the angel who explains these things to the seer is strikingly inappropriate to the picture drawn in the preceding verses (1–5). Instead of the luxurious woman who is there the central figure, it is the beast upon which she rides that is now made prominent, and this is interpreted not as the Roman Empire, upon which the glory of the city of Rome is based, but as one of the five past emperors, who is to come again and to treat the woman as an enemy, by which Nero must be meant. It is clear that this is not the original meaning of the image in *vv.* 1 ff. There the woman and the beast belong together as the Empire and its metropolis; here, on the other hand, the beast is represented as the personal enemy of the woman—that is, the city of Rome. That is quite another thought, entirely foreign to the original sense of the picture in 1–5. But the interpretation in 7 ff. does not merely contradict the original meaning of the vision in 1–5; its own individual features do not agree with one another. The seven heads of the beast are interpreted in two different ways in verses 9 and 10, as representing the seven

THE APOCALYPSE 457

hills upon which *Roma septicollis* lies, and as the seven
kings, *i.e.* Roman emperors. The former is appropriate to the proper interpretation of the woman as
the city of Rome, which is finally given in verse 18;
the reference of the heads to the emperors is only
interpolated in order to prepare the way for the
identification, to which the author attaches special
importance, of the beast with Nero, which in verse
10 f. he clothes in the enigmatic words: "The five
(kings) are fallen, the one is, and the other is not
yet come, and when he comes he shall continue only
for a little time. And the beast that was and is not,
is himself the eighth, and at the same time (one) of
the seven, and goes down to destruction." It is
not open to doubt that here, as in xiii. 3 and xiv.,
there is a reference to the popular legend regarding
Nero's return. Now two forms of this legend were
current. Originally it was believed that Nero was
not dead, but had taken refuge with the Parthians,
intending with their support to return and revenge
himself upon Rome. In this form the legend is
found in the *Sibylline Oracles*, in several passages
in the fourth and fifth books, dating from the
years 70–80; Suetonius, too (*Nero*, xlvii., l.), and
Tacitus (*Hist.*, i. 2, ii. 8) report that in the year 69
a pseudo-Nero appeared in Greece and was quickly
suppressed, while another in the time of Vespasian
and Titus wormed his way into the confidence of the
Parthians and nearly succeeded in inducing them to
undertake a campaign against the Romans, but later,
in the time of Domitian, he was handed over by them
to the Romans. Later, however, the legend took
the form that Nero was indeed really dead, but would

return again from Hades as a demonic being, equipped with demonic powers. In this form it is first found in a *Sibylline Oracle* which dates from the time of Hadrian, but it probably goes back to a much earlier period. This is the form of the legend which seems to be implied in Apoc. xvii. 8: "The beast was, and is not, and is about to come up out of the abyss," if this is to be understood as meaning a return from Hades, which would certainly seem to be the most obvious explanation of it. In the following verses, however, it is said of the same beast that it will be the eighth (emperor), and that, in league with the ten kings (of the East), it shall make war upon the harlot Rome and destroy her (11–13, 16 f.); which seems to imply the earlier form of the legend, the return of Nero, who is not supposed to have died, accompanied by the Parthians. The question may be raised whether both can be united, in the sense that the rising up of the beast "from the abyss," verse 8, only refers to the demonic character of the returning Nero, not to his return from among the dead; or whether we have here two forms of the legend side by side, which might be explained by a working over of the interpretation in verses 7–18 (itself an interpolation into the original picture) by the hand of the final editor of the whole work? This last hypothesis has a further piece of evidence in its favour. The ten horns of the beast are interpreted in verse 12 as ten kings who have not yet received a kingdom, but who, nevertheless, receive authority as kings for a short time, and give their authority to the beast by joining cordially with him in making war upon the harlot. By these we may understand the vassal-princes of the Parthian Empire, by means of whose confederate power Nero was to carry out his campaign of vengeance against Rome. But how does this agree with verse 14, where it is said that these ten kings shall make war upon the Lamb, and that He with His called, chosen, and faithful shall overcome them? It is clear that this struggle of the kings with Christ and His Church has nothing in common with the campaign of the Parthian princes against Rome; on the contrary, they contradict one another, for in that struggle the kings are a God-opposing power which is defeated by Christ as the Lord of lords; in the campaign against Rome, on the other hand, they are victorious, and execute judgment upon the ungodly city according to the will of God. Obviously, therefore, verse 14 has been interpolated by a Christian apocalyptist into a text which originally did not deal with the struggles and victories of Christianity, but only with the expected victorious campaign of the Parthians in alliance with Nero against Rome, the same theme upon which numerous variations are played in the fourth and fifth books of the Jewish *Sibyl*, dating from the time of Vespasian. But the "kings of the earth" play yet a third rôle in the course of these two chapters, that, namely, of the allies and companions in guilt of the same harlot Rome of which they appear as the enemies in xvii. 16 ff. According to xvii. 2, the kings of the earth have committed fornication with the great harlot, and therefore they weep and wail for her fall (xviii. 9). This judgment is here executed directly by God Himself, who causes the proud city to be devoured in one day by fire, without the aid of Nero or the

Parthian hosts. That was the original form of the vision of the great harlot which was announced in xvii. 1–5, and described in chapter xviii. In this ground-document, which probably originally belonged to the "little book of revelations" of x. 9, and therefore dates from the time of Gaius Caligula,[1] a later hand has altered the reference of the beast to Nero, and has interpolated the allusion to his campaign of revenge against Rome, and this, indeed, is made to occur, in xvii. 10, under the sixth emperor, that is (since the three short-lived usurpers of the year 68 are evidently not taken into account), under Vespasian. This redactor of the earlier story of judgment saw in Rome no longer only the wanton city, "the mother of harlots and all abominations" (xvii. 5), but also the tyrant who is drunk with the blood of the saints and prophets and all the slaughtered upon earth, and for this reason he added to xvii. 5, verse 6a, and also inserted xviii. 20 and 24. He did not, however, expect the judgment to take place under Vespasian, but under his successor, Titus, the coming seventh emperor; for that Rome should have seven emperors was for him a dogmatic postulate, since the traditional dragon of the abyss had seven heads; moreover, it might well appear to him appropriate that the judgment upon Rome should begin under that emperor who, as the destroyer of Jerusalem, had filled up the cup of the blood-guiltiness of Rome towards the

---

[1] The command to the people of God to depart from Rome in order to avoid sharing in the guilt and punishment (xviii. 4) implies the existence of a considerable Jewish colony in Rome, and must therefore date from a time preceding the expulsion of the Jews from Rome by Claudius in the year 53.

THE APOCALYPSE 461

Jewish people. For this reason the present sixth emperor was to be succeeded by a seventh, who was, however, to continue only for a short time, since men thought that the hoof-beats of the Parthian host which should wreak vengeance in his days could already be heard in the east. The short reign of Titus, who died of a fever, is an accidental coincidence with his prophecy, which looked to quite a different fulfilment. He was to be followed, according to the apocalyptist, by an eighth emperor who was one of the seven, namely, the victorious avenger, Nero, who, as soon as he has fulfilled his allotted task, shall likewise go down to destruction.[1] When, however, all these expectations of the Jewish Apocalypse had remained unfulfilled, and, instead, Titus had been followed by Domitian, the enemy of the Christians, and perhaps also by Trajan, the author of our Apocalypse could no longer use this vision of the judgment upon Rome in the form in which tradition had handed it down to him. He allowed, it is true, the return of Nero to stand, but he was no longer to come from the Parthians but from Hades (verse 8, and perhaps even verses 3 and 14, in chapter xiii.), and no longer as the enemy of Rome but as the enemy of Christ and the Church. Similarly, he made the Parthian princes

[1] Perhaps these words, καὶ εἰς ἀπόλειαν ὑπάγει, are not from the same hand which wrote the Nero prophecy, but are, like verse 8, from the hand of the final editor, who possibly thought of the "eighth" emperor as the Emperor Domitian, who had appeared in the meantime (and perhaps had also departed), whom it was possible to regard as a "second Nero." We cannot, however, lay much stress on this, since the original author of verse 10 f. can hardly have meant by the "eighth who is one of the seven" anyone else than Nero.

marching against Rome into the powers hostile to Christ (perhaps with special reference to the Roman provincial officials as organisers of the persecution of the Christians), whose assaults Christ and His Church should victoriously resist (xvii. 14). To "the blood of the saints" (xvii. 16) he adds that of the martyrs of Jesus, and to the prophets, xviii. 20, also the Apostles. In this way our author, the seer John, adapted the Jewish apocalyptic fragment regarding the judgment upon Rome in chaps. xvii. and xviii. to his own purpose, as a prelude to the universal judgment of the world to which he makes the transition in chapter xix.

The execution of the divine judgment upon earth is preceded by a heavenly hymn of triumph celebrating the commencement of the reign of God, and the blissful marriage of the Lamb with His pure bride, whose glorious robe is not, like that of the great harlot, of purple and red, but of shining white linen, symbolic of the righteousness of the saints (verse 7 f.). The Old Testament figure of the marriage of Jahwe with Israel is here transferred to the Christian Church as the bride of the Lamb, as was done indeed already in the parables of Jesus (Mk. ii. 19; Mt. xxii. 2 ff.), and by the Apostle Paul, 2 Cor. xi. 2; Eph. v. 26 f. The resemblance of these heavenly scenes of triumph to the similar scenes and hymns in vii. 9 ff., xi. 15 ff., xiv. 1 ff., allows us to recognise in them all the hand of John the Apocalyptist, who loves to insert these bright pictures from the heavenly world as contrasted interludes between the terrors of the earthly scenes of judgment; the latter he has adapted from apocalyptic tradition, the former are his own creation.

The hymn of jubilation over the approaching marriage of the Lamb is appropriately followed by the benediction upon those who are bidden to the marriage feast, to which is added a solemn asseveration of the truth of these promises (verse 9). It is uncertain—and also unimportant—whether the speaker here is the angel of xvii. 1 or another. Noteworthy, however, is the warning which is emphasised both here and in xxii. 8 against the worship of angels, who are, after all, only fellow-servants of the seer, and of his brethren who hold the testimony of Jesus, "for the testimony of Jesus is the spirit of prophecy" (verse 10). This is a significant saying, which is no foreign interpolation but expresses the inmost conviction of the prophet, who sees in the inspirations of his spirit of revelation the true testimony of Jesus, independent of all human mediation and historical tradition, *i.e.* he is convinced that he possesses in this the most genuine Christian truth. In this conviction, which the author shared with the "brethren," the prophetically gifted Christians of his time and environment, lie the roots from which grew up the "spiritual gospel" which is named after John (the prophet!).

The description of the judgment begins in xix. 11 with the imposing picture of the Messiah descending from the opened heavens, a rider on a white horse who is called "Faithful and True," "for in righteousness doth He judge and make war"; His eyes are like flames of fire, and upon His head are many diadems, and a name written which no man but himself knoweth (and His name is called "the Word of God"), clothed in a garment dipped in blood, and followed by the heavenly hosts upon white horses and in white linen garments; out of His mouth proceedeth a sharp sword to smite the peoples; He shall rule them with a sceptre of iron, and He treads the wine-press of Almighty God; on His garment, upon His sword-belt, is written the name "King of Kings and Lord of Lords." Then an angel cries from the sun, summoning the birds of the air to "the great feast of God," viz. to devour the flesh of the slaughtered kings and princes, horses and riders, bond and free, small and great. Then the beast and the kings of the earth and their hosts are gathered together for the decisive battle against the Messiah and His (heavenly) armies. Whether there is an actual battle is not clear, for the seer sees the end at once: the beast, and the lying prophet who persuaded men to worship the beast, are overpowered and thrown alive into the lake of fire that burneth with brimstone, the rest are slain by the sword which comes forth from the mouth of the Messiah, and their carcasses are devoured by the birds. Though it is clear that this picture of judgment is in the style of the Jewish apocalyptic, we are not justified by that in refusing to ascribe it to the author of the Apocalypse, for whom, as for all the Christians of his time, the hoped-for victory of Christ was naturally clothed in the outward forms associated with the realistic Messianic hope of Judaism. It was Gnosticism which first began the spiritualisation of this realistic eschatology which we find fully carried out in the Johannine Gospel. But this innovation by no means found universal acceptance. If even towards the close of the second century Irenæus still earnestly believed in the sensuous glories of the millennial kingdom, and Tertullian found edification in the picture of the bloody judgment which the returning Christ would execute upon the heathen, we certainly cannot wonder that a Jewish-Christian prophet at the end of the first or beginning of the second century, in face of imminent persecution, strengthened his own faith and that of his churches with the traditional pictures of judgment which he derived from Judaism. When Christ was thought of as the "King of kings and Lord of lords coming to judgment," He inevitably assumed, even for the Christian consciousness, the traditional traits of the Jewish Messianic King, the righteous judge and awful avenger, who rules the peoples with His iron sceptre, out of whose mouth goes a sharp sword, and who treads the wine-press of the wrath of God, so that blood flows down in rivers—three figures which to our taste are unattractive, but which were obviously favourite figures in the Jewish-Christian apocalyptic; they are found repeatedly in our Apocalypse even before chap. xix., namely, in ii. 27, xii. 5, i. 16, xiv. 19 f., and are derived from Ps. ii. 9; Isa. xi. 4, lxiii. 3 ff.; Joel iv. 13; Psalms of Solomon xvii. 24, 35. The repellent picture, too, of the great feast of God at which the birds of prey gorge themselves on the corpses of the slain (verse 17 f.) is an almost literal imitation of the picture of judgment in Ezek. xxxix. 17 ff., where, almost immediately before, are mentioned the enemies of God—Gog and Magog—whom our author introduces in the next chapter. In all this we clearly recognise the common stock of apocalyptic material which the Christians shared with the Jews.

There seems to me, therefore, no sufficient ground for supposing that the author of the description of the judgment in chaps. xix. and xx. took it from a special Jewish source such as we have seen reason to infer in chaps. xi.–xiii. and xvii., xviii. Nor can I find in this chapter any reference to heathen myths. The beast and the lying prophet have been taken over by our author from the chapters we have just referred to, where the figures in question, though they are of course of mythical origin, have already been modified by a Jewish writer; he seems, however, himself to have invented the designation "lying prophet" for the second beast, and thus to have given to this rather enigmatic figure a more definite significance as a religious deceiver, just as in xvii. 8 and 14 the beast representing the Emperor Nero and his ten confederate kings is given a religious and Christian instead of a Jewish political significance. A similar Christian interpretation of a traditional apocalyptic mystery is found in verse 13 compared with verse 12. In verse 12 it is said that the Messiah bears a name which no man knoweth but Himself, by which, according to apocalyptic modes of speech, is probably meant some mysterious magic word with wonderful powers;[1] this attribute of the apocalyptic Messianic figure has then been interpreted either by our author himself or some later interpolator by the addition " His name is called the Logos of God," which is probably to be understood in the specific sense of the Johannine

---

[1] Bousset rightly points in his *Commentary*, p. 495, to the analogous case of the mystical word in ii. 17; *cf.* also the "hidden name" of "strong power" which in Enoch lxix. 14 is conferred upon the Archangel Michael.

Logos-Christology. Since the application of this conception to Christ occurred among the Gnostics before the time of John the Evangelist, it is not quite impossible that the author of the Apocalypse was already acquainted with it, and, just because it was a name of Christ which was as yet only known in esoteric circles, may have given it here as the solution of the enigma. But it appears to me more probable that this sentence, which does not fit in very well with the context, is a marginal gloss from a different hand, which some copyist has interpolated into the text. In any case, this explanation of the mystical name (verse 12) is strikingly out of relation with the Jewish conception of the Messiah which prevails throughout this whole scene of judgment. In chap. xx. the description of the judgment is continued. In the first place, the ancient devil-dragon (*cf.* xii. 9) is cast into the abyss of hell and shut up there for a thousand years. During this period a share in the kingly rule and judicial status of Christ is given to the risen martyrs who have given their lives for the testimony of Jesus, and to all Christians who amid persecution have been faithful to their confession and who have not received the mark of the beast, while the remainder of the dead do not rise until the end of this thousand years. The partakers in this "first resurrection" are therefore a chosen band which is not subject to the "second death," but, joined in priestly and kingly dignity with God and Christ, enjoys a preliminary blessedness. After the lapse of this thousand years, Satan is loosed from his prison and again goes forth to assemble the peoples of the earth, with Gog and Magog at their head, to battle.

They march against the beloved city (Jerusalem), but are consumed by fire from heaven. The devil who deceived them is cast into the sea of fire, where, along with the beast and the prophet of lies, he suffers endless torment. Then the seer beholds the ruler of the world (God), before whose face heaven and earth flee away, sitting upon a great white throne, and before the throne stand all the dead, who have now risen from Hades, both small and great. They are judged according to their deeds, which stand written in the open book of judgment and in the book of life. He whose name is not[1] written in the book of life is cast into a lake of fire along with the (personified) death and the princes of hell. This is the "second death," the final damnation.

This description of the drama of judgment as taking place in two acts, separated by the thousand years' reign of the Messiah upon earth, follows a Jewish tradition, the first trace of which is found in Enoch's vision of the "ten weeks" (xci. 14 f.), but which later appears more distinctly in the Apocalypse of Baruch (xl. 3) and in 2 Esdras (vii. 28 f.), and is further developed in the Talmud. The basis of this conception of an earthly and temporally limited kingdom of Messiah, lies in the need which Jewish theology felt of reconciling the old prophetic hope of an earthly exaltation of the people of God with the expectation which arose, from Daniel onwards, of a super-earthly condition of final blessedness. Regarding the duration of the preliminary reign of the Messiah, opinions varied in the Jewish theology[1] between 40 years

[1] Weber, *Altsyn. Theol.*, p. 355 f.; Schürer, *N. Tle. Zeitgesch.*, ii. 457 f.

THE APOCALYPSE 469

(= Israel's sojourn in the desert), 400 years (Israel in Egypt), 600 or 1000 years (a day of the cosmic week, Ps. xc. 4), 2000 years (a third of the cosmic week corresponding to the 2000 years before, and 2000 after the law), finally even 7000 (corresponding to the seven days of the marriage feast). The conception, too, of a temporary fettering of the evil spirits in subterranean dungeons and abysses of flame recurs frequently in the Apocalypse of Enoch, *e.g.* x. 4 ff., xii. f., xviii. 14 ff., xxii. 4–14, where there is mention of places of imprisonment in Hades for the preliminary punishment of all wicked spirits. These conceptions of the Jewish eschatology were connected with widely current myths. According to the Persian eschatology,[1] the dragon Azi Dahak, after he had been overcome by the divine hero Thrætaona and imprisoned in the depths of the earth, is loosed at the end of 9000 years by the anti-god Angramainyu and helps the latter in the last decisive battle against the kingdom of Ahura Mazda. The Orphic myth,[2] too, tells how the Titans, after being conquered by Uranus and cast into Tartarus, again broke loose and craftily laid wait for Dionysus, the son of Zeus; after they have slain him and torn him to pieces they are burnt to ashes by a thunderbolt of Zeus. That myths of this kind influenced the Jewish eschatology is highly probable, but our apocalyptist doubtless merely followed the Jewish-Christian tradition without

---

[1] As exemplified in the writings of Parseeism—which are, however, no doubt later—Bundehesh and Bahman Yast. *Cf.* Hübschmann, " Persische Eschatologie" in the *Jahrb. für prot. Theol.*, 1882; and Stave, *Einfluss des Parsismus auf das Judentum*, p. 175 f.
[2] Rohde, *Psyche*, p. 410 ff.

thinking of its ultimate roots. The names of the God-defying powers, Gog and Magog, who came forth to the battle, are derived from Ezek. xxxviii. and xxxix., where Gog the King of Magog, represents the powers of the world which are hostile to God, as in Enoch lvi. they are represented by the Parthians and Medes. In Jewish eschatology[1] Gog and Magog are the standing names for the last enemies of God who are to be overcome, though there is some uncertainty as to whether the battle with them takes place before the Messianic reign or at the close of it, the latter being, however, the customary conception. In this also, therefore, our author follows the lines of the Jewish theology, from which, too, he simply takes over the description of Jerusalem as "the beloved city" where the Messiah has His seat during His millennial reign, so that we are not justified in concluding that this must be derived from a source written before the destruction of Jerusalem.

After the defeat of the last enemies, begins the consummation of all things (chap. xxi.-xxii. 5), the scene of which is a new heaven and a new earth, the old having disappeared; whether this comes about as the result of a burning of the world, or in some other way by a creative transformation and renewal of the old world, is not said. The expectation of a renewal of the world goes back to Isa. lxv. 17, and is a standing article of faith in the Jewish apocalyptic; the only point on which opinion was divided, was, whether the renewal of the world should precede the Messianic period, or follow it, the former view appearing in Enoch xlv. 4 f., the latter in 2 Esdras vii. 30 f. and

[1] Weber, *Altsyn. Theol.*, p. 369 f.

in the theology of the Talmud.¹ After this the seer beholds the manifestation of the "New Jerusalem," which descends from heaven like a bride adorned for her husband, and hears a voice from the throne, saying: "Behold the tabernacle of God is with men, and He shall dwell with them, and they shall be His peoples, and He shall wash away all tears from their eyes, and there shall be no more death, nor suffering, nor crying, nor pain—for the first things are passed away: behold, I make all things new. These words are faithful and true. I am Alpha and Omega, the beginning and the end. I will give unto him that is athirst of the fountain of the water of life, freely. He that overcometh shall inherit these things; and I will be his God, and he shall be My son. But the cowardly, and unbelieving and defiled, and murderers and fornicators, sorcerers and idolators, and all liars, shall have their part in the lake of fire, which is the second death" (*vv.* 3-8). In this passage the seer describes, in his own characteristic phraseology, the glorious picture of the consummation of all things which he beheld in vision, and with this he might have closed his work. But he felt bound by tradition, and to the tradition belonged a more detailed description of the New Jerusalem, which he did not feel justified in withholding from his readers. He therefore adds a new vision, in which he is carried up by "one of the angels which had the bowls" unto a high mountain from which he is able to see the holy city, Jerusalem, in all its detail. The description which follows in xxi. 11–xxii. 5, unites earthly with supernatural traits in a strange and wonderful picture. On the one hand,

¹ Schürer, *ut sup.*, p. 459; Weber, *ut sup.*, p. 380 ff.

it is a new earthly Jerusalem, with walls and gates that can be measured, adorned with Oriental splendour, the capital of the world-ruling Jewish nation, to which the heathen nations and their kings bring their glories as tribute. On the other hand, there dwell in this earthly city God Himself and the Lamb, whose presence not only takes the place of the former Temple, but also replaces the sun and moon and every kind of light, for the glory of God is the light of it, so that there is no more night there; moreover, the mystical features of Paradise are transplanted to this city; the stream of living water goes forth from the throne of God and the Lamb, and beside it stands the tree of life, which yields its fruit every month (for the twelve tribes of Israel) and whose leaves are for the healing of the heathen. In this, Ezekiel's picture of the new Jerusalem (Ezek. xlvii.) is combined with the Paradise legend into an ideal picture of a glorified, but still essentially earthly and Jewish Jerusalem, which contrasts markedly with the heavenly Jerusalem where God shall dwell with universal mankind, and these all without distinction shall be His people and His sons, where old things are passed away, and all things have become new (xxi. 3–8). If we notice, further, that the description of the New Jerusalem in xxi. 10 is introduced in a way which does not harmonise with its having already appeared in verse 2, the conjecture is justified that the author has taken his second picture (xxi. 10–xxii. 5) from a Jewish source, and has only given it a Christian colouring by certain additions. Among these are the placing of the Lamb beside God in xxi. 22 f., xxii. 1, 3 (in both passages, the addition is

THE APOCALYPSE 473

awkward), further, the names of the twelve apostles of the Lamb on the twelve foundation stones of the city, corresponding to the names of the twelve tribes of Israel, upon its gates (xxi. 14, *cf.* 12). Whether the absence of a temple in the New Jerusalem (xxi. 22) is to be ascribed to our author, or whether he found that in his Jewish source, may be left an open question.

In xxii. 6–21 the author adds to his prophecies a concluding word of edification which recalls the introduction in chap. i. As there (i. 4) God was represented as surrounded by the bodyguard of the seven spirits who stood before the throne, so here he is called "the God of the spirits of the prophets." These originally mythical star-spirits (*sup.*, p. 405 f.) whom Parseeism and Judaism made into a guard of honour for God, are here given a new significance as mediators of the prophetic revelation, partial manifestations of the one spirit of prophecy (xix. 10), which here divides itself into a plurality of spirits (1 Cor. xiv. 32) corresponding to the manifoldness of its operations. John then solemnly affirms that he has heard and seen all these things (by the aid of the spirit of revelation, which is again represented here as an angel who shows him these things) and that he has received the express direction not to seal them, that is, to keep them secret, but to make them known; for the time of fulfilment is at hand. Then Jesus is introduced, speaking in person: " Behold I come quickly, and My reward is with Me, to give to every man according to his work. I am the Alpha and the Omega, the first and the last, the beginning and the end " (*cf.* i. 17, ii. 8, and the same said of God in i. 8). "Blessed are they that wash their robes" ("keep His commandments" is doubtless an explanatory gloss), "that they may have a right to the tree of life, and to enter in at the gates of the city" (the heavenly Jerusalem). "Without are the dogs" (unbelieving heathen), "and sorcerers and fornicators, and murderers and idolators, and every one that loveth and maketh a lie. I, Jesus, have sent My angel" (not the prophet, but the spirit of revelation, i. 1) "to testify unto you these things for the churches. I am the root and the offspring of David, the bright and morning star" (v. 5, ii. 28; Isa. xi. 1, xiv. 12). Thereupon the spirit of the prophet, and the bride (the Christian Church) say "'Come,' and let him that heareth say 'Come,' and let him that is athirst come; and he that will, let him take of the water of life freely" (xxi. 6). Then follows a warning from the author to the readers of these prophecies, not to add anything to them or to take anything from them, at peril of their salvation (verse 18 f.). Finally the fundamental thought of this book of revelation is summed up once more in a solemn liturgical antiphonal between Jesus and the Church: "Yea, I come quickly." "Amen; come, Lord Jesus." To the epistolatory introduction, i. 1-3, corresponds the customary epistolatory conclusion: "The grace of the Lord Jesus be with the saints."

In spite of all the various material which has been worked up in this Apocalypse, from oral and written, Christian and Jewish, tradition, its spirit and language remain from beginning to end essentially the same. It is the work of a prophet who, in a time of difficulty, at the beginning of sore temptations, seeks to strengthen the Christian churches in their faith by directing their glance towards the blessed consummation in which all conflicts and troubles of the present shall find their victorious issue. As a battle-cry and word of encouragement it not only had a great significance for his own time—the beginning of the persecutions—but retains its value for all times, a value which is increased, not diminished, by the fact that we have learned to distinguish between its religious spirit and purpose and the fanciful forms in which they are embodied.

www.ingramcontent.com/pod-product-compliance
Lightning Source LLC
Chambersburg PA
CBHW031305150426
43191CB00005B/84